ACADEMIC RESEARCH
AND WRITING

ACADEMIC RESEARCH AND WRITING

Inquiry and Argument in College

Linda S. Bergmann

Purdue University

Longman

Boston   Columbus   Indianapolis   New York   San Francisco   Upper Saddle River
Amsterdam   Cape Town   Dubai   London   Madrid   Milan   Munich   Paris   Montreal   Toronto
Delhi   Mexico City   São Paulo   Sydney   Hong Kong   Seoul   Singapore   Taipei   Tokyo

Executive Editor: Lynn Huddon
Senior Marketing Manager: Sandra McGuire
Senior Supplements Editor: Donna Campion
Production Manager: Denise Phillip
Project Coordination, Text Design, and Electronic Page Makeup: Electronic Publishing Services Inc., NYC
Cover Designer/Manager: Wendy Ann Fredericks
Cover Photo: © Hill Street Studios/Blend Images/Getty Images
Senior Manufacturing Buyer: Roy Pickering
Printer and Binder: R. R. Donnelley & Sons/Crawfordsville
Cover Printer: R. R. Donnelley & Sons/Crawfordsville

For permission to use copyrighted material, grateful acknowledgment is made to the copyright holders on pp. 336–337, which are hereby made part of this copyright page.

Library of Congress Cataloging-in-Publication Data

Bergmann, Linda S., 1950
    Academic research and writing: inquiry and argument in college / Linda Bergmann.
        p.   cm.
    Includes bibliographical references and index.
    ISBN 978-0-321-09184-0
    1. English language—Rhetoric. 2. Persuasion (Rhetoric) 3. Academic writing. 4. Critical thinking. I. Title.

PE1431.B53 2009
3808′ .0420711—dc22   2009023878

3 4 5 6 7 8 9 10—DOC—12 11 10

Longman
is an imprint of

www.pearsonhighered.com

ISBN-13: 978-0-321-09184-0
ISBN-10:   0-321-09184-1

Contents

CHAPTER **3** Using Academic Sources Responsibly:
Understanding Plagiarism 47

CHAPTER **4** Moving from Inquiry to Argument 60

CHAPTER 7 Revising and Editing to Meet Audience Expectations   129

CHAPTER 8 Adapting Writing for Professional Audiences   141

A Quick Guide to Documentation 206

Readings 237

Preface

I began writing this textbook because I could not find a research writing textbook that would help my class achieve the goals I had for it, goals which included students' not only learning *how* to write researched papers relatively successfully, but also understanding *why* they were required to take a course teaching them to do so. I wanted a textbook that would teach the skills students need to produce effective researched writing in a variety of genres and that would at the same time show students some of the purposes of research in colleges and universities and encourage them to identify themselves as novice members of that larger researching community.

Academic Research and Writing: Inquiry and Argument in College is a result of that search and these goals. The book is directed at college students who have had some experience with writing and research in high school or college composition, but who need to extend their skills and knowledge in order to undertake the more demanding work of reading and writing in their chosen academic or preprofessional fields. It is designed for one or two semester first-year composition courses, second semester courses focused on researched writing, and some upper-level research writing courses. The book builds on students' existing knowledge about research and writing and encourages them to extend that knowledge by seeking out assumptions and practices about reading and writing research specific to the fields they hope to enter. It starts by suggesting general strategies for reading and evaluating sources and arguments, but it moves from general academic skills to particular genres of researched writing, and it repeatedly demonstrates that writing must be understood within the framework of larger conversations involving disciplinary and workplace expertise. It resists the idea that the writer—any writer—is engaged in a solitary pursuit.

The book, then, operates from the assumption that the general academic research practices of argumentation, research, and using sources effectively do not stand alone; they are embodied in fields of inquiry and argument in college. As a textbook, *Academic Research and Writing: Inquiry and Argument in College* resists the temptation to simplify academic writing as a single, unified discourse, recognizing instead that there is no "one-size fits all" quick fix for learning to conduct research and use sources. It acknowledges that there are major differences in discourse practices throughout the university and in the professional work students are preparing for, differences that students must negotiate in their progress toward expertise in a field. It aims to be an *introduction* to learning about research and researched writing, to offer a beginning for (rather than the conclusion of) a learning process that students will continue as they move through their college careers and beyond.

The concept of "field" is central to the book, providing an entrée into different genres, audiences, and rhetorical situations. The book suggests starting points for students to appreciate what it means to enter a field of study through reading and through actively engaging in the intellectual life of the college or university, and it encourages them to synthesize the varying and sometimes contradictory academic expectations they encounter as they move from general education to more specialized study. *Academic Research and Writing: Inquiry and Argument in College* aims to make students' transition to the discourse of their field smoother and more conscious than is often the case, by showing them connections between the assignments students are often given and the research projects that many faculty conduct and write about. In spite of the obvious differences between faculty and student research, I am convinced that students who see the larger research endeavors of the university can gain a clearer sense of participating in a meaningful process of learning and discovery that is theirs—but not theirs alone. Such students have the opportunity to buy into the life of the university in a particularly meaningful way.

THEORETICAL UNDERPINNINGS

My thinking about research in general and this textbook in particular is deeply rooted in concepts of disciplinarity articulated in this country over the past decade by such scholars as Charles Bazerman, James Paradis, Paul Prior, David R. Russell, and David Smit, among others. The instructions, exercises, and readings in *Academic Research and Writing: Inquiry and Argument in College* are based on the idea that writing is always part of an activity system that includes wider professional conversations and practices shared by participants in a dynamic of evolving knowledge. The book contextualizes writing in several ways:

1. It directly describes research as part of larger systems of activity within a discipline, and it addresses differences in discourse conventions among disciplines. The book seeks to dispel the idea that the different demands made by different courses and teachers are arbitrary; instead, it represents these differences as aspects of how knowledge is produced and used by different fields.
2. It admits that transferring knowledge from general writing instruction to specific genres in specific disciplines is part of a complex initiation into a disciplinary community. It does not seek to describe all the conventions, genres, and fields a student may encounter, but it acknowledges that different expectations hold in different fields, and it explains how and why students should expect to work in different ways as they move through their coursework.
3. It encourages students to examine texts for information about genre and field expectations and to consider for themselves how genres, conventions, and audience expectations differ in different parts of the university.
4. Finally, and about this I have some reservations, the book invites instructors to construct the research writing course itself as a community of learners and researchers—a kind of "school version" of an activity system—so that students can experience working among a group of peers. By reading at least some common texts, working in topic-based research groups, presenting research to the class, and reviewing each others' work, students can have something of the experience of writing in a discourse community in which knowledge is created, shared, and transferred among a group of people doing similar work and engaging with similar questions.

This approach has several potential advantages, the most important of which is that students are asked to write to a real audience with whom they have some shared knowledge; their discourse can be part of actual conversations, both about the sources they read and with the audience to whom they write. It encourages students to think rhetorically: to think of research not merely in terms of following rules for good writing or effective research in general, but more fully in terms of understanding the expectations and needs of a known and potentially demanding audience. Although the book invites students to join in the research function of the university, it positions them as novices, learning the processes of doing research and writing about it, not as "finished" experts who are expected to have completed this learning process before taking the course or even by the time they have finished their final projects.

To this end, the book offers a series of reading and writing assignments centered on topics related to education, knowledge, and learning to write. I chose these readings and activities based on the assumption that teaching writing and critical thinking is an activity most composition instructors have in common, whether we have other roles as medievalists, Americanists, or specialists in rhetoric and composition. Readings about academic life and learning to write offer perhaps the closest we can come to a shared body of expertise that students too can recognize as part of their experience of schooling. This body of readings also fits into the traditional assumptions that composition courses are a means of helping students make the transition into college education and life, and that reflective reading and writing help students make this transition most effectively.

I have some hesitation about a textbook's limiting the topics for students' research in this way because many instructors are reluctant to impose a single topic or discipline on a diverse body of students; a single focus for the class restricts students' freedom to choose their own topics and so deemphasizes some aspects of invention. Therefore, I leave it to the individual instructor to decide how much to use the specific readings and activities I chose. The Instructor's Manual suggests ways to emphasize or deemphasize my own selections and alternative ways to use the textbook.

WHAT CONSTITUTES RESEARCH?

Readers of this book will realize that I am clearly inclined toward teaching students to conduct library research, particularly online library research. One thing that unites the production of knowledge in most fields is that new knowledge starts from investigating what is already known, and finding and reading previous research is the primary way researchers do that. The book does offer opportunities for conducting interviews and researching subjects from primary sources, and some instructors may want to focus on this kind of assignment. However, I remain convinced that contemporary undergraduates need to learn to find, read, understand, and evaluate the work that previous researchers have done in order to recognize the conversation in which their own work can and should be taking part. This is not a matter of academic learning only. When they graduate, our students will become working citizens, people who should understand something about how to read, use, and contextualize the ongoing work of university researchers. This need is particularly strong at the present time because the amazing growth of technologies over the past decades has both expanded the potential of information literacy in exciting ways and also raised questions of ownership, authority, and value that need to be discussed and evaluated both in the university and by the public. Our students are part of that public or about to enter it, and understanding how to access and use academic research will, I believe, give them stronger and more informed voices in those conversations.

For example, academic research in both genetics and law has led to the application of DNA evidence in hundreds of criminal cases, sometimes reversing decades-old decisions. This research affects professionals in law and law enforcement, as well as citizens trying to understand the American system of justice. Another example: academic research in entomology has been used to fight insect infestations that threaten the trees in many yards, parks, and forests. Such research impacts professional practices in forestry, recreation management, and related fields, but it also impacts individual homeowners, who might find much-loved and expensive parts of their landscapes threatened by infestations or by attempts to fight them. Popular books like *Freakonomics: A Rogue Economist Explores the Hidden Side of Everything*, by Steven D. Levitt and Stephen J. Dubner, have made thousands of readers aware of economics as a field of study. And of course there are constant applications of university research in medicine, dentistry, agriculture, chemistry, and other fields, applications that are so continual that it is hard to notice each one individually unless we are working in a field that uses them or until they impact our lives directly. Moreover, the greatly increased accessibility of that research on the World Wide Web makes the abilities of people outside of universities to understand academic arguments, contextualize academic research, and evaluate sources of information more crucial than they may have been in the past, when such research was less broadly and immediately accessible.

The practices of researching and writing have almost completely changed over the past twenty years, and this book acknowledges these changes. I assume that students using this book have access to computers and the Web and that they need to use these technologies ethically and efficiently for research, writing, and image production. I know that many students use computer technologies with more ease and comfort than some of their professors, but writing instructors still have much to teach students about how to use them to produce exciting, effective, and ethical researched writing. I use the term "researched" writing by design. The book introduces and describes a variety of ways in which research is communicated within the university and beyond. Students are provoked to consider genre as a dynamic configuration of a writer's purpose, readers' needs and expectations, and common practices within a community. The exercises at the end of every chapter offer instructors and students choices not only about what they will research, but often about in what genre that research will be presented, and the range of assignments addresses different levels of formality appropriate for different audiences and purposes. The exercises are grouped at the end of each chapter so that instructors can decide which assignments they think most useful for their class and integrate them into their syllabi in different ways. No instructors could or should try to use all of these suggested exercises, nor should instructors hesitate to modify them or design assignments more appropriate to their particular students.

WRITING AS A RECURSIVE PROCESS

Writing instructors tend to talk about writing and learning to write as a recursive process, but research writing courses are often focused on using recursivity to develop a single, final product. This book attempts to reflect how academic and professional researchers often use and reuse materials from project to project, and from genre to genre, document to document. The writing process addressed in *Academic Research and Writing: Inquiry and Argument in College*, then, is punctuated by a series of genres that students are invited to adapt and reuse as their thinking develops throughout the semester. For example, the working bibliography students compile in Chapter 5 and the summaries and syntheses they write in Chapter 6 may be revised and adapted for use in a literature review and annotated bibliography assigned in Chapter 7, for the personal research paper in Chapter 9, and for the argumentative research paper in Chapter 10. However, not every piece of work needs to be reused. Student writers, like all the rest of us, are entitled to some dead ends and fresh starts, as they both learn how to be researchers and discover what they want to learn about. The book encourages students to reflect on these issues rhetorically, not merely to follow directions for converting text from one genre to another.

The book does not eliminate the long argumentative research paper because this kind of research project is still required by many undergraduate programs. However, it provides linked examples of the development of a number of distinct documents that taken together comprise two sustained sample projects, one project addressing plagiarism and the other project addressing the use of international graduate students as teaching assistants in undergraduate courses. The book provides series of written examples of student researchers' work on both of these topics, as they move from general practices such as choosing a topic and constructing a general working bibliography, to meeting genre expectations for proposals, annotated bibliographies, and research papers (one a personal or "I-Search" paper in Chapter 9, and the other a more traditional argumentative paper in Chapter 10).

USING SOURCES APPROPRIATELY AND ETHICALLY

The book devotes an entire chapter to issues of plagiarism and intellectual property. Plagiarism has become a big issue in contemporary culture, and instructors and students alike cannot help being aware of the proliferation of Web sites for sharing and purchasing papers and then of sites aimed at catching what are seen as cheating students and plagiarized papers. My intention in devoting a full chapter to this topic is to move away from teaching a simple "thou shalt not" approach to thinking about the appropriate use and attribution of sources. Like many other members of the rhetoric and composition community, I fear that plagiarism-detecting tools establish an "us versus them" relationship between teachers and students that ultimately inhibits learning. Instead of focusing on initiating students into the values of our institutions and fields of study, too often instructors find themselves in the role of detectors, enforcers, and judges—not teachers. My intention in Chapter 3 is to move beyond this cat and mouse approach to defining and apprehending plagiarism, and, in the spirit of "Defining and Avoiding Plagiarism: The WPA Statement on Best Practices" (http://hwpacouncil.org/positions/plagiarism.html), to teach students to think about their own citation practices in the context of larger and more complicated issues concerning intellectual property. I address this issue early in the book to emphasize the importance of appropriate use of sources as a means by which students enter the discourse community of the university and its disciplines and by which they establish ethos as writers. Using sources appropriately and ethically is at the heart of the ethics of the university, not something tacked onto the end of a project. Moreover, it can take time and practice for students to distinguish their own thinking from that of others, and understanding why this effort is important is a crucial early step in that process.

I do not mean to minimize the problem of student cheating; I have often felt personally insulted when discovering—often by chance—that students have submitted to me work that is not their own. However, as Rebecca Moore Howard and others have pointed out, there are distinct differences between intentional cheating (such as buying or borrowing a paper) and the less obvious ways students appropriate ideas and words, particularly the process she calls "patchwriting," that is, strategies novice writers use when they do not yet feel in control of the knowledge they need to fulfill the assignments they are given. Learning to use sources ethically and effectively is a *learning* process, and this chapter addresses it as such. Moreover, it is not just a process of learning about how to use citations; it is also an interplay of discovering the place of one's own thinking in the intellectual resources of a field and of using those resources to develop expertise. This chapter aims to teach students to understand how using sources fits into the complex process of learning to understand and participate in a field of study or work.

THE CONVERSATIONS OF SCHOLARS

At the heart of the book is the idea that students should be brought into conversation with an intellectual community as it actually functions, with some members passionately maintaining a position and others puzzling over ideas and rethinking what might seem to be settled questions. Real intellectual communities are seldom very neat, and students mature as thinkers by recognizing and participating in serious disagreements among experts about important issues. I want students to see themselves as members of an academic community and to understand how and why academic communities make demands on their members to produce knowledge and use it well. I envision the students using this book as learning to see themselves as novices learning their fields, rather than as outsiders looking in. I also see them as individuals growing and changing through the process of becoming educated, a process that good teachers are still going through in their own lives. I do not consider the end of a course or the granting of a degree to be the *end* of education; these are temporary markers in a process of learning that spans most careers. My aim is to help students to understand what academic research does and to use it to enrich their own lives, whatever career paths they follow.

ACKNOWLEDGMENTS

This book, written over eight long years, owes much to the encouragement and support of nearly all my friends, colleagues, and students at Purdue University, who encouraged me in this work over that time.

I owe a very great debt to Lynn Huddon, my editor at Longman; to her assistant editor Rebecca Gilpin; and to Virginia Blanford, who took over and pressed on while Lynn was on leave. I am also most grateful to the fine reviewers Lynn and her colleagues found to review my manuscript in its many drafts. Without the encouragement of some of these reviewers, who saw what I was trying to do even when it was far from accomplished, I would not have had the courage to proceed. Several reviewers provided exceptionally good ideas for organizing material that I just could not seem to organize on my own. Sometimes reviews are hard to read: like our students, teachers want everyone to love our work at first sight or at first draft. But I really do appreciate the thought and effort that went into the praise, the critique, and the suggestions that were such an important part of my own writing process.

These reviewers are as follows: Timothy Brady, Wayland Baptist University; Nancy J. Brown, Lourdes College; Deborah K. Chappel, Arkansas State University; Huey Crisp, University of Arkansas–Little Rock; Alison Ganze, Western Kentucky University; Jonathan Hall, Rutgers University; Laura Halliday, Southern Illinois University; Susanmarie Harrington, Indiana University Purdue University–Indianapolis; Mary L. Otto Lang, Wharton County Junior College; Leticia Y. Lopez, Bellevue Community College; Susan Miller-Cochran, North Carolina State University; Bryan Moore, Arkansas State University; Lyle W. Morgan, Pittsburg State University; Ed Moritz, Indiana University Purdue University–Fort Wayne; Carol L. K. Smith, Chandler-Gilbert Community College; Rosanna West Walker, Lane Community College; Linda Woodson, The University of Texas at San Antonio.

The following friends, students, and former students helped draft, revise, and proofread various drafts and parts of the book, and some of them tried out all or parts of it in their classes (giving me much good feedback). Insofar as I can, I locate them by their current name and institutional affiliation, in alphabetical order: Dana Bisignani, Purdue University; Jessica Clark, Ph.D., Assistant Professor and Writing Center Director, Christopher Newport University; Danielle Cordaro, Purdue University; Elizabeth Cummins, Ph.D., Professor Emerita, Missouri University of Science and Technology; Dana Driscoll, Ph.D., Assistant Professor, Oakland University; Misty Farrar, Purdue University; Debra Huffman, Ph.D, Assistant Professor, Indiana University/Purdue University Fort Wayne; Jaisree Jayaraman, Purdue University; Erin Karper, Ph.D., Associate Professor, Niagara University; Judith Yaross Lee, Ph.D., Professor, Ohio University; Lu Liu, Ph.D.; Wendy Madore, Purdue University; Megan Hughes Morton, Ph. D., Assistant Professor, Geneva College; Sarah Johnson Pope; Deborah Rankin, Northwest Vista College; Morgan Reitmeyer, Purdue University; and Tony Russell, Purdue University.

CHAPTER 1

Argument in Academic Writing
Some Essential Concepts

Academic writing involves two interacting processes: argument and inquiry. The kinds of argument and means of inquiry vary considerably from field to field, but with some practice they are identifiable. To succeed in most college writing, students need to understand and participate in some of the conversations that are going on in every academic and professional field. In short, you need to be able to recognize and evaluate arguments, make successful inquiries, and finally make arguments of your own.

THREE APPEALS IN ARGUMENT: ETHOS, PATHOS, LOGOS

One useful way of looking at argument was first described by Aristotle in the fourth century B.C.E. Aristotle examines three aspects of argument, otherwise known as appeals: *logos* (the appeal to reason), *pathos* (the appeal to the reader's emotions), and *ethos* (the appeal to the writer's character). *Logos* involves evidence from the material, external world and reasonable ways of deriving conclusions about this evidence. *Pathos* involves appealing to and making an impact on the audience. *Ethos* involves the self-representation of the speaker or writer, how he or she establishes and maintains credibility, authority, and expertise. Aristotle would have preferred that all arguments be merely logical, but he admitted that given the frailty of humankind, pathos and ethos are effective and necessary strategies. Contemporary *rhetoricians* (people who study how arguments are made) are interested in how these appeals interact with each other. In different disciplines, logos, pathos, and ethos are applied differently, but all arguments can be considered in terms of the presence and nature of these three appeals—or their absence.

In academic writing, an acceptable argument is neither an opportunity to vent personal animosity nor a mere statement of personal opinion or preference. To maintain an acceptable, credible ethos, researchers normally need to demonstrate knowledge of their field and to relate new knowledge to what is already known in a way that seems reasonable. They expect their work to be evaluated by a knowledgeable and critical audience. For example, the excerpt below from biologist Jacob Bronowski's review of

James Watson's account of the discovery of DNA illustrates how scientists evaluate each other's work in an atmosphere of respectful mutual criticism and argument and how, while doing their best to interpret accurately what they see in their observations or experiments, they always leave room for doubt:

> [The book] will bring home to the nonscientist how the scientific method really works: that we *invent* a model and then *test* its consequences, and that it is this conjunction of imagination and realism that constitutes the inductive method. The models in science are not always as concrete as those which Crick and Watson put together with their hands; Albert Einstein could not have made a visible model of his space-time; and yet space-time *is* a model, and so is every discovery, and it takes its power from the closeness with which the consequences that flow from it match the real world.
>
> Building models with one's hands is an engaging task, during which the builder becomes attached to his model and is tempted to gloss over its faults. Since most models are wrong and have to be discarded, however attractive they seem, it is therefore helpful to have two people at work, so that each may be ruthless with the other. This is a point that Francis Crick has made and it comes out firmly in this book—the progress of science depends on criticism. This is why there are no scientific critics in the sense that there are literary critics in their own right. Criticism is a necessary and positive function in science, but it has no independent status; and if you cannot make and take it without anger, then . . . you are out of place in the world of change that science creates and inhabits. (381–82)

However, even though scientists work in a professional world of controversy and contention, they do not usually rely heavily on pathos, and so direct appeals to the readers' emotions seem out of place in their academic writing. Ethos is maintained by a detached professional voice and clear articulation of the research method and the means by which data are analyzed.

In most other fields as well, researchers consider logical argumentation to be the primary way professionals interpret information and exchange knowledge, and they expect an academic argument to offer an informed thesis, to be supported by credible evidence, and to be presented with "good reasoning." In general, in making a good argument, a researcher

- draws conclusions warranted by the evidence;[1]
- takes into account the evidence and arguments against his or her own position, refuting the alternatives or modifying the claim accordingly;
- uses evidence honestly;
- manages ethos and pathos appropriately for the discipline and the purpose;
- and avoids the major logical fallacies that come from over-generalizing, assuming that an exceptional case is typical, and appealing excessively to personalities and emotions.

None of these aspects of argument exists in isolation because they are rooted in the expectations of particular fields and in the specific purpose of a particular piece of writing. Academic writers are very careful in constructing arguments because they expect knowledgeable fellow researchers in their field to read and evaluate their research. Part of the process of *peer review*, a concept described by Jacob Bronowski in the previous passage, and which will be discussed more fully in Chapter 2, is the attempt by colleagues to find problems with each other's arguments, particularly gaps in the evidence (methodological problems) and lapses in the reasoning with which the case is made (logical fallacies).

CONSENSUS AND CONTROVERSY

Textbooks in most fields, particularly at the introductory levels, focus on *consensus*, on what "everybody knows" and what most practitioners in a field agree constitutes good theory and good practice. However, as students learn more about any field, they come to see that it is full of controversies, ongoing disagreements among experts about what data mean, how evidence should be interpreted, or how research should affect practice. These controversies are often based on important differences. For instance:

- In the field of communication, some scholars consider the most important communications to be public statements like speeches and announcements, while others consider the informal interpersonal communications between individuals to be more significant.
- In psychology, some researchers attribute individual differences to learned behaviors, while others attribute them to physiological factors.

Scholars and experts writing for others in their field tend to focus more on the controversies, problems, misinterpretations, reinterpretations, and arguments in their field than on the consensus that almost everyone in the field agrees on. In communicating their research, scholars construct arguments, supported by evidence appropriate to their field, to fill gaps, to correct errors, and to apply data or methodologies from one context to another. But, as Bronowski insisted, they leave room for doubt, since knowledge always grows and changes as data accumulate and paradigms shift. The Nobel Prize–winning physicist Richard P. Feynman describes this necessary doubt as both the beginning and the end of the scientific process:

> The first is the matter of judging evidence—well, the first thing really is, before you begin you must not know the answer. So you begin by being uncertain as to what the answer is. . . . The question of doubt and uncertainty is what is necessary to begin; for if you already know the answer there is no need to gather any evidence about it. Well, being uncertain, the next thing is to look for evidence, and the scientific method is to begin with trials. But another way and a very important one that should not be neglected is to put together ideas to try to enforce a logical consistency among the various things that you know. It is a very valuable thing to try to connect this, what you know, with that, that you know, and try to find out if they are consistent. And the more activity in the direction of trying to put together the ideas of different directions, the better it is . . . Authority may

be a hint as to what the truth is, but is not the source of information. As long as it's possible, we should disregard authority whenever the observations disagree with it. (103–104)

Feynman looks at "authorities" as a starting point, not an ending point; when conducting a scientific experiment, a researcher does not know the answer to the question, and thus seeks to extend knowledge, not merely repeat it. A researcher doesn't have a real inquiry if the answer to the question is already known.

PARADIGMS AND WARRANTS

Rational arguments are possible because people within fields of study and work share a consensus concerning basic assumptions, procedures, and practices. They agree about the appropriate ways to ask and answer questions, and about what questions can be asked within a field. These *paradigms* (to use a term applied by the historian of science Thomas Kuhn) may change over time. Kuhn uses as an example the idea that the sun revolves around the earth, a paradigm shared by most intelligent and educated people until the seventeenth century, when it became clear that the Copernican paradigm of a sun-centered (solar) system offered a simpler explanation for the movements of planets and stars that had been revealed by the increasingly improved telescope lenses of that time (68ff). In the nineteenth century, a similar paradigm shift occurred in medicine as the germ theory of disease replaced the idea that the cause of illness was bodily humors (fluids) being out of balance.

Paradigms may shift, but warrants (as defined by Stephen Toulmin in the 1950s) are even more basic assumptions. Because they rest on often unexamined assumptions about what is good, true, and (in some fields) beautiful, warrants tend to be quite stable. Scientists tend to share the warrant that the simplest explanation for a phenomenon is more reliable than a complicated one. For example, during the century or so before the Copernican theory was widely accepted, the lenses used in telescopes were greatly improved, and astronomers could see and chart more planets and stars and their movements in relation to each other. They had to make increasingly complex and awkward charts and models to explain the movements of planets and stars through spheres that almost everyone believed circled the earth and constituted the heavens. Putting the sun instead of the earth at the center of what came to be known as the solar system allowed for a much simpler model and clearer explanations of what they had observed, and because most scientists assume that the simpler explanation is more apt to be true, the paradigm shift was warranted.

Many academic fields also share the warrant that a valid theory must be capable of being disproved by later research ("falsifiable"). This warrant offers the room for doubt that Feynman wrote about. Most fields also share the warrant that material explanations outweigh nonmaterial explanations. Thus, for example, physicians look for physical explanations for illnesses, and astronomers look for material explanations for the sudden appearance of a comet. In the sixteenth century, however, a supernatural explanation would have seemed warranted to most people—witchcraft, perhaps, or a miracle. Or, to use a fictional example, I might firmly believe that an airplane I am riding in is held up in the air by the force of my will to keep it flying, but there is no way to measure and prove or disprove that proposition about the strength of my will. The basic principles of aerodynamics, however, have been measured over the decades and refined to adapt to new evidence, in response to the doubts Feynman sees as necessary to science. The results of mechanics and physics are falsifiable by experiment, not dependant on assertion alone.

Arguments about warrants can be deep and bitter, since they involve basic beliefs about goodness, truth, and beauty. To say that someone's conclusions are unwarranted can draw a clear line in the sand. A clear example identifying warrants and showing how they shape arguments can be seen in David Brooks's *New York Times* (op-ed) opinion piece "Virtues and Victims," (p. 241 in the Readings). Brooks compares two different warrants for understanding an incident at a university in which several lacrosse players were accused of rape after a party. Brooks's point was not about the players' innocence or guilt, which he assumed would be settled in the courts, but about two ways of looking at what happened: as an issue of personal responsibility or as an issue of the social and cultural setting of the university in its town and of athletes in the university. The courts found the athletes to be innocent, but Brooks's piece about this incident is useful for understanding these two different ways of framing responsibility: individual responsibility versus social values. Although a rape would be judged "bad" by adherents to both warrants, Brooks points out that the arguments about whom to blame and how to avoid such incidents in the future look very different, depending on the warrant on which they rest. Warrants, then, can contain fighting words and can also preclude argument, since arguments depend on the arguer and the audience sharing pretty much the same warrants about how things work.

On the other hand, although some warrants are absolute (either/or), they can also be more subtle. For example, some people might argue from the warrant that *both* personal morality and institutional culture contribute to bad behavior. Because warrants involve basic assumptions that are often left unstated, they can be tricky to identify, and developing research skills requires practice in identifying warrants in both sources and your own inquiries. Identifying, analyzing, and making arguments help clarify how warrants connect evidence through general, often unstated principles, and can help you identify where your own warrants overlap or contradict the warrants of other arguments or each other.

THE STRUCTURE OF AN ACADEMIC ARGUMENT

While writing can vary according to the audience, purpose, and demands of a particular project in a particular field, there are some common, recognizable ways in which arguments are usually structured. Recognizing these features can help you make the necessary transitions from field to field.

FOCUS POINTS: UNDERSTANDING ARGUMENTS

■ Although an argument can start with a topic or a question, it moves to make a *claim*, which is stated in a *thesis* statement (argument to be made) or *hypothesis* (proposition to be tested).

- Claims are arguable—not a matter of feeling or taste (like chocolate is the best flavor, or football is my favorite sport).

- The writer and the audience must share warrants concerning what constitutes evidence and about how the world works. For example, it is extremely difficult for a contemporary physician with standard scientific training to argue with a person who believes that disease is caused by witchcraft, since neither accepts the other's evidence.

- An argument about a claim that pretty much everyone believes is probably not much of an argument; there must be room for the doubt Feynman writes about. However, a well-supported claim that questions what most people believe may be worth arguing. For example, a claim like "Competitive sports are an important aspect of higher education because they inspire loyalty in the fans and build character in the players" will probably not make for a compelling argument to an audience of American sports fans—because it will seem obvious. On the other hand, Murray Sperber's claim in *Beer and Circus: How Big-Time College Sports Is Crippling Undergraduate Education*, that big-time competitive sports at universities are damaging to both athletes and nonathletes, is a claim that he can and does vigorously argue for by assembling reasons and evidence for an audience concerned about a presumed decline in academic achievement in college. In turn, his claim has given rise to further counterarguments about the benefits of college sports in response to his challenge. Notice that although they make different claims, both sides of this argument share the warrant that universities can and should contribute to the health and character of all students and that these characteristics can be measured in various ways; they differ primarily about the means to this end and the measurements they use.

■ In any argument, the claim is supported by reasons, the grounds on which the writer will support the claim.

■ The reasons are in turn supported with evidence, the documented results of investigation. In the humanities, evidence is found in the sources consulted, that is, literary works in literature courses, or historical documents (or accounts of them) in history. In science, the evidence consists of the documented results of experiments, systematic observations, and calculations. Many of the social sciences use both kinds of evidence.

- Most of an argument consists of supporting the reasons by presenting and defending evidence and by refuting conflicting evidence to show that it is wrong or irrelevant to those reasons.

- Sometimes writers can find direct, clearly relevant evidence to support an argument; other times they assemble other kinds of support, such as definitions, comparisons and analogies, and appeals to the needs and values of the particular audience.

- Sometimes arguments are supported by secondary arguments with claims, reasons, and evidence of their own, and reasons are defended by making subordinate arguments that contribute to the primary claim.

■ In U.S. academic discourse, when a paper is constructed as an argument, the major claim is usually stated in the introduction of a paper and set in the context of current knowledge in the field; often the sequence of reasoning that will be followed is also stated or suggested. Most of the body of the paper lays out the evidence for the reasons and shows how they support the claim. The conclusion, then, reiterates the claim and discusses its significance to the field.

■ You can usually find the major claims, reasons, and organization of the evidence in a piece by skimming it. Try highlighting the first sentence of each paragraph of a source you are working with, as well as the first and last sentences of the introduction and conclusion. The highlighted sentences will usually produce an outline of the argument.

EXAMPLE 1.1 *An Argument in Biological Ethics*

Francine Patterson and Wendy Gordon, researchers in gorilla behavior, argue that gorillas deserve to be considered moral beings, like humans, because they share some fundamental mental qualities with humans, including intelligence, emotionality, the capacity for creative expression through language and other means, and self-awareness (70–71). They support each of these reasons with experimental evidence that shows that gorillas possess these qualities to the extent that some humans, such as young children and the mentally disabled, possess them. The warrant for their claim that gorillas are entitled to moral rights we normally consider uniquely human is that all beings should be consistently classified according to the qualities they are observed to have.

Question

What alternative warrants (i.e., underlying assumptions about how beings should be classified) might lead to a different argument and a different conclusion, even if we accept the evidence for gorillas' mental capacities that results from the researchers' documented experiments in teaching and testing gorillas?

EXAMPLE 1.2 *An Argument in Sociology*

Eviatar Zerubavel argues that our memories are not completely individual, but result from our participation in a particular community of knowledge, a social group (for example, a nation, a tribe, or a religion) that sets rules by which we remember (89). His main reason is that many members of the same group hold similar memories, which he attributes to how the social group constructs its history into stories. These shared stories are shaped by certain beginnings (or births) of eras often marked by particular discoveries; they distinguish between history and prehistory and create specific traditions of memory, so that individuals remember events they were not personally involved in and share the feeling of belonging to the social group (i.e., we can feel pride in our nation's founders, even if our own ancestors recently immigrated from another country). His evidence includes the inclination of almost every society to write histories, pass along oral traditions, preserve historical sites, and commemorate particular events, which he supports with examples spanning disparate social groups. The warrant for his argument is that similarities in the way people think are caused by the influence of a group to which they belong.

Questions

Suppose you assumed (as some social scientists do) that similarities in the way people think are caused by the inherent truth of what they observe and experience? Or by their own individual experiences and perceptions? How would those different warrants affect the argument described above? What alternative claim(s) might be made?

EXAMPLE 1.3 *An Argument in Educational Administration*

The Readings section contains an article by Alfie Kohn, which argues that grade inflation is a myth that diverts attention from the real problem with grading: that grading impedes rather than fosters learning. The underlying warrants for this argument are that the purpose of education is learning, which is impossible to measure accurately, and that students and teachers share this purpose. There are two main claims in this argument:

1. Kohn supports the claim that grade inflation is a myth with three reasons:
   - that accounts of grade inflation are based on false information,
   - that no one has actually proven that students today get As for work of a quality that once received Cs or Ds,
   - and that the warrant that there can be "an objectively correct evaluation of what a student (or an essay) deserves" is outdated and wrong.

   He supports these reasons by refuting the conclusions drawn by earlier researchers on the grounds that their evidence is unreliable, that they fail to refute alternative interpretations, and that they are tainted by a conservative political bias, and by citing data from a U.S. Department of Education analysis of student grades, assumed to be a highly reliable source, that grades have not risen, but actually declined, over the years.

2. Kohn supports the claim that grading impedes learning by arguing against the underlying warrants of the opposing argument:
   - that the purpose of education is ranking students,
   - that stringent grading improves learning,
   - and that grades are a good motivation for student learning.

   He supports these arguments with evidence drawn from published research that demonstrates that students learn better from internal motives and from teachers who expect them to succeed rather than to compete.

Questions
- When you read this piece, you may notice that Kohn refutes the warrant that what a student learns can be effectively measured by merely condemning this idea as outdated and simplistic, whereas he provides considerable evidence to refute the idea that grades are an effective motivator. In what ways are these different kinds of warrants?
- How does a writer distinguish between warrants that need to be defended and warrants he can expect the audience to share?
- Why might Kohn have chosen simply to dismiss the warrant about measurement?

EXAMPLE 1.4 *An Argument in English Studies*

In a well-known article, reprinted in the Readings section, Jane Tompkins argues that all attempts to see the past are affected by the points of view of historians and of contemporary witnesses, but that nonetheless researchers can make reasonable conclusions about past events by comparing the various accounts with a critical mind. Like Kohn, she makes two claims, the second building on the first.

1. Her first claim, that all attempts to see the past are affected by point of view, she supports by arguing that both distinguished historians and firsthand witnesses are products of their times and cultures, which shape what they see, what they think needs to be recorded, and how they describe what they see. As evidence, she analyzes excerpts of texts first by historians and then by eyewitnesses (such as a woman held captive) about relations between white people and Native Americans.

2. Her second claim, which modifies the first, is that we can still reach reasonable conclusions about the past by "piecing together facts from contradictory evidence and convergent points of view," a claim she supports by demonstrating this kind of "piecing together" and the presumed facts available as a result.

Questions

- In what ways is Tompkins' argument similar to Zerubavel's?
- What do these examples suggest about the different kinds of evidence used to support arguments in different academic fields?

VISUAL ELEMENTS IN ACADEMIC ARGUMENTS

Like other writers, academic researchers often support their writing with visual elements, but usually they are informational, not emotional. For instance, a magazine article might make an effective case for famine relief with a picture of a weeping mother; a scholarly argument, on the other hand, might instead use visuals like a chart of the ages of famine victims. Scientists and social scientists designate visuals as figures—including charts, tables, graphs, and occasional diagrams. Researchers in these fields expect to be able to "read" the (logical) argument of the paper from the figures, which render quantifiable data in a visual format. In businesses and most administrative work, an organizational chart helps both employees and clients find their way around (see Fig. 1.1).

In most fields in the humanities, researchers use visuals less often (except in fields like art history), and the visuals (like maps, portraits, etc.) are used more to supplement the argument than to make it. For example, the map in Figure 1.2 gives a clear picture of the relative sizes of the United States and Mexico before the Mexican War in 1846–1848, a picture that could be used as evidence for several different arguments. When pictures are used—as they often are, for example, by historians and biographers—they are sometimes collected together in one or two sections set off from the rest of the text.

A good place to look for maps, pictures, and other visuals that may be freely used for noncommercial sources (like research or teaching) is: en.wikipedia.org/ wiki/Public_domain_image_resources. Be sure to check the policy for using the image to be sure that you may download it and use it as you intend. For example, students might be allowed to use a visual in a paper, but not on a Web site. This is the owner's decision, not the user's. Be sure to cite visuals as you cite other sources, unless you create them yourself. The issues of copyright and plagiarism will be discussed more fully in Chapter 3.

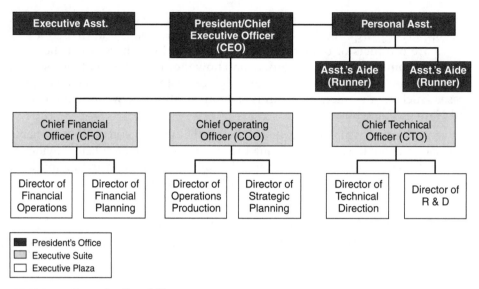

FIGURE 1.1 Organizational Chart

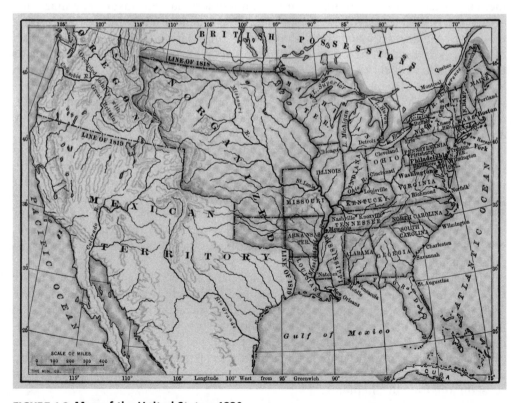

FIGURE 1.2 Map of the United States, 1830

ARGUMENT AND PERSUASION

Persuasion draws on elements of argument, but persuasion attempts not just to convince, but to move the reader to action or to a major change of mind. Academic readers tend to be persuaded by strong evidence, good reasoning, and an ethos of expertise in the field. A persuasive researched argument not only argues its own case, but demonstrates its relation to other knowledge in its field. A strongly persuasive researched argument can change the shared knowledge or standard practices in a field, as Watson and Crick's "Molecular Structure of Nucleic Acids" did in genetic research. The persuasion is rooted, however, in the evidence; the authors maintain their ethos as scientists by retaining distance from their conclusions, leaving the room for doubt discussed by Richard Feynman. For example, in reporting their discovery of how DNA works, an important breakthrough in the life sciences in 1953, James Watson and Francis Crick merely claim that "We wish to suggest a structure for the salt of deoxyribose nucleic acid (D.N.A.). This structure has novel features which are of considerable biological interest."[2]

The possibility of persuasion lies at the heart of much academic writing; every researcher wants to have a recognizable impact on the field. On the other hand, persuasion can have manipulative aspects as well, as when a writer relies excessively on appealing to the reader's emotions (pathos), and when a writer simply asserts in an appealing way claims that are not proven or assumptions that are not stated and defended. Advertisers regularly persuade people to buy a product or accept a particular view on an issue by appealing primarily to the emotions of a target audience, and many successful marketing campaigns demonstrate how the force of an emotional appeal (pathos) or the pull of a celebrity endorsement (ethos) can tempt people to ignore major failures of reasoning. That is why logical fallacies abound in the popular media, where pathos and ethos tend to be more prevalent than logos. Advertisers rely on their success at persuading people to buy a particular brand of soft drink or car by the attractiveness of its commercials, the image it seems to project, and praise by popular or attractive people. Most advertisements rely on fallacies, as do many political discussions on talk shows, commentary programs, and blogs—and so contemporary Americans get used to hearing people make illogical leaps between ideas.

FALLACIES

Fallacies that undermine good arguments occur when the connections among claims, reasons, and evidence are faulty or nonexistent. These gaps often come from the desire to make a strong argument, a desire that can tempt writers to assemble all the supporting evidence they can find (even the dubious bits), to exaggerate their position's strength and relevance, and to ignore contradictions, exceptions, and counterexamples. Of course, deliberate misrepresentation should not be part of the process of argument, and unless there is clear evidence of intent to deceive, you should assume that fallacies in the academic arguments of faculty and students are unintentional. However, when they are exposed, *mistakes* detract nearly as much as *lies* from the credibility of an argument. Since most academic researchers write primarily for critical peers in their field like the scientists Bronowski describes earlier in this chapter, they know there is a good chance that their mistakes will be caught and exposed in reviews of their work—and so they try very hard to avoid them. Academic argument, to be persuasive, must be logical—and that implies that the researcher must be willing to change positions if new or better evidence shows that a claim is false. In short, academics' arguments rely on research to provide the evidence to support their claims.

FOCUS POINTS: COMMON LOGICAL FALLACIES

As you practice finding and using research, watch your reading and writing for major logical fallacies that involve generalizing from insufficient evidence and appealing excessively to personalities and emotions. Notice that in the following examples one fallacy often breeds another. There are many ways to generalize from insufficient evidence, but these are some of the most common:

- **Hasty generalizations or false generalizations:** This fallacy assumes that an exceptional case is typical, or assumes erroneous relations between individuals and classes of things.

  Example

  Women should not work outside the home if they want to be happy. My mother was always a stay-at-home mom, and she is the happiest woman I know.

  This mother might be an *example* of a happy homemaker, but is she a *typical* example? How do you know? How would you respond to a counterexample of a happy working mother?

  Example

  I cannot take a course in Chinese-American history because I am not Chinese.

  Courses in ethnic and gender studies (African-American Studies, Women's Studies, Asian Studies, etc.) are neither limited to people of that race or gender, nor are they taken by all people who belong to it.

- **Appeals to ignorance:** Not knowing something is a good reason for investigating it, but ignorance is not good evidence to support a reason.

  Examples

  Because we do not know the consequences of abolishing grades, we need to maintain the traditional system of grading.

  Because social scientists disagree about the effectiveness of teaching students to drink more responsibly, these scholars should not bother to investigate this strategy any longer, but simply focus on promoting abstinence.

- **False absolutes:** Absolute claims should rarely—if ever—be asserted (even if you believe very strongly in them) because one exception is all that is necessary to falsify an absolute claim. "All" and "none," "always" and "never" are disproved by one exception. A single second example negates the claim that a thing is "unique" or that your hypothesis is proven. Modifying your claim to admit the possibility of exceptions or alternatives does not weaken it but allows it to bend to accommodate new evidence without breaking. This is why Feynman, a deeply committed scientist, insists on the necessity of entertaining some doubt about what seems certain. Here are some other examples of false absolutes that would benefit from allowing for exceptions by using modifiers like "most," "many," "few," or "seldom."

  Examples

  Successful students never depend on the pressure of a deadline to get their work done.

  All scientists understand that facts change over time as new experimental results are obtained.

■ **False dichotomy/false division:** When you claim that things fall into two or three categories, you should be positive that there can be no other. It is more often the case that there is some intermingling between the categories and some outlying data.

Examples

> You are either in favor of having special classes for students whose first language is not English, or you are against this practice.
>
> There are only two ways of understanding the immune system: through the observation of large populations or through controlled experimentation on individuals.

Many people are of two minds about serious issues, and new methodologies are always possible in every field. As with modifying absolutes, you strengthen your argument by acknowledging the gray area rather than letting the reader find exceptions that support a counterargument.

■ **False cause:** Cause and effect are very hard to prove. Demonstrating that one event happened before another does not necessarily mean that the earlier one caused the later. They may be totally unconnected, they may stem from the same cause, or they may be the result of multiple causes rather than merely one.

Examples

> I got an A on the paper because I turned it in on time.
>
> The French Revolution occurred because of the example of the American Revolution a decade earlier.

You usually need to make an argument about cause, not just assume or assert it. If you added to the first statement "and the teacher cares more about papers being turned in on time than anything else," you'd have a reason that looks very much like a false generalization, and thus a reason in need of evidence to support it.

■ **False analogy:** Analogies are an important means for making an argument, particularly when there is little or no direct evidence to support a point, but they should not be the argument's only support. An analogy is only as valid as the resemblance of the features being compared. For example, an epidemiologist might use rates of disease in rat populations to predict rates of disease in human populations; the validity of the argument would lie in the extent to which the two species are comparable, which could be established by citing other studies in which rat populations predicted similar effects in human populations. A false analogy is one in which the comparison cannot be defended or has not been sufficiently defended.

Examples

> Notice how the following false analogies also try to arouse pathos:
>
>> Denying on-campus parking to students would be like denying a life jacket to a drowning man.
>>
>> A computer is like a human brain, only faster and more accurate.

These are exciting words, but to be reasonable, the analogy must be explored and defended.

FOCUS POINTS: EMOTIONAL FALLACIES

Many of the fallacies above also involve pathos and ethos as well as logos. Emotional fallacies come from inappropriate, irrelevant, and excessive appeals to ethos (the authority of the writer) or pathos (the emotions of the reader). Here are some more gaps in reasoning to watch out for in your reading and to avoid in your writing:

- ■ **False authority:** When you use an authority to support your claim, you need to be sure that he or she has actual authority in that particular field. A Nobel Prize–winning biologist like James Watson is probably not an expert in economics or population dynamics.

  Example

  > Dr. Jones, winner of the prestigious Smith Award in Physics, has stated that the Civil War had little to do with slavery.

- ■ **Guilt (or credibility) by association:** A person's affiliation with a certain group (like a religion or a political party) does not necessarily mean that his conclusions are biased or untrue, although the affiliation might influence his thinking; likewise, an affiliation does not necessarily mean that his conclusions are accurate or fair, although relevant credentials and associations can be marks of credibility. (See the discussion of "Evaluating Sources" in Chapter 2.)

  Example

  > Because Professor Abbot has served as an influential advisor to the Reagan administration, his advocacy of free market economics is suspect.

  Closely related to this fallacy is the *ad hominem* fallacy, in which a person's ideas are discredited solely because of who he or she is or because of qualities the audience might find distasteful.

  Example

  > Since Dr. Anderson is known to be an atheist, her statistics on hunger in Michigan cannot be accepted as accurate testimony before the state legislature.

  It is possible to make a case for the unfairness, or bias of a source, but the reasons must be directly relevant to the claims, and the case must be argued, not accepted as given.

- ■ **Bandwagon:** Even though most people believe in an idea or practice, even though it is customary, or even though it may be rapidly gaining in popularity, it is still necessary to argue—that is, show reasons and evidence—why the idea or practice would be useful in a particular situation. Moreover, what everyone knows or does can change drastically from generation to generation, as was the case when "everyone" knew that the sun revolved around the earth.

  Example

  > Because all colleges with any claim to keeping up with contemporary technology are requiring students to purchase laptops and PDAs, our university should follow this lead.

  This can be the basis for an argument for or against such requirements, depending on the particular circumstances of a school's faculty or student body, but by itself it is merely an assertion in need of defense.

- ■ **Slippery slope:** It can be tempting to assert that a step in one direction will inevitably lead to the worst conceivable results, particularly when you are arguing about issues with ethical implications. Seeing a potential future abuse can be a useful way of thinking or rethinking an issue, but predictions alone are not an argument for or against a future outcome. If a claim for a chain of results (devastating or beneficial) is made, it must be supported by reasons and evidence that demonstrate that the predicted effects might actually occur.

Example

> If teachers start to distinguish between buying term papers and faulty citation, eventually everything students hand in will be plagiarized.

Generations of students and teachers have struggled with this issue, but most students still do their own work. People can stay on slopes, even slippery ones, for a long time.

■ **Appeals to tradition:** What has been done in the past may not continue into the future, and not everyone benefits from, believes in, or engages in traditional behaviors, functions, and activities. The argument for or against the value of a practice must be made, not simply stated.

Examples

> Owning your own home is good because it is a central aspect of the American Dream.

> It is a mistake to allow women into the higher-earning professions, since men have always been the primary breadwinners in a family.

■ **Appeals to spite and ridicule:** Clearly, these are not arguments, but name-calling, which is never appropriate in academic discourse. Such emotional appeals can set up a false dichotomy in a particularly nasty way.

Examples

> Only an idiot would . . .

> Any self-respecting engineer knows . . .

Spite and ridicule are often used in propaganda, particularly when one side has no respect for the other. Think about the caricatures of politicians in newspaper cartoons, for example. And for a particularly vicious example, see the World War II propaganda poster in Figure 1.3.

FIGURE 1.3 "Warning" Poster
Appeals to the emotions like this, combining fear and ridicule, are common to all sides during wars and in intense ethical and political debates.

VISUAL FALLACIES

Although we often tend to believe what we see more than what we read, visuals can also be fallacious. For example, photographs may be cropped to make crowds seem larger or smaller than they actually were, and they can leave out matter that modifies or contradicts the point the writer wants to make. Even worse, current computer technology allows for rearranging photographs, so that people from different photographs can be made to seem to be talking with each other, backgrounds can be changed, and so on. Graphs can be designed so that the visual elements make differences look smaller or greater than the numbers they are designed to represent. In the excerpt from his book *The Visual Display of Quantitative Information* (p. 303), Edward Tufte calculates a "lie factor" for false graphics, by dividing the size of an effect as seen in the graphic by the size of the effect the data supports. Tufte asserts that lying through visual design—like any other form of deception—is not only wrong, but ineffective in making an argument. As with most deceptions, once the attempt to deceive is uncovered, the credibility (ethos) of the writer or designer is severely undermined. When evaluating sources with visuals, you may find Tufte's "lie factor" a useful means of assessing reliability.

Exercises

1.1 RECOGNIZING AND ANALYZING ELEMENTS OF ARGUMENT

1. Read the opinion piece in the Readings by one of the following authors: David Brooks, Robert Macfarlane, or Rebecca Moore Howard. With one or two of your classmates, identify elements of logos, ethos, and pathos in the piece.
2. Next, identify the author's claim(s), reasons, evidence, and warrants(s). Highlight these parts of the argument with different colored highlighters or underline them with different colored ink. If any warrants are not stated, decide what they are and write them down.
3. Write a brief response that addresses the author's argument and use of references.
4. Repeat this process with an opinion piece you find for yourself in the op-ed (Opinion and Editorial) section of a newspaper.

1.2 FINDING FALLACIES

With one or two of your classmates, select advertisements from different kinds of magazines, and one or two television advertisements that seem convincing or that you particularly enjoy. Collect at least five different advertisements.

1. Identify the audience that each advertisement seems to be aimed at.
2. Identify at least five of the fallacies listed above. Look for these fallacies, particularly the emotional fallacies, in the pictures, as well as in the words. Write a short description of how one of the advertisements uses pictures and text to appeal to the emotions in order to persuade the reader/viewer.
3. Repeat this analysis using another printed advertisement or television commercial aimed at a different audience.
4. Review three of the op-ed pieces in the Readings, and disclose any fallacies you find in these authors' reasoning.
5. Collect some examples of solicitation letters that come in your mail or on Web sites you visit. Review three of them to identify their warrants. Then, disclose any fallacies you find in the letters.

1.3 MAKING FALLACIES

Write your own examples of five of the fallacies described in this chapter, and then explain how they could be exposed or modified. If you like, design at least one visual, and explain how it works to entice the reader to accept unreasonable assertions. How do pictures contain fallacies and how can researchers expose them?

1.4 QUESTIONS FOR FURTHER CONSIDERATION AND INFORMAL WRITING

Write an informal reflection on one of the following topics:

1. How well does your own sense of "argument" and "controversy" accord with the way those concepts are discussed in this chapter? How similar and different do academic arguments seem from everyday disputes?
2. What controversies have you been involved in? Describe how warrants allowed you to resolve them or prevented you from doing so.
3. Have you encountered any controversies in your major field of study or in another academic discipline? Are any controversies discussed in the textbooks you have used so far? How would you describe how changes (or advances) in knowledge in your field have been represented to you?

CHAPTER 2

Reading, Evaluating, and Responding to Arguments

One of the challenges of college work is that the readings often seem more complex than those you are used to, and understanding them may require more background information than the books assigned in high school. These increased expectations may be especially apparent as students progress from reading textbooks written for students to reading books and articles written for more informed and specialized audiences. Textbooks give students the "common knowledge" that introduces them to a field of study, and they usually represent a consensus view of the field. On the other hand, books and articles written by researchers for fellow researchers in their field—members of the same academic "discourse community"—are more apt to focus on a controversy or gap in knowledge. Researchers writing for their peers expect their readers to bring considerable common knowledge to their reading, and they may not repeat that common knowledge directly, except when introducing their topic. Thus, they may leave out pieces of information that newcomers need in order to fully understand the reading. For instance, an American Civil War historian writing for her colleagues might not mention the dates of the war, since she would assume that those dates are common knowledge in the field. A Shakespeare scholar writing for other experts in the field might not define terms like *first folio*. Moreover, researchers writing for their peers often use *jargon*, or professional terminology, without defining it (like "folio" in the previous sentence). All of these factors can contribute to a student's uncomfortable sense of entering a conversation in the middle—which is, in a way, what all newcomers to a field do. You can, however, increase your comprehension of readings in unfamiliar fields if you try to pick up the cues writers give regarding their audience, purpose, and argument.

READING FOR CUES TO AUDIENCE, PURPOSE, AND SIGNIFICANCE

Cues to Audience (Who Are "We"?)

Researchers addressing an audience of researchers in their field usually start out by establishing the context for their argument. Sometimes they will directly state the context for the argument as a consensus, using phrases like *"It is generally believed . . ."* or *"Established practice recommends. . . ."* It is very important to developing the writer's credibility (or ethos) that these actually are general beliefs or established practices and that the audience of researchers agrees with the writer about what the consensus in the field is. One way to establish this credibility is to draw on the work of authorities in the field, and researchers often make references to earlier published work to establish the common knowledge and to create the context for a particular inquiry. Some cues to what everyone knows are

- *we/our*
- *of course*
- *it is widely believed that*
- *the fact that*
- *there is general agreement that*

You can find even more information about the audience by looking at the acknowledgments page, citations list, and sources cited in footnotes or endnotes. These parts of a publication can reveal the immediate audience envisioned by the academic researcher.

Establishing that there is a consensus often includes a formal appraisal of previously published research, called a "literature review" (see Chapter 6). In this case, "literature" means publications in the field, *not* creative writing. The literature review both demonstrates the researcher's expertise (ethos) and moves toward the controversy to be addressed: what is unknown or mistaken in current knowledge that the current research will resolve. In the process of reviewing previous research, the writer normally indicates its value to the present project, addresses its shortcomings, and states the purpose of the present study in relation to past work in the field. The writer may also use the literature review to move from consensus to controversy, laying the groundwork for extending a line of thinking or showing that an accepted claim is wrong. Look for verbal cues to the writer's position such as:

- *on the other hand*
- *however*
- *more recent studies suggest*
- *more convincing research suggests*
- *to extend this line of research*

Cues to Purpose

To identify the purpose of a piece of writing, look for language that addresses two common general purposes of academic research: increasing understanding of an issue or advocating good choices about potential actions. Look for what the writer wants the piece to do:

- explore an idea
- extend an idea or approach
- change a way of thinking about a subject

- correct a misconception
- put an established concept in a new framework
- adopt a new methodology
- change a practice
- another purpose (Identify it.)

An author who is advocating a particular course of action usually makes that very clear, but it may be more difficult to catch the author's purpose if it is primarily a matter of changing or resolving ideas. Usually by the end of the introduction, the writer's purpose is clear; sometimes the writer will directly assert it by saying something like

- *The purpose of this investigation is to . . .*
- *This study will show (or argue) that . . .*

Near or at the end of the introduction, the research writer usually makes the major, overall claim for which the piece will argue, either as a thesis statement, or, in a scientific report, as the hypothesis which the investigation is meant to prove or disprove. The major claim may sometimes be merged with a statement of purpose. In this case, some writers use direct cues to announce their claim:

- *The point of this paper (or argument, or line of thinking) is . . .*
- *My point here is . . .*

This kind of statement is often used at key places in academic writing, where claims and reasons are stated and reiterated. As you read academic articles, you will find that these statements are quite common, even though writers in most academic fields are advised to avoid such direct statements (particularly those using "I" or "we"), and some handbooks assert that they are not acceptable.

Cues to Significance

Finally, most academic writers consider the greater significance of their research to understanding in the field—how the results of that investigation change or modify the consensus addressed at the beginning of the piece. Look for points where the writer mentions "significance" in the introduction and anticipates it throughout the work. The significance, however, is usually most explicitly discussed in the conclusion. A significant piece of research usually changes something about how people in the field think, work, or practice, and perhaps influences those outside the field as well. Some writers may be subtle about the significance, like Watson and Crick, whose work with DNA was mentioned in Chapter 1. They coyly understate that their findings "are of considerable biological interest" (737–38), because they anticipate that their fellow scientists will appreciate the great importance of what they have discovered.

By carefully reading for the cues writers give about their audience and purpose, and by noticing when writers use the terminology of argumentation—such as *argument, claim, warrant, reason,* and the looser term *point*—you can increase your ability to follow even complex arguments and to understand the conversation of a field you might not yet be very familiar with.

ANNOTATING READINGS

In addition to highlighting cues to argument, annotation can include a more complete process of highlighting, underlining, and taking notes in the margins of sources. While marginal note-taking is a very valuable means of understanding an argument, you can annotate only sources you own—printouts, photocopies, some electronic files, and your own books and journals. It is unethical—and illegal—to write in library books, although you can photocopy parts that seem to be useful or particularly difficult to understand and annotate your own copies.

While you may be asked to produce an annotated bibliography (that is, a list of sources with summaries and evaluations written for an audience), annotations you make on texts while reading are made for yourself, and in some cases they can replace taking notes. Because you are the audience, you have considerable flexibility about how to make annotations and for what purposes: for example, to help you understand the reading, to organize it in your mind, or to record your initial responses to it. You might also flag things that you do not quite understand, to return to after you have read more deeply in the field.

It can be very tempting to highlight or underline everything, but that defeats the purpose of annotating. One way to keep highlighting from taking over is to highlight (preferably in different colors) mainly two kinds of passage: those that carry the writer's argument and those you do not completely understand. Marginal comments can be a big help when you return to a piece after further reading and reflection on the topic. Your comments can identify key points of reasoning, make connections from part to part, and record your first responses. They can also identify relations you see among sources and record how you think a source might fit into your thinking about the topic. By rereading annotated sources, you can expand or contradict initial responses as seems appropriate. You need not always annotate by hand. If you can move the document into MS Word, you can highlight and comment electronically.

FOCUS POINTS: READING ARGUMENTS

The following guide to reading arguments offers a structured approach to understanding and evaluating difficult writing. This focused reading takes some thought and very close reading—usually more than once—but it can help you identify the line of the author's reasoning and locate the information with which to evaluate reliability. As students move into a major field, they begin to pick up the specialized knowledge that writers in a field expect their audience to have and to acquire the specialized vocabulary that can make reading academic writing difficult at first. More than one reading of a text is often necessary; often fully understanding a complex argument begins only on a second or third reading.

- If there is an abstract (that is, a summary printed just before the piece begins, and usually separated from the main body of text), how much does it tell you?
- What does the writer count as "already known" in the field? Who does this author say has this common knowledge?
- What is the author's preliminary thesis or statement of purpose? What cues does the author use? Why does the author claim it is important?
- How does the writer fit his or her claims into the argument? Does the writer have to make a case for the validity of the evidence? How is this accomplished?

- With what reasons are the claims supported? What kinds of evidence does the writer use? Does the writer refute any conflicting evidence? What cues are used? What reasons are given?

- How is the evidence represented? Examples? Charts? Graphs? Quotations?

- What is the writer's conclusion? Does the writer raise any new ideas in the conclusion? How is the significance of this research established? What cues are used to do this?

- What can you tell about the audience the writer is addressing and about the warrants the audience will accept? From what field is the author coming to the topic? Does the author ever use "I" or "we"? If there is a "we," who does it include? What are the effects of the author's use of formal and/or informal language?

- How does the author relate to the sources cited as the argument develops? Does the author agree or disagree with them? What cues does the author use? How often does the author summarize, paraphrase, use short quotations, and use long, set-off quotations?

READING FOR THE ARGUMENT IN A SAMPLE OPINION PIECE

"The Dangerous Myth of Grade Inflation" (p. 260), by education writer Alfie Kohn, is a good sample argument on which to try using these focus points. The article was first printed in *The Chronicle of Higher Education*, a weekly newspaper for a non-specialized academic audience—faculty in all fields, college administrators, and professional college and university staff members—and was later printed in a collection of Kohn's essays directed to the general public. The article refers to other articles and studies, but it is an opinion piece, an interpretive essay published in the opinion section of a professional newspaper. Kohn can expect a highly critical reading from his academic audience, some of whom have considerable expertise in his field and many of whom have strong feelings about his argument. Although his article has no formal citations, the author refers to other publications by using parenthetical references that allow his readers to find those sources, and in a note at the end he directs readers to his Web page for more complete citations. Ellipses (. . .) indicate material left out.

Kohn addresses what seems to be common knowledge in the field. Where does it come from and who has it?

Complaints about grade inflation have been around for a very long time. Every so often a fresh flurry of publicity pushes the issue to the foreground again, the latest example being a series of articles in *The Boston Globe* last year that disclosed—in a tone normally reserved for the discovery of entrenched corruption in state government—that a lot of students at Harvard were receiving A's and being graduated with honors.

Kohn gives a specific source for his claim about common knowledge.

He repeats that this knowledge has been common for a long time.

The fact that people were offering the same complaints more than a century ago puts the latest bout of harrumphing in

Kohn is making fun of this series of articles.

perspective, not unlike those quotations about the disgraceful values of the younger generation that turn out to be hundreds of years old. The long history of indignation also pretty well derails any attempts to place the blame for higher grades on a residue of bleeding-heart liberal professors hired in the '60s. (Unless, of course, there was a similar countercultural phenomenon in the *1860s*.)

> Another repetition: this knowledge has been common for a long time.

Yet on campuses across America today, academe's usual requirements for supporting data and reasoned analysis have been suspended for some reason where this issue is concerned. It is largely accepted on faith that grade inflation—an upward shift in students' grade-point averages without a similar rise in achievement—exists, and that it is a bad thing. Meanwhile, the truly substantive issues surrounding grades and motivation have been obscured or ignored.

> Kohn is setting readers up for a counterargument: his thesis. Scholars do not accept ideas "on faith": they demand evidence.

> This is the thesis: it is closer to a final thesis than to a preliminary thesis.

The fact is that it is hard to substantiate even the simple claim that grades have been rising. Depending on the time period we're talking about, that claim may well be false. In their book *When Hope and Fear Collide* (Jossey-Bass, 1998), Arthur Levine and Jeanette Curteon tell us that more undergraduates in 1993 reported receiving A's (and fewer reported receiving grades of C or below) compared with their counterparts in 1969 and 1976 surveys. Unfortunately, self-reports are notoriously unreliable, and the numbers become even more dubious when only a self-selected, and possibly unrepresentative, segment bothers to return the questionnaires. (One out of three failed to do so in 1993; no information is offered about the return rates in the earlier surveys.)

> This is the author's first claim in support of his thesis: that the "common knowledge" about grade inflation (although it has been common knowledge for a long time) is false.

> Kohn cites published evidence *against* his claim; experts would note that Jossey-Bass is a highly respected publishing company in the field of education.

> Kohn points out the unreliability of data that comes from self-selected reporting and the incomplete data from the earlier surveys used for comparison.

To get a more accurate picture of whether grades have changed over the years, one needs to look at official student transcripts. Clifford Adelman, a senior research analyst with the U.S. Department of Education, did just that, reviewing

> Kohn directly proposes a more reliable and more "accurate" source of data. Then he adds two more sources that he considers more reliable.

transcripts from more than 3,000 institutions and reporting his results in 1995. His finding: "Contrary to the widespread lamentations, grades actually declined slightly in the last two decades." Moreover, a report released just this year by the National Center for Education Statistics revealed that fully 33.5 percent of American undergraduates had a grade-point average of C or below in 1999–2000, a number that ought to quiet "all the furor over grade inflation," according to a spokesperson for the Association of American Colleges and Universities. (A review of other research suggests a comparable lack of support for claims of grade inflation at the high-school level.) . . .

> In moving toward his second claim, that grades are not effective motivation for learning, Kohn starts with "common knowledge" about motivation but moves quickly into expert knowledge.

Grades motivate. With the exception of orthodox behaviorists, psychologists have come to realize that people can exhibit qualitatively different kinds of motivation: intrinsic, in which the task itself is seen as valuable, and extrinsic, in which the task is just a means to the end of gaining a reward or escaping a punishment. The two are not only distinct but often inversely related. Scores of studies have demonstrated, for example, that the more people are rewarded, the more they come to lose interest in whatever had to be done in order to get the reward. (That conclusion is essentially reaffirmed by the latest major meta-analysis on the topic: a review of 128 studies, published in 1999 by Edward L. Deci, Richard Koestner, and Richard Ryan.)

> Kohn uses a "meta-analysis" as evidence for this claim. In a meta-analysis, experts in a field review a large body of relevant studies to assess agreement and disagreement in a field and often to suggest directions for future research.

Those unfamiliar with that basic distinction, let alone the supporting research, may be forgiven for pondering how to "motivate" students, then concluding that grades are often a good way of doing so, and consequently worrying about the impact of inflated grades. But the reality is that it doesn't matter how motivated students are; what matters is how students are motivated. A focus on grades creates, or at least perpetuates, an extrinsic orientation that is likely to undermine the love of learning we are presumably seeking to promote.

> Kohn repeats his second claim, that grades are poor motivation for learning, distinguishing between the "common knowledge" of nonexperts, and the "common knowledge" of experts.

Three robust findings emerge from the empirical literature on the subject: Students who are given grades, or for whom grades are made particularly salient, tend to display less interest in what they are doing, fare worse on meaningful measures of learning, and avoid more challenging tasks when given the opportunity—as compared with those in a nongraded comparison group. College instructors cannot help noticing, and presumably being disturbed by, such consequences, but they may lapse into blaming students ("grade grubbers") rather than understanding the systemic sources of the problem. A focus on whether too many students are getting A's suggests a tacit endorsement of grades that predictably produces just such a mind-set in students.

Kohn offers evidence for his claim that grades are not the best motivation for learning with a reference to empirical research that demonstrates the ineffectiveness of grades as motivation for genuine and sustained learning.

These fundamental questions are almost completely absent from discussions of grade inflation. The American Academy's report takes exactly one sentence—with no citations—to dismiss the argument that "lowering the anxiety over grades leads to better learning," ignoring the fact that much more is involved than anxiety. It is a matter of why a student learns, not only how much stress he feels. Nor is the point just that low grades hurt some students' feelings, but that grades, per se, hurt all students' engagement with learning. The meaningful contrast is not between an A and a B or C, but between an extrinsic and an intrinsic focus.

Kohn argues against a study that identifies grade inflation by pointing out the study's limitations.

Kohn connects grade inflation claim to motivation claim.

Precisely because that is true, a reconsideration of grade inflation leads us to explore alternatives to our (often unreflective) use of grades. Narrative comments and other ways by which faculty members can communicate their evaluations can be far more informative than letter or number grades, and much less destructive. Indeed, some colleges—for example, Hampshire, Evergreen State, Alverno, and New College of Florida—have eliminated grades entirely, as a critical step toward raising intellectual standards. Even the American Academy's report acknowledges that "relatively undifferentiated course grading has been a traditional

Notice how this transition moves the two claims toward his conclusion.

People in the field would recognize these programs, since they are acknowledged leaders in student assessment.

practice in many graduate schools for a very long time." Has that policy produced lower-quality teaching and learning? Quite the contrary: Many people say they didn't begin to explore ideas deeply and passionately until graduate school began and the importance of grades diminished significantly.

If the continued use of grades rests on nothing more than tradition ("We've always done it that way"), a faulty understanding of motivation, or excessive deference to graduate-school admissions committees, then it may be time to balance those factors against the demonstrated harms of getting students to chase A's. Ohmer Milton and his colleagues discovered—and others have confirmed—that a "grade orientation" and a "learning orientation" on the part of students tend to be inversely related. That raises the disturbing possibility that some colleges are institutions of higher learning in name only, because the paramount question for students is not "What does this mean?" but "Do we have to know this?"

Kohn returns to his opening idea: that "common knowledge" is based on tradition, not evidence.

Here is Kohn's statement about the significance of his argument—and it offers a serious accusation.

A grade-oriented student body is an invitation for the administration and faculty to ask hard questions: What unexamined assumptions keep traditional grading in place? What forms of assessment might be less destructive? How can professors minimize the salience of grades in their classrooms, so long as grades must still be given? And: If the artificial inducement of grades disappeared, what sort of teaching strategies might elicit authentic interest in a course?

Kohn repeats his conclusion. Notice the "punch" in the final sentence—it repeats the point, using a few, very blunt words.

To engage in this sort of inquiry, to observe real classrooms, and to review the relevant research is to arrive at one overriding conclusion: The real threat to excellence isn't grade inflation at all; it's grades.

For a complete list of sources, go to www.alfiekohn.org/teaching/gisources.htm.

EVALUATING SOURCES

The quality of any argument depends directly on the sources it uses for evidence and support. Evaluating sources has always been a necessary skill for students writing research papers, but it has become somewhat more complicated with the advent of the World Wide Web because of the sheer quantity of information available on it. Many instructors complain that too many students start—and finish—their research by entering their topic into a search engine like Google or Yahoo! and using whatever turns up. This section offers criteria for evaluating sources and suggestions for finding sources likely to be most credible to an academic or professional audience.

Arguments and Expertise: Peer Review

It is useful to students to know about peer review because one of the goals of a college-level research writing course is knowing how to evaluate sources. Because a peer-reviewed book or article can generally be considered to fit within the boundaries of its *discipline*—another name for a field of study and practice—you can usually expect peer-reviewed sources to be credible.

An important feature that distinguishes academic writing from writing for a mass market is that it has been reviewed by other specialists in its field before it is published. As the quotation from Jacob Bronowski notes in Chapter 1, "criticism is a necessary and positive function in science," and that necessary criticism is made by other scientists in the field. Most other academic fields also depend on this kind of critical reading by other experts.

While experts may not entirely agree on how to interpret new information—if they did, there would be no need to continue research or argument—most people working in a particular field agree on common knowledge in the field, on methods of discovery and interpretation, and on what arguments are warranted. Articles in peer-reviewed journals and books published by peer-reviewed presses are considered authoritative because they have been read by several of the author's peers, who have good reasons to be critical because they often are competitors for funding, awards, reputation, and other rewards of scholarship.

Peer review is one important and reliable criterion for judging a text when students are new to a field because peer-reviewed sources are generally recognized as having authority in a field of study. This does not mean that all peer-reviewed sources agree, because they do not. Nor does it mean that you cannot or should not read anything that is not peer reviewed. However, when you draw information from more general sources, you often need to be more careful about judging their reliability for yourself.

Peer Review among Researchers

Here's how peer review works: if a history professor sends a book proposal or manuscript about the Civil War to a university press, it will be sent to several other history professors who have published books on the Civil War, and these peer reviewers will determine whether or not the book should be published. The reviewers will use their own expertise to evaluate the manuscript on grounds of the accuracy of its evidence, the logic of its argument, and the contribution it makes to the arguments and controversies in its field of study. Peer review actually begins before the book is written, when the researcher may compete with peers on proposals for research funding and preliminary publications, and it continues after the book is published, when it is further evaluated in published reviews by still other experts. If the published book turns out to be widely read by other experts in its field, subsequent researchers will cite it as a source, even if they intend to refute it. The same peer-review process is used for articles in scholarly and scientific journals. While no review process that involves human beings can be 100 percent effective, peer review works reasonably well to make sure that research published in books by university presses and in scholarly journals is acceptable to other experts in the field. Other sources, like encyclopedia entries, magazine articles, and books for a general audience are useful sources for general readers, but they may reflect an editor's idea of what specialists wrote and of how to present it to a wider public, or they may project a single author's point of view apart from the context of a field of study. Sources written for a general audience may smooth over controversies in a field, or use those controversies to discredit the value of expertise.

Peer Review in the Professions

Peer review takes place in every academic field—biology, zoology, civil engineering, medicine, literature, and so on—because it offers a workable balance between maintaining a stable body of knowledge and responding to newly discovered information. Although peer review of published work is most common in academic research, similar processes of peer review take place in other professions. For example, many professions have a certifying process (involving taking an exam and obtaining a license to practice) overseen by a professional board of peers. Boards of specialists license physicians to practice in specific fields like pediatrics or internal medicine. Law school graduates must pass their state's bar association exam before they can practice as lawyers. These groups of professional peers uphold standard procedures to decide who has sufficient knowledge to practice and to determine what constitutes good (and ethical) practice. The publications of professional associations are also peer reviewed, not only their journals (like *The Journal of the American Medical Association*), but also manuals and other resources for practitioners. Usually the title pages of such publications will list the names and institutional affiliations of members of the editorial board responsible for peer review.

Peer Review among Students

For students, the process of peer review often begins in groups in which students develop and test each other's growing expertise in a field. Many students start informal study groups to help them master new material. In some courses students are required to form research groups in which they can develop enough common expertise to read each other's developing inquiries. Such research groups develop shared expertise in an area of investigation through the processes of discussing developing drafts, compiling bibliographies (lists of sources consulted), and carrying out projects together. One of the useful effects of this peer group work is that reading and responding to each other's writing helps students directly experience how their own writing communicates to actual, visible readers who are interested in the topic and who need to know what has been discovered about it. Peer review helps students create and participate in an academic discourse community and prepares them for the teamwork expected in a wide range of future professions.

FOCUS POINTS: EVALUATING SOURCES

It is important to remember that while the following questions can be helpful, it is not sufficient to simply run through a checklist to evaluate sources. While overt propaganda and deception are reasonably easy to spot, some sources—books, articles, and Web sites—cleverly misrepresent themselves as thoughtful, unbiased purveyors of information, when they are actually promoting political, religious, or social agendas; others are written by writers who do not have sufficient expertise to know about or argue with alternative explanations or interpretations. Because the questions in the checklist that follows may not give rise to consistent answers, student researchers need to constantly weigh the criteria against each other and make difficult decisions about the credibility of sources they find.

1. Is the book or article peer-reviewed? That is, has a body of experts already evaluated it?
   - You can generally assume that a book has been peer reviewed if its publisher has the words "University Press" in its name. There are some other presses that use peer review for their books (NCTE Press, Heinemann, Routledge, Earlbaum, etc.). When in doubt, ask your instructor or a reference librarian.
   - Peer-reviewed sources usually make specific references to other peer-reviewed sources and have the "scholarly apparatus" appropriate to the field, such as footnotes, endnotes, parenthetical citations, and/or bibliographies. Questions 2 and 7 in checklist 2-1 (Reading Arguments) can help you locate some of the information you need to evaluate the reliability of sources.
   - The "Acknowledgments" section of peer-reviewed books usually mentions and thanks colleagues at the writer's institution and other universities, and may list government or foundation grants that helped pay for the project. However, students should not use the presence of acknowledgments as the only criterion for evaluating a source because sometimes authors of sources that are not peer-reviewed also acknowledge the help or inspiration of others, and some sources of funding are highly partisan.

   Example
   See Figure 2.1.

   - Scholarly journals have editorial boards listed on the title page or a page next to it, and these editors' university affiliations are identified.

   Example
   See Figure 2.2.

2. What kind of piece is it?
   - In a newspaper or magazine, is the piece a news article, a feature article, an opinion piece, or an editorial?

   Example
   See Figure 2.3.

   - In a peer-reviewed journal, is the piece a research report or article, a review essay, an editorial commentary, a letter or commentary in response to a previously published article, or something else that you can identify? Research reports, articles, and review essays are considered more reliable

Academic
Charisma *and the*
Origins
of the Research
University

William Clark

THE UNIVERSITY OF CHICAGO PRESS
CHICAGO AND LONDON

Notes

here make use of a number of conventions. Notes in reference to
ls use an abbreviation schema under Abbreviations. All other citations
iography. Page citations in most notes are made in terms of the now
se of *f* for one page following the page number listed, and of *ff*
es. I have omitted the periods conventionally called for in this citation
xample 40f. becomes 40f and 108ff.becomes 108ff and so on.

CHAPTER ONE

77; 1986; Foucault 1975; Latour 1987; 1990; Becker and Clark 2001.
975, 150.
Marx and Engels 1966, 1:31–60. See also Funkenstein 1986.
76a, 563 (1956, 571); emphasis of "expert" in the original.
r 1976a, 122ff (1956, esp. 122ff).
76a, 129 (first quotation), 578f (second quotation, emphasis in original
ird quotation, emphasis in original omitted);(1956, 129, 586f, 129).
3 1958, 73. On Baroque courtiers, see Biagioli 1993.
1 from Brandenburg-Prussia 1894–1936, 3:577.
r 1953, 13 (quotation); see also 12ff. On the above, see Brandenburg-
Prussia 1894–1936, 3:582f; Heinrich 1931, 11f; Bleek 1972, 63ff.
    10. On the above, see Heinrich 1931, 13; Dorwart 1953, 189ff; Rosenberg 1958, 160;
Bleek 1972, 41, 69; Johnson 1975, 49ff, 218ff; D. Willoweit in Jeserich et al. 1983–88,
1:346ff; Jeserich in ibid., 2:304; Raeff 1983, 158ff; on bureaucracy in general, see Weber
1976a, 551ff (1956, 559ff).
    11. Justi 1758, 2:63f (quotation).
    12. See Justi 1760–61, 1:3ff; 2:73ff; 1782, 3ff, 10, 15f, 56f, 254ff; Sonnenfels 1771–77,
1:132 (quotation); from Zincke 1742–43, 1:296ff, 319f, 322 (quotation); see also Darjes
1756, 397, 425ff; Dithmar 1755, 154, 172; Förster 1771, 196ff; in general, Small 1909;
Brückner 1977, 229ff; Stolleis 1988–92, 1:366ff, esp. 374, 379ff.
    13. On the next paragraphs, see Justi 1755, 1:173f, 184, 212ff, 231f, 290ff; 1758, 1:496;
2:56, 63f, 251, 263f; 1760–61, 1:481ff, 505ff, 685f, 698ff; 2:19ff, 37ff; 1782, 34f, 43ff, 59f, 159ff.
    14. Justi 1755, 1:xiii–iv, xxiii–iv, 235f.
    15. Justi 1755, 1:107; 1758, 2:611 (quotation on giving a gracious audience); 1760–61,
2:47ff, 67f (quotation on freedom of thought), 68ff; 1782, 254ff.
    16. On Catholic protests contra commodification, see Nicolai 1783–96, 4:682.

| 515 |

FIGURE 2.1

Bibliography

Abelard, Peter and Héloïse. 1962. *Historia calamitatum.* Edited by J. Monfrin. 2nd ed. Paris: Vrin.

ADB. 1875–1912. *Allgemeine Deutsche Biographie.* 56 vols. Repr. Berlin: Duncker & Humblot, 1967–71.

Aepinus, Franz (*praeses*). 1702. *Moralitas Graduum Academicarum . . . contra Fanaticos praesertim, asserta. . . .* Johann Carlquist (*resp.*). Rostock.

Albers, Bruno, ed. 1900–12. *Consuetudines Monasticae.* 5 vols. Monte Cassino: Soc. Ed. Castri Casini.

Albrecht, Helmuth and Armin Hermann. 1990. "Die Kaiser Wilhelm-Gesellschaft im Dritten Reich (1933–1945)." In Vierhaus and Brocke 1990, 356–406.

Alexander, Jeffrey. 1985 [1982–83]. *Theoretical Logic in Sociology.* 4 vols. Berkeley: University of California Press.

Allport, Gordon and Leo Postman. 1947. *The Psychology of Rumor.* New York: Holt.

Amelunxen, Clemens. 1991. *Zur Rechtsgeschichte der Hofnarren.* Schriftenreihe der juristischen Gesellschaft zu Berlin, 124. Berlin: de Gruyter.

Amerbach, Vitus. 1550. *Variorum carminum.* Basel.

———. 1571. "Oratio de doctoratu philosophico (ante-1557)," fol. 351v–70r in *Tomus primus orationum Ingolstadiensium.* Edited by Valentin Rotmar. Ingolstadt.

Annan, Noel. 1999. *The Dons: Mentors, Eccentrics and Geniuses.* Chicago: University of Chicago Press.

Anon. n.d.1 *Themata medica de beanorum. . . .* n.l., n.d. [Munich UB: 8° H.lit. 1913: 50].

Anon. n.d.2 *Theses inaugurales. . . .* n.l., n.d. [Göttingen UB: 8° Sat. I, 7265].

Anon. n.d.3 *Curiöse Inaugural-Disputation von . . . Professoren-Burschen. . . .* n.l., n.d. [Göttingen UB: 8° H.1.p. II, 112/15; 8° H.1.p. II, 10810].

Anon. 1476 [ca. 1476–81]. *Manuale scholarium.* Heidelberg (?). Repr. in Zarncke 1857, 2–48.

Anon. 1726. *Vernünftiges Studenten-Leben.* Jena.

Anon. 1778–79. *Briefwechsel dreyer akademischer Freunde.* 2 vols. 2nd ed. Ulm.

Anon. 1782. *Abhandlung was die Universitäten in den kaiserlichen, königlichen Erblanden sind, und was sie seyn könnten.* Prague/Vienna.

Anon. 1790. "Gedanken eines akademischen Bürgers über Öffentliche akademische Disputation . . . ," by J. B. In *Journal von und für Deutschland* 7/11:480–89

Anon. 1797. "Das gelehrte Schauspiel, oder forma dat esse rei." In *Allgemeiner Literarischer Anzeiger,* 1279–80.

| 567 |

Acknowledgments

ıder, Amos Funkenstein, Robert Westman, and M. Norton ed me and the original research. In addition to continued help re, the work and I have enjoyed the support, individually, of Lorraine Daston, Nick Jardine, Peter Reill, Hans-Jörg Rhein- Sabean, Simon Schaffer, and Rudolf Vierhaus, and, institu- ryn Mawr College, the Society of Fellows in Humanities at iversity, the Max-Planck-Institut für Geschichte in Götting- Aax-Planck-Institut für Wissenschaftsgeschichte in Berlin. ectual stimulus and support came from Peter Becker, Hans er, Marina Frasca-Spada, Heidrun Friese, Martin Gierl, ner, Ernst Hamm, Anke te Heesen, Klaus Hentschel, Isabel nka Rublack. David Sabean read and commented on the an- : revision, and Simon Schaffer and Nick Jardine on the penul- rine Rice brought the book through its ultimate revision. made the book more readable and more correct in form. vas read and commented on by Simon Werrett.

Chapter 2 was read and commented on by Alix Cooper. This is a revision of "Parades académiques: Contribution à l'économique politique des livrets universitaires," translated by Marielle Aujollet, *Actes de la recherche en sciences sociales,* December 2000, 135: 6–24, based on a paper presented at *Inconscients adacémiques,* organized by Pierre Bourdieu, Olivier Christin, and Franz Schultheis, 3–4 December 1999, Université Neuchâtel.

Chapter 3 was read and commented on by Martin Gierl.

Chapter 4 was read and commented on by Jane Caplan and John Gascoigne. This is a revision of "On the Table Manners of Academic Examination," pp. 33–67 in *Wissenschaft als kuturelle Praxis,* edited by Hans Erich Bödeker, Peter Reill, and Jürgen Schlumbohm (Vandenhoeck & Ruprecht, 1999), based on a paper presented at *Wissenschaft als kulturelle Praxis,* organ-

| 629 |

FIGURE 2.1 *(continued)*

COLLEGE ENGLISH

THE JOURNAL OF THE COLLEGE SECTION OF THE NATIONAL COUNCIL OF TEACHERS OF ENGLISH
PUBLISHED SINCE 1939

FIGURE 2.2

THE NEW YORKER

MARCH 9, 2009

COVER *"Downsized," by Bob Staake* DRAWINGS *William Hamilton, David Sipress, Zachary Kanin, Matthew Diffee, Mort Gerberg, Ariel Molvig, Mike Twohy, William Haefeli, Gahan Wilson, Bruce Eric Kaplan, P. C. Vey, Robert Mankoff, Mick Stevens, Alex Gregory, Charles Barsotti* SPOTS *Laurent Cilluffo*

www.newyorker.com

FIGURE 2.3

SPECIAL ISSUE: MELVILLE THE POET
Guest Editors, Elizabeth Renker and Douglas Robillard

3 From the Mast-Head

ARTICLES

9 ELIZABETH RENKER AND DOUGLAS ROBILLARD .... Melville the Poet: *Introduction*

17 DAVID DEVRIES AND HUGH EGAN .... "Entangled Rhyme": *A Dialogic Reading of Melville's Battle-Pieces*

35 FAITH BARRETT .... "They Answered Him Aloud": *Popular Voice and Nationalist Discourse in Melville's Battle-Pieces*

51 MARY K. BERCAW EDWARDS .... "An Old Sailor's Lament": *Herman Melville, the Stone Fleet, and the Judgment of History*

65 MATTHEW GIORDANO .... Public Privacy: *Melville's Coterie Authorship in John Marr and Other Sailors*

79 LYON EVANS .... "Tears of the Happy": *The Design of Darkness in "To Winnefred" and "The Year"*

NOTE

97 DENNIS BERTHOLD .. Ekphrastic Composites in "At the Hostelry": *Van de Veldes, Tromps, and Trompes l'Oeil*

POEMS

107 HERMAN MELVILLE...... Selections from *Battle-Pieces, John Marr,* and *Weeds and Wildings*

REVIEWS

141 Robert Milder, *Exiled Royalties: Melville and the Life We Imagine* by JOHN WENKE

146 Timothy Marr, *The Cultural Roots of American Islamicism* by BRIAN YOTHERS

N KELLEY .... *All Astir*

BERT K. WALLACE .... *Melville Birthday Lecture: "What Melville Means to Me"* A Discussion with Rinde Eckert and Ricardo Pitts-Wiley

tracts

IZABETH RENKER .... Melville and the Meaning of Genre

TER NORBERG.............. From "Fragments" to "Rammon": Poetry as Consolation

LT NOTT...................... Melville's "The Encantadas": Genre and the Discourse Community of *Putnam's Monthly*

ON CORNER .... "An Unaccountable Pair": Genre and Value in *The Confidence-Man*

WYN KELLEY........................... "Free Robe and Vest": Melville and the Uncollected Fragment

FIGURE 2.4
Table of contents with section headings that identify kinds of pieces, from *Leviathan: A Journal of Melville Studies* 9.3 (2007).

than editorial comments and the responses of readers—even of prominent or authoritative readers.

Example

See Figure 2.4.

- On a Web site, are you looking at a personal Web site, a governmental or institutional site, or a site for a recognized and reputable organization? ("Recognized" and "reputable" can be ambiguous terms, which is one reason why evaluating sources is always a matter of judgment.) Was the piece written for the Web, or first published in print and then archived on the Web? Is it from a newspaper, a major magazine, a blog, or an academic journal? Whether it is an archived print publication or an original Web publication, was it peer reviewed?

3. Do sources from newspapers and magazines seem to adhere to the ethical codes of journalism?
   - Journalistic codes of ethics (i.e., The American Society of Newspaper Editors' "Statement of Principles" www.asne.org/kiosk/archive/principl.htm and the Society of Professional Journalists' "Code of Ethics" www.spi.org/ethics_code.asp) date back to the 1920s. These codes, followed by the most reputable newspapers and magazines, bind journalists to high standards of truth, accuracy, impartiality, and fair play.
   - Although major newspapers usually adhere to journalistic codes of ethics, it can be hard to tell whether smaller, newer, more popular, or more politically committed publications do so. If a journalistic piece seems one-sided or unfair or if it makes what seem to be inflated claims for a position, ask your instructors and librarians what they know about it. An inflated claim is one that uses absolute terms like *always, never,* or *unique* or that attributes a wide array of results to a single factor; if a claim seems too good (or too bad) to be true, the source merits a closer, more critical examination.
   - The extent to which the writer's opinion is supposed to shape the piece varies depending on whether it is published in a news article, a feature article, or an editorial.
     - A news article aims to document information—who, what, when, where, and how—and to record responses from significant participants or analysts.
     - A feature article develops an interpretation as it presents information.
     - An editorial tries to persuade readers to share a particular interpretation or to respond to a call to action.
   - Usually newspapers give clear cues about what kind of piece a given article is (for example, editorials are often printed on a page labeled "Opinion"). *However, ethical journalists are responsible for factual accuracy in all these genres.* This means, for instance, that responsible journalists cannot misrepresent facts to support an editorial or opinion piece. Misrepresentation includes fabricating evidence, making a composite source seem like a single person, and taking quotations out of their original context.
   - In many publications, these codes of ethics are taken very seriously; for example, in 2003 the *New York Times* was wracked with scandals involving the fabrication of stories and staff writers publishing the work of their assistants as their own. The newspaper appointed a "public editor" at that time, who

explains (and sometimes disagrees with) editorial decisions about what is printed and why.

4. Does the piece seem to adhere to a code of ethics in a professional field or discipline?
   - As professions define themselves as distinct fields of practice, they usually establish codes of ethics that define acceptable practices in that field—what practitioners may and may not do without risking the disapproval of their peers.
   - Codes of ethics for specific professions are available on professional association Web sites. The Center for the Study of Ethics in the Professions at the Illinois Institute of Technology maintains an online collection of most of those codes of ethics, organized by profession. To take a look at these codes, see the following Web site: www.iit.edu/departments/csep/publicwww/codes/index.html.

5. How up-to-date is the source?
   - Information in newspapers may be quickly rendered obsolete by breaking news, which often reveals new information that may contradict the observations of early witnesses.
   - Books have a somewhat longer "shelf life" than articles, but their importance varies from field to field, and how long they remain current depends on how much they have been cited in more recent books and articles.
   - In any field, a book or article over 15 years old that has not been cited in a considerable number of more recent sources is probably not a very important source.
   - In the humanities, books are considered the most important publications. Peer-reviewed articles over 10 years old have probably been surpassed by more recent articles and books, although some articles that have presented groundbreaking arguments may continue to be cited for much longer.
   - In the sciences and most social sciences, articles are considered more important than books because they are more current (they make it into print faster), and you should not consider an article over five years old to be current unless you have good evidence to the contrary (for example, if it is still frequently cited in more current articles).
   - The "classics" in a field may be read for decades or even centuries, but they carry a different kind of authority as they become classics. For instance, B. F. Skinner and Sigmund Freud were crucial figures in psychology 50 and 100 years ago, respectively. They are still cited in histories of science and in some inquiries in literary or cultural studies, but they should not be cited as evidence for current claims in psychology, a field that has shifted considerably since their times.
   - Some "classics" are not disproved; they are built upon until the original insights become commonplace. The Watson and Crick article that articulated the structure of DNA in 1953 is such a classic; this work has been built upon significantly over the years, but the double helix model remains "common knowledge" in genetics and related fields.
   - Historians and others writing about history may use old sources as well as more recent ones to draw evidence from the past.

6. Is the source cited by, and relied upon, by others in the field?
   - Do other authors cite this source or refer to it? Because research is ordinarily conducted and published when there is controversy or a gap in a field of knowledge,

other authors may substantially disagree with a source—but even when there is disagreement, the fact that researchers cite it indicates that the source is important enough to refute. When you begin doing research in a field, you will find that many of the authors use each other as sources. This is the visible *discourse community* of the field. Writers who frequently show up on lists of works cited are probably authors whose work you too should read.

- Does the source refer to other researchers known to be authorities in the field? Does the source use and reflect on data that other sources in the field use, or relate new data to existing, accepted data? Be wary about sources that claim to refute an entire field or to discard all or most previous research. Most paradigm shifts take place only after considerable discussion by experts about how to interpret puzzling data.
- Is the author a recognized authority *in this area* of study? You may have heard of the author, but consider whether other writers in this field use this writer as a source or reference. For example, it would be unusual for a chemist to be considered a reliable source in American history.
- When in doubt, ask an instructor—or several—in the field, and consult with a research librarian.

7. What is the author's purpose?
   - Most authors have a purpose and make an argument. Almost all published research proposes an argument or interpretation; there would be no reason to publish if it did not. People do research because there is a controversy or a gap in knowledge, and the purpose of most credible published research is to interpret or explain the result of an experiment or an investigation—seldom do "the facts speak for themselves." There are controversies in every field, and in some fields there are very deep differences among experts and the way they look at data. A writer who is making an argument will make a case for his or her interpretation based on the evidence. If the interpretation refutes earlier work, the researcher may argue for a reinterpretation of earlier results in the light of new evidence or a new theory, but researchers seldom reject earlier knowledge out of hand. Be careful to distinguish between *argument* and *bias*. An argument is a legitimate aspect of much academic writing, but a biased argument omits or distorts evidence to support its claims.

8. How and how much is the source biased?
   - A writer's position is always a factor in a piece of writing, and the way the writer represents himself or herself can impact the argument. Does the writer's ethos seem like a legitimate professional position, or does the purpose of the argument seem personal—not clearly connected with the writer's area of expertise? When evaluating bias, ask how clearly the writer states her position. Does there seem to be a hidden agenda? What warrants does the writer state or assume? Are they in accord with others you have read in the field? How much room for doubt does the writer admit? A nuanced position that allows for or carefully considers possible exceptions is often more reliable than an "always" or "never" stand.
   - An *overly biased* writer may twist and distort evidence in order to make a point. An overly biased writer may merely dismiss earlier research or ignore evidence,

rather than refuting it; may engage in personal (or *ad hominem*) attacks on those who hold other points of view (including name-calling and guilt by association); or may use other logical fallacies like bandwagon, slippery slope, false dichotomy, or appeals to tradition, spite, or ridicule.

- As Jacob Bronowski observes in the passage quoted in Chapter 1, scholars and scientists normally disagree with each others' methodologies and conclusions. However, they seldom accuse each other of deception or falsification, which are serious violations of professional ethics. Such accusations may indicate that a source is unfairly biased.

- What do your fellow students and instructor(s) think about a source? If a number of people warn you away from a source because they think it is biased, you too should be wary about its reliability. Although the decision about the reliability of a source is yours, remember that part of your work in making an argument is to convince the audience. If you know that your audience considers a source unreliable, you need to make a case for its reliability, and so consider whether that secondary argument will strengthen or weaken your larger claims.

EVALUATING THE RELEVANCE OF SOURCES

While reliability is very important, when you are engaged in a research project, you need sources that are directly relevant to the particular question you are considering. When you first start reading about a particular topic, almost everything a writer discusses may seem related to it, and the sources used by writers you read early in the process can be a good place to find more to read. But try to develop your own questions as soon as possible, so that you can focus your reading and research on the particular question you want to consider, rather than on the topic in general. If you write down your questions and responses from the outset of a project, you will have a record of your thinking as it develops, and when you review your responses to a particular piece of writing, you will probably find questions, points of agreement and disagreement, and other reactions that can move you toward a particular question and guide your finding and selection of sources.

When reviewing your responses, look for central ideas and key terms that you have identified as interesting to you. Then review the writer's use of sources, to see if you can find those terms repeated in the writer's summaries and in the titles of the sources he or she uses. Don't look only for sources that agree with you, but do look for sources that speak to the points that you want to investigate further.

For example, if you were to start an inquiry with Alfie Kohn's article, "The Dangerous Myth of Grade Inflation," and decide you want to think more about and perhaps write about motivations for learning, you might turn to the review of 128 studies by Edward L. Deci, Richard Koestner, and Richard Ryan that Kohn mentions in his article, a reference which was posted on Kohn's Web site and is available in the version of the article later published in a collection of his essays. Because this review article is now over 10 years old, you might want to skim the review for key terms and for the names of writers the reviewers considered important at the time. Then, you could do an author search (see Chapter 5), looking for more recent articles by these authors, particularly articles that have "grades" and "motivation" in their titles. Kohn refers to other studies that discuss the issue of grade inflation, but these are less likely to be of use for a study on motivation, even though they are important to making Kohn's point. Keep in mind that his inquiry is not the same as yours; while you can and should use a previous author's research on a related topic, your own research decisions should be based on the question *you* want to investigate.

Learning to skim is necessary for effective decisions about the relevance of a piece to your own work. Reading the introduction, the conclusion, and the first sentences of paragraphs will show you the scope of a piece. Recognizing a writer's use of key terms can help you decide whether you will be able to use a piece in your own work. It helps if you write down these responses and reflections as you make them, so that you can avoid backtracking later.

EVALUATING ONLINE SOURCES

Even though the Internet has revolutionized the research process in the past 10 years, the same criteria work for evaluating electronic sources as well as printed texts. The challenges of evaluating Web materials come not only from the sheer quantity of information available online, but also from its highly variable quality. The Internet has vastly increased the quantity of information available to everyone with access to the Web, but it is important to remember that *almost anyone can put anything on the Web for any purpose*—usually more easily and cheaply than publishing in print. When you are doing research online, then, you need to be even more careful about who produced the documents you are consulting and whether they are credible to an audience who knows the field you are studying.

The easy freedom to put things on the Web makes it very attractive, but this same freedom can leave you vulnerable to mistaken or deceptive Web resources. Remember that some Web sites look very professional and official but carry highly biased, distorted, or deceptive information. Of course, you should expect that information put online by a political organization will be biased toward its candidates and principles, but that information is not necessarily deceptive. However, there is a difference between sites that admit their political stance (the Web site of a political party, a candidate for office, or a political blog or influence group), and those that hide their position. For example, some extremist political organizations post information that most mainstream historians or political scientists would find misleading. If information about who created the site is not available on the first page of a site, follow links such as "about us" to see whether a site you have located has a semi-buried affiliation, and ask yourself why that affiliation may be hidden. Deceptive sites *pretend* to be unbiased, which should lead you to be very suspicious about accepting their posts without considerable investigation.

When evaluating Web sites, use the same criteria you would use for evaluating a print document, but with a more critical eye. As with print media, you need to know what kind of page you are looking at, who wrote it, and when it was produced. Always ask yourself whether your readers will think a source you cite is reliable, and, if you have doubts about a site, ask your instructors or a librarian to help you make an evaluation. In general, when doing research for academic papers, try to keep in mind the differences between sources available through your university library and the databases it provides access to, and sources generally available on the World Wide Web. Try to stay within the library's Web resources and to use databases located on the library's Web site. These will lead more directly to peer-reviewed sources and to the more reputable magazines and newspapers.

FOCUS POINTS: EVALUATING MATERIALS ON THE WEB

In order to do the best academic research, you need to find sites that are reliable and relevant, and that offer the best possible resources. In addition to the general considerations for evaluating sources, here are some further considerations specific to sources found on the Web.

- ■ *What sort of document have you found?* A commercial site (.com), an organizational site (.org), a college or university site (.edu), and so forth? A personal Web site? An archived print document? A piece of an online discussion from a listserv that has been archived? A piece from an online journal? A blog?

- ■ *Who wrote the document*, or what organization adopted it? Was it peer reviewed? Is the person or organization considered a reputable source in the field? Is it cited by other sources you have encountered—particularly by print sources? Is the person or organization subject to any ethical code?

  - • Be sure to click on any link that offers information about the person or organization behind the Web site, such as "About us," the name of the organization, or the name of the person to whom it belongs.

  - • A print document archived online is as reliable as it was when in print (unless it has become outdated).

  - • A personal or organization Web site or blog is only as reliable as the person or organization that created it; you should rely on such sources primarily when researching the blogger (since the blog can tell you what the person thinks), but you will have to make a case for their reliability if you use them as evidence for an argument. Sometimes blogs can lead you to useful sources on very contemporary topics, through links to journals, articles, and other sites, but, as always, you must evaluate these sources critically.

- ■ *What is the purpose of the document?* Is it clearly stated on the front page, or do you have to dig to infer it? Are the document and format suitable for the purpose? Can you detect bias in the coverage the document offers?

FINDING THE MOST RELIABLE, RELEVANT, AND USEFUL SOURCES FOR ACADEMIC RESEARCH

Say that you are researching New Wave French Cinema of the 1950s. The Internet has abundant resources for your search, some more promising than others. Using the criteria in Focus Points: Evaluating Materials on the Web, let's evaluate two examples.

At first glance our preliminary Web search has yielded some results (see Example A). We have a site that provides a place to start and some useful preliminary information from which to start. However, we still need to check for contact, copyright, and publishing information before we can determine whether or not this site is a credible one from which to quote.

This is a .com Web site, which tells us that it is a commercial site. It is not an organizational or university Web site. It appears to be informational but also appears to sell films.

The site seems to have some helpful links for finding out more information on the topic and also includes a Links page that may lead to other bibliographic information.

The site gives examples and summaries of some well-known films of the period but does not offer expert commentary or peer-reviewed references.

Example A—Web Research on French Cinema #1

When we click the Contact link, we do not get any indication of authorship, copyright, or publication information.

The actual contact link takes us to a Web form that does not include a persons name or e-mail address. Sources without publication information (author, publisher, date modified) are difficult to cite and usually indicate that they are not credible sites for quoting.

Example A—Web Research on French Cinema #2

This Web site is a .edu site, which means that it is a university-sponsored site. For this site, then, we already know that the name of the publishing organization is the name of the university.

This site also names the article clearly and provides an author name and affiliation information. This article appears to be from the Wisconsin Studies in Film series.

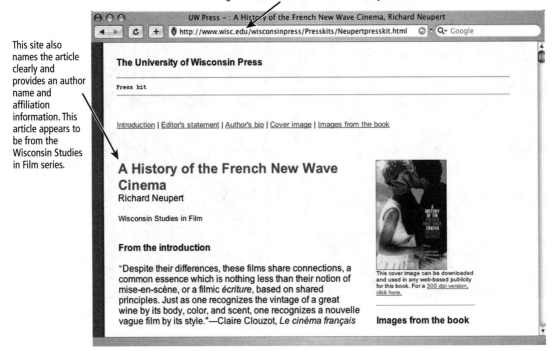

New Wave suitable for advanced undergraduates and all specialists in the study of French film. I predict that Neupert's work will immediately become the standard English-language reference on the French New Wave.' I think so too, and the result is an important addition to the scholarly wing of our cinema studies list, and to our growing focus on European cinema."—Raphael Kadushin

Author's bio

Richard Neupert is associate professor of film studies at the University of Georgia. He is the author of *The End: Closure and Narration in the Cinema* and his translations include *Aesthetics of Film* and *French New Wave: An Artistic School.*

Return to the regular Web page for *A History of the French New Wave Cinema*

Home | Books | Journals | Events | Textbooks | Authors | Related | Search | Order | Contact

If you have trouble accessing any page in this web site, contact Kirt Murray, Web manager. E-mail: kdmurray@wisc.edu or by phone at 608-263-0733.

Updated April 16, 2009

© 2009, The Board of Regents of the University of Wisconsin System

This site includes background information on the author that helps us to determine the author's credibility as an expert in the field. It also provides the names of other publications that can expand your research horizon.

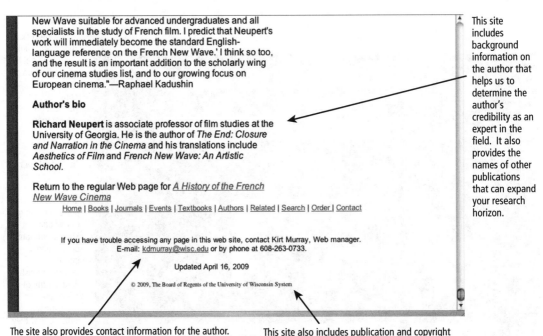

The site also provides contact information for the author.

This site also includes publication and copyright information, which will be used in your bibliography.

Example B—Web Research on French Cinema #3 & #4

In our second search (see Example B), we find an article on the history of New Wave Cinema. Here again we will apply our evaluation criteria in order to test the credibility of the site.

Our second search has yielded much more promising results by way of credibility thus far. However, we should check the bottom of the page for more information that will help us to finally determine credibility.

ADDITIONAL SOURCES FOR EVALUATING MATERIALS

For additional discussions and examples useful for developing your ability to evaluate Web sources, consult the following sites. Many of these sites were created by reference librarians at colleges and universities to help students locate and identify reliable sources on the Web. You will benefit most, however, by consulting your own library's Web page to see what help your library offers with finding and evaluating online sources and learning what other "information literacy" resources your instructors and reference librarians recommend.

www.ithaca.edu/library/training/think.html   "ICYouSee: T is for Thinking: A Guide to Critical Thinking About What You See on the Web." This recently updated site built by a reference librarian has been on the Web for nearly 15 years. Students find it clear and easy to use.

www.library.jhu.edu/researchhelp/general/evaluating/index.html   This is a short list of considerations about the reliability of sources from the Sheridan Libraries at Johns Hopkins University.

gateway.lib.ohio-state.edu/tutor/   This larger and more complex site from the reference department at The Ohio State University offers both information and interactive tutorials (available to users anywhere). There are special sections on Careers and Employment, History Research, and News Sources.

www.lib.purdue.edu/rguides/tutorials.html   Purdue University reference librarians have compiled this body of resources, including tutorials on topics for beginning students through advanced researchers. You may sign in as a guest and use most of the informational materials offered.

RESPONDING TO (AND IN) ACADEMIC WRITING

When you are reading and taking notes on a topic, it is almost inevitable that you will respond to your sources, both positively and negatively, and you can use those responses to start exploring potential arguments about your topic. While it is important to maintain a clear distinction in your mind, and particularly in your notes and papers, between other writers' ideas and your response to them, by no means should you try to squelch your responses, since they will help you direct your research, discover what you want to argue, and suggest how you might organize that argument. The word *response* brings to mind a reflex—something automatic and outside of conscious control. While responses to readings may start with a reflex, those first thoughts can be modified by conscious thinking and by reflecting about the field's conventions (that is, its usual ways of doing things, some explicit and some implicit) and the warrants (basic assumptions) it accepts. Response is an important part of the research process; as researchers read sources, they decide how they might fit into an argument being constructed and how they work in relation to each other.

- How well does the research fulfill its purpose; that is, how well does it do what the researcher says it will do?

- Is the evidence convincing?

- What are the warrants of the argument—the underlying assumptions that the argument depends on? Can you tell if they are the usual warrants in the field? To what extent do you share them?

- Does the writer acknowledge and refute alternatives to the conclusions reached?

- Is the research thorough, and is the methodology appropriate? (These issues can be hard for a person new to a field to judge; take particular notice when you find articles that evaluate other research on these grounds.)

- Is the argument reasonable? Review the list of logical fallacies in Chapter 1 and consider whether the writer exploits any of them.

These are not the only possible grounds for response, but they are common ones. In a response, you provoke an interaction between the written piece and your own thinking on the topic. When writing a response, you are expected to be reasonable—but not necessarily impartial. "Being reasonable" includes representing accurately what was written, responding to what the writer said rather than who the writer is, and acknowledging when your basic assumptions about values or how things work (i.e., your warrants) differ from those of the writer. Although a response need not be written as a polished argument, it can help you to think about making a case in relation to a reading or readings. If you misrepresent what the writer said, the case falls apart as soon as the mistake is pointed out. If you attack the personal qualities of the writer or question the writer's ethos, you must be sure that you are willing and able to support that attack, and that those qualities are relevant to the article you are responding to. It is very important to recognize where you share warrants with the writer to whom you are responding, and where you differ.

Exercises

2.1 READING A SOURCE

1. Read the piece by Alfie Kohn in the Readings, highlighting cues to audience, purpose, and argument.
2. Answer in writing the questions in Focus Points: Reading Arguments (p. 21) that are not addressed by the annotated excerpt of this article. You may be asked to do this work with a small group so that you can discuss your understanding of the argument.
3. Write a list of the parts of the piece you still do not understand, discuss them with a partner or small group, and then reread the article, looking for clarification. Take notes as you read that record your opinions and responses to the author's argument.

2.2 RESPONDING TO A SOURCE

1. Using another source from the readings, highlight parts that seem important, write in the margins why you highlighted them, and record any immediate responses you have. Also note the parts of the piece that you do not understand.

2. Answer, in writing, the questions in Focus Points: Shaping Your Responses (p. 44).

3. Review your answers and notes. Write a response to the piece, based on one or more questions from the list that seem most applicable to your thinking about the piece.

4. Write a short paragraph reflecting on how useful these questions were for increasing your understanding of and response to the piece. What questions would you add and/or eliminate?

2.3 EVALUATING RELIABILITY

1. Write a short (350–400 words) evaluation of the reliability of the article on grade inflation by Alfie Kohn (p. 260), based on the criteria in Focus Points: Evaluating Sources (p. 29). Focus your discussion on the criteria from the list that you think most appropriate to this particular source, and explain your choice.

2. Discuss your evaluation with a small group, considering which of Kohn's sources seem more or less reliable and how this affects his argument. What other kinds of sources would you want to consult if you were writing a paper on grade inflation?

3. Does your consideration of reliability change your response to the piece? If so, make a list of changes you might make in your response. If not, make a list of how Kohn's use of sources helps support your response.

2.4 EVALUATING TWO WEB SITES ON THE SAME TOPIC

A Google search on Cosmetics and Safety yielded 19,600,000 hits. Two near the top of the list were:

www.cosmeticsinfo.org/   What's in Cosmetic and Personal Care Products? Source: The Personal Care Products Council (industry trade group)

www.cosmeticsdatabase.com/   Skin Deep Cosmetic Safety Database. Source: Environmental Working Group

1. These two sites were found on a search for information about the safety of cosmetics. Consider what the point of view of each site is. Do you think that either or both of them are biased? How are they biased and what makes you think so?

2. Write a short account of how the perspectives of these sources differ. Consider whether you consider one or both of them overly biased and how you might be able to use them in an inquiry of your own.

3. Repeat this exercise with two sites found in a search on a topic of your own choosing.

2.5 READING AND RESPONDING TO COMPLEX ACADEMIC WRITING

Articles written for a more specialized academic audience can be very difficult for a newcomer to understand. For this exercise, you may be asked to read and respond to the piece by Jane Tompkins (p. 289). This is a source from which examples of claims and evidence were drawn in Chapter 1. Tompkins' piece is a very unconventional scholarly article, because it is constructed as a personal account of the writer's research process, not as an impersonal account or finished argument. Tompkins breaks some of the rules of academic writing in order to make a point about the nature and limitations of historical research. Even though it may not be the best model for typical academic research writing, it is useful to read because it shows the process of academic discovery in action—like the personal account of your research that you may be assigned in later chapters. Reading Tompkins' inquiry demonstrates the experience of research clearly driven by a question, or, more accurately, by a sequence of questions. Tompkins makes a complicated argument, and you should expect to read it several times in order to understand what the author is saying.

1. During the first reading, use the annotation strategies described at the beginning of the chapter. On this first reading, highlight the thesis statement—or question—and the first

sentence of every paragraph. Highlight her cues to audience, purpose, and argument. In the margins, ask questions, record responses, and mark parts that you do not understand.

2. Use the Focus Points: Reading Arguments (p. 21) to assist your second reading of this piece. As you read, notice how the author moves back and forth between summarizing and responding to sources.

3. Reread the piece a third time, this time identifying the sentences or parts of sentences that indicate the author's responses to sources consulted. In the Tompkins piece, what you do not identify as response should be primarily summaries of and quotations from the works she consulted.

4. List the cues the author uses to show when and how she is representing the thinking of others and when she is representing her own thinking.

5. With a discussion group, consider how the author's summaries prepare for and justify her responses to the works consulted. How does the author use quotations from sources in this piece? On what grounds does she consider the sources to be authoritative?

6. Consider the following questions with a discussion group:

   • Given Tompkins' discovery that researchers always see the past and that witnesses perceive the present through eyes affected by their own cultural assumptions, what is the value of doing historical research at all?

   • How do Tompkins' questions change and develop as she works her way through the topic of "Indians"?

   • What is the effect of Tompkins' violating the convention that academic writers not include personal experiences in their research? Why might she have chosen to present an unconventional ethos in this article?

7. Finally, use these informal reflections as a start for writing a response to some aspect of the author's piece. For example, you might consider Jane Tompkins' use of "I," her idea of history, her dismissal of absolute objectivity, or her conclusion that meaning in history may be tentative, but is still possible. Compare your responses to those of another writer in the class who responded to a similar aspect of the reading.

8. Reread your response and consider with your group on what warrant(s) you grounded it. How do warrants you would accept differ from the author's warrants, and from the warrants of other members of your discussion group? Describe audiences that would and would not share them. How might you need to reframe your response to incline a reader to consider your response, even though he or she does not share your warrants?

CHAPTER 3

Using Academic Sources Responsibly
Understanding Plagiarism

Most professional style manuals devote considerable space to citations and references, practices that give writers a formal, recognizable way to acknowledge their use of other writers' thinking, research, and arguments. Correct attribution of words, ideas, and concepts is very important to practicing researchers, since the accusation of plagiarism can lead to loss of a job, a reputation, and the chance for professional advancement.

The Modern Language Association (MLA) is the largest professional association of English and foreign language professors. Here is the definition of plagiarism from that organization's style manual for students, a definition that closely resembles definitions of plagiarism used in most American universities:

From "Documentation and Plagiarism":

> Derived from the Latin word *plagiarius* ("kidnapper"), *to plagiarize* means "to commit literary theft" and to "present as new and original an idea or product derived from an existing source" (*Merriam-Webster's Collegiate Dictionary* [11th ed.; 2003; print]). Plagiarism involves two kinds of wrongs. Using another person's ideas, information, or expressions without acknowledging that person's work constitutes intellectual theft. Passing off another person's ideas, information, or expressions as your own to get a better grade or gain some other advantage constitutes fraud. Plagiarism is sometimes a moral and ethical offense rather than a legal one since some instances of plagiarism fall outside the scope of copyright infringement, a legal offense. . . .
>
> A complex society that depends on well-informed citizens strives to maintain high standards of quality and reliability for documents that are publicly circulated and used in government, business, industry, the professions, higher education, and the media. Because research has the power to affect opinions and actions, responsible writers compose their work with great care. They specify when they refer to another author's ideas, facts, and words, whether they want to agree with, object to, or analyze the source. This kind of documentation not only recognizes the work writers do; it also

tends to discourage the circulation of error, by inviting readers to determine for themselves whether a reference to another text presents a reasonable account of what that text says. Plagiarists undermine these important public values. Once detected, plagiarism in a work provokes skepticism and even outrage among readers, whose trust in the author has been broken.

The charge of plagiarism is a serious one for all writers. Plagiarists are often seen as incompetent—incapable of developing and expressing their own thoughts—or worse, dishonest, willing to deceive others for personal gain. When professional writers, such as journalists, are exposed as plagiarists, they are likely to lose their jobs, and they are certain to suffer public embarrassment and loss of prestige. Almost always, the course of a writer's career is permanently affected by a single act of plagiarism. The serious consequences of plagiarism reflect the value the public places on trustworthy information. (*MLA Handbook*, 52–53)

Many experts in plagiarism distinguish between two types of plagiarism:

- Deliberate cheating, that is, buying, borrowing, or stealing a paper and handing it in as your own, with or without minor revisions;

- Questionable research practices, that is, using undocumented or poorly documented pieces from various sources, without distinguishing clearly among quotation, paraphrase, and summary, and without citing the sources properly (Howard, "Plagiarism").[1]

Clearly the first category describes acts of deception; there is no way to give a citation for a purchased or borrowed paper. The second kind is more closely described in the passage from the *MLA Handbook*: the failure to give credit to the researchers who preceded you. This kind of plagiarism can have consequences as serious as outright deception, and it can be harder to be sure when you are doing it. It also raises questions of motivation (honest mistake, hasty composition, conscious importing of chunks of other texts to fill in blanks) that can be hard to judge fairly. It is crucial in academic writing to learn to avoid misuse and miscitation of sources—accidental or not. Other kinds of writing also demand similar care about the "ownership" of writing. See, for example, the pieces in the Readings by Robert Rivard and Doris Kearns Goodwin.

PLAGIARISM AND PROFESSIONAL ETHICS

Notice that the *MLA Handbook* considers plagiarism to be an *ethical issue*, not a *legal issue*. According to professional ethicist Michael Davis, ethics are a matter of group consensus: "*Ethics consists of those standards of conduct that, all things considered, every member of a particular group wants every other member to follow even if their following them would mean he has to follow them*" (25, his italics). Even though ethical violations may not always be criminal (i.e., against the law), you may face blame, sanctions, or expulsion from a profession, school, or other group if you violate its ethics; simply not knowing the rules is usually not an excuse. University faculty adhere to the professional ethics established by their discipline and university, and students are expected to follow similar ethical standards. Two of the most serious ethical violations for students and professional researchers alike are fabricating data or evidence and submitting someone else's work as their own. By enrolling in a university and then registering for classes, students acknowledge compliance with its standards of ethical behavior, which are usually spelled out in the college catalog and/or student handbook. By the time they get to college, most students know that plagiarism can get them into big trouble: failure on a paper or in a course, or even suspension or expulsion from the university. But they may not know why.

FACULTY AND PLAGIARISM

Why would university faculty care so much about "using another person's ideas or expressions in your writing without acknowledging the source" that they would give up the convenience of doing so in their own work? Faculty members have a very strong concern about plagiarism because many of them depend on their writing as well as on their teaching for their position in the university and for their reputation in their profession. If someone publishes another researcher's ideas as his or her own, the person who initially did the work does not get credit for considerable time and effort and may lose out on the real, material rewards that can come from academic research: promotions, salary increases, professional honors, and awards. Therefore, professors are willing to expend time and effort on giving credit to their sources, and they expect their students and colleagues to do the same. In Michael Davis's terms, the advantages of having colleagues who are careful about crediting sources are worth the bother of exerting that kind of care themselves.

Intellectual property can also be a workplace issue. Because the origins and ownership of ideas is so very important in contemporary American life and work, it is generally expected that people who have made it through college, or into positions where they do work that involves writing, understand that they cannot represent someone else's work as their own. The consequences of plagiarism in the workplace are often harsh. For example, Robert Rivard's op-ed piece in the Readings shows the scorn of an editor for a colleague who did not follow the basic ethical expectation that a journalist (even a weatherman) does not represent another person's work as his own. Rivard absolutely rejects the pleas of the audience who would overlook what he sees as the weather broadcaster's clear violation of journalistic ethics.

STUDENTS AND PLAGIARISM

One of the ways the ethics of intellectual property directly concerns students is that the student who turns in someone else's work as his or her own may be gaining an unfair advantage over students who do their own work. However, there is another reason why students should care about plagiarism. The university is a teaching institution, and one of its functions is to give students credentials—a diploma. Most of the people who may become your employers or clients assume that a diploma means that a college graduate has adequately mastered certain advanced skills and acquired certain knowledge. The student who passes off another's work as his or her own may not have achieved this mastery. This pretense of learning cheats the students who have actually mastered the material sufficiently to be able to write about it; moreover, it is dangerous, since our world runs on the assumption that people credentialed as experts actually have expertise. Would you want to drive your car over a bridge built by someone who plagiarized her work in an engineering course? Again, looking back to Davis's definition of ethics, the advantages of living in a world in which credentials have real meaning is worth the effort of actually requiring students to write their own papers—not just download them. It pays to avoid plagiarism because the consequences—for people in the workplace as well as students—can be very grim, at best tremendously embarrassing and at worst severely damaging to a career.

Some Reasons Students Plagiarize

Four common reasons students plagiarize are as follows:

1. They do not understand the conventions of citation in the university or in a particular field.
2. They run out of time and panic.
3. They do not understand the material they are working with well enough to summarize and respond to it effectively.
4. They do not consider themselves to be part of the ethical community that rejects plagiarism and believe that cheating is acceptable if it leads to academic success.

Not much can be done about reason 4. From what we read in the newspapers, this is made to seem a common attitude among students, but instructors with considerable classroom experience know that while it exists, it is not as common as some people claim. Students in group 4 operate under a different set of warrants than the rest of the university, and unless those warrants can be changed, nothing much can be done except policing them. Much more common, in most instructors' experience, are students who do not document sources appropriately for the first three reasons, which are often combined.

It takes a long time to master citation practices, and many students get hung up on small points like how to punctuate references. The small points are important to maintaining a professional ethos, but the most important aspects of citation are to let a reader go back to your sources and to place your ideas in the context of what others in the field have said and done. In order to learn when and how to cite sources, reading a style guide is a start. But to become really proficient, you need to ask questions of your instructors and to notice how other writers use sources and identify them.

Sometimes students are tempted to buy or borrow a paper because they run out of time. It is easy to say that students should always leave themselves plenty of time to write. However, there is no one who has not, at one time or another, run out of time and panicked. Nonetheless, panic is not an acceptable reason to purchase or borrow a paper. There are several possibilities if you run out of time to write a paper—none of them are as good as writing a fine paper and getting it in on time, but they are always better than violating academic ethics:

- Talk to your instructor and request an extension, even if it will mean a lowered grade.
- Write a mediocre paper. If it is a paper that involves using one or more sources, be sure to cite every source whenever you refer to it. Your paper may not have much independent thought or original response, but it will be better than not having a paper or cheating to obtain one.
- Ask for the opportunity to revise the paper and get to it immediately.

If you find yourself in a panic more than once a year or so, rethink your study habits and priorities.

Often students put off writing a paper or working on a project because they do not understand the material they are working with. Entering a new field can involve learning a new vocabulary and figuring out new ideas expressed in unfamiliar ways, and this is often very difficult. It's useful to recognize that you are lost early enough to discuss a text with your friends, your instructor, or a tutor. Try reading each source more than once, marking what seem to be important points and annotating it with your questions and responses. Use the Focus Points: Reading Arguments in Chapter 2 (p. 21) to guide your reading, and then discuss your responses. The more you work in a field, the clearer the sources you work with will become, and the easier it will be to respond to them.

AVOIDING PLAGIARISM

It would be easier to understand and avoid plagiarism if the actual practice of writing were as simple and straightforward as the MLA definition implies. Reread that definition at the beginning of this chapter and consider how clearly it applies to all the kinds of written work you have done or know about.

Like the Texas weather broadcaster in Rivard's piece, a student who downloads an essay from the Web or recycles a piece from the fraternity or sorority files and submits it as his or her own is simply ignoring or defying the ethical standards of the university, and, in the opinion of most university faculty and administrators, fully deserves whatever penalties the university imposes. But understanding and avoiding the more subtle kinds of plagiarism (which might be the result of careless or unclear understanding of using sources) are not always so simple. Even professional writers occasionally run into trouble. From time to time you will read in the press about writers who are accused of "lifting" chunks of their books from previous publications by other authors. Usually they are soundly scorned and chastised by their peers and colleagues, and the book may be withdrawn from publication. At such times, it seems as though it should be a simple enough matter for an author to distinguish between his or her own ideas and someone else's, but sloppy note-taking and recordkeeping can add up to a big, career-endangering mistake even for experienced researchers. Consider, for example, how the allegations of plagiarism against the popular and prolific historical writer Stephen Ambrose severely damaged his reputation. See, in the Readings, the remorseful explanation by historian Doris Kearns Goodwin of her own professional failure, which explains how her plagiarism occurred, without excusing it; also look at Abigail Witherspoon's account of students who willfully violate the ethics of the university.

USING SOURCES TO ESTABLISH TRUST AND COMMUNITY

Using sources well is a matter of credibility as well as trust. Citation is as much a matter of *using* the authority of acknowledged sources to support your own argument as it is a matter of avoiding theft of intellectual property or misrepresenting your work. By reviewing the previous research to develop a line of argument, researchers demonstrate their understanding of and participation in a field and their involvement in its larger conversations. Academic writing acknowledges and draws on earlier work, and by citing previous sources, you not only take part in an ongoing conversation but also establish your credibility as a participant. By citing reliable sources, researchers indicate awareness of other participants in the conversation and acknowledge its history, thereby establishing their own ethos, which is the expertise that allows them to take an informed position in the field.

Using sources entails not only bringing these earlier "voices" into a conversation, but also finding a way to write in the language of the field in your own voice—a process, as will be noted in Chapter 6—that takes a long time to perfect.

BROADER ISSUES OF INTELLECTUAL PROPERTY: WHO OWNS IDEAS?

Acknowledging the work of others in your writing is part of an ongoing process of learning and one that requires continual attention. Understanding who really "owns" a piece of writing can be complicated, because writing and learning are not simple acts and are seldom done alone or in discrete units. Students read textbooks for most courses and are expected to repeat and use the information they learn on exams and in papers. Some coursework requires not only imitation but also memorization of texts, definitions, formulae, or processes.

FOCUS POINTS: ORIGINAL IDEAS AND COMMON KNOWLEDGE

Most "original" ideas come from years of mastering a field of study. Within all fields, there is much "common knowledge," which is not common for students because they have not yet encountered it. These contradictions are fertile grounds for discussion of how and when claims can be made about the ownership of ideas, as suggested in the questions that follow.

- To what extent are your ideas your own? How much does your thinking reflect what you have read or heard? Can you always tell the difference between your own thinking and the things you have read or learned?

- Can you sort out who said what and remember where they said it first? And is there any point in doing so? Once you say or write something, to what extent does it remain yours, and to what extent does it belong to the person who hears or reads it? Is "originality" ever possible?

- If you find yourself repeating someone else's idea as your own, to what extent does your intention matter? If a student is supposed to be in a learning situation, isn't the very point of education to gain ideas and information that you did not have before?

- What does originality mean if your "own" idea was discovered centuries ago and has been debated for generations, but you did not know about it?

- To what extent is imitation an important way of learning the basics in a field? When does imitation turn into misuse of someone else's ideas or violating the author's copyright? How does memorizing a definition from a textbook and using it to answer an exam question differ from cutting and pasting a definition from an online dictionary into a paper? What kind(s) of attribution are necessary in these cases?

- How does computer technology change the nature of intellectual property? For example, how does the ease of downloading music, newspaper articles, and pictures change people's understanding of "ownership"?

- How compatible is a free flow of information or a free ranging of mind with a strict policing of ideas?

We learn in ways we are not always totally aware of, extracting ideas and information from lectures, discussions, and brainstorming sessions that we do not always fully remember. During the college years, a student may read hundreds of books and articles. Sometimes students are asked to memorize texts or material, and sometimes they are asked to imitate other writers or speculate about how a writer from the past might have responded to a contemporary situation. All of these are reasons for thinking about intellectual property in a wider framework of common, professional, and personal ideas, a way of thinking that includes, but is not limited to, simply avoiding plagiarism.

Plagiarism and Imitation

Imitation can be not only a form of flattery, but also a method to learn organization, style, and ease of expression. In the past, memorizing texts and imitating a writer's style were important learning practices—as they still are in some countries and some American schools.

Learning through Imitation

In the following passage from his autobiography, Benjamin Franklin describes consciously using imitation to learn to improve his style, understanding, and vocabulary as a writer.

> About this time I met with an odd Volume of the Spectator [an English magazine that published literature and social commentary]. I had never before seen any of them. I bought it, read it over and over, and was much delighted with it. I thought the Writing excellent, and wish'd if possible to imitate it. With that View, I took some of the Papers, and making short Hints of the Sentiment in each Sentence, laid them by a few Days, and then without looking at the Book, tried to complete the Papers again, by expressing each hinted Sentiment at length and as fully as it had been express'd before, in any suitable Words that should come to hand. Then I compar'd my Spectator with the Original, discover'd some of my Faults and corrected them. But I found I wanted a Stock of Words or a Readiness in recollecting and using them, which I thought I should have acquir'd before that time, if I had gone on making Verses, since the continual Occasion for Words of the same Import but of different Length, to suit the Measure, or of different Sound for the Rhyme, would have laid me under a constant Necessity of searching for Variety, and also have to fix that Variety in my Mind, and make me Master of it. Therefore I took some of the Tales and turn'd them into Verse: And after a time, when I had pretty well forgotten the Prose, turn'd them back again. I also sometimes jumbled my Collections of Hints into Confusion, and after some Weeks, endeavor'd to reduce them into the best Order, before I began

to form the full Sentences, and complete the Paper. This was to teach me Method in the Arrangement of Thoughts. By comparing my Work afterwards with the original, I discover'd many faults and amended them; but I sometimes had the Pleasure of Fancying that in certain Particulars of small Import, I had been lucky enough to improve the Method or the Language and this encourag'd me to think I might possibly in time come to be a tolerable English Writer, of which I was extremely ambitious. (11–12)

Questions

- Would it make sense to accuse Franklin of plagiarism for using this kind of imitation as a learning process?
- Does the fact that Franklin was working alone, teaching himself to write, make any difference?
- What kinds of imitation have you used as a student? Memorization? Imitating an author's style? Using models to learn a new genre?
- How is imitation different from plagiarism? How is it similar?

Plagiarism and Copyright

Copyright is a *legal* issue, in contrast to the primarily ethical issue of plagiarism. Copyright laws ensure that writers and other creators of various kinds of texts (including music, pictures, films, software, etc.) maintain ownership of their work for at least a limited period of time. Copyright laws give authors (or the person or company that owns the copyright) ownership of the work—including the right to reproduce it, to modify it, and to grant permission for its use or modification by others. Copyright is justified on the grounds that it creates an incentive for writers to produce new material; they can sell it or the right to reproduce it to publishers, filmmakers, and other outlets, and thus receive compensation for the time and effort they put into creating the text.

Copyright issues bear some similarities to plagiarism issues, and both revolve around the idea of getting "credit" for your work, but plagiarism is an issue of attribution (who claims to have written what) and copyright is a matter of permission for use (who has permission to reproduce what). Thus, it is possible to plagiarize a piece without violating copyright. If, for example, a student buys a paper and submits it as his or her own, or if a friend gives him or her permission to submit in his own name something she has written, this constitutes plagiarism, even though it does not violate copyright. And if you photocopy a book or download a copyrighted image and reproduce it, you may be violating copyright, even though you leave the author's or artist's name on it and fully acknowledge your source. It can be easy to violate copyright when constructing Web sites, particularly when downloading visuals, since the images and texts on the Web are so easily accessible that they seem to be free. Many of them, however, are protected by copyright. Many Web sites have copyright statements attached to them, allowing or limiting their use.

Another area in which you may have had contact with copyright issues is the music industry, which has been waging an active battle to maintain control over music protected by copyright in the face of widespread file swapping. The people who share files look at the practice as sharing a resource, whereas many of the artists and the companies who own the copyright to works of music look at it as sharing resources that the sharers do not actually own, that is, as theft. This issue has led to a renewed and vigorous discussion of the extent to which intellectual property can be owned, of what rights are inherent in that ownership, and of how long that ownership can and should last. Copyright is a limited right, always balanced against "fair use," that is, the right of the public to have access to ideas, information, and entertainment. Copyright protects the right of authors, at least temporarily, to the profits derived from their work, but it does limit the circulation of information. This can be a serious problem in academic research, which depends on access to information. The extent and limits of copyright and fair use are generally determined by civil lawsuits, and rest on the body of legal decisions generated since the first American copyright laws were passed in the nineteenth century. New forms of art and entertainment raise new copyright issues. For example, consider the practice of "sampling" in music. Should it be seen as homage to older recording artists? Imitation? Parody? Or merely theft of the original artist's work? Should the inventiveness of musicians finding new frames for old performances be subordinated to the rights of artists to maintain the integrity of their own performances? There are no easy answers to these questions.

PLAGIARISM, COLLABORATION, AND TRUST

Collaboration in group projects can complicate issues of who is responsible for what and who owns what part of a written document or of an idea. This issue has immediate application to students, who are often expected to work in research groups or teams. Many students find group work a mixed experience. When everyone contributes to a project with energy and intelligence, group work can be a compelling means of learning. However, this is not always the case. Sometimes group members feel exploited, particularly when some think they are doing more work or higher quality work than other group members. Moreover, group work can lead to disagreements about who owns the documents a group produces, and how such documents should be handled, including the following:

- Should a group member put a document produced by the group into a personal portfolio?
- Should a group member incorporate that document or the research from the group project into a later work to be submitted as her own?
- At what point does an expanded or modified work derived from a group project become the individual's own product?
- If an individual member uses part of the group's work, what kind of documentation or acknowledgement seems fair?

As you work with groups, try to keep track of what constitutes "common knowledge," that is, knowledge generated and shared by the research group or entire class, and what ideas or pieces of work seem to "belong" to an individual person. However, the answers to these questions vary significantly from field to field, and you should keep these questions in mind as you work in various courses and enter your profession.

USING SOURCES TO ENTER THE CONVERSATION IN A FIELD

In spite of all these issues and disciplinary differences, most instructors agree that students must not only avoid cheating, but also learn to identify the sources that they quote from, paraphrase, or summarize (see Chapter 6). Many college instructors take a hard line on this issue. In many classes, the discussion of plagiarism often boils down to a grim series of warnings about misuse of sources and rules about formatting references. However, the ethics of documentation and citation are not only a set of prohibitions such as "do not download papers from term paper mills" or "do not lift pages or paragraphs from published sources and insert them into papers without adequate references." Ethical citation is also a means of connecting with and drawing on the knowledge of a field—of an academic community. If you view the use of sources as part of the normal practices of a profession or field of study, a set of practices closely tied to its other activities (like conducting experiments or reading manuscripts), the processes of citation and documentation may seem less like a mountain of busywork and more like a means of establishing a place and a voice in that community. Using sources well shows that you understand the value of research at a university (where original thought is very highly valued) and helps you to place your own writing in the larger context of a field. Using sources well helps you see the circulation of knowledge that takes place as researchers read and respond to each other's work. A new researcher is entering a conversation in which integrity is expected, and citing previous work serves to indicate shared values and growing expertise.

Exercises

3.1 PLAGIARISM AND ARGUMENT

Read the piece by Doris Kearns Goodwin in the Readings. Consider how she uses argument to explain and apologize for her mistake. Discuss with a small group the following questions and then write a short response to one or more of them.

1. Goodwin published this piece in *Time*, a popular, high-circulation news magazine, not in a professional journal. Considering the discussion of professional ethics earlier in this chapter, what purpose might addressing this wide popular audience serve?
2. Is the purpose of the piece more to apologize for or to explain her plagiarism? Do you find this to be an acceptable explanation? Is it an effective apology?
3. How does she incorporate an explanation of the work of an historian into the piece? What kind of ethos or professional position does she assume? What effect does this ethos have on you as its reader? Do you think it would affect one of her fellow historians the same way?
4. What is the effect of the first paragraph of this piece? How well does it succeed in arousing your sympathy? Does this appeal to pathos effectively support her claim?
5. Compare Goodwin's explanation of her plagiarism to Rivard's critique of Albert Flores' plagiarism (see Readings). How comparable are Goodwin's and Rivard's underlying assumptions about right and wrong use of sources?

3.2 IDENTIFYING MISUSE OF SOURCES

Summary drawn from Doris Kearns Goodwin's "A Historian Explains Why Someone Else's Writing Wound Up in Her Book"

Doris Kearns Goodwin describes how fourteen years ago, not long after the publication of *The Fitzgeralds and the Kennedys,* she received a communication from author Lynne McTaggart to the effect that material from her book on Kathleen Kennedy had not been properly attributed. Goodwin realized that McTaggart was right. Though Goodwin's footnotes repeatedly cited McTaggart's work, she left out quotation marks for phrases taken word for word. Goodwin had assumed that these phrases, drawn from her notes, were her own words, not McTaggart's words. She made the requested corrections, and the matter was completely laid to rest—until the *Weekly Standard* published an article reviving the issue. The larger question for historians is to understand how citation mistakes can happen.

1. Compare the summary paragraph above to the paragraph from which it was drawn in Goodwin's full article printed in the Readings. Highlight the phrases that were changed in the paragraph above. Many people would identify an imitation this close as plagiarism even though the source is identified and a few words are changed, because the sentence structure is the same, with only a few changes in vocabulary and elimination of the authorial "I."
2. With a small group of your classmates:
    *   Put quotation marks around all groups of three or more words "lifted" from the original.
    *   Rewrite the paragraph with the book closed, working to get the author's point rather than her words across. (Remember that a summary also needs a reference.) If you find that you've used any of her phrases—three or more words in a row—put quotation marks around them.

Repeat this process with the following paragraphs:

Summary from Robert Rivard's "What Every Student Knows: Thou Shall Not Copy"

Editors at the *Express-News* faced no dilemma when they decided to stop publishing Flores' weather column when an alert copy editor discovered that Flores was putting his name on the work of others. No readers canceled their subscriptions, although a few did threaten to. Even if there had been cancellations, editors would have been free to act. The *Express-News* would fire any columnist or reporter caught taking the work of others and passing it off as their own. Flores' departure from KENS clearly occurred in the aftermath of events there. The newspaper did not employ Flores or compensate him for his column. They did not employ or compensate KENS meteorologist Bill Taylor, whose weather column appears twice a week in the *Express-News*. KENS management, in turn, does not employ or compensate *Express-News* writers, such as columnist Edmund Tijerina, who appear on their news programs. Both companies are equal partners in MySanAntonio.com, their shared news and information Web site, but the talent exchange is just that, a collaboration.

Summary from Alfie Kohn's "The Dangerous Myth of Grade Inflation"

The fact that people were offering the same complaints more than a century ago puts the latest bout of complaints in perspective, like those quotations about the disgraceful values of the younger generation that turn out to be hundreds of years old. The long history of indignation also pretty well invalidates attempts to place the blame for higher grades on the liberal professors hired in the 1960s. (Unless, of course, there was a similar counter-cultural phenomenon in the 1860s.) Yet on campuses across America today, academe's usual requirements for supporting data and reasoned analysis have been suspended for some reason where grade inflation is concerned. It is largely accepted on faith that grade inflation—an upward shift in students' grade-point averages without a similar rise in achievement—exists, and that it is a bad thing. Meanwhile, the truly important issues surrounding grades and motivation are obscured or ignored.

3.3 CORRECTING MISUSE OF SOURCES

Choose a paragraph from one of the Readings or from a source of your own choice.

1. Revise it slightly, like the paragraphs above. With your group, discuss what you did to change it.
2. Put quotation marks around all groups of three or more words "lifted" from the original.
3. Rewrite the paragraph with the book closed, working to get the author's point rather than his or her words across. (Remember that a summary needs a reference too.)
4. Write a short comparison of the three different versions of the passage. Give your own account of how you moved from making minor changes in wording (a process often considered plagiarism) to representing the author's ideas in your own words.
5. Prepare a visual presentation to demonstrate the process of moving from patch-writing to composing.

3.4 SHORT RESEARCH PROJECT

In small groups, undertake the following investigations, taking notes on your queries.

1. Find your institution's plagiarism policy in student and faculty handbooks. How does it define academic honesty, particularly in relation to intellectual property? How detailed is the policy? Does the tone seem instructive or punitive?
2. Search your college's Web site for other, more local policies—in departments, the library, the writing center, and even on particular course syllabi. What additional concerns are addressed in these policies? What questions are raised and answered? Do the definitions of plagiarism vary much? How about the tone—the interplay between the writer of the policy and the students for whom it is written?
3. Search the Web to find plagiarism policies of other colleges and universities and compare them with your own school's policy. Try to find at least one college with a formal, explicit honor code (like the University of Virginia or one of the military academies like West Point or Annapolis). How does a traditional honor code supplement the school's plagiarism policy? Using the name of the university and plagiarism as keywords, search for how violations of the honor code have been handled.
4. If your groups know any students at these schools or have had contact with them online, ask them for their point of view on plagiarism issues at their school. Consider carefully the reliability of their answers.
5. Take a look at the Statement on Plagiarism on the Council of Writing Program Administrators Web site: www.wpacouncil.org/positions/. How do you think it could be adapted to the needs and practices of your own class or English department? Do you see any problems with applying it?
6. Search your campus newspaper archives (either in print or on the Web) for news stories about plagiarism in the last five years. Are there any points of contention?
7. Take a look at one or more of the online "term paper mills" (like www.schoolsucks.com/, www.123helpme.com/, www.1millionpapers.com/, www.the-paper-doctor.com/, www.cheathouse.com/, etc.). How do their statements of purpose and values echo and defy definitions of plagiarism and academic honesty posted by the colleges you have examined?
8. Write an account of your research, either as an essay or a PowerPoint presentation, that reflects on what you think are the most significant of your group's findings. Compare accounts with your group members, considering the different significances you have focused on.

3.5 ADDITIONAL READING AND INFORMAL WRITING OR RESPONSE

1. Read Abigail Witherspoon's "This Pen for Hire: Grinding Out Papers for College Students" in the Readings (p. 276).
2. Reread the piece, this time highlighting the parts of the essay in which Witherspoon demonstrates that she does not belong to the profession that accepts the ethical prohibition of plagiarism. Where does she position herself and what basic assumptions about educational institutions does she establish as warrants for her way of thinking? Also note the parts of the argument that you have the most intense response to—either positive or negative.
3. Write a response to Witherspoon's paper, using one of the following questions as a starting point:
   - The disputes concerning the nature of intellectual property notwithstanding, can you identify any ethical common ground shared by various groups within a college? Can you see a consensus between the different layers of the university (i.e., students, administration, faculty) concerning what constitutes cheating and what constitutes fair use or fair sharing of intellectual property, or do you see mostly differences?
   - Which laws or rules about intellectual property do you and your friends normally observe? Which do you ignore? What are the major differences between the rules you follow and the rules you ignore?
   - Do you find yourself more inclined to value the protection of intellectual property or the free dissemination of knowledge and information? Does your inclination have anything to do with your field of study?

CHAPTER 4

Moving from Inquiry to Argument

Almost all researched writing involves taking a reasoned stand among consensus and controversies that other researchers have addressed and about which there is some disagreement. For example, you might investigate the advantages or drawbacks of organic farming, or the extent to which early education programs impact success in secondary schools. Notice, however, that even though these questions address controversies, they do not lend themselves to "yes" or "no" answers. Writing about the consensus and controversies in a field can help you understand the field better and develop more nuanced responses to your sources. Understanding how and why experts agree and disagree can help you move from researching a topic to making an informed argument about it.

MAKING CHOICES ABOUT TOPICS

Finding a topic for a researched project in college can be challenging because you must find a topic you care enough about to live with for some time. However, keep this process of choice in perspective. "Choosing a topic" from scratch is not a process much used in the workplace or even in academic research. Even though research is part of the work of many professions, the topic seldom needs to be searched for. The topic is usually simply there, as part of what a company produces or a case requires. An engineer may be asked to do background research on a certain manufacturing process, a medical researcher might look into the treatment of a disease by a certain drug, and a lawyer or paralegal might be asked to conduct research on a designated legal precedent. Academic researchers usually base their current research on questions unearthed in their past work or pursue projects for which they have proposed and received funding. Only occasionally does a researcher start from scratch, researching a totally new and different topic. These outside constraints and the need for continuity are major aspects of inquiry for most researchers.

If a specific topic is not provided by an outside source, most researchers find topics by a combination of reviewing what they have already done, talking about their semi-formulated responses and ideas with friends and colleagues, and browsing potential sources. They may cycle several times through these approaches to a topic until they find an idea that provokes a question or an argument. Like many students, even experienced researchers often find this phase of a project very frustrating.

THE ETHICS OF RECYCLING YOUR OWN WRITING

Many scholars who publish their research consistently use and reuse pieces of their own work, moving ideas, sentences, and sometimes paragraphs from a synthesis to a proposal to the draft of an argumentative paper. This practice is legitimate for students to follow as well, provided that you do it within the context of a single course, using your own, unpublished writing, to which you hold the copyright. Students who are required to write an argumentative research paper often find it more satisfying when they can draw on earlier versions of their work such as proposals, annotated bibliographies, summaries, and syntheses.

While some of the projects in the remaining chapters invite you to revise, rethink, and resubmit a series of pieces based on the same body of reading and research, it is usually considered unethical for students to submit work done in one course for an assignment in another course. There is something apparently inconsistent to this prohibition, since some faculty teach the same course many times, updating their notes and assignments as necessary. And invited speakers often give the same lectures over and over again to different audiences. For students, however, the point of taking a course is to learn to do new things, not to demonstrate what you already know, and so you are expected to do new work for every course.

On the other hand, sometimes you may begin an area of research in one course that you would really like to continue in another. If you should want to "recycle" a piece of work from a previous course, in a writing course or any other, propose to the instructor what you want to do and ask for permission to extend your earlier research. The instructor may want you to show him the earlier piece and explain (orally or in a written proposal) how you intend to produce a different or more mature version of the earlier project. You should expect to have to convince the instructor that you are proposing a major rethinking or expansion of the earlier work. You may need to demonstrate that the continuity gained from continuing an investigation outweighs the advantage of exposure to a new set of issues. If you propose to revise or continue an earlier project, you should be willing to take "no" for an answer, if that is the instructor's decision.

FINDING A TOPIC FOR INQUIRY

Unlike many researchers in the workplace, students must often find a topic that interests them. What follows is a process to help choose and define a topic. This is not, however, a series of linear steps that you can follow and be done with but a recursive process, in which you can and should go back and forth from step to step until you find a research question in which you see the potential for projects that interest you (see Fig. 4.1).

Step 1: Decide on an Area of Interest

Most students start by deciding on a general area for inquiry and then experiment a bit to see what might be done with it. The goal of this sometimes messy process is to find an issue that not only interests you but also contains questions about which an argument

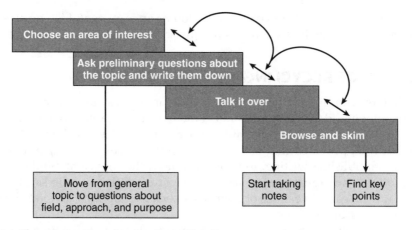

FIGURE 4.1 Choosing an Inquiry as a Recursive Process

can be made by people with similar warrants or basic assumptions. These questions must also provide a basis for reasoned argument within a field of study or work.

One place to start this process is by rethinking work you have already done, looking for a related issue you are interested in pursuing further. Some of the readings in this book touch on issues that might offer a starting place for an inquiry, for example, plagiarism, grading, and the way universities work. Each of those issues raises questions that could make good topics for inquiry and which draw on your experiences as students.

Suppose you wanted to pursue an issue about intellectual property. Some questions you might consider are:

- who owns "code" in computer science;
- the practices of parody and/or sampling in music or comedy, and the extent to which they violate the intellectual property rights (or artistic integrity) of the original artist;
- preventing or detecting plagiarism (What are the effective means? How much effort should be put into this?);
- recent attempts by movie producers to extend copyright protection;
- the history of plagiarism as a concept, and how it has changed over time; and
- the ethics of downloading music or other materials from the Web.

Or you might explore topics about professions and professional life:

- how professions like teaching or law or nursing have changed over time;
- whether and how physicians can maintain professional status in face of the growing power of HMOs and if they should try;
- how much responsibility nurses should be expected to take on;
- how schools can deal with the current shortage of science instructors;
- the effects of high-stakes testing on public education; and
- the effects of "No Child Left Behind" legislation, either locally or nationally.

There are many other topics you could consider. For example, you are apt to have questions about the field you want to major in, the profession you are aiming for, or a field that you want to learn more about. Once you decide on a field, start looking for the important issues that its researchers and practitioners are facing. You could also start an inquiry about activities that interest you, like computer games, music, sports, or movies; or you could start with social issues you care about, like global warming or genetic research. Look for news or magazine stories that mention academic research about the issue. Look for the aspects of the activity or issue that involve controversy or disagreement.

Step 2: List Preliminary Questions

With a small group of classmates, start describing what you already know about the topics that seem most interesting to you and generate some specific questions you might raise about these general topics. Use this discussion to decide on the general topic you will research and then to determine several possible ways of looking at it. Write down questions and new ideas as they arise in the discussion. For example:

- If you want to write about psychology, do you want to work with clinical psychology, experimental psychology, or physiological psychology? What are the relations between these subfields?

- Think about a problem or social practice, such as cigarette smoking, and consider what approaches different fields like medicine, psychology, marketing, and environmental engineering might take. Which approach do you most want to investigate?

- Draw questions from the kinds of controversies you find in a field that interests you. Are there controversies about safety issues (e.g., the safety of a particular medical treatment), ethical issues (e.g., what the social impact of building a dam might be), or issues of practice (e.g., the most effective way to teach students for whom English is a second or third language)?

Your questions should move toward greater specificity as you think and talk about your topic. If you start with several questions at the same level of generality, choose the one you like best and focus on that one. The more you write down your questions and responses, the better you will remember them as you take notes and do library research, and the more valuable this preliminary work will be to you later in the process.

A project analyzing how plagiarism affects college work might start with questions like these:

- A teacher once suspected that I had plagiarized. What do teachers look for when they grade papers to see if students have plagiarized? How do they know if the student plagiarized on purpose? Does it make a difference?

- What are teachers doing to prevent plagiarism? Some teachers at my school always fail students who have plagiarized. Who decides on these penalties? Do some teachers try to prevent plagiarism without using scare tactics?

A project examining the role of international teaching assistants at large universities might start with questions like these:

■ Many classes at my school are taught by international TAs. How many? Are the numbers similar at other universities? Why do universities use TAs from other countries? What kind of training do TAs get before they teach? Is there some kind of requirement that must be met for training TAs, especially international TAs?

■ I've heard some other students complain about taking courses with international TAs. What problems do these students complain about? Are there students who like having international TAs?

■ What are some of the issues being discussed by university faculty and administrators regarding international TAs? Is this a controversial issue for your college or university? What are this university and others doing about it?

Step 3: Talk It Over

You need not develop your topic alone; most researchers work in groups, ranging in formality from the relatively tight and hierarchical collaboration of scientists and their students in a laboratory to informal networks of humanities researchers working in the same general subject area. Take advantage of any familiarity your classmates, instructor, and friends have with the questions that interest you, and discuss the possibilities for your investigation with them, taking notes on your emerging ideas and recording possible objections to them. It may seem unnecessary to take notes on these early discussions, but they can be very useful as you move into planning and drafting your project(s).

Your general purpose at this early phase of the process is to decide where to focus your inquiry; your purposes for specific projects will emerge from the assignments you undertake.

Step 4: Browse and Skim

To better understand the extent and context of what you already know about your questions, use what you know about finding and evaluating sources to locate and skim a few preliminary sources.

■ Look for items in magazines, newspapers, and your textbooks that refer to academic research about your topic. Keep a list of these potential references and try to find a few in the library.

■ Look for controversies in the field that will help you formulate questions that direct the inquiry.

■ As you browse and skim preliminary sources, continue discussions with your research group about what issues seem to be important in the field and which controversies seem most interesting.

■ Browsing can be more efficient when you understand the way much academic writing is structured. The end of the introduction and the beginning of the conclusion are major points at which readers expect to see a statement of the overall argument. Beginnings of paragraphs very often refer back to the main issue and may introduce a line of reasoning or major supporting evidence. The ends of paragraphs often recapitulate and extend the point.

■ As you move from a general topic to a specific issue or question, narrow your conception of how relevant particular sources may be to your specific inquiry, and narrow the focus of your browsing accordingly.

Identifying Key Words

Identify key terms used by an author or authors in a field. Key words are important words in the title and throughout the piece that may be repeated from source to source. For example, most of the words in the title of this textbook are key words: "Academic," "Research," and "Argument." In some readings, the key terms may not be this obvious, but they are always words that writers use to organize their ideas, that compilers of databases use to sort and retrieve sources, and that readers can, in turn, use to search for additional related sources. For some publications, authors are instructed to provide key words in order to ensure that their work can be retrieved by the particular academic community the author is addressing.

■ If a journal article provides a list of key terms on its first page, highlight them as you read. In some electronic formats, you can use the search function to help you locate them and then analyze the places where they are used and the frequency with which they are repeated.

■ If no key words are given, identify and highlight words that seem particularly important to the meaning of the article, particularly terms that you notice being repeated throughout the source. Becoming aware of key words will also enable you to find additional relevant sources through key word searching, to sort your own notes as you move from note-taking to drafting, and to start building coherence into your drafts early in the writing process. Using key words that are typical in a field also indicates your growing expertise and then helps establish your ethos.

Recognizing Authors' Cues

Authors also often provide cues to help readers identify key points.

■ Look for the authors' cues to audience, purpose, and significance (see Chapter 2).

■ Look for the authors' cues to the argument in a thesis phrase:

The point of this paper [or argument, or line of thinking, etc.] is to . . .

■ Look for transitional cues:

Another reason this is important is . . .

■ Look for cues to inferences and conclusions:

This implies that . . .

It naturally follows that . . .

■ Look for self-references (*what I really mean is . . .*), which may creep into a piece when the author is stating or reiterating a crucial point. Writers in the sciences and many social sciences, however, rigorously avoid personal pronouns, and so their cues can be harder to spot.

Skimming

As you read, annotate, highlight, and take notes on the following:

- Identify issues of consensus ("what everybody knows") and of controversy, which are often indicated by cues to agreement and disagreement. Look for questions and controversies that do not invite simple "yes" or "no" answers.

- Identify specific claims the sources make.

- Take brief notes on where the authors position themselves within which controversies and which other authors they cite as representing various sides or approaches.

- Keep in mind the fallacies described in Chapter 1, and make notes when you find writers using them.

- List key words, meaningful terms that recur within a source or within a body of sources.

- List the warrants the sources share or do not share.

- Save this preliminary exploration to use as your inquiry proceeds.

Then make a preliminary idea map for your own use. It might look like a conventional outline, like a "point/counterpoint" argument, or like a series of islands of information and argument that you connect with arrows when you can. If you do not know where you stand, it is not necessary to fully commit to a final position, or even to completely shape your question(s) at this point, although you will have to do so eventually. Simply get as close as you can and record what you are thinking at this point.

Step 5: Choose Relevant Sources

This process of browsing, responding, and discussing your topic will be more efficient if you skim initial sources to judge whether a source is directly relevant to your issue, whether it may be background information, or whether it seems only marginally relevant. For example, if you were writing a paper on plagiarism in college:

- Recent sources that use terms like "plagiarism" and "college" or "university" in the title and as key words at the beginnings of paragraphs will probably be relevant to your inquiry.

- Recent sources that discuss cheating in college in general may offer some background but may be only marginally relevant.

- As you move toward a thesis, the range of relevance should narrow. For example, inquiring into "how common plagiarism is in universities" or "how universities combat plagiarism" will narrow the range of relevant sources.

- When you find a possible source, skim it to see how much it contributes to your inquiry. If it seems like a good fit, keep a reference for it for a "working bibliography" (described in Chapter 5), with whatever comments might help remind you to look at it again. It is sometimes useful to read a source that fascinates you carefully all the way through, even if it is not strictly relevant, since it may help you formulate your approach. Clearly, this kind of reading is less useful when you are seriously pressed for time.

■ When checking the references in a recent source, you may find references to earlier sources that use key words directly relevant to your own project. Think about the age and quality of these older references, using the Focus Points in Chapter 2.

■ To establish your ethos in the field, aim to find the most important, authoritative, and reliable references concerning your issue, without packing your work with irrelevant references.

TAKING EFFECTIVE NOTES

The progression from finding a topic for inquiry to taking notes from sources is not very clear, because there is no clear boundary between consulting preliminary sources and continuing the inquiry. Finding and assembling sources involves exploring a field and listening to its conversations until you find yourself taking a position in them. Generally, writers start researching rather widely, and then narrow their research as they hone in on an issue and discover the opinion they are developing toward it. Because this process may stretch over a significant period of time, you can make research projects easier by taking good notes and keeping them well-enough organized to find them again when needed. As a specific inquiry becomes clearer, researchers generally find that some of their early work is not directly relevant. They put those notes in a separate set of files, for possible use on later projects.

Taking notes on your responses and developing questions can help you make informed decisions about what sources are most relevant as the research process goes on. With good notes, you can spend more time developing your responses and reasoning and less time backtracking to find and understand work you have already done. Good notes also help researchers avoid accidental plagiarism, as was described in Chapter 3.

The concept of "good notes," however, has changed considerably over the years. In the past, many researchers took notes by hand on index cards, which could later be sorted and arranged in various ways. While some researchers still take notes this way, many do not. Taking notes by hand often involves transcribing electronic text into handwriting and back into electronic text, a process that provides at least two opportunities to introduce errors like dropped words, misspellings, and transposed integers. With the advent of photocopying and computer technology, most writers collect and store research electronically. Many writers find that taking notes on a computer is preferable to writing notes by hand because the researcher can move text from notes to draft to revision by cutting and pasting, *not retyping*. Moreover, electronic files often provide easier ways to distinguish notes about sources from responses to them. For example:

■ Attaching reference footnotes to specific quotations can let you transfer references from notes to drafts.

■ Using the comment feature to record your responses to materials can distinguish your own thinking from that in the sources. You can also use a different font or color to maintain this distinction. If you are using your own computer, bookmarking online materials allows easy access to them as your ideas develop.

As you start taking more extensive notes, review the annotation and reflection strategies described in Step 4: Browse and Skim, remembering that the acts of reading and writing are recursive and that even very experienced researchers move backward and forward.

There are still times when notes are taken by hand, such as when recording field observations or conversations. There are social and logistical inhibitions to using computers in some of these situations, although they are diminishing. For example, sometimes it is hard to take notes on a laptop in a one-on-one meeting or when visiting a site about which you need to write a report. In those cases, you may need to take notes on paper as you go along and transcribe them later. However, these conventions are changing with the increasing technical sophistication and popularity of electronic notebooks, handheld computers, and personal digital assistants, which seem less intrusive than conventional laptops. The tiny, inexpensive digital audio and visual recorders now available can be expected to bring about even more changes.

FOCUS POINTS: TAKING RESEARCH NOTES FROM TEXT

- *Start taking notes by skimming and reading selectively*, looking for particular issues that interest you within a wider topic and for sources that refer to each other or to the same sources. Consider the relevance of sources by quickly skimming them, identifying in your notes (by highlighting and making annotations on your own print copy or on electronic text, if possible) those parts you might want to return to. Sometimes it helps to indicate, either on the source itself or in a separate prewriting file, your impression of how useful you think some sources will be. Record citation information even when just starting to skim, in case you later decide to return to a source you originally thought irrelevant.

- *Examine the sources for reliability.* (Refer to Focus Points: Evaluating Sources, p. 29.)

- *Keep copying errors from creeping into your draft* by taking notes electronically and cutting and pasting quotations (once you've double-checked them for accuracy). When working from electronic sources, you can sometimes cut and paste sentences and paragraphs from sources directly into your notes. However, whether you copy or cut and paste, be careful to avoid unintentionally plagiarizing. Failing to indicate clearly when you are using someone else's ideas and exact words is considered to be a serious form of plagiarism—*even if you cite the source.*

- *Distinguish between a source's ideas and your own* by using a different font or highlighting color. Choose a method and use it consistently.

- *Put quotation marks around quotations copied from the source* and pasted into notes, even short quotes (2–3 words in the same order), and keep track of page numbers at the end of each paraphrase, summary, and quote. Even long quotations should be put in quotation marks as you cut and paste or copy; you can decide later what kind of punctuation (quotation marks or indentation) should be used in the final draft.

- *Clearly indicate in the notes when the author is quoting or paraphrasing another source* and whether the author is agreeing or disagreeing with other sources. If possible, copy the author's citation into your notes, in case you want to use the "embedded citation" in your own paper.

- *Collect the information you think you will need from each source, **once**,* preferably electronically, and cut and paste from your original notes into the drafts you write. Avoid rewriting reference list entries, because every rewrite risks introducing error in content or format. You can write the reference information at the beginning of a file for each source, or as a footnote attached to the citation; in either case, be sure that the information stays with your notes about a source, even if you use only part of the notes when drafting.

■ *Go back to the sources and double-check all quotations* before ending a session of reading, note-taking, and copying to make sure that they are exact and have the necessary reference information. This practice can prevent a lot of backtracking later. If possible, keep electronic or hard copies of sources in case you need to go back and check for accuracy. If you get confused about context or authorship, it pays to be able to check sources quickly and easily.

Collecting Reference Information

When working with sources, always collect the information you need for references as you go along, because backtracking is time-consuming and frustrating. Many journal articles put a complete reference on the first page, and now that photocopying and downloading are such common practices, if your source has such a reference, you can merely cut and paste it into a file for sources, or photocopy and file it. Different citation styles require slightly different information, but you will have most of what you need if you collect the following information:

■ For all sources, record the author, title, and year of publication.

■ For books, add the place of publication, publisher, and edition if it is not the first.

■ For articles in journals, add the journal name, volume and issue numbers, and page numbers.

■ For articles in magazines and newspapers, add the publication name, full date, page numbers, and section number for newspapers divided into sections.

■ For online sources, keep the information from the medium of initial publication, and add the URL and date you accessed the site (such as the journal or newspaper an article came from).

Consult the Quick Guide to Documentation at the end of this book, which is a short reference for formatting information for particular styles.

EXAMPLE 4.1 *Sample Preliminary Notes for Paper on Plagiarism*
See Chapter 8 for a draft of this paper.

Plagiarism

Sources Used

Howard, Rebecca Moore. "Forget about Policing Plagiarism. Just Teach." *Chronicle.com*.

Chronicle of Higher Education, 16 Nov. 2001. Web. 17 Jan. 2008.

McGrath, Charles. "Plagiarism: Everybody Into the Pool." *New York Times* 7 Jan. 2007:

C33. Print.

"Online Tool Helps Universities, Colleges Fight Plagiarism." *Community College Week* 15.12

(2003): 18. Print.

Robillard, Amy E. "We Won't Get Fooled Again: On the Absence of Angry Responses to Plagiarism in Composition Studies." *College English* 70.1 (2007): 10–31. Print.

Straw, Deborah. "The Plagiarism of Generation 'Why Not?'" *Community College Week* 14.24 (2002): 4–6. Print.

Consensus

Plagiarism is easier and more common on college campuses than ever before (Howard, "Online Tool," Straw).

Plagiarism is a problem.

Online plagiarism is even easier.

Cheating/dishonesty vs. misunderstanding or insufficient knowledge (called "patchwriting" by Howard).

Controversy

Difference between cheating and "patchwriting"? (Howard)

Difference between stealing and developing ability to use sources?

My response: How do we identify motives? How to be fair when we know some students cheat?

Developing as writers/writing as development

Punishment or education???

Should schools pass students who do not understand how to use sources and so "patchwrite"? If so, at what levels?

Questions

Should teachers be held responsible, in part, for giving their students opportunities to plagiarize? (Howard, Straw, Robillard)

Is the increase in plagiarism due to an inherent change in the values/assumptions of today's students? ("Online Tool," Straw, McGrath)

What kind of values do I want students to have and schools to help maintain? How can this be done?

What about the time I was wrongly accused of plagiarizing? Did it hurt me? Why or why not?

EXAMPLE 4.2 *Sample Preliminary Notes for Paper on International Teaching Assistants*
See Chapter 9 for preliminary and final drafts of this paper.

International TAs

Sources Used

Davis, Stephen F., and Jason P. Kring. "A Model for Training and Evaluating Graduate
Teaching Assistants." *College Student Journal* 35.1 (2001): 45–51. Web. 8
August 2008.

Johnson, Susan M., and Xia Li Lollar. "Diversity Policy in Higher Education: The Impact of
College Students' Exposure to Diversity on Cultural Awareness and Political
Participation." *Journal of Education Policy* 17.3 (2002): 305–320. Print.

Sarkodie-Mensah, Kwasi. "The International Student as TA." *College Teaching* 39.3 (1991):
115–16. Print.

Smith, Rosslyn, et al. "Crossing Pedagogical Oceans: International Teaching Assistants in
U.S. Undergraduate Education." *ASHE-ERIC Higher Education Report* 8 (1992): n. pag.
Web. 6 Nov. 2008.

Consensus

How to train graduate teaching assistants is a major issue in higher education (Davis and
Kring, Smith).

Achieving diversity is a priority for most universities and can be beneficial to students
(Johnson and Lollar, Smith).

Teaching opportunities help graduate students (Davis and Kring).

Both ITAs and their students are responsible for cultural conflicts and breakdowns in
communication (Sarkodie-Mensah, Davis and Kring).

ITAs will probably continue to be an aspect of education at big universities. If there is a
problem, it is not apt to go away.

My response: My school does not have graduate students. Is this an advantage or a
disadvantage to me? My school does have some faculty from foreign countries who were
educated abroad and who use accented English. How does the issue of ITAs relate to the
issue of international faculty members?

Controversies

Is this really a problem? How to deal with it?

Americanization of ITAs

Professional development for ITAs

My response: Should these good things take place at the cost of tuition-paying American under-graduates?

International understanding for undergraduates

Globalization—what do American students need to know about foreign countries?

My response: Yes, this is dismal. Few of us even know a foreign language very well—much less its culture and customs. Many of us have never been out of the United States. Can we compete?

Questions

What is the best method for evaluating and training ITAs?

Is it enough to just have education programs for the TAs, or should the students be educated as well?

Deciding on an Appropriate Level of Detail

Take more detailed notes whenever you read material you *know* you want to put in your paper or when you discover something highly unusual or unexpected in the source, such as an example that really stands out, a line of reasoning that you have not seen before, or warrants that are not usually applied to the issue.

- All the time you are taking notes, keep actively thinking about what specific questions you might pose concerning this material, how it might modify your argument, or how you could synthesize it with other materials.

- In general, take notes in great detail only in rare book rooms and similar situations where you cannot borrow, photocopy, or download the source—under those circumstances do take copious notes.

- You can cut and paste an interesting but probably irrelevant piece from a source into your notes, making a marginal note to yourself. If you are working with hard copy, annotate your proposed use for it and your response. But try to keep your focus on pieces that are directly relevant to your topic.

- Photocopying or printing out sources to reread can be helpful as you develop a clear thesis and anticipate the need to review the sources most relevant to it. But keep relevance firmly in mind as you choose materials to copy.

If the research is going well, most researchers, while skimming sources or taking detailed notes, start responding to the author or seeing important connections among sources. This is an important step in understanding the field, finding your own position in it, and ultimately formulating a thesis, so do not ignore these responses. However, as suggested previously, be sure to distinguish responses from notes on your sources by using a different colored pen or a different kind of font or color, or by highlighting. The important thing is to choose a system that suits you and use it consistently. When returning to notes after a period of time, you must be able to distinguish your own language, ideas, and responses from those drawn from a source, and the easiest and most reliable way is to consistently indicate whose ideas are whose while you are taking the notes.

REAL-TIME NOTE-TAKING

Taking notes on books, articles, or Web sites is easier than taking notes on lectures or discussions because you can usually go back and reread written texts another time to make sure you got the argument right and caught the author's cues about main points and positions. Taking notes on a lecture, discussion, or other nonrepeatable kinds of event requires that as you listen you anticipate the organization, recognize the main points, and decide how much detail you may need later. This kind of note-taking can be important, however, because taking real-time notes accurately contributes to your ethos—and not only in school. Good notes are the raw material for a number of crucial professional activities, such as producing minutes of meetings, writing a memo recapitulating your understanding of a meeting or conveying its results to your colleagues, and moving from an oral agreement to a binding contract.

Taking notes on a lecture is probably the easiest kind of real-time note-taking because lecturers tend to use the same kinds of cues as writers, and in the same places, only more strongly and consistently. They are apt to repeat key terms to be sure listeners catch them. Many lecturers use the "tell them what you're going to tell them, say it, then tell them what you've told them" model, which gives the audience the chance to catch important terms and concepts missed or misheard the first time. Taking notes on a discussion—which may go anywhere—requires sorting through a lot of detail as it goes along, because unless there is a strong discussion leader, there may not be much control over the pattern of the discussion, leaving the note-taker to determine which points are most important. Taking notes on a phone conversation, a meeting, an interview, or an onsite visit requires similar decisions about the meaning and purpose of the event and about which details to record; how you make these decisions will depend on the purpose of the report you anticipate writing from the notes.

FOCUS POINTS: REAL-TIME NOTE-TAKING

- Record the time, place, and speaker's name accurately. When taking notes in situations where there is more than one speaker, make sure you attribute remarks correctly or write down that you are not sure exactly who said what.
- Look for and identify the main points as well as you can as you listen. Good speakers use verbal markers and cues and repeat their main points and key terms.
  - In a standard lecture format, the speaker summarizes what she or he is going to say, repeats the key words and cues as the points are developed, and recapitulates them in the conclusion. If you miss a point, listen for it to be repeated.

- When taking notes on discussions, which can seem to ramble, listen for explicit links to points made by earlier speakers. These cues often mark the beginning of an agreement, disagreement, or elaboration.

■ Decide on the level of detail you are trying to capture, and make sure your record is as accurate as possible.

- If you realize you've opted for too much or too little detail, change your strategy immediately and go forward with the note-taking—*don't try to go back.*
- Identify statements you suspect you may not have recorded accurately. Some writers use a question mark in the margin, before and after a questionable note, or use a consistent color to highlight points about which they are uncertain. If you later decide to quote or paraphrase, you will need to clearly remember how reliable each part is.

■ If there is a chance for follow-up, ask questions to clarify the details you did not understand the first time.

■ Listen for speakers' references to sources and try to record them accurately.

■ As soon as possible after the event has ended, review your notes, filling in the blanks and adding whatever else you remember. "Debrief" yourself and any collaborators, and record your immediate responses, clearly indicating that they are *responses* rather than notes.

MOVING FROM NOTES AND RESPONSES TO ARGUMENT: FINDING A PRELIMINARY THESIS

In Chapter 1, the idea of the thesis was raised as an essential point of developing an argument: "Although an argument can start with a topic or question, it moves to make a claim, which is stated in a thesis statement (argument to be made) or hypothesis (proposition to be tested)." While scientific genres like laboratory reports usually begin with an hypothesis, many genres in other fields begin with a thesis: an argument that will be supported with evidence and that often refutes other ways of thinking about the topic. However, the actual process of writing tends to be recursive, and many writers start drafting before they have a final, argumentative thesis, using instead a "preliminary thesis" that they will revise as their argument becomes clearer (see Fig. 4.2).

Often, a preliminary thesis resembles an hypothesis because it is posed as a question yet to be answered. In moving from inquiry to argument, think about moving from a question to an arguable position. A preliminary thesis with potential is a clear, succinct question that a researcher finds as he or she surveys a field. You can start developing that question by reviewing your early browsing and skimming.

■ Review the list of the initial questions raised in Step 2: List Preliminary Questions and your responses to the sources you have read.

■ Talk with a group of your fellow researchers, and shape your responses to fit the kinds of researched projects assigned.

■ Based on your browsing, skimming, and library research, find a controversy that interests you, and use it to formulate a working question to guide your research. Write the question down; you can refine it later.

■ Make sure the question does not invite a "yes" or "no" answer, but rather a "why," "how," or "to what extent" approach and that it addresses an ongoing controversy rather than a single position.

EXAMPLE 4.3 *Revised Thesis Question for a Paper on Plagiarism*

Topic: Plagiarism in college

Question: Is plagiarism a problem in colleges?

Controversy: Different responses to plagiarism

Revised question: What different responses to plagiarism are made by university faculty and administrators?

EXAMPLE 4.4 *Revised Thesis Question for a Paper on International Teaching Assistants*

Topic: Resistance to international graduate teaching assistants in undergraduate courses

Question: Why do American undergraduates often resent being taught by international teaching assistants?

Controversy: How to understand and respond to students' resistance to international graduate teaching assistants

Revised question: Why do some undergraduates resent being taught by international graduate teaching assistants, and what do university administrators do about it?

After narrowing and shaping your research questions, start writing a claim for which you might argue. Next, write a short statement of the value or importance of what you propose to do—what larger question or concern it answers. In short, ask yourself right from the start—"So what?" This need not be an earthshaking significance. Your research may not uncover the definitive answer to the question, but you should be able to foresee the significance of your work for your audience—your fellow students and instructor.

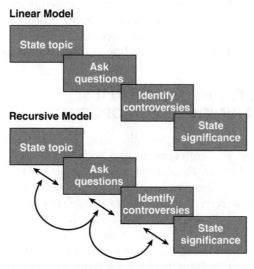

FIGURE 4.2 Formulating a Preliminary Thesis

If you have not had much experience constructing a thesis, you will find that this too is a recursive process. The following template offers a way to construct a preliminary thesis from your notes, discussion, thinking, and questions. The following formula for thesis development is derived from *The Craft of Research*, an excellent advanced research guide written by Wayne Booth, Joseph Williams, and Greg Colomb. As with all formulas, use this one if it helps you understand what a thesis should do, and only as long as it continues to help. Over the years, many teachers and researchers have found this to be a useful way to start to organize their thinking.

I am going to look at _____, in order to find out _____, because it will address or resolve this larger problem: _____.

EXAMPLE 4.5 *Preliminary Thesis for Paper on Plagiarism*

I am going to look at *plagiarism at American colleges*, in order to find out *how much of a problem it is and how colleges have tried to solve it,* because it will address the larger problem *of how to teach students moral thinking and ethical behavior.*

EXAMPLE 4.6 *Preliminary Thesis for Paper on International Teaching Assistants*

I am going to look at *the complaints about the use of International Teaching Assistants in American Universities* in order to find out *how much of a problem it is and how some major universities have dealt with it* because this information *may help* solve the larger problem of *how best to adapt American students and international instructors to each other.*

Although you may not yet be ready to make a final statement about the results of your inquiry, a formulation like this can help distinguish what will be most relevant as you search for, skim, and take notes on additional sources. Again, like most formulas, it is useful only insofar as it helps you organize and state your ideas. Therefore, consider this preliminary thesis as the start of another recursive process—you can and probably will return to it several times to bring it into accord with your growing understanding as you move deeper into the process of reading and writing about your topic.

USING YOUR NOTES AND RESPONSES: MOVING FROM THINKING TO PROPOSING

Research is presented in different genres—that is, in different forms that may have different purposes, audiences, and conventions, and which may vary from field to field. The genres described throughout this book invite you to call up and rework notes and previous assignments related to your inquiry. Many researchers work this way; it is easier not to have to start with a blank screen, and it allows you to refresh your memory about what you already know about a topic. This recursive approach to writing, like the recursive approach to choosing a topic and conducting research, demands that you read your own work critically, adapt your thinking to what you learn over the course of a project, and embrace the idea that good writing demands revision. As you pursue an area of research, your thinking about the topic may change substantially from the initial questions or preliminary thesis. Instead of trying to fit the results of an inquiry into a preexisting thesis, researchers use a recursive, revision-oriented approach, in which the writer revises the thesis to new results of the inquiry. Moreover, as Richard Feynman affirmed in the passage quoted in Chapter 1, a researcher cannot know the answer to a question before conducting the research. Preliminary research raises questions and helps focus an issue; later research can deepen, and quite probably change, your understanding of the topic.

Proposing Research

A proposal is written to persuade a specific reader or group of readers to accept a project before the major research is begun or while it is in its early stages. For example, a researcher thinking about writing a book proposes the project to an editor, much as students beginning major research projects may be asked to propose them to the instructor who will assist with and evaluate them. Proposals are also commonplace in business, the professions, and community work; they constitute a formal request for support and a promise of what will be produced. In a research proposal, you need to convince your reader:

- that you have identified an important problem or controversy,
- that you have a sound approach to resolving it, and
- that you have both the knowledge of the field and the resources necessary to complete the project successfully.

Proposing a project serves two purposes, in addition to providing experience in writing in an important professional genre. First, a proposal can help you more clearly see and shape the purpose and direction of your research. Second, a proposal can demonstrate more clearly than your less formal work that you have a viable project, that you are finding and thinking about your sources, and that you are developing claims about your topic.

Drafting a Research Project Proposal

Research proposals are usually based on only preliminary research into a particular question, although usually the proposal writer has at least some experience in the field. Like other genres of researched writing, a proposal should demonstrate that you understand the claim in relation to the consensus in the field and should suggest how the conclusion might impact the way an audience (either inside or outside the field) thinks or acts about an important controversy. You are not expected to have a finished conclusion at the beginning of a project. However, the proposal should show that you know enough about the work in the field to take part in its conversations, and it should convince its audience that you have a definite plan to follow from the proposal to the final finished product or products. Although students can expect that their teachers will accept most project proposals sooner or later, outside the classroom, proposals are almost always in competition with other proposals and the acceptance rate may be low.

A proposal is written to be judged—either accepted or rejected. Passing a serious and competitive review, then, is central to the purpose of a proposal and must shape the writer's conception of its audience. Because of the competitive nature of most proposals, three aspects of proposal writing are particularly crucial: meeting deadlines, staying within length limitations, and providing all the information requested in the call for proposals.

Sometimes a request (or "call") for proposals provides an outline or a set of questions to be answered, in which case the writer should follow that guidance very closely. The writer should also identify key words in the call and repeat them in the proposal.

FOCUS POINTS: PROPOSAL QUESTIONS

In general, a proposal should answer the following questions and will usually follow this general order. In the following list, the questions in bold type should be answered directly. The questions in italics are underlying questions; they may be answered less directly, but they will certainly matter to the readers (evaluators) of the proposal.

- **What is the problem?** *Why should we care about it? To what larger conversation in the field is it relevant?*
- **What is your solution?** *Why should we think this solution will work?*
- **How are you going to arrive (or how did you arrive) at your solution?** *Why should we think your approach to this project will be successful?*
- **What product will be the outcome? When will it be finished?** *Why should we believe you?*
- **What resources will be used/needed? What will it cost?** *Are the expenditures appropriate? Do you have sufficient funding? Will the outcome be worth it?*

FOCUS POINTS: DRAFTING AN EFFECTIVE PROJECT PROPOSAL

You should follow these steps to make sure you are creating an effective proposal:

- Review your questions and thesis.
- Consider the kind(s) of documents you have been assigned. How can you shape your inquiry to produce these genres?
- Look at what you have already written about your research and responses, your argument and its significance.
- Write a first draft of the proposal, answering the questions above to propose the documents you expect to produce from your inquiry.
- Rethink and revise your proposal to highlight your expertise in the field and to address the audience who will be reading it. Consider the knowledge the readers (evaluators) will have—and will expect you to have. At what time will the audience expect citations and references? In the proposal itself? In the working bibliography? In an annotated bibliography produced near the end of the project?

EXAMPLE 4.7 *Sample Proposal for an Inquiry about Plagiarism*

This is a proposal for a series of assignments based on a student's inquiry into why plagiarism is a problem in universities and what universities can and should do about it.

> Plagiarism is a very important issue for college students, because failure to
>
> understand what it is and how to avoid it can lead to serious consequences. I became
>
> interested in plagiarism because when I was in high school I was accused of plagiarizing
>
> a paper. I had a vocabulary that was larger than most of my fellow students, and that

made one of my English teachers believe I had plagiarized an essay on Herman Melville. At the time I thought this was completely unfair, but now that I've done some reading about plagiarism, I've started to understand how it could happen. The problem I want to work with really has two parts. One is the question of why plagiarism is such a big problem in universities, and how they are dealing with it. I will investigate Web sites that sell term papers as well as anti-plagiarism sources and articles from various places about when plagiarism occurs and how it can be fought. The other part is how students can learn to avoid plagiarism—through learning good citation practices, but also by developing an ethic of independent thinking that would make copying someone else's work literally unthinkable.

My project will have three major products. First, I will produce an annotated bibliography that describes and evaluates some of my reading about plagiarism, derived from the working bibliography written for the assignment in Chapter 5. Second, I will write an "I-Search" paper that describes the process of my research and relates what I have learned from the sources to my own personal experiences with using sources and being accused of plagiarism and to my ideas about independent thinking. Finally, working with my research group, I will participate in creating a Web site designed to teach students how to avoid plagiarism and how to think about it. The Web site will include links to bibliographies and resources about plagiarism, links to our school's plagiarism policy and to policies at other schools, guides to using sources carefully and responsibly, and other materials designed to be informative and comprehensive about the issue. Our focus will be on how to avoid plagiarizing, but we want to base it on a fully comprehensive understanding of plagiarism, not simply preach about how plagiarism is bad and how to cite sources.

EXAMPLE 4.8 *Sample Proposal for an Inquiry about International Teaching Assistants*
This is a proposal for an argumentative research paper about why international teaching assistants are seen as a problem and what can be done about it:

At many large research universities, undergraduate students take many of their first- and second-year courses with graduate teaching assistants. While most courses in fields like English and History are taught by American graduate students, international teaching assistants are very common in mathematics, science, and engineering fields. Many undergraduates consider taking courses taught by international graduate students to be a major problem with their education. They complain that they cannot understand their teaching assistants, that their TAs do not understand American students and their expectations, and that they are getting an inferior education because they are not being taught by Americans.

In my research project, I intend to investigate the use of international teaching assistants in order to see whether they actually hurt the education of American undergraduates. I will look at why universities hire these students, taking a look at the history of the practice of using graduate students to teach undergraduates. I will try to find out about how the graduate teaching assistants are trained for their positions, and the special problems they face in adjusting to American academic life and expectations. I will also investigate whether there are programs to help American undergraduates adjust to instructors from other countries, which I think are in place at some universities.

The most important part of my research will be trying to find evidence that will let me argue that having international teaching assistants is actually an advantage for American undergraduates. These instructors can give us exposure to foreign countries and different languages, and give us experience in hearing and accepting accents and ways of speaking and thinking that are different from the ones we are used to. In many high schools, we seldom run across anyone who is very different from us. Even if there are some international students in a school, it is even rarer to have people of other nationalities, religions, and languages in positions like teachers. It is easy for American students to live separately from people who seem different, but this is not very good preparation for a working world that is increasingly international. I think it is a very good opportunity to learn to understand and respect instructors with different styles of speaking, behaving, and thinking, and I hope to find evidence that will allow me to make a convincing argument about this experience.

My project is going to result in an argumentative research paper. My thesis at this point is as follows: I am planning to investigate why American students have difficulty adjusting to international teaching assistants in order to argue that instead of complaining about instructors with foreign accents and different educational experiences, we should appreciate the value of studying with TAs from other countries and cultures.

REVISING A PROPOSAL

Because proposals are so important, they are generally reread and revised several times before submission. The questions with which you started must all be fully addressed without going over the page, word, or time limit. The following self-evaluation offers a means to review a proposal and shape your revisions of it. Notice that the revision questions ask you to consider major rhetorical issues about how you represent your project to a reader. Although these questions do not directly address editing sentences, your language will often become clearer as you reconsider how to say precisely what you intend to communicate. Remember that clarity and correctness are very important to readers of proposals.

FOCUS POINTS: SELF-EVALUATION FOR REVISING THE PROPOSAL

Reread the proposal, marking the draft where appropriate and writing down the answers to the following questions.

- What is the purpose of your project? Describe in informal words what you intend to do with the results of your inquiry. Does the proposal clearly state your plans?
- What is the larger significance of this investigation—what bigger question might it answer, and how does it fit into the current literature in the field? Are these relationships clearly stated? Is your plan for the project clearly directed toward achieving it?
- What parts of the proposal do you really believe in? Indicate this in the margin.
- What parts of the proposal seem weak to you? Are there points where you are not sure that a reader could follow it? Are there parts that you have other questions about, either questions about whether your representation of the issue is accurate or questions about the clarity of what you have said. Identify these parts in the margin, and write your specific question(s), either in pencil or by using the comment function of your word processing program.
- Consider how the topic, question, or significance could be restated even more clearly and precisely.
- Have you edited the proposal for sentence accuracy and clarity and then proofread it carefully? Since proposals tend to be competitive, you should not run the risk that your audience will interpret poor proofreading with poor performance on the project.

Exercises

4.1 FINDING A TOPIC

1. Review the research you have done so far. Follow the Steps toward Finding a Topic, taking notes on how your thinking about the topic has changed as you work through the process.
2. Decide on a topic or question. Find a preliminary source with references, and look for sources you might use to develop your topic.
3. Write down the questions you have about the topic, and record (using a map, outline, list with arrows, or whatever method you find comfortable) what you see as the relationships among them. Make a shorter list of questions that you would like to pursue in more detail.
4. Take preliminary notes on your experience with reading and thinking about the topic so far.

4.2 WRITING A PRELIMINARY THESIS

1. Generate a preliminary thesis from this early work, using one of the processes described in this chapter (or another that works for you).
2. Make a list of the key words you have identified.
3. Assemble your list of sources you think you will need to consult. What additional sources will you need to produce the writing assignments for which you will use it?
4. Let your preliminary thesis sit for a few days while you look for these additional sources. Then go back to your thesis to decide whether you like this question well enough to continue working on it. If not, try to find a way to use the research you have already done in a way that is more interesting to you. Since defining your project is a recursive process, try asking new questions and talking them over with classmates and your instructor. Go back through as many steps as necessary to find an issue you can enjoy working with.
5. Either revise your questions and thesis, based on your rethinking of the project, or redefine your topic.

4.3 QUESTIONS FOR DISCUSSION AND INFORMAL WRITING

1. Using the notes you took while searching for your topic, describe the process you used to find your topic and initial sources. How might you do it differently next time?
2. How has your understanding of your topic changed as you have read in the field? Can you see your topic in terms of some of the concepts of argumentation that have been raised so far, such as warrants, reasons, examples, and so on? What kinds of reasons and evidence do you expect to find to support or extend your ideas?
3. At what point can a student writer assume sufficient expertise to write with at least a semblance of authority about an issue about which experts disagree? What is a student's responsibility to the field? To your classmates and research team? To a larger public?

4.4 PROPOSING A RESEARCH PROJECT

Follow the guide to writing proposals in Focus Points: Proposal Questions (p. 78) and Drafting an Effective Project Proposal (p. 78). If you are producing a series of different projects, the proposal should demonstrate how they build on each other. (See Sample Proposal for an Inquiry about Plagiarism, p. 78.) If you are working toward a long argumentative paper, the progress toward this final product should be the focus of the proposal, with preliminary work clearly leading to that final product. (See Sample Proposal for an Inquiry about International Teaching Assistants, p. 79.) Whether your proposal is written or oral, consider carefully how to convince your audience (the class and your teacher) that you have identified an important problem or controversy, that you have a sound approach to resolving it, and that you have both the knowledge of the field and the resources necessary to complete the project successfully.

1. Write a proposal of no more than 500 words. Identify the significance of your prospective work, the issues you will examine, and the documents you will produce.
2. Prepare and give an oral proposal presentation of no more than ten minutes that fulfills the same goals as a written proposal would. You should not read your presentation or speak from notes of more than a few key words. (The expectations for oral presentations that Professor Way outlines in Chapter 7 are widely held in business and the professions.)
3. Augment your presentation with visuals and request questions at the end. See Appendix A for information about developing oral presentations and Appendix B for constructing effective visuals. Prepare a short summary of your proposed project as a handout to distribute at the end of the presentation.
4. Use Focus Points: Self-Evaluation for Revising the Proposal (p. 81) to revise the written proposal or to evaluate and reconsider the oral proposal.

CHAPTER 5

Using the Library and Its Databases Effectively

Contemporary libraries are Web sites at least as much as they are buildings, and many students and faculty use the library Web site more than the physical building. In most academic libraries, the rows of card catalogs have been replaced or at least supplemented by the library's online catalog, and all sorts of reference resources are available online. This development has made research much faster and easier in many cases, and has made a great number and wide variety of sources available to more people than would have been imaginable a generation ago. However, although the Web can be a tremendous resource for students, it is a dangerous resource because *anybody can put up a Web page on any topic for any reason* and at much less expense than publishing in print. Because the Web offers such great freedom to circulate information, researchers using the Web need to be particularly careful to know the source of information they find there and to evaluate it carefully.

General open Web searches (like Google searches) give results of varying quality. While they may provide some useful sources, often the results reach into the tens of thousands. By contrast, library Web sites (both university and public) provide databases that allow researchers to filter results, including options for limiting searches to specific genres and dates and for accessing only peer-reviewed sources. Peer review (i. e., evaluation by recognized experts within a particular academic discourse community), as discussed in Chapter 2, generally ensures greater reliability of sources accessed on the Web because readers know that experts in the field have examined and critiqued these sources before publication. However, even when conducting research through library databases, you need to consider the credibility of the documents you choose. Peer review is only one criterion to consider. Other criteria include when the source was written, who published it, the qualifications of the author, and the source's relevance to your topic. But compared to open Web searches, it is often easier to find reliable and relevant sources on library Web databases.

As you search library databases, be sure to consciously follow your links and to occasionally check the Web addresses you access. Sometimes, a few mouse clicks can move you out of the library and into the general World Wide Web. Information literacy involves not only knowing how to find information, but how to evaluate, organize, and use it. The more easily evaluated sources are apt to end with specialized domain names, like the suffix **.edu** (indicates a college or university) or **.gov** (indicates a government body). You may also find material at URLs with other common suffixes: **.mil** (military), **.net** (network organization), **.org** (nonprofit organization), and **.com** (commercial).

Some university and government Web sites serve as the original medium of publication for current and useful information. Others provide access to articles or other material originally published elsewhere. In these cases, look for the citation for the original publication. However, although **.edu** denotes a college or university address, be aware that a tilde (~) in an **.edu** address may indicate the site of an individual who is authorized to use a university's Web address (a student, for example), but it does *not* indicate authorization or authentication of the material on the page by the university. Students and faculty at American universities have considerable freedom to put materials and links on their Web sites, material that is only as reliable as its source.

LEARNING TO NAVIGATE THE LIBRARY

Your instructor may invite a college librarian to give a workshop or library tour as an introduction to finding and using library resources. In addition, your library's home page will lead you to both the catalog and whatever special services are available to students. Use this information as a starting point, and then try to get to know your library for yourself.

One of the most important resources in every college library is the *reference* desk; reference librarians really know how to find things, and they tend to enjoy the search. Although they may be put off by students who come in at the very last moment and expect a librarian to do their research for them (and who would not resent that sort of imposition?), reference librarians are usually willing to help students not only locate sources but also understand the process of finding them.

Some libraries have e-mail or telephone reference services as well, which can be a big help when you are working from a distance and just cannot figure out how to find something—or when you are not even sure what you are looking for. Many university library Web sites have extensive online workshops on information literacy, including, for example, research guides, tutorials on searching for and evaluating sources, databases, and direct access to a reference librarian. A short list of those is provided on page 88.

RESEARCH TOOLS ON THE LIBRARY SITE

■ Most college and university library Web sites provide access to a range of databases. Databases allow you to search online bibliographies (lists of publications in various disciplines, accessible by subject, author, title, and key words), to download abstracts (summaries) of articles, and sometimes to download full journal articles.

■ Library Web sites usually subscribe to dictionaries, encyclopedias, and other online reference materials and sources and to services like *JSTOR*, which allow you to access complete journal articles without paying for them yourself.

■ Libraries also usually subscribe to major newspapers and newsletters. These may be accessible directly on the Web, but often charge direct users for downloading articles or for using their archives (to find articles older than a week or a month). These services are generally free to library users through library subscriptions.

FOCUS POINTS: EFFECTIVE SEARCHING PRACTICES

It can be easy to get lost when searching for information on a topic. The key to good research—on the Web or elsewhere—is to start early.

- Give yourself time to consult with librarians and professors, who may be willing to help even if they are not immediately available at the moment you make a request.
- Give yourself time to make mistakes and get lost.
- Give yourself time to request books and articles through interlibrary loan.
- And give yourself time to follow your own interests as you move from a general topic toward a specific inquiry.

As you find and collect sources, keep in mind the questions raised in Chapter 2 about their validity and relevance.

SEARCH ENGINES AND DATABASES

As you plan your research questions, try to sharpen and refine them from broad research questions to more specific ones. Similarly, as you move forward in your research, you should refine your search methods. Be sure to keep in mind the ethos of your eventual paper by considering how the research you choose to include in your project demonstrates your own credibility and reliability.

General search engines (like Google or Yahoo!) can be useful to locate people, institutions, and some products, but they can sidetrack students learning to do academic research. For example, a recent search for the word *plagiarism* on Google Scholar yielded over 42,900 entries—clearly many more than anyone could possibly evaluate. Search engines leave much of the work of evaluation to the user, even with the most effective key word searches, because they arrange sources by popularity, not credibility. Everyone knows that search engines and other general reference tools like ask.com and Wikipedia can be very useful for checking matters of common knowledge, but because they list sources in the order of how frequently they are accessed, they can also lead users to unreliable sources and incorrect information. They must be used with caution and common sense. Table 5.1 (p. 86) documents some of the differences between databases and general search engines.

Sometimes general search engines provide results from databases that are not available to the general public or that charge a fee for use. Remember that as a student at a college or university, you have free access to many of those databases if you access them through your library. For example, databases like *LexisNexis* and *JSTOR* must be accessed through a library's site because libraries pay a subscription fee to provide users with these exclusive services. In Appendix C there is a list of databases, organized by research fields, to which many university libraries subscribe. Your university librarians and course instructors can recommend the databases that are best suited to your particular research questions.

POPULAR SOURCES ONLINE

At an early stage of an investigation, it can be useful to consult sources written for the general public to get a sense of the public impact and recent developments

Table 5.1 Differences between Databases and Open-Access Web Sources (available through general search engines)

	Databases	Search Engines
How to Access	Usually accessed through a library. They are purchased by subscription. Most college and university libraries purchase access to a sizable number of databases (although you may need to use a university-networked computer to access them, or a password provided by the university's Information Technology department). Public libraries often offer access to some databases as well, usually through their own, on-site networked computers.	Offer free access to open-access sources on the Web. Sometimes specific sites (like newspapers or photograph repositories) will charge a fee for access to resources; often resources are free and open to the public.
Kinds of Sources Accessible	Limit the sources they collect and retrieve those relevant to particular academic or professional communities. Users expect these sources to have been published in journals or other publications relevant to a field. Often users can limit searches to peer-reviewed publications.	Not selective about the *kinds* of sources they lead to. If you search a person's name, for example, you are apt to find a broad range of material, such as the person's Web site, newspaper articles that mention the person, the person's posts to a discussion list, as well as archived publications the person has written. If you search a topic, you will draw a similar range of sources.
Arrangement of "Hits"	Usually allow the researcher some selectivity about what is chosen and how it is arranged. For example, you can search a person's name in an "author search" or a "subject search" and determine the range of time you want the search to cover. Often the researcher can select the order in which the references should be listed.	Normally list sources in the order of those most frequently accessed. Frequency of access is not usually a good indicator of the reliability of a source.
Relevance of Coverage	May be more or less general, but even a general academic index will be limited to areas normally studied by students and scholars. The more focused databases are limited to a specific disciplinary field (for example, the *Modern Language Association Bibliography, LexisNexis,* or *Business Source Premiere).*	Do not distinguish among fields of study or interest, unless the user limits the field with "and" or "not" commands. For example, if you want to find online writing labs, searching "OWLS" brings up sources about birds, insomniacs, and other irrelevant topics. Doing an "Advanced Search" may improve the relevance, but not necessarily the reliability, of the search.

involving your emerging topic. To find such sources, search the topic in a magazine and newspaper index like *Newspaper Search* or *Wilson Reader's Guide* or the *New York Times*. In these indexes you may find sources that lead you to discoveries and public controversies, information that can suggest the larger significance and potential applications of your inquiry.

Consulting newspapers, magazines, general or commercial Web sites, and personal Web sites or blogs that link to online articles from newspapers and magazines are also common ways to get background information. As with all sources, it is necessary to consider their reliability, particularly since these sources report breaking news, which may change from day to day, and they sometimes offer reports of research that may not be correct and complete. Even the best newspaper and magazine reporting can misinterpret the conclusions of experts. In working with sources online, as much as with print sources, it is important to distinguish between news stories, which claim to merely report on what happened; feature stories, which offer more synthesis and thus more room for interpretation; and editorial or opinion pieces, including blogs, which offer a commentator's opinion of ongoing events, often with limited documented support. In magazine journalism these distinctions are less clear, since magazines feature longer articles with more interpretation of events rather than breaking news. In general, remember that a newspaper or magazine writer is usually a professional journalist who may write on a large range of issues, whereas the author of a peer-reviewed book or journal article is an expert with advanced training in a specialized field.

Web Sites and Blogs

You should be careful about consulting personal Web pages and blogs when doing academic research, unless you are doing research on the person who owns the Web site or runs the blog. These resources can provide an introduction to a topic and links to peer-reviewed publications and news stories, but, as with every other source, you need to constantly evaluate the links you are directed to. Some personal Web pages are the pet projects of recognized experts in their field or deal with a specific issue, and if they are reliable sites, you will be directed to them by other reliable sources or by your instructor. For example, some researchers put extensive bibliographies on their areas of interest, direct links to their archived publications, or links to important resources they have collected on their Web sites.

It is impossible to ignore blogs because they have become such an important means of communication and controversy over the past five years. However, blogs raise even more difficult questions about accuracy because they are usually created specifically to convey the blogger's opinions and responses to events. Commentary on blogs often consists of immediate responses to a post rather than reliable information. Moreover, bloggers may link to sources of high or low reliability. So, while blogs can be useful sources of information, particularly background information, and can offer good examples of persuasion, in academic research they should be approached with caution, and with the question of whether your readers will find them to be authoritative sources. For example, if your class has a blog, how authoritative would you consider it to be? Is it a trustworthy source of information or a site for testing ideas, extending inquiries, and trying out conclusions? Such a blog can host very useful explorations, even though it might not be a particularly reliable source of information.

Unreliable Web Sites

When writing academic papers, try to do most of your research by searching the library Web site, going to the library when necessary. Unless directed to a Web site by a reliable source (a reference librarian or instructor), leave searches of the entire Web for the very beginning of your inquiry, or for when you have time to look for "extras," not for the main body of your research. Be aware that when searching the Web, you may run into apparently reliable Web sites that are totally unreliable for various reasons, including strong bias, the intent to deceive, or a lack of specialized knowledge. An important aspect of building your expertise in a field and your ethos as a research writer is learning to identify such sites. See Chapter 2 for a review of how to evaluate reliability.

RESOURCES FOR RESEARCHERS ON THE WEB

There are some open-access Web sites that are very useful to researchers for tracking down particular details of common knowledge as well as for finding references. However, remember to use these resources with some care, as they may turn up both reliable and unreliable sources and information.

Ask.com <ask.com>: Formerly known as AskJeeves.com, the Ask.com search engine uses a specialized algorithm that considers both click and subject-specific popularity in order to produce results that represent reasonably authoritative Web sites. Users may search by subject term or by asking a question.

Bartleby.com <bartleby.com>: While the Internet is full of dictionary, quotation, and online book sites, few feature so many in one place as Bartleby.com. Bartleby features diverse reference works, including fiction, poetry, thesauri, grammar handbooks, presidential inaugural addresses, etiquette guides, and even cookbooks. Users can search for specific quotations or use the home page subject guide to search for available works.

Google Books <books.google.com/>: Often online search results will lead you to Google Books, an online project in which libraries around the world scan books into PDF format. However, be aware that only out-of-copyright texts and books for which the publisher has given permission appear as full texts. Nevertheless, Google Books is a powerful resource and frequently provides lengthy portions of texts (often including tables of contents and indexes) that researchers can use in order to evaluate a book (whether or not to purchase it or check it out from the library), get missing bibliographic information (page numbers, publisher names, and locations), or find additional sources (cited in the text or in the index).

Google Scholar <scholar.google.com/>: The Google Scholar project provides scholarly references that often appear in full-text versions. Those that do not can usually be accessed through your library website. Some general Web search results link to Google Books.

Infomine Scholarly Internet Resource Collections <infomine.ucr.edu/>: The Infomine project puts librarians from several institutions to work for you. This librarian-driven database produces results appropriate for university research and offers links to e-journals (some of which require access through your university library), articles, maps, directories, and other databases. Users choose a search field (for example, Business & Economics, Cultural Diversity, Visual & Performing Arts), then search by term.

Information Please <www.infoplease.com/>: The Information Please Web site offers information on a wide range of topics. It features encyclopedia, thesaurus, atlas, and dictionary entries, as well as news links, helpful charts, and statistics. Information Please is a good place to start if you are searching for a research topic or for ways to whittle a topic down.

Know Play? <www.kplay.cc/reference.html>: KnowPlay? is a general information site that gathers several online references on a single home page where users can select the types of works they want to reference and enter search terms to find relevant results. KnowPlay? features online dictionaries, thesauri, quotation guides, an acronym finder, atlas searches, and other resources.

LibrarySpot.com <www.libraryspot.com/>: LibrarySpot.com is another librarian-driven resource project. It provides links to help users find libraries, and it features links to reference sites and online books and magazines.

Refdesk.com <www.refdesk.com/>: Sometimes researchers simply are not aware of all of the resources available to them. The refdesk.com resource site is subtitled "Fact Checker for the Internet." Some users may find the home page a bit overwhelming, as it includes links to hundreds of pages; however, refdesk.com orders these links into easily understood categories. There are clear links to newspapers, magazines, reference works, genealogy sites, almanacs, style and writing guides, and much more.

Wikipedia <en.wikipedia.org/>: Wikipedia is a very useful research tool, but it too should be consulted with care because its wiki format allows anyone to post or edit entries (although its editors now exert some control over entries). Both the MLA and APA style guides give warnings about the reliability of this site. Students tend to consider it a great resource for general background and as a means of locating sources, but you should be aware that entries may or may not be accurate at any given time, and you should check information found here against other sources.

INDEXES AND DATABASES

Because your researched papers should reflect understanding of some of the academic research connected with your topic and because this reading can be difficult, you should start looking at peer-reviewed sources early in the research process. After a preliminary look at popular sources, a good place to move is to a general academic index like *Academic Search* or *Periodicals Index Online*. If you are not sure about what the field you are working with is called or which indexes to consult, ask your instructor and/or a reference librarian for help. On many university library Web sites, indexes can be sorted by fields, as in the list in Appendix C: Databases. This kind of help can be very useful for specialized research projects.

The databases you use most often depend on your field of study, and they may change as you progress through college. Check your library's Web site to get a specific list of resources to which your library subscribes. It is seldom necessary to use more than a few databases for a source search, since sources tend to be listed on all applicable databases, although perhaps in different ways. It is most useful to learn to use a few databases well and to understand how to access sources from them. The first page of a database indicates the scope of the resources, and the help function on each database explains the particulars of how to search with it. Some databases commonly found on the Web sites of college and university libraries appear in Appendix C.

STARTING ONLINE LIBRARY RESEARCH

Searching by Author

Searching by author can be more efficient than searching by key words. Once you find a few recent articles on the topic you are researching, use the works it references at the end of the article or in endnotes or footnotes to find those sources by author or title. Their reference lists will yield additional, potentially relevant sources. Pay particular attention to authors whose works are cited by more than one of your initial sources, since they are probably quite important (see Fig. 5.1).

Some databases provide the full texts of articles, whereas others provide only references and perhaps abstracts (see Fig. 5.2). In that case, look up the journal title in the online library catalog. Most university libraries make some journals available electronically, but others are still available only in bound volumes in the library. Some articles may be available only through interlibrary loan, which can be either electronic or paper-based.

If the database you are using does not provide the full text of an article you think you need, you might try another, more specialized database. However, as noted previously,

---

References

Battig, W. F., & Montague, W. E. (1969). Category norms for verbal items in 56 categories: A replication and extension of the Connecticut category norms. *Journal of Experimental Psychology Monograph, 80* (3, Pt. 2).

Brown, A. S., & Halliday, H. E. (1991). Cryptomnesia and source memory difficulties. *American Journal of Psychology, 104*, 475–490.

Brown, A. S., & Murphy, D. R. (1989). Cryptomnesia: Delineating inadvertent plagiarism. *Journal of Experimental Psychology: Learning, Memory, and Cognition, 15*, 432–442.

Dorfman, J. (1994). Sublexical components in implicit memory for novel words. *Journal of Experimental Psychology: Learning, Memory, and Cognition, 20*, 1108–1125.

Identify multiple sources by experts in the field.

FIGURE 5.1 Bibliographic References

You may identify the names of persons commonly associated with the field you are researching (A. S. Brown's name, for example, comes up twice), or you may use the article names to find elements of research that you are lacking.

Source: Patricia L. Tenpenny et al. "In Search of Inadvertent Plagiarism." *The American Journal of Psychology* 111.4 (1998): 529–59. [JSTOR key word search: "Plagiarism"]

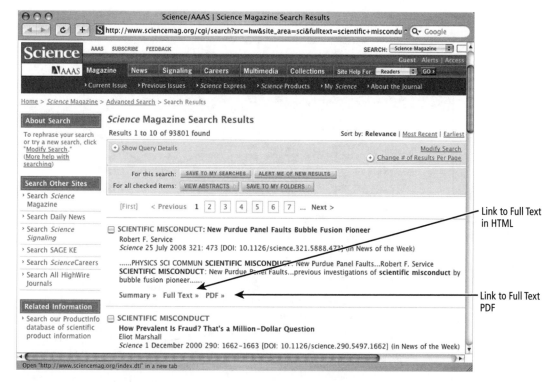

FIGURE 5.2 Database Search

Library databases can lead you to peer-reviewed journals and well-known publications that will offer summaries, abstracts, and often, links to full-text HTML or PDF documents.

Source: Science Magazine key word search: "Plagiarism"

very recent or very old articles in some journals may be available only in print format. In that case, look up the journal title in the online library catalog. If the library does not have the source you need, consult a reference librarian for help.

To find books, use the authors' names to search your library's catalog. If your library catalog does not list a book you need, conduct a broader search in a database like *WorldCat* (see Fig. 5.3).

A final hint: you can often e-mail references or documents to yourself and then save them in your source file until ready to use them. Some PDF documents cannot be cut and pasted, but sources put directly on the Web can often be transferred into Word after you send them to yourself, so that you can highlight and annotate them.

Searching by Key Words

If you cannot start with a source that provides references, or if you have found some initial sources but want to widen your search, use a key word search on an academic database to scan the field and browse for sources. As was noted in Chapter 4, as you gain experience reading in a field, you will be able to identify key words in a reading. If you keep a list of key words from the beginning of the inquiry, you will have a good starting point for a key word search in a database. For example, a preliminary list of

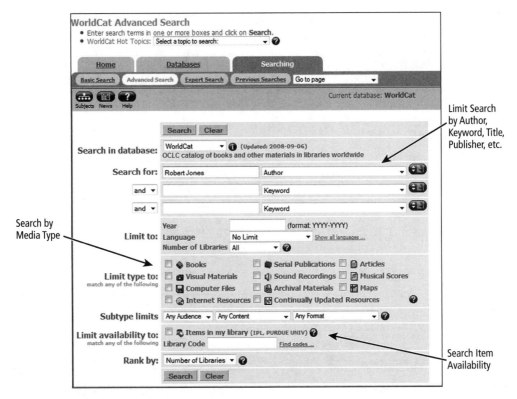

FIGURE 5.3 *WorldCat* **Search**

WorldCat lets you search by several criteria at once, including author, key word, title, and subject. You can also limit your results by date, the type of media, and availability.

Source: WorldCat home page

key words for Alfie Kohn's article might be: grades, "grade inflation," motivation, learning, measurement.

FOCUS POINTS: SEARCHING BY KEY WORDS

Searching for a single, common key word can call up many sources, many of which are not directly related to your topic See Figure 5.4 and the list below for ways to refine your search.

■ To limit the search to a manageable number of hits, try using two key words, connected by *and*. Note also that putting quotation marks around two or more words used together, like "grade inflation," indicates that they should be treated as a single term. It takes some experience with particular databases to find key terms that yield the sources you are looking for. For example, a search on *ERIC*, an education database, for the key words "grade inflation" and "college" yields 77 citations, which can then be sorted by date; a search for "grade inflation" and "motivation" yields a more manageable 12 citations, but even some of them might not be useful to your inquiry.

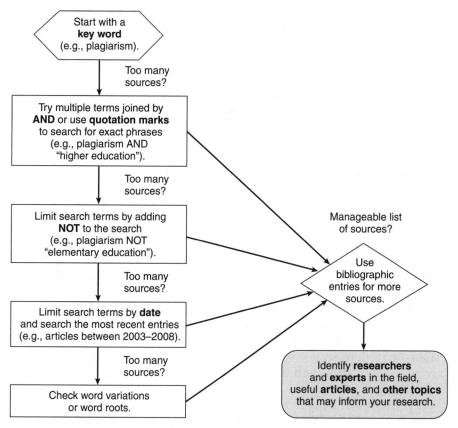

FIGURE 5.4 Flowchart for Searching by Key Words

- If a key term has more than one possible meaning, you can use "not" to limit searches to the meaning you are looking for. For example, you might use "OWL not bird" to look for information about online writing labs.

- Consult the more recent of the first sources you find, and they will lead to further sources, authors, and related key words. An author search derived from sources found through a key word search may yield particularly relevant sources.

- To find references to sources that may be listed under several variations of a word, use the root of the word. For example, "Antarctic explor" will pick up both Antarctic exploration and explorers, but will still limit the search to a single topic.

KEEPING TRACK OF SOURCES

As researchers deepen their reading about a topic, they not only gather information and ideas about the topic but also use their responses to begin constructing an argument. Because research is such a recursive process, researchers often need to reexamine sources consulted earlier in the search, so they find it useful to start a working bibliography from the outset of an inquiry. A working bibliography is a list—formatted according to the style guide you are using—of all the works you have consulted, heard of, or thought about looking for. You might think of it as a "master list" of sources, a list that you can assemble for yourself, or that you can create and share with a group of fellow researchers. You can draw on the working bibliography over time to find or document sources for various papers, talks, and other projects. Instead of searching through your entire body of notes, you can consolidate brief information about sources and the information necessary for citing them in one master list. In order to avoid backtracking, start keeping track of possible sources from the beginning of a search.

CONSTRUCTING A WORKING BIBLIOGRAPHY

Remember that a working bibliography is a list of sources, both those you have consulted and those you have collected and intend to consult. A working bibliography is a way to keep your sources under control as you go along; it is work that you can either do alone or share with a group working with the same general topic of inquiry. A working bibliography with well-formatted references can be the source of references for any number of papers and projects. While references should be formatted according to the style specified by your instructors, you can add notes to yourself about things you want to remember. For example, you might indicate that you suspect a source's reliability, that some sources seem out of date, or that various sources seem to complement or contradict each other. As you work on your projects, keep adding to the bibliography, but delete items only rarely; at a later phase of a project, you might decide you want to use sources you discarded earlier, and the working bibliography makes them easy to find again.

Writing a working bibliography also entails formatting references early in the research process. Formatting references is a skill that takes considerable practice. Many instructors pay close attention to format because this kind of accuracy can be important in their own research: well-formatted citations let other researchers find sources quickly and easily, and a well-constructed and well-formatted reference list serves as a mark of professionalism that contributes significantly to the credibility—the ethos—of the work.

MLA AND APA STYLES

The sample bibliographic entries throughout this book are in MLA (Modern Language Association) style because it is most commonly used in English Departments and composition courses. Basic rules for using MLA, American Psychological Association (APA), and Chicago Manual of Style (CMS) are available in the Quick Guide to Documentation at the end of this book. You may need to consult these organizations' published manuals for more complicated citations (the *MLA Handbook for Writers of Research Papers*, 7th edition [2009]; the *Publication Manual of the American Psychological Association*, 6th edition; or *The Chicago Manual of Style*, 15th edition).

Most libraries keep these manuals in their reference collection, and most writing centers have copies available for students to consult. Some online guides to common citations in these styles are also available. If you are required to work in a style that does not seem to suit your career plans, do not be too dismayed: all styles change over time, and therefore what you need to know is not a specific format but rather how to look up and follow a set of conventions that change with the advent of new technologies.

Learning to format references takes a lot of practice. It is not necessary to memorize the rules for formatting references in a particular style, although you should become familiar enough with them to know what information about sources to collect as you do library research (see Chapter 4). It *is*, however, necessary to keep a style guide at hand when formatting references and to consult it continually. If you take down the necessary information as soon as you start thinking about your inquiry, you can modify it to reflect correct MLA, APA, or other citation style when it comes time to construct a bibliography or draft a paper.

FORMATTING REFERENCES

Formatting references while constructing the working bibliography, particularly if you work with a group doing research in the same area, saves time and effort later because these references will not have to be formatted again (although you will need to recheck the formatting). When it comes time to use sources for a project, extract from the working bibliography only those references you used for that particular project. Cutting and pasting from a fully formatted bibliography is much easier and usually more accurate than trying to construct the bibliography from scratch at the last minute. Using a bibliography program like *Endnote*, if you have access to it, can be a great help with formatting. However, to use these programs effectively, the user still needs a basic understanding of what belongs where and why, and of how a particular kind of bibliography should look.

EXAMPLE 5.1: *A Working Bibliography in MLA Style for a Paper on Plagiarism*

Plagiarism Project: Working Bibliography

Boyle, James. "Who Stole the Goose?" *Campus Technology*. 1105 Media, 31 Oct. 2003. Web.

11 Nov. 2008.

Crace, John. "Higher Education: Cut and Paste job: As Plagiarism Engulfs the US and

Threatens the UK, a New Advisory Service Has Been Launched To Track Down Our Own

Academic Cheats." *Guardian* [London] 15 Oct. 2002: 10. Print.

Directessays.com. Direct Essays, 2003. Web. 27 May 2007.

Essayfinder.com. Paper Stores Enterprises, 2000. Web. 1 Sept. 2008.

Feldt, Brandon. "English Professors Discuss Solutions for Plagiarism." *Daily Vidette*. Illinois

State University, 27 Jan. 2003. Web. 17 Nov. 2008.

Flores, Christopher. "Allegations of Plagiarism Continue to Mount against Historian."

Chronicle.com. *Chronicle of Higher Education*, 1 Jan. 2002. Web. 17 November 2008.

Foster, Andrea L. "Plagiarism Tool Creates Legal Quandary." *Chronicle.com*. *Chronicle of*

Higher Education, 17 May 2003. Web. 17 Nov. 2008.

Garinger, Alex. "Plagiarism Cases Jump During Fall." *Chronicle*. Duke University, 13 Jan.

2003. Web. 17 Nov. 2008.

Haberling, Michael. "Maintaining Academic Integrity in Online Education." *Online Journal of

Distance Learning Administration* 5.1 (2002): n. pag. 3 Dec. 2003. Web. 11 Nov. 2008.

Hotessays.com. Hot Essays, 2003. Web. 2 Sept. 2008.

Howard, Rebecca Moore. "Forget about Policing Plagiarism. Just Teach." *Chronicle.com*.

Chronicle of Higher Education, 16 Nov. 2001. Web. 17 Jan. 2008.

---. "Plagiarisms, Authorships, and the Academic Death Penalty." *College English* 57.7

(1995): 788–806. Print.

Hunt, Russell. "Four Reasons to be Happy about Internet Plagiarism." *Teaching Perspectives*

5 (2002): 1–5. Web. 19 June 2008.

Iacocca, Lee. "Internet Encourages Student Plagiarism." *Daily Bruin* [Los Angeles] 5 Nov.

2002: 1. Print.

Jerome, Richard, and Pam Grout. "Cheat Wave." *People* 17 June 2002: 82–83. Print.

Mallon, Thomas. *Stolen Words*. San Diego: Harcourt, 2001. Print.

McGrath, Charles. "Plagiarism: Everybody Into the Pool." *New York Times* 7 Jan. 2007:

C33. Print.

"Online Tool Helps Universities, Colleges Fight Plagiarism." *Community College Week* 15.12

(2003): 18. Print.

Peloso, Jennifer. *Intellectual Property*. New York: Wilson, 2003. Print.

Plotz, David. "The Plagiarist: Why Stephen Ambrose Is a Vampire." *Slate*. Washington Post

Newsweek Interactive, 11 January 2002. Web. 25 February 2008.

Randall, Marilyn. *Pragmatic Plagiarism: Authorship, Profit, and Power*. Toronto: U of Toronto

P, 2001. Print.

Rivard, Robert. "What Every Student Knows: Thou Shalt Not Copy." *San Antonio Express-

News*. Hearst, 11 Oct. 2002. Web. 12 Nov. 2008.

Robillard, Amy E. "We Won't Get Fooled Again: On the Absence of Angry Responses to

Plagiarism in Composition Studies." *College English* 70.1 (2007): 10–31. Print.

Scribner, Mary Ellen. "An Ounce of Prevention: Defeating Plagiarism in the Information

Age." *Library Media Connection* 21.5 (2003): 32–35. Print.

Silverman, Gillian. "It's a Bird, It's a Plane, It's Plagiarism Buster!" *Newsweek* 15 July 2002:

12. Print.

Spigelman, Candace. "The Ethics of Appropriation in Peer Writing Groups." *Perspectives on*

Plagiarism and Intellectual Property in a Postmodern World. Ed. Lise Buranen and Alice

M. Roy. Albany, NY: SUNY Press, 1999. 231–40. Print.

Straw, Deborah. "The Plagiarism of Generation 'Why Not?'" *Community College Week* 14.24

(2002): 4–6. Print.

Turnitin.com. iParadigms, 2003. Web. 31 Aug. 2008.

Exercises

5.1 FINDING THE LIBRARY

1. With a research partner, visit your campus library. You may need to consult the library's Web site first for some basic information. Take notes on the following:
   - Where is the library located?
   - Does your campus have one or two centralized libraries, or a larger number of smaller, discipline-specific locations?
   - What hours are they open?
   - Where are services for undergraduates located? If there are several libraries, make your visit to the undergraduate library.
2. Look for and collect copies of the library's informational handouts. Libraries usually distribute these handouts or brochures near the circulation desk (where you check out books) or the reference desk (where you go for help in finding material).
   - Is there a physical card catalog in the library, or has the catalog become completely electronic? If there is a card catalog, does it reference all the library's books or just materials acquired before a particular year? Where are current issues of periodicals located? Where are back issues stored?
   - Where are general reference tools, such as encyclopedias, dictionaries, almanacs, and specialized bibliographies? Where are the MLA and APA style guides located?
   - Does the reference department offer any special services for undergraduates? Are those services online or in the library? For example, many academic libraries have online tutorials, "ask a librarian" e-mail features, telephone hotlines, and other help for students working on research projects.
   - Are there other kinds of student services located in the library? Some libraries house writing centers, computer labs, rooms with high-end computer resources that students can use to experiment for incorporating sound and video in their projects, and even a coffee shop. What services does your library have for students to use?
   - Where are photocopiers available? How do you purchase a copy card?
   - Are there quiet areas of the library for independent work?
   - Are there rooms available for group work?
3. Find a print encyclopedia. **Make a photocopy of an article related to your inquiry.**
4. Browse the other reference tools near the encyclopedia. Take notes on resources you might find useful.
5. Using an author or key word search, look up a peer-reviewed book related to your topic in the library catalog, find it in the stacks, and **make a photocopy of its title page.** Look in the book's list of references, and photocopy references for at least two books and two journal articles that might be useful to you. If the author references any other kinds of sources (for example, Web sites or government documents), also copy one or more of those references.

6. Write a short response to what you found in the library, ending with a list of questions you still have about finding and using its resources.

5.2 EXPLORING THE LIBRARY'S WEB SITE

Use this exercise as a means of collecting some of the references and sources needed to construct a working bibliography.

1. Observe how the library's Web site is organized—the major divisions of information, and how they are related to each other.
   - How does the Web site compare to the physical layout of the library, that is, the circulation and reference areas, and other special features of the library?
   - What help for learning research skills is available online?
2. Go to the online library catalog. There is usually a "quick search" option. Using the book references you collected in the library, search for their catalog entries first by title, then by author, until you reach the full citation. This is usually on a page by itself and includes the title, author, publication information, catalog number, and availability. Using the "browse" function, search for other books by the same author and for other books categorized by some of the same key words. **Make printouts of the full citations for at least three books you find in this way.** Choose books that seem likely to be useful sources for your proposed inquiry.
3. In the online catalog, search for the two references to journal articles you found in Exercise 5.1. Start the search by looking for the journals by title. Are they available online? Does the library have a print version? Many academic libraries are part of a state or regional system, from which you can also order books and articles. If this is the case with your college library, expand the search to the libraries in this wider system.
4. Find an encyclopedia on the library's site, preferably one specific to your field, such as the *Dictionary of Literary Biography, World Statesmen,* or *Access Science.* **Look up an aspect of your topic and make a printout of the entry.** Browse to locate other reference tools— a dictionary, almanac, etc.—available on the library's Web site.
5. Find the indexes and databases to which the library subscribes. Describe how they are categorized, and write down the names of three you think you will use most.
6. Find one of the general indexes like *Academic Search Premier* (for the humanities and social sciences).
   - Find citations for two sources in journals that may be relevant to your project, starting with references from sources you have already found. Find at least one relevant full-text journal article available through the library's indexes.
   - Using the author, subject, and key words from a source you have already found, try author, key word, and subject searches on the database to find additional sources.
   - Make printouts of at least three references to articles in periodicals.

5.3 WORKING ON THE WEB

1. Try the same author, key word, and subject searches on a general search engine like Google.com or Ask.com. While your library home page might offer access to these resources, remember that they are general Web resources that take you outside the library and onto the general World Wide Web. What are the differences in results? Does this comparison illuminate some of the advantages and disadvantages of using these search engines?
2. **Make a printout of one of the most interesting items you find relevant to your topic.** Evaluate this source using the Focus Points for evaluating reliability and relevance in Chapter 2. How reliable does it seem?

3. Find the *New York Times,* the *Washington Post,* and your local newspaper online. Search these sites by key words essential to your inquiry. Find an article relevant to your inquiry, and determine whether it is a news story, a feature story, or an opinion piece. **E-mail an article to yourself, if you can. Print it out.** What kind of costs or restrictions, if any, does the paper place on retrieving articles? If the newspaper charges for articles or searches, try to find free access to it through the library's databases. Ask a librarian or consult the library Web site's help function if necessary.

5.4 CONSTRUCTING A WORKING BIBLIOGRAPHY

1. Using the references you found in the Exercises 5.1 and 5.2 and sources you found while doing the browsing suggested in Chapter 4, start constructing a working bibliography for your inquiry. If some classmates are working on topics relevant to yours, your instructor might encourage you to pool your references. If working with a partner or small group, discard duplicate references.
2. Remember that a working bibliography is a list of *potential* sources, not a list of works you have actually read; some of them you will use, and others you will skim and reject. At the beginning of an inquiry, the working bibliography is more like a pool of references you can draw from than a reflection of work you have completed. That will come later, in the reference list you construct for each project.
3. Using the MLA or APA style guide in the Quick Guide to Documentation at the end of this book, and consulting an APA or MLA manual when necessary, format each reference until you think it is perfect. Next, as a group, review the entries for mistakes, using the following process:
   - One person should read the citation out loud, reading the punctuation as well as the information.
   - One person should find a sample citation for a similar source in the Quick Guide to Documentation.
   - Other group members should check the citation against the sample for mistakes. Consult the MLA or APA style manual when you find a citation that doesn't fit the short list of examples in the Quick Guide to Documentation in this book.
4. Arrange the list in alphabetical order by the last names of the first authors.
5. Exchange your bibliographies with another group and proofread them. Correct any mistakes your exchange group finds. Look for a pattern to the mistakes, and reread the instructions and examples that address these patterns.

5.5 USING THE LIBRARY TO FOLLOW A RESEARCH CAREER

*Choose one of the writers of a peer-reviewed source that interests you, and examine his or her research career. This project will be most useful to you if you are actively thinking about this researcher's field as a career or if you are considering a project for which this writer's research is particularly pertinent to your own inquiry. Take notes on the information you find as you pursue this information and collect all reference information. Unless your instructor tells you otherwise, **do not for any reason call, write, or e-mail the person you are researching to request this information. That's like asking the object of your research to do your research for you.** If you uncover gossip or rumors about this person, consider whether they are found in a reliable source and whether they are relevant to your purpose, which is to write a profile of your subject as a researcher.*

1. Read a peer-reviewed article by the researcher. Read the source closely, using Focus Points: Reading Arguments from Chapter 2 (p. 21).
2. Make a list of the information the source gives you about the researcher. What field is he or she in, who is he or she writing for, what reference style does the source use? Identify key words in the article. Add your own responses in a clearly distinctive format.

3. Look the researcher up on a library index in his or her field, and make a list of the other books or articles he or she has written. Whether using APA or MLA reference format, for the time being, arrange the entries in chronological order to highlight the development of the research career.

4. Try doing a search on a Web search engine like Google. To what different kinds of sites that reflect the life and work of this researcher does this general Web search bring you? Take notes on any new information you find about the researcher.

5. Search for the researcher's professional Web site, which may be housed at his or her university. Many scholars include their *curriculum vitae* (CV) on their websites. A CV is like a resume, but much longer and more complete. If the CV is available online, what information does it give you? Sometimes scholars provide direct links from their Web sites to archived articles they have written. If your researcher has done this, take a look at those sources.

6. Use the researcher's university's search function to find other materials for the profile, such as course descriptions, syllabi, class notes, and news stories about the researcher.

7. Either write a profile of the researcher or develop materials (slides and reading notes) for an oral profile of this researcher's work.

8. Write a short reflection on what your inquiry has shown you about how this researcher's work has developed over time. Or write a short reflection on the relationship between the researcher's writing, public activities, and teaching.

CHAPTER 6

Using Sources Effectively

The abilities to find and document sources and to develop an argument about or interpretation of them have many applications in school and on the job. The genres of researched writing used in academic disciplines include the argumentative research paper (often called a term paper), the proposal, the annotated bibliography, the book review, the literature review, the personal research report (often called an "I-Search" paper, the name given to it by Ken Macrorie, an early advocate of this genre). You may be asked to a build a Web site based on library research. You may be asked to simply report on your research, or to use it as a starting point for experimentation or observation in the laboratory or on field observations. Usually oral presentations and the visuals that support them are rooted in extensive research. Research reports in the sciences (lab reports) and social sciences, although their formats differ from papers in the humanities, usually begin with a review of the previous research that led to the hypothesis currently under investigation. All these genres of researched writing involve similar strategies for finding and evaluating sources, taking notes, and using quotations, summaries, and paraphrases skillfully. However, when and how sources are used and how they are cited vary for different kinds of writing and from field to field. Thus, these general information literacy and research writing skills must be adapted to meet discipline-specific expectations for format, style, and means of presentation in specific academic fields.

SKILLS FOR ACADEMIC INQUIRY: QUOTATION, PARAPHRASE, SUMMARY, AND SYNTHESIS

There are four basic means for using sources when writing researched papers and reports: quotation, paraphrase, summary, and synthesis. These techniques help writers progress from taking notes to drafting. It is always necessary to cite sources as you use them and to consistently distinguish between your own words and ideas and those of your sources.

1. *Quotations* are exact repetitions of a writer's work. Quotations are less often used in disciplines that use APA (American Psychological Association) style than those who use MLA (Modern Language Association) style because arguments in most

disciplines that use APA depend more on summary and synthesis of previous research than on close analysis of texts.

2. *Paraphrases* are restatements of the writer's ideas in your own words, following the source closely in the order in which an argument is developed or evidence is laid out. Paraphrases must be clearly identified as such, by direct attribution to the author, because they can be mistaken for your own thinking.

3. *Summaries* give an overall representation of a writer's argument or part of one, and also must also be identified as representing the ideas of the original as they are moved from notes to drafts.

4. *Syntheses* draw on more than one source in order to show relationships among methodologies, assumptions, and conclusions.

Summaries and syntheses of other writers' work make up the "literature review" that opens most academic papers and provides the context for most academic arguments. Any aspects of understanding or response that occur to you while taking notes and working with sources make drafting a researched paper easier, so write your interpretations, questions, and responses into your notes, using a consistent method (font, color, etc.) to distinguish your voice from the voice of the author.

Quoting

Quotations always must be exact copies of the original, whether copied or cut and pasted, and in your notes they should always be enclosed in quotation marks and accompanied by a reference to the source. One convenient way to keep references attached to citations while taking notes and drafting is to attach a footnote to each quotation, which can then travel with the citation as you use the source for various projects. Add each source to your working bibliography, so that you can easily copy it into the reference pages of each project.

FOCUS POINTS: USING QUOTATIONS

- Remember that whenever you reproduce a source's wording, *even for a few words*, you must put quotation marks around it. You may not add or delete anything from the quoted text, unless you use brackets (for adding) or ellipses (for deleting).

- Be very careful not to take a quotation out of context in a way that changes or distorts its meaning. For example, Jacob Bronowski's statement quoted in Chapter 1 would be severely misrepresented by cutting out a few words of that statement, even if ellipses were correctly used. Notice the difference between the following statements:

   [The book] will bring home to the nonscientist how the scientific method really works: that we invent a model and then test its consequences, and that it is this conjunction of imagination and realism that constitutes the inductive method.

   [The book] will bring home to the nonscientist how the scientific method really works: that we invent a model . . . and that it is this conjunction of imagination and realism that constitutes the inductive method.

- When taking notes, copy quotations when you want the exact wording of a source, or when you think you might want it later. If you do not completely understand a claim or a piece of evidence, making an exact copy allows you to go back to it later, when further reading in the field may give you a better understanding of it. However, you should resort to that kind of copying as little as possible, since it can lead to a paper that simply pieces together quotations rather than using them to make an argument. To write effectively you need to *understand* your sources, not just *repeat* them.

■ When you use notes to draft a paper, it is advisable to state the point or purpose of a quotation *before you use it* and to integrate shorter quotations smoothly into complete sentences. This is a way to demonstrate your understanding of the source and guide your readers to share it. For example:

Alfie Kohn claims that there is no data to confirm that more students in the present than in the past receive higher grades for less real achievement: "The bottom line: No one has ever demonstrated that students today get A's for the same work that used to receive B's or C's."

FOCUS POINTS: PUNCTUATING QUOTATIONS

It is important to distinguish word-for-word quotations of sources from paraphrases and summaries in your own words, and correct punctuation is the way to make this distinction clearly and effectively. The rules for punctuating quotations are relatively simple, but they need to be followed consistently. These rules follow Modern Language Association (MLA) style, because quotations are rarely used in fields that use American Psychological Association (APA) style.

Authors' Names

The first time you use an author's name, you should use the full name, *without* honorifics (Mr., Miss., Professor, Dr., etc.). For later reference, use only the last name. *Never* refer to an author by first name only.

Short Quotations

■ In contemporary American practice, short quotes are put in double quotation marks.

■ In the following example from Benjamin Franklin's biography, the spelling and capitalization of the original are maintained, even though they are now obsolete.

■ If the author's name is mentioned before the quote, only the page number goes in the parenthetical citation. The period that ends the final sentence follows the final parenthesis.

■ In the following example from the *MLA Handbook*, notice how the quotation is fused to the writer's text to produce a single, grammatically correct sentence.

■ Since the author is not cited before the quotation, the last name is included in the parenthetical citation.

Short Quote Following a Complete Sentence

Benjamin Franklin describes how he learned to write through imitating *The Spectator*, an English magazine: "I bought it, read it over, and was much delighted with it. I thought the Writing excellent, and wish'd if possible to imitate it" (532).

Short Quote Integrated into a Sentence

It is crucial for students to learn to document sources well because it "not only recognizes

the work writers do; it also tends to discourage the circulation of error" (*MLA Handbook* 52).

Long Quotations

■ A long quote (three or more lines; one or more complete sentences) should be set off by indenting the entire quote one inch—or ten spaces. Notice in the example below that when long quotes are set off, quotation marks are *not* used around them.

■ Use long, set-off quotations when it is important to get the exact words of a particular passage or when the author's style is very important and you need a long quote to get across its impact. However, they should be used sparingly, since they can look like "padding" and may suggest that you do not understand the material well enough to summarize it. Moreover, many readers admit to skipping over them, and this can dilute the impact of your argument.

■ It is particularly important to introduce long quotes, so that your reader can see the point in a single reading. Use the same spacing (double or single) for the set-off quotation that you use for the document itself.

Punctuating Introductions to Quotations

■ When using a quotation in a paper, it is more effective to introduce it than to just let it "speak for itself."

■ If the introductory statement is a complete sentence, follow it with a colon.

■ If the introductory statement is integrated with the quotation to make a complete sentence, use a comma only if you would use a comma if the quotation marks were not there. If the introductory statement would need a comma without the quotation, follow it with a comma.

Quote Following a Complete Sentence

Alfie Kohn claims that there are no data to confirm that more students in the present than in

the past receive higher grades for less real achievement: "The bottom line: No one has ever

demonstrated that students today get A's for the same work that used to receive B's or C's."

Quotes Integrated into Sentences

As Alfie Kohn argues, "the long history of indignation" over grade inflation is usually ignored.

Alfie Kohn observes that "the long history of indignation" over grade inflation is

usually ignored.

Quotes within Quotes

Put quotations within quotations in single quotation marks, as in the example below. However, quotes within set-off quotes are punctuated normally, with double quotation marks.

Quotes within Quotation Marks

Alfie Kohn observes that a report from "the National Center for Education Statistics revealed that fully 33.5 percent of American undergraduates had a grade-point average of C or below, a number that ought to quiet 'all the furor over grade inflation,' according to a spokesman for the Association of American Colleges and Universities."

Set-Off Quotes

Alfie Kohn raises serious questions about the reality of grade inflation by citing highly reliable sources:

> To get a more accurate picture of whether grades have changed over the years, one needs to look at official student transcripts. Clifford Adelman, a senior research analyst with the U.S. Department of Education, did just that, reviewing transcripts from more than 3,000 institutions and reporting his results in 1995. His finding: "Contrary to the widespread lamentations, grades actually declined slightly in the last two decades." Moreover, a report released just this year by the National Center for Education Statistics revealed that fully 33.5 percent of American undergraduates had a grade-point average of C or below in 1999–2000, a number that ought to quiet "all the furor over grade inflation," according to a spokesperson for the Association of American Colleges and Universities.

Sentence-Ending Punctuation

The basic rule is that commas go inside quotation marks, and periods do so if the sentence ends with the last quotation mark. However, there are several important variations:

- When a parenthetical citation immediately follows the quotation, the sentence does not end with the final quotation mark, and so the period follows the final parenthesis.

- Question marks and exclamation points go inside only when they are part of the quotation. When they are not part of the quotation, they go outside. Commas go within the quotation marks, but semicolons and colons go outside them. For example:

Alfie Kohn asserts, "The bottom line: No one has ever demonstrated that students today get A's for the same work that used to receive B's or C's."

Mike Rose admits that "there is no single profile of the Good Teacher" (9).

Why did Mike Rose reject the idea that "there is no single profile of the Good Teacher" (9)?

Ellipses, Brackets, and [Sic]

- Use ellipses when you cut away a piece of a quotation. Be very careful not to change the author's meaning by cutting a part away. Do not use ellipses at the beginnings or ends of quotations, unless there is a real possibility of misunderstanding without them. Ellipses consist of three dots, separated by spaces. Use a period before the ellipses to show that a sentence ends before the ellipses begin (and thus the number of dots totals four in those cases).

■ Use brackets to add to the quotation any material necessary to understand it. The bracketed material can clarify words or expressions in the original text that could be ambiguous when read out of context. In the following example, the bracketed material replaces and clarifies what the author is referring to by "the two."

■ The term "sic" set in brackets is used to indicate that the preceding material is original to the source, not the invention or mistake of the quoter. For example, the archaic capitalization and contractions in the quotation from Franklin above could have been followed by [sic] to indicate that they were part of the original. Using [sic] is a judgment call, but it is preferable to avoid it unless there is the possibility of serious confusion or misreading. This did not seem to be the case in quoting Franklin.

Ellipses . . .

Alfie Kohn draws on the distinction between kinds of motivation:

> With the exception of orthodox behaviorists, psychologists have come to realize that people can exhibit qualitatively different kinds of motivation: intrinsic, in which the task itself is seen as valuable, and extrinsic, in which the task is just a means to the end of gaining a reward or escaping a punishment. The two are not only distinct but often inversely related. . . . But the reality is that it doesn't matter how motivated students are; what matters is how students are motivated. A focus on grades creates, or at least perpetuates, an extrinsic orientation that is likely to undermine the love of learning we are presumably seeking to promote.

Brackets [ ]

> Alfie Kohn observes that "the two [intrinsic and extrinsic motivation] are not only distinct but often inversely related."

PARAPHRASING EFFECTIVELY

Paraphrases follow the thinking and wording of the author closely and may include some short quotations like those in the examples above. As when you use quotations, the best way to distinguish your thinking from that of the source is to name the source at the beginning of the paraphrase and (when using MLA style) to follow the paraphrase with the page number in the source from which it was taken. Paraphrasing when taking notes can be used to follow a line of reasoning in detail, but it is risky because it is easy to reword it when actually writing the paper, bringing it back so close to the original (whether or not you intend to) that it will seem like plagiarism—using another writer's words without attribution. If you feel you must closely follow the reasoning of a source by using a paraphrase, consider quoting directly in your notes and writing the paraphrase later, when you draft the paper. If there are cases where this is not possible, leave reminders to yourself when you paraphrase, so that you know what you have in your notes when using them later. As with a direct quotation, introduce each paraphrase, end it with a page number (when available), and attach a reference.

> Alfie Kohn observes that people who blame grade inflation on the liberal excesses of the
>
> 1960s are ignoring the fact that people have been complaining about it for centuries.
>
> Alfie Kohn argues that there is no documented evidence that grade inflation has
>
> taken place.

SUMMARIZING APPROPRIATELY

Summaries, an important aspect of note-taking, are also written in your own words, but they cover more of the source in a more general way. Being able to summarize what a writer said accurately, briefly, and without distorting the meaning is a crucial academic skill. A summary of a whole work (sometimes called an abstract) recapitulates the major claim the author makes in a piece, the reasons that support the argument, and the conclusion reached. Although summaries are sometimes assigned and written for their own sake to demonstrate that you have read and understood an article, in research writing they are primarily used to establish the context of an argument and to bring in evidence from other researchers to support a line of reasoning. Keep those uses in mind while summarizing sources and when deciding how much detail to include from a particular source. Like other uses of sources, summaries should be clearly distinguished from your response to the material; although your response is important, the summary should never change or distort the meaning of the original piece. The length of any summary should depend on how you plan to use it in the project and on how central its argument, reasoning, or evidence is to your own developing argument.

FOCUS POINTS: EFFECTIVE SUMMARIZING

- *Attach a reference to the summary* so that you have the material for a bibliographic entry. Remember that the source for a summary needs to be cited, even if you are describing a writer's general approach or argument, and even if you are not using any direct quotations in it.
- Clearly indicate in the notes when you are speaking for yourself and when you are summarizing another work. The clearest way to distinguish your own thinking from that of your source is to name the source before summarizing, just as you would before quoting or paraphrasing it. If you consistently mark your responses (by highlighting or using a different font) while taking notes, you can easily distinguish them from your summaries of sources.
- *If you use an author's summary*—from an abstract or concluding paragraph—as a starting place for your own, *make sure that you do not simply copy it into your paper.* Try restating the author's summary in your own words, and then decide what additional information is needed for the purposes of your project. It may help to close the source while you summarize, so that you are forced to think through the

main ideas until you fully understand them before putting them in your own words. Then check that the summary accurately represents the source. If it does not, a quotation might be preferable at this stage of your inquiry.

- *Let the author do some of the work of summarizing* by looking at the central argument (or thesis) of the piece, which usually can be found at the end of the introduction, and which is often reiterated at the beginning of the conclusion and referred to at the beginnings of some paragraphs. You can usually find the major claims, reasons, and organization of the evidence in a piece by skimming it. Try highlighting the first sentence of each paragraph of a source you are working with, as well as the first and last sentences of the introduction and conclusion. How close do the highlighted parts bring you to a summary?

  Unfortunately, when dealing with any sizable work, following this method closely will produce a summary that is far too long and that includes explanations, supporting elements, and other peripheral material. In a piece from a newspaper or magazine—like Alfie Kohn's piece on grade inflation and Robert Rivard's piece on plagiarism in the Readings—the paragraphs are usually too short for this to be an effective strategy. But reading for the writer's statements of argument and purpose—wherever they are located—can provide a good start for summarizing.

- *Identify key words by skimming first lines* and construct a summary around them.

A Simple Format for Learning to Summarize

If you are new to summarizing, here is a simple framework for getting started. This strategy is adapted from instructions for formulating a thesis given in *The Craft of Research*.[1] If you are already experienced at summarizing, you may find this process to be too rigid and formulaic to let you say what you need to say, so do not hesitate to adapt the process to suit the texts you are working with and to your purpose in summarizing them—or to drop the process when it fails to help you frame your understanding of a source:

- *The author [full name] raises [name the problem] with [state the purpose];*
- *The author [last name or pronoun] argues that [state main claim] by observing that [state main reasons];*
- *The author [last name or pronoun] concludes [describe conclusion and/or recommendations]; and*
- *The author [last name or pronoun] proposes [state significance or implications where appropriate].*

EXAMPLE 6.1 *Building the Summary*

Here is a summary of Alfie Kohn's article on grade inflation that follows the process described above:

Alfie Kohn raises the issue of grade inflation in order to argue that it is not really a problem

in most universities. He observes that contemporary students are at least as knowledgeable as those of a century ago and suggests that concerns about grade inflation rest on misreadings

of data not directly relevant to measuring student learning. He concludes that claims about

grade inflation derive from an uncritical acceptance of the idea of competitive grading, and

proposes that competitive grading itself is destructive of intellectual effort and detrimental to

educational excellence.

This is a very short summary, only ninety words, yet it gives a precise overview of Kohn's piece and gives appropriate weight to the points Kohn stresses. Here's how it works:

1. Alfie Kohn raises the issue of grade inflation in order to argue that it is not really a problem in most universities. [*The first sentence of the summary states the problem, repeats the central claim of the article, and gives Kohn's purpose: to refute the idea that grade inflation is a problem.*]

2. He observes that contemporary students are at least as knowledgeable as those of a century ago, [*The second sentence gives the major reason supporting Kohn's claim*]

3. and suggests that concerns about grade inflation rest on misreading data not directly relevant to measuring student learning. [*and the reason why the other side is wrong.*]

4. He concludes that claims about grade inflation derive from an uncritical acceptance of the idea of competitive grading [*The third sentence shows Kohn's reasons for discrediting the warrant for the other side (which constitutes much of Kohn's strategy in this article) . . .*]

5. and proposes that competitive grading itself is destructive of intellectual effort and detrimental to educational excellence. [*. . . and gives Kohn's conclusion, which attests to the larger implications of his argument.*]

Notice that this summary covers the entire argument specifically; it does not move to a higher level of generality than the author uses, but it does leave out the supporting evidence and most of the context. It is preferable to keep a summary as near as possible to the level of specificity in the source. For example, this summary could move to a more general level by starting with a statement that Alfie Kohn addresses an issue in American higher education of considerable concern to faculty, students, and parents; this may be true, but that statement is too general to begin a short summary of Kohn's article.

The summary also includes the author's name; a final draft would indicate page numbers (when available) for any material closely derived from the source, meeting the need for accurate documentation. If a longer summary is required, more detailed support could be added to each of the four sections, and the line of reasoning established, in order to more fully describe Kohn's argument. In the example below, the additions have been bolded. Notice that the additions are primarily the main reasons for his position.

EXAMPLE 6.2 *A More Detailed Summary*

Alfie Kohn raises the issue of grade inflation in order to argue that it is not really a problem

in most universities, **suggesting that grade inflation is actually a myth based on false** information, insufficient proof, and an unjustified belief in the objective validity of grades. He documents the unreliability of research attesting to grade inflation and attributes the conclusion that grade inflation is undermining American higher education to the conservative political bias of some researchers. Kohn observes that contemporary students are at least as knowledgeable as those of a century ago, citing data from a U.S. Department of Education analysis of student grades, and suggests that concerns about grade inflation rest on misreading data not directly relevant to measuring student learning. He concludes that claims about grade inflation derive from an uncritical acceptance of the idea that grading should be competitive and from the assumption that stringent grading effectively motivates learning. Kohn proposes that competitive grading itself is detrimental to education and destructive to educational excellence, citing evidence that students learn better from internal motives and from teachers who expect them to succeed than from competition for grades.

Question

What would you expect to be the key words in this article?

How Purpose Affects Summary

Clearly, summarizing is an important step in progressing from taking notes to writing an argument of your own. You can shape summaries to the purpose of your projects as you go along, and later synthesize summaries of multiple sources to develop your thinking about your topic even further. In the Readings, the excerpt from the introduction to Mike Rose's *Possible Lives: The Promise of Public Education in America* summarizes the book and explains the order of the evidence used to argue that there is much that is good in American public education. His evidence is embedded in his account of site visits to a range of schools across the country that, he argues, can and should be considered successful. He begins and ends by addressing the purpose of the book: "I hope not so much for prescription as for an opening up of the way we think and talk about public schools" (9).

A writer using Rose's book as a source might summarize this passage in ways that are relevant for a number of different purposes. Each of these sample summaries uses a different aspect of Rose's introduction as a starting point for a response, analysis, or argument.

1. *To support a position or offer evidence for it:*

> Not everyone believes that public school education in America is hopeless. For example, Mike Rose assembles case histories of schools that provide effective and engaging instruction to support his argument that American public education for the most part works (8–9).

Notice that even though this summary is setting us up for a response—probably a positive response—to Rose's argument, it nonetheless accurately conveys what the passage says.

2. *To argue against its conclusions, assumptions, or methodologies or to point out weaknesses in the evidence it uses:*

> Mike Rose assembles case histories of selected American schools to argue for the success
>
> of American public education and for the "decency and achievement" these schools foster.
>
> However, the actual experience of the majority of teachers and students cannot be ade-
>
> quately represented through a handful of case studies, which may or may not be typical.

The phrase "selected American schools" prepares for a negative response by emphasizing the selectivity of this sample, whereas the first summary emphasized its geographic breadth. The summary, even though asking us for a negative response to the material, accurately states what the passage says.

3. *To explain (and possibly adopt) a writer's methodology:*

> Mike Rose describes his travels from school to school across America, observing class-
>
> es, talking with high school teachers, university faculty, and students, considering
>
> particular practices and projects in terms of their local populations and their condi-
>
> tions of life. This study will follow a similar plan, but limit the "journey" to neighbor-
>
> hoods within a single city.

This short summary offers more details about Rose's methodology, which the writer intends to imitate.

4. *To gather evidence about one focus of the writer's work. (For example, a writer examining urban education might summarize only Rose's references to schools in Los Angeles, Chicago, and New York City):*

> When considering urban schools, Mike Rose examines the interplay of relationships
>
> between students and teachers, schools and communities, and reform movements and
>
> individual lives.

This writer may be moving into an analysis of the interactions among similar relationships in some other aspect of urban life, summarizing this aspect of Rose's work to establish the terms of analysis.

As you work with sources, you will find additional purposes for summarizing sources; the direction your argument takes and the kinds of claims you make will determine what information should be summarized from a source and the appropriate length of the summary. It cannot be stressed too often, however, that it is crucial to summarize accurately and fairly, which means making sure you do not change the author's ideas, even when you take them out of their original context, and especially when you disagree with them. As well as being unethical, such inaccuracy would seriously undermine your credibility—your ethos as a writer.

WRITING AN ANNOTATED BIBLIOGRAPHY

An annotated bibliography is a list of sources relevant to an inquiry, alphabetized by the author's last name. Each source is summarized and evaluated, usually in no more than a short paragraph or two. Published annotated bibliographies serve as reference guides for other researchers, and finding a recent one related to your research can offer an expert introduction to the literature and a strategy for navigating through it. Sometimes researchers write more informal annotated bibliographies for themselves, in order to keep track of their sources when working on a long-term project. They are often assigned in upper-level courses in the humanities.

FOCUS POINTS: STRATEGIES FOR WRITING AN ANNOTATED BIBLIOGRAPHY

■ Copy the citations from the working bibliography into a new file; focus on sources you have read and are likely to use in later projects.

■ Evaluate your sources in terms of reliability. See the Focus Points on Evaluating Sources and Evaluating Materials on the Web in Chapter 2, pages 29 and 40. Discard sources that do not seem reliable or that are irrelevant to your inquiry, unless you have a special reason for including them, for example, exposing their unreliability as part of your response.

■ Find additional reliable and relevant sources to add to the bibliography until you have enough to demonstrate the scope of your inquiry and to meet the requirements of the assignment.

■ Consider your audience: your class and your instructor. Are you writing for a research group with considerable knowledge in common, or for an audience that has an interest in your topic but less knowledge about it than you do? Consider the balance of common and disciplinary knowledge appropriate for this audience.

■ Write a summary for each source chosen. For some of the sources you may be able to draw on notes, summaries, and responses from previous exercises. Revise this earlier work to fit into the summary/response format and to reflect what you have learned later in your inquiry; write new annotations for sources not yet summarized.

■ Write a new or revised response to each source. Start by considering criteria for evaluating the entries:

• what part the source plays in your emerging argument,

• how it relates to the other sources,

• how it has affected your thinking, and

• how you might use it in another project.

■ Compare your earlier responses to these new ones, and consider how they have changed. Consider how the sources may be useful for future projects based on this inquiry.

■ Make sure the entries are in alphabetical order, and write a short introduction to the bibliography that describes its purpose, how much of the inquiry it covers, and what other sources or kinds of sources are needed to complete the inquiry.

■ In a longer bibliography (30 or more sources), you can divide the bibliography into sections with subtitles; if you do so, the introduction should also explain what each section covers.

EXAMPLE 6.3 *Sample Annotated Bibliography for a Paper on Plagiarism*

Plagiarism: An Annotated Bibliography

This bibliography describes and documents my reading so far for an investigation of plagiarism and possible solutions to it at American universities. I decided to focus my early reading on specific cases and places, in order to give me a sense of the "common understanding" of the issues. Most of the articles examine specific cases of plagiarism or responses to it, at specific American schools. They identify plagiarism as a problem that needs to be solved, without paying much attention to defining it or questioning whether it is a problem at all. The pieces by Rebecca Moore Howard and Candace Spigelman, however, do make the issue more questionable, and I will need to examine the individual cases reported in the popular press to distinguish between fraud and mistakes. At the same time, it is important to test that distinction against descriptions of specific cases to make an argument about whether or not it is a useful distinction.

Feldt, Brandon. "English Professors Discuss Solutions for Plagiarism." *Daily Vidette*. Illinois
State University, 27 Jan. 2003. Web. 17 Nov. 2008.

This university newspaper article describes how professors at Illinois State University consider possible solutions for the growing plagiarism issue. They discuss preparation for writing in both college and high school atmospheres, and suggest that some students do not understand the different aspects of plagiarism and/or how to cite correctly. They also consider the impact of the fact that some teachers tend to give nonspecific directions for papers and assignments.

This article supports my research by providing several different problems that cause plagiarism as well as a few possible solutions. It considers many of the same issues I plan to touch upon, particularly the unexplained issues.

Foster, Andrea L. "Plagiarism Tool Creates Legal Quandary." *Chronicle.com*. *Chronicle of
Higher Education,* 17 May 2003. Web. 17 Nov. 2008.

This article touches upon the law and copyright infringement. It shows the critical issues concerning computer programs that have emerged since universities began using them. The article also gives reactions to the possible copyright infringing services.

The article can help my argument by covering the legal aspects of the situation. It also helps me get a broader understanding of plagiarism as an intellectual property issue.

By being able to fully understand the situation, I can write a thorough report on the issue, addressing legal issues as well as moral issues.

Garinger, Alex. "Plagiarism Cases Jump During Fall." *Chronicle*. Duke University, 13 Jan.
2003. Web. 17 Nov. 2008.

This article reaffirms the increasing rate of plagiarism in our school systems. It focuses on a study done at Duke University, discussing problems with plagiarism over the past few years.

This article might work as additional background information for my research.

Haberling, Michael. "Maintaining Academic Integrity in Online Education." *Online Journal of
Distance Learning Administration* 5.1 (2002): n. pag. 3 Dec. 2003. Web. 11 Nov. 2008.

This article refutes the idea that plagiarism and other forms of cheating occur more often in online courses than in face-to-face courses. Comparing plagiarism cases in both kinds of classes at Baker College in Michigan, the author (the president of the college) argues that this is not necessarily so. In fact, it may be easier to detect plagiarism in online courses. For one thing, teachers of online classes have a larger record of students' writing, since most class participation is done in writing. It can be easier for a teacher to spot plagiarism when he or she is used to a student's normal writing style and abilities. The article describes how to do a "search in reverse" on search engines to detect plagiarism and includes a pretty funny story about students plagiarizing their college application essays and getting caught.

This article extends the question of plagiarism to online courses, which I have not really thought much about in this project.

Howard, Rebecca Moore. "Forget about Policing Plagiarism. Just Teach." *Chronicle.com*.
Chronicle of Higher Education, 16 Nov. 2001. Web. 17 Jan. 2008.

This article seems like a simpler version of the earlier article in *College English*. Instead of considering what students do when writing, it tells teachers how to deal with plagiarism in their courses. Howard does not seem to think that there is a "plague" of plagiarism, and she reminds teachers that they do not want to be police. She looks into some of the reasons why students may cheat, and talks about how professors' working conditions can help them assign papers that students do not want to cheat on.

This article seems to be blaming colleges and professors for students' cheating. It does raise the question of how professors should be teaching classes.

---. "Plagiarisms, Authorships, and the Academic Death Penalty." *College English* 57.7
(1995): 788–806. Print.

This article makes the issue of plagiarism much more complicated than some of the
others. The author thinks that plagiarism should be given a different definition, so that
cheating is seen differently than "patchwriting." Both of them are bad, but they are not the
same thing, in her opinion. Schools should rewrite policies to make that difference clear, and
teachers should teach students how to use sources better, even though it takes a long time.

This article makes my thinking about this research more complicated. It also makes
me wonder how the schools and teachers in the other articles defined plagiarism. Which
cases were really cheating, as compared to making mistakes?

Jerome, Richard, and Pam Grout. "Cheat Wave." *People* 17 June 2002: 82–83. Print.

This article discusses one specific disagreement that occurred in Piper, Kansas, and
one legal outcome of the current debate on plagiarism. It also considers the effect of the
court decision upon the student and the school.

This article provides a strong case study of the impact of plagiarism on a community.
Also, by showing that there is more than one side to the issue, I should be able to raise
awareness of the importance and growing magnitude of the issue at hand.

McGrath, Charles. "Plagiarism: Everybody Into the Pool." *New York Times* 7 Jan. 2007: 33. Print.

This article talks about some high-profile plagiarism cases that have occurred over
the last couple of years. It also discusses how students that plagiarize often suffer harsher
consequences than their professors who are guilty of the same thing.

I will probably use one of the statistics from the end of the article about students
who reported cheating by using the Internet. The article also discusses Richard A. Posner's
The Little Book of Plagiarism, which may be another good source to consider.

Robillard, Amy E. "We Won't Get Fooled Again: On the Absence of Angry Responses to
Plagiarism in Composition Studies." *College English* 70.1 (2007): 10–31. Print.

This article talks about plagiarism from the side of the Composition instructor. It tells
how frustrating it can be for teachers to play the role of a policeman when grading papers,
but it also explains the dilemma involved with dealing out punishment to plagiarizing
students and what that means for their self-esteem and careers.

This article supports the point of view of the teacher on plagiarism and will contrast nicely to other articles that discuss it from the student's point of view and that of other professionals.

Silverman, Gillian. "It's a Bird, It's a Plane, It's Plagiarism Buster!" *Newsweek*

15 July 2002: 12. Print.

This article pertains specifically to students stealing from the Internet. It raises the idea that plagiarism is partially due to the nature of students' lives. It suggests that students are either too busy or too free to do other things, and so they tend to do homework at the last minute, which causes them to turn to plagiarism.

This article supports different points of view on plagiarism, the point of view of the schools and the point of view of the student. By looking at several different viewpoints I can make a better response to the issue.

Spigelman, Candace. "The Ethics of Appropriation in Peer Writing Groups." *Perspectives on Plagiarism and Intellectual Property in a Postmodern World*. Ed. Lise Buranen and Alice M. Roy. Albany, NY: SUNY P, 1999. 231–40. Print.

This article discusses how students talk about and think about intellectual property in writing groups that are part of a class. It discusses the problem that some courses want students to work alone, so that their ideas are always theirs alone. The writer quotes the students discussing their feelings about where ideas come from and the need to credit people as well as books for influencing their thinking.

This article will be useful because it makes the idea of plagiarism more complicated. The author doesn't just quote people for and against plagiarism, but students trying to understand what to do in different situations.

Straw, Deborah. "The Plagiarism of Generation 'Why Not?'" *Community College Week* 14.24 (2002): 4–6. Print.

This article explains the rising complications with plagiarism specifically upon the high-school level and also on the collegiate level. It uses statistics from universities and high schools around the country to represent this idea while also including quotes from various school officials. The article considers the part the Internet has played in the growing incidence of plagiarism. After introducing the problem, the article questions who is likely to be an offender. It suggests that the higher entrance requirements at colleges cause students in high schools to try and get the highest grade point averages that they can, even if it means plagiarizing. The article concludes by providing possible ways of attacking the dilemma.

The source is a credible one that gives me ample information to create a sound base for my research. This article provides a background scene I can use to help the audience to better understand the situation. Also, it gives me statistics to prove that the situation exists and is becoming more of a problem every year.

Questions

1. What kinds of sources does the writer of the bibliography use? How directly do they address his particular project?

2. Do you agree with the writer's assessment of the reliability of the sources in this bibliography? Which ones seem questionable? Why?

3. How precise are the summaries? Where should they be clearer?

4. What are the criteria for the responses? Are they applied consistently? Do they seem reasonable? How could they be improved?

5. The audience for this bibliography seems to be primarily the writer himself. How might it be adapted to communicate the content and value of the sources to another audience, for example, to an audience more interested in reading about plagiarism than in writing about it?

6. How informative is the introduction? How might it be revised to disclose more clearly the researcher's purpose in writing the annotated bibliography?

MOVING FROM SUMMARY TO SYNTHESIS: ESTABLISHING RELATIONSHIPS

A synthesis shows one or more significant relationships among sources. Synthesis draws on techniques of comparison and contrast, but it demands acknowledging nuanced relationships among sources and guiding readers through them. For example, to explain the consensus of a significant body of opinion in a field, you can draw on the ideas of a number of authors, attributing variations of ideas or different approaches to the appropriate source. Synthesis uses your responses to make judgments, and the success of a synthesis will depend in large degree on how good your judgment is and how well you understand the sources in the context of their field. Although a synthesis may be based on your response to the sources and may point toward your developing argument, like other uses of sources, it requires a fair and accurate reflection of what the source actually says.

Summarizing accurately and for a purpose is a good starting point for synthesizing, and the purposes suggested for summaries in the previous section can be expanded into the governing purpose for a synthesis. The key to writing an effective synthesis is to show the relationship of sources—often different in kind and in purpose—to each other and in relation to a field or an issue. Synthesis is also used to set a context for an argument. Synthesis requires more than merely pasting a number of summaries together, but requires that you identify and even argue for a particular relationship among the sources. An effective synthesis not only brings together a body of information from a number of sources, but also—and most importantly—provides the reader with a map to navigate the field. Before you can write an effective synthesis, you must reach a clear idea about the relationships among the sources and how they fit into the field to serve as a guide for your readers.

A synthesis can draw on a variety of organizing principles, depending on the topic and purpose of the paper you are writing. The topic and purpose should be evident in a topic sentence that orients the reader to your intentions. For example, a synthesis might:

1. **Establish considerable overall consensus in a field or among a group of writers, with which you might be preparing to agree or disagree.**
    *   Although they might disagree on some particulars, most physicians agree that mental and physical processes affect each other in subtle but important ways.
    *   These historians define *professionalization* as a sequence of activities a group of practitioners consciously undertakes to move from amateur to professional status, including forming an organization that distinguishes insiders from outsiders and producing documents like codes of conduct, codes of ethics, and requirements for entry.
    *   Rebecca Moore Howard's distinction between cheating and incomplete learning initiated a body of research that takes a developmental view of teaching students to incorporate sources into their writing.

2. **Claim more or less sharply divided sides to the issue (a dichotomy), either to identify specific sources typical of opposite lines of reasoning or to identify the range of thinking about the issue.**
    *   The scholars who address issues of plagiarism tend to fall into two camps: those who look at all instances of "borrowing" stories, ideas, phrases, or complete texts as wrong; and those who distinguish cheating from allusion, "sampling," and inadequate documentation.
    *   While most physical education departments have come to emphasize competitive sports, a few hold on to an older ideal of providing personal fitness education for all students, an ideal that has regained some popularity in recent years.
    *   Current thinking about plagiarism ranges from the position that any almost any form of unattributed imitation is wrong, as seen in the work of Thomas Mallon, to the motive-based distinctions recommended by Rebecca Moore Howard.

3. **Show several points of view from which the issue can be analyzed, resulting in differing predictions about outcomes or prescriptions for courses of action.**
    *   Studies of international teaching assistants tend to focus on either the effects of their teaching on American undergraduates or the impact of teaching American students on the education of international graduate students.
    *   While downloading music from the Internet looks like a reasonable use of freely available resources to many of those who do it, it looks like theft to the record companies. For some recording artists, the issue is less about compensation and more about maintaining artistic control over their material.

There are variations on these strategies that can be used to articulate the "state of the field" you have been studying. Two kinds of synthesis very common in academic fields are the history of an idea, issue, or controversy within a field, and the literature review (in this context, "literature" means published previous research in a field, not creative writing). A crucial factor in all kinds of synthesis is how well the writer establishes and maintains a clear and consistent presence (possibly personal, but not necessarily so) as a guide through the material. Notice the tone of assurance in the previous examples.

Because synthesis can be used to document the agreement or overlap among significant groups within a field or to define a common warrant for argument among authors writing about different topics, it can help you to understand the larger significance of your inquiry, as well as to establish a context for a claim. For example, the following synthesis shows how the readings by Mike Rose, Rebecca Moore Howard, and Alfie Kohn—arguments about different topics—are all founded on similar warrants about the nature of learning.

EXAMPLE 6.4 *Synthesizing Warrants*

What has been called the "progressive" view of education considers the human interaction of teacher and student to be the most essential aspect of learning. Underlying this way of thinking are the assumptions that teachers and students are naturally interested in teaching and learning as much as they can, as well as they can; that teaching and learning are personal and interpersonal activities, best conducted in a nurturing environment; and that benign self-interest and good will can serve as sufficient motivation for good work. Thus, for example, Alfie Kohn argues that the "external" motivation of the tough grade is not only unnecessary, but detrimental to the educational process. In a similar vein, Rebecca Moore Howard assures us in "Forget about Policing" that "patchwriting" students will grow out of the practice as they gain enough understanding of a field to use their own words, which they will do more effectively under the guidance of an understanding teacher than a firm disciplinarian. Mike Rose undertakes his journey across America to look at people more than at institutions, to consider the possibility of educational reform as "the day-to-day human reality of social change" (8). These progressive educators assume that the essential honesty and good will of people working together are more important for learning than are rules and institutional structures.

Such a synthesis could be used as the introduction to a thesis arguing for or against the progressive assumptions outlined in the last sentence. It could also serve as the basis for a much longer synthesis, which would include summaries and perhaps longer quotations and more paraphrases from the sources to illustrate the range of agreement and nuances of disagreement within that general consensus. Or it could serve as a basis for a reflection on or response to these authors' positions.

REVIEWING THE LITERATURE

The process of inquiry demands close and critical reading that distinguishes among sources that establish a context, sources that suggest claims or reasons for use in an argument, and sources that provide important evidence to support your reasoning. When you find sources difficult to understand, use Focus Points: Reading Arguments (p. 21) to help you work your way through them. Once you can summarize accurately the overall point and purpose of a source, you can consider more fully what role it would best play in your project.

FOCUS POINTS: WORKING WITH THE LITERATURE

■ Some sources may agree with the argument you are constructing and others might disagree; as a research writer, you need to demonstrate the degree of agreement and disagreement among the sources (i.e., the extent of the controversy) and to give reasons for your own position toward them.

■ Writing a critical synthesis of sources is called "reviewing the literature" in most fields. The term *literature* in this case does not mean creative writing or fiction, but the previous publications in a field (for instance, the literature of suicide prevention or the literature of eating disorders). The term *critical* means that the writer makes judgments about the accuracy, relevance, and value of the sources.

■ Most academic studies start with a short review of the literature to set the context for the argument or hypothesis to be examined. There are also standalone surveys of the literature, such as the annotated bibliography and literature review. Examples of literature reviews can be found in the Readings, particularly in Jane Tompkins' "'Indians': Textualism, Morality, and the Problem of History" and in Motoko Rich's "Digital Publishing Is Scrambling the Industry's Rules."

■ All variations of "working with the literature" involve taking clear research notes, writing summaries and syntheses, and addressing a particular audience, in many cases an audience that knows the field in general but is less familiar than you with the specific issue.

■ As with other kinds of writing from sources, a good first step toward producing either an annotated bibliography or a literature review is to review what you have already written, such as your notes, the working bibliography, and summaries and syntheses written for previous assignments. Skim through this earlier work to review your ideas, and then extract what you consider the most reliable, interesting, and important sources to include in your selection. Based on your developing expertise:

• Select the sources that seem most relevant for appraising the context and significance of your inquiry.

• Identify sources that provide background for your project and decide how much background is needed.

• Identify sources that offer evidence for or against your reasons.

• If you find sources that you strongly agree or disagree with, make note of those responses. Keep these written responses so that you can apply them to evaluating the evidence, warrants, or reasoning in those sources. You might modify or change those evaluations as the project develops.

• Sources do not speak for themselves; you must explain how you are using them to support your position. Your voice—your response to the sources—should be clearly distinguished from the voice of the source, whether you are using summary, paraphrase, or quotation.

■ The purpose of reviewing sources is to decide how to synthesize them into a coherent document. This reviewing and synthesizing can help not only to organize the sources, but even more importantly, to reveal gaps in the research that should be filled. You can cut and paste pieces of earlier summaries, syntheses, and responses into the developing draft—provided that you bring the references with them and clearly distinguish your own responses from the authors' voices.

■ As you work with the literature, recheck the formatting of the sources taken from your working bibliography. Even experienced researchers make mistakes with formatting references because this work demands an attention to detail difficult to sustain, and mistakes are easier to recognize when you put the bibliography aside for a while. This is also a good time to double-check the spelling of authors' names and of words in titles. As always, make certain that you have clearly distinguished quotations from paraphrases. If you are not sure, go back to the source and check.

WRITING A LITERATURE REVIEW

A literature review is a synthesis that demonstrates how sources reflect and build on each other, that provides a map through the previous literature, and that develops an understanding of a particular question. Often literature reviews convey an argument, support a point of view, or evaluate the sources in relation to each other. Literature reviews serve a number of purposes:

■ *Many papers assigned in college courses are extended literature reviews*, in which students are asked to review, synthesize, and formulate an interpretation of what has been previously written about an issue.

■ *Some literature reviews serve as the introduction to a paper*, setting the context for the thesis or hypothesis, or giving the history of previous investigations. (See Focus Points: Synthesizing the History of a Field, page 123.)

■ *Literature reviews can also be used as evidence to explore or support claims.* For example, Jane Tompkins' essay, "'Indians': Textualism, Morality, and the Problem of History," printed in the Readings, uses a long review of literature, first of historians and then of eyewitnesses, to lead to her final conclusions about the limitations of history.

■ *Some long literature reviews, called "review essays," are published to summarize and evaluate the significant publications in a field* over a period of time, so that readers can keep up with the research. These review essays, which consider important recent publications in the context of a longer history of consensus or controversy in the field are common in history, literature, and various humanities and social science disciplines. They are also found in journals like *Science*, to help scientists keep up with developments in fields other than their own specialty, or like the *New York Review of Books*, which serves a similar purpose in the humanities and social sciences. The literature review by Robert Macfarlane, "The Burning Question" (in the Readings) is aimed at an even more general audience.

■ Carefully consider to whom and for what purpose you are presenting this information. Are you writing to an audience with considerable knowledge about a particular domain, or to an audience with interest in the field, but little knowledge about it?

- Choose the sources that seem most valuable to your research projects.

- Follow a process similar to the one proposed for writing an annotated bibliography: draw on your notes, summaries, syntheses, and responses, to re-see and reevaluate your reading in the field, as you develop a position toward the sources in your inquiry. Add to the literature review by referring to additional sources at points where they illuminate or contradict your initial sources or raise questions yet to be researched.

- Like any synthesis, a literature review needs a clear and purposeful organization, derived from an interpretation of the meaning of the sources. Referring to your written responses, consider the relationship of the items in the literature to your topic and to each other. Reflect on how the various sources relate to a central question or purpose, especially if your sources do not fit neatly into a preestablished framework.

- Extract from your working bibliography the references for the sources used in the review and paste them in alphabetical order at the end of the review.

These questions for self-evaluation reflect the audience orientation of the literature review and may help you to address its purpose more clearly. They may also point out where the relationship among sources needs to be clarified or reconsidered.

- Reread the paper. Describe in informal words the criteria by which you have selected and evaluated the sources it reviews for reliability and relevance. Did you make those criteria clear in the introduction?

- How well does the literature review reflect how your research relates to questions being asked by researchers in its field? Can you state this relationship more clearly?

- Has the review established a context for an argument derived from your inquiry?

- Does the review anticipate the larger significance of your inquiry—the "so what?" How can you make this significance more precise?

- What parts of the literature review do you really believe in? Highlight them, and explain with a note in the margin.

- What parts of the literature review seem weak to you? Are there points where you are not sure your readers can follow you? Or parts where you are uncertain about your accuracy or clarity of expression? Highlight those parts and write your specific questions in a marginal note.

REVIEWING THE HISTORY OF KNOWLEDGE WITHIN A FIELD

As suggested previously, many research studies begin with a short history of the development of ideas about a topic in its field. This kind of synthesis provides a context for the inquiry and demonstrates the existence and importance of the gap that the researcher proposes to fill—either a lack of knowledge or a presumed mistake in previous understanding or interpretation (Booth, Columb, and Williams 185). Recounting the history of a topic or of a field's approach to it also helps establish the writer's ethos as an authority by demonstrating that the writer has done the necessary groundwork and is building upon existing common knowledge in the discipline. Many academic writers use this kind of synthesis as an introduction to their claims, but researchers in different fields give the history of their research issue in different ways.

In the humanities, a disciplinary history may go back several centuries, if a question has been central to the field. In the sciences, on the other hand, researchers seldom trace questions very far into the past, but they often look one or two steps back into past understanding of a question, to provide a context for the present research project or interpretation of results. When writing to specialists in a very narrow field, researchers sometimes refer only to the problem itself, expecting their audience to already know the history of attempts to solve it. For example, in their groundbreaking paper on DNA, mentioned in Chapters 1 and 2, Watson and Crick give the history of the problem in three short paragraphs, mentioning only two earlier studies (one not yet published), before they go on to state: "We wish to put forward a radically different structure. . ." (337–38).

FOCUS POINTS: SYNTHESIZING THE HISTORY OF A FIELD

- Identify stages of development and acknowledge shades of agreement and disagreement among your sources over time.

- Consider whether the controlling assumptions, or central warrants, of the field remain substantially the same over time, or whether there were major paradigm shifts at particular historical moments.

- Make sure your chronological sequence is accurate, and use one or two particular sources to represent each important stage.

- Keep in mind the different uses for which you might use this history, and the different audiences for different projects. For example, this history may be adapted later to serve as a draft of the introduction to another paper or as background material for a Web site.

- End the historical synthesis with a current controversy that needs to be resolved and, if applicable, identify the historical precedents for the stand you expect to take.

- Add references drawn from your working bibliography, and proofread the piece.

DISTINGUISHING VOICES

Even though interpretation is crucial to synthesis, writers need to be careful not to misrepresent what the sources say. Whether you agree or disagree with an author or position, it is important to represent the position fairly and accurately before arguing for or against it. The transition from summary to response must be absolutely clear. One way to show the difference between your own thinking and that of a source is to name the author of the source before citing it. It can help to return immediately to using your own words and tone, which will seldom be as fully professionalized as that of an expert. It can, however, be difficult to show when you are returning to your own thinking and your own voice, particularly in fields that do not allow the use of "I" and when using online sources that lack page numbers. Another way is to use transition words as cues when moving from the source to your voice:

- *On the other hand . . .*
- *To question this line of reasoning, however . . .*
- *Jones's ideas have dominated the field for a decade, but . . .*

Reading out loud and listening to the voices can help you hear whether or not you have made the distinction.

MAINTAINING A POINT OF VIEW

Researchers use sources in a number of ways, as you have already discovered:

- Sometimes writers use sources to provide authoritative evidence to support a claim.
- Sometimes they agree with the source's argument and want to extend it or build on it in some way.
- Sometimes writers use a source to distinguish their own position from that of the source, or to argue against it.
- To make their attitudes toward their sources clear, writers use cues to indicate where there are consensus and controversy and to state their own agreement or disagreement with a source.

It is important to distinguish your own position from the positions of your sources, not just to avoid a charge of plagiarism (see Chapter 3) or to avoid misrepresenting the source. Maintaining a consistent point of view reflects your judgments about the issues in your inquiry—and thus provides grounds for your argument.

In "The Dangerous Myth of Grade Inflation" (see Readings, p. 260), Alfie Kohn cites an often-quoted source in order to critique its methodology and conclusions; his rhetorical cues to agreement and disagreement are in italics:

> The fact is that *it is hard to substantiate even* the simple claim that grades have been rising. Depending on the time period we're talking about, *that claim may well be false.* In their book *When Hope and Fear Collide* (Jossey-Bass, 1998), Arthur Levine and Jeanette Cureton tell us that more undergraduates in 1993 reported receiving A's (and fewer reported receiving grades of C or below) compared with their counterparts in 1969 and 1976 surveys. *Unfortunately,* self-reports are *notoriously unreliable,* and the numbers *become even more dubious when only a self-selected, and possibly unrepresentative,* segment *bothers* to return the questionnaires. (One out of three failed to do so in 1993; no information is offered about the return rates in the earlier surveys.)

Notice that his claims about his source's methodology are not absolute—he leaves room for argument—but they are clear. He is not criticizing the methodology of surveys, but pointing out the unreliability of this particular survey because it does not meet criteria most social scientists consider necessary for generating reliable survey data. Kohn is equally clear about his agreement when he cites sources that support his argument:

> *To get a more accurate picture* of whether grades have changed over the years, one needs to look at official student transcripts. Clifford Adelman, a senior research analyst with the U.S. Department of Education, *did just that*, reviewing transcripts from more than 3,000 institutions and reporting his results in 1995. *His finding*: "Contrary to the widespread lamentations, grades actually declined slightly in the last two decades." *Moreover*, a report released just this year by the National Center for Education Statistics revealed that fully 33.5 percent of American undergraduates had a grade-point average of C or below in 1999–2000, *a number that ought to quiet* "all the furor over grade inflation," according to a spokesperson for the Association of American Colleges and Universities. (*A review of other research suggests a comparable lack of support* for claims of grade inflation at the high-school level.)

Writing much more personally and informally, as suits the newspaper opinion (or op-ed) piece "What Every Student Knows: Thou Shall Not Copy" (see Readings, p. 255), Robert Rivard clearly takes issue with readers who sent e-mails criticizing the firing of a local weatherman for representing downloaded weather reports as his own. The cues are again italicized:

> I've personally read more than 125 e-mails and letters now, the majority of them critical of editors and KENS management. To sum up our critics: We like Albert and do not think he deserved to lose his column or his job.
> *Many of those protesting our decision scare me.*
> What's wrong with what he did, anyway, they demand? Doesn't everyone do it, both at the *Express-News* and throughout society? Who do we think we are, acting against such a popular television personality? Isn't plagiarism something only journalists think is wrong?
> *Thank God for the teachers who have written in our defense.*

Although Rivard's informal tone here would be more appropriate for an "I-Search" paper than for a more formal research paper, he too offers strong and clear cues to his disagreement with the complaining readers and to his agreement with the teachers who disparage plagiarism.

Notice that these writers do not let sources "speak for themselves" or by themselves. Instead, they engage their sources in conversation in order to make a point. Although sometimes a writer's stance toward sources is direct agreement or disagreement, in academic writing the response is often nuanced, neither completely agreeing nor completely disagreeing with a source. Writers often find some validity in a source despite shifts in the consensus of their discipline. They may find some useful information in a source, even if they disagree with its conclusion. The more complicated the response to the source, the clearer the writer's rhetorical cues need to be.

In academic writing, writers are apt to respond to their sources as members of a discipline or of a group within it, in which case they adjust their ethos to mediate between a personal stance and what they identify as a conventional professional consensus. Therefore, it is useful to notice when a writer uses "we" or "us" and to consider who is included in those collective terms. For example, who is included and excluded in "our" when a writer says, "from our best evidence . . ." or "our usual position is . . ."? Writers often use a plural pronoun like "us," rather than the personal "me," when invoking a collective professional consensus rather than a personal opinion. To be effective, however, the pronoun must reflect actual consensus—a warrant or position that many or most people in the field would accept—or the argument can be dismissed as "unwarranted" and the writer perceived as not authoritative.

One way to practice conversation between writers and their sources is by using these cues when writing responses to sources throughout the inquiry. By consciously using cues to represent how the sources contribute to your growing body of reasoning and evidence and to point out arguments you find compelling or weak, you can lay groundwork for your argument as you write in other genres.

Exercises

6.1 PRACTICING QUOTATION

Working with one of the sources in the Readings, or with a source related to your developing topic, write the following kinds of quotations. Use the guidelines for punctuating quotations in this chapter.

1. A quotation of a single sentence that is introduced and followed by at least one sentence of your own.
2. A set-off quotation of 3–5 sentences, clearly and specifically introduced.
3. A quotation of 3–8 words that is integrated into a sentence of your own.

6.2 PRACTICING PARAPHRASE

Starting with the quotations you have already written, write three paraphrases that restate the author's meaning in your own words.

1. Consider how much of the context of the quotations you need to include in order not to alter the author's meaning and presumed intention.
2. Read the paraphrases of some of your classmates. Did any of them seem to come too near to the author's wording at any point? If there is any doubt, help each other rephrase them.

6.3 PRACTICING SUMMARY

Working with the same source, try summarizing, using one of the strategies described in the chapter.

1. Write a summary of about 150 words.
2. Discuss with a group of your classmates:
   - How well do you think your summary is structured?
   - Does the "formulaic strategy" seem too constricting?
   - How did you—or could you—modify it?
3. Trying to summarize often shows writers where they do not really understand a source. Highlight parts of the original source that you still are not clear about.
4. Identify which key words you included in the summary.

5. Write another 150-word summary using a different source.
6. Review the summary and condense it into summaries of one or two sentences that are appropriate for each of the four purposes demonstrated in this chapter (pp. 110–111). If you have another purpose in mind, you can substitute it, but be sure to identify it.
7. Discuss your revisions with your group, taking particular care to look for distortions of the author's meaning, and revise as necessary.

6.4 WORKING WITH SUMMARY AND SYNTHESIS

1. Take one of these summaries, and with a small group of students consider how it might be used to shape a synthesis involving the other readings in the research you have consulted in your inquiry.
2. Read at least two or three related sources in your working bibliography. Write a synthesis of the sources, based on important aspects of their claims or reasoning.
3. Working with the group, consider how the syntheses could be modified to be used for different purposes (see pp. 117–119). Write an opening statement for each kind of synthesis.
   • Highlight the words that serve as cues for the different purposes and describe how the opening statements change as you move from purpose to purpose. Using another color, highlight key words.
   • Add cues and key words as needed.
   • Make a list of those cues for later reference.

6.5 SYNTHESIZING SOURCES

1. To help organize your own thinking, write a synthesis of five sources relevant to your topic, identifying both the consensus and the controversy in the field you are working with. If there is an historical aspect to the controversy, this can be a good way to organize a synthesis to be adapted into an introduction.
2. Follow the synthesis with your preliminary thesis statement. Did the synthesis provide enough context to identify your argument as part of an ongoing conversation in its field? If necessary, revise the thesis to make it more specific or to show the significance of your project more clearly.
3. List any other possible significance of or uses for the research you are doing. What can be done with what you expect to show, and why does it matter?
4. With a group of fellow students, consider the revisions needed to make this synthesis, which you wrote to help organize your own thinking, to make it work to provide an argument for other audiences: the group, your class, and your instructor.
5. Based on these analyses, write a short paragraph or a bulleted list that describes the direction in which you plan to take the inquiry.

6.6 LISTENING FOR VOICE IN A SYNTHESIS

Work in groups of four for this exercise.

1. Each group member should take a part to read, and the writer should listen. One person should read any direct quotations, one should read summaries and paraphrases, and one should read the writer's part, including reflections, responses, transitions, and thesis.
2. Discuss what you heard; the writer should take notes on the discussion.
   • Does the writer's voice clearly guide you through the relations among the sources?
   • How authoritative does the writer's voice sound? Is it convincing without being arrogant? How might it be modified?

- How accurately were the sources summarized, as far as you know? Did the writer's voice clearly distinguish summary from response?
- How convinced were you by the synthesis? What could be improved?

3. Repeat this activity with other members of the group.

6.7 QUESTIONS FOR DISCUSSION AND INFORMAL WRITING

1. How has your understanding of your topic changed as you have deepened your reading in the field? How would you describe the state of your inquiry at this point in the process?

2. Can you see your topic in terms of some of the concepts of argumentation that have been raised so far, such as warrants, main claims, thesis, reasons, and evidence?

3. What kinds of reasons and evidence are you finding to support your ideas? What more can you foresee needing to support your thesis?

4. At what point can a student writer assume sufficient expertise to write with at least a semblance of authority about an issue of disagreement to experts? What is the student's responsibility to the field? To your classmates and research team? To a larger public?

CHAPTER 7

Revising and Editing to Meet Audience Expectations

Writers of all kinds know that revision is an important part of the writing process. It is not a punishment for poor performance or busywork for people with nothing better to do; rather, for most writers, it is the most important thing they do to increase how well they get across what they are trying to communicate. For many writers, it is also an important means of *discovering* what they are trying to say; seeing a draft of a project on the screen or page helps them judge more effectively the extent to which they have examined their research, how convincingly they have recorded it, what remains to be said. Editing is often defined as the aspect of revision that focuses more closely on sentences and on language-related elements. Although some students and teachers think of editing primarily as the correction of mistakes, the most effective editors not only correct sentences, but concentrate on how well a writer's choices about language lead to effective communication, to a good working relationship between the writer and the audience, and to clear connections among ideas and evidence. Learning to be an effective editor of your own work helps you hear your voice come through your writing and to use it as you think appropriate for different audiences, purposes, and occasions.

Students are often advised to start revising for larger issues before fine-tuning sentences for correctness and clarity. There are good reasons for this advice. It can be a waste of time to edit a paragraph into perfection, only to cut it entirely out of the paper. Even worse, the commitment you can feel after doing serious editing can make you reluctant to throw out a particularly eloquent paragraph that you later realize to be irrelevant, inconsistent with the argument, or just plain wrong.

The rationale for addressing conceptual issues before editorial corrections, useful as it can be for understanding the difference between revising and editing, does not reflect the actual practices of many experienced writers. Some writers might write a full draft, go back over it asking revision questions like the ones in Focus Points: Revising for Coherence (p. 130), revise the draft, and finally work at the sentence-level corrections that contribute to their readability and credibility. However, other writers combine revising and editing, using a recursive process of writing, going back and forth over the revising and editing phases of the process, trying to say more exactly what they mean at the same time as thinking about how to organize it and what needs to be added and deleted. Those larger concepts are conveyed through words and sentences, and usually good editing makes concepts and relationships among them clearer, especially in particularly important sentences like those at the beginnings and ends of paragraphs.

No matter in what order they do it, all writers have to deal with both conceptual revisions and editing after writing a first draft. If you haven't revised papers much, try starting with the big-picture issues unless you discover that another revision process works better for you. However, it is not a problem if you correct sentence errors as you revise for conceptual issues, or interrupt drafting to revise or rethink your ideas— provided that you continue to make reasonable progress toward completing the next draft. You need to figure out revision processes that work for you, to discover those processes that let you produce the most successful paper possible in the amount of time available to write it.

Some writers make printouts of their work, penciling in changes, which they then transcribe to the computer. Other writers—usually people who have had reliable, ongoing access to computers for most of their lives—do all their revising and editing with the text on screen. The medium you use for editing depends in part on whether you have better access to paper for printing or computers on which to work. If access to these resources is not an issue for you, use the method that you find most comfortable.

If your campus has a writing center, it can be very helpful to take your paper there for a consultation at one or more phases of the writing process, and certainly when you feel stuck. Most writing centers can give you further help in revising and editing papers (although they will *not* do that work for you), and they have handbooks and other resources available for student writers. One advantage of using your writing center is that having an outside reader can provide a valuable perspective on how well a draft communicates what you are trying to say.

FOCUS POINTS: REVISING FOR COHERENCE

Students often wonder if a paper "flows"—whether they have made sufficient connections from part to part. One way to check for coherence is to use the strategy for reading discussed in Chapters 2 and 6: extract the beginnings and endings of paragraphs to see if the connections between them are clear. Making the following "revision outline" can help you see where you need to make connections and use transition words and phrases.

1. Copy the first and last sentences of the introduction and conclusion and paste them into a separate document, with a space between each sentence.

2. Copy the first sentence of the middle paragraphs.

3. Read through this "sentence outline."
   - Does the order of the topic sentences seem basically reasonable? If not, how might you rearrange the paragraphs?
   - Can you follow the movement from sentence to sentence? If not, try revising these sentences so that they summarize the story or argument, adding transitional phrases or clauses to connect to the preceding paragraphs.
   - Try to identify key words and to incorporate them into these sentences.
   - Revise the sentences in the outline so that one claim leads to the next, as if you were writing a summary extracted from them. Then reinsert these sentences

back where they came from. Save the new version under a different name, in case you want to go back to the earlier version.

4. Review connections among key words, reconsider the development of your argument, and revise the paragraphs as necessary to fit the revised topic sentences.

5. Read the paper through. Revise again if what you are trying to say seems either unclear or overly repetitive.

MAKING EFFECTIVE TRANSITIONS

A revision outline can help you judge the overall coherence of the paper. However, even if the ideas are clear and the progression makes sense, almost all papers need to be revised for transitions. Writers see the relationships among their ideas from the inside, but transitions show those relationships to a reader. When you read your draft, you may see that some of the connections you should have written into it are still in your head. Transitions are particularly necessary in arguments, because the potential relationships among ideas in arguments can be so diverse: you can agree or disagree, modify and adapt, give examples, resolve apparent contradictions, and so on.

FOCUS POINTS: REVISING TO IMPROVE TRANSITIONS

■ Use transition words and terms to show specific relationships between ideas:

Addition: *Moreover, furthermore, in addition, also, and, not only . . . but also, first . . . second . . . third*

Negation or contrast: *however, on the other hand*

Cause and effect: *thus, therefore, hence*

Part and whole: *one aspect, one explanation*

Repetition: *in other words, that is, in short*

Transitional commands: *take this, consider this, to repeat*

■ Sometimes writers simply say what they are doing ("On the other hand," "for example, "to restate the question," "the most convincing reason"). You can also use a rhetorical question (that is, a question that you intend to answer) to make a transition, but rhetorical questions seem too informal to readers in many academic fields, particularly in the sciences and social sciences.

■ Use key words: You can build coherence by repeating important terms as the paper builds. For example, a "find" search for "grade inflation" on Alfie Kohn's argument (reprinted in the Readings and discussed in Chapter 2), shows that the term *grade inflation* occurs at least once and often twice in each paragraph, usually in the first or last sentence. *Grade, grades,* and *grading* are liberally scattered within the paragraphs, and variations on *inflation* are also used. Because these key words refer directly to important elements of the inquiry or argument, they keep readers focused on the issue and seldom seem repetitive.

• Make a list of terms you consider central to your understanding of your research, and then do a "find" search of the entire paper, counting when and where you used those key terms.

- Look for key terms among the words in the introduction, which established the context for the piece. In the process of drafting, writers often drop the words used in the introduction. Do a "find" search on the key words in the introduction to check whether you have dropped them later in the paper.
- Also look for key terms in the conclusion. Do a "find" search for any words that seem important to the conclusion, to see how often they are used in the paper. If you have not used these words before, consider how you can prepare for your conclusion by using them earlier in the paper.
- To strengthen your transitions, move as many of these key words as possible into the sentences in your revision outline.
- Put transition words and repeated words and concepts at the beginnings of sentences and paragraphs.[1] This is a good way of moving from sentence to sentence within a paragraph, and it is particularly useful for moving from claim to claim, from paragraph to paragraph, and from claim to support or from claim to reasons.

EXAMPLE 7.1 *Building Coherence with Transitions*

The following excerpt from James Paul Gee's book about video games (discussed more fully in Chapter 8) offers a good example of how effective transitions build coherence. As he moves from paragraph to paragraph, Gee arranges his sentences so that transitions and repetition of key words occur at the beginning of each paragraph. "Know" and "social practice" are key terms that the first sentence of the passage below repeats from preceding paragraphs. He uses these terms in various parts of speech ("know" and "knowledge") in order not to sound repetitive, and he reinforces the concepts with synonyms ("recognize") and references ("the same thing"). The italics show how key terms, a transitional command (*"Take something so simple as the following sentence about basketball"*), and repeated words and concepts are placed near the beginnings of sentences:

> *One can know a good deal about a social practice*—such as arguing before the Supreme Court, carrying out an experiment in nuclear physics, or memorializing an event in gang history through graffiti—without actually being able to participate in the social practice. *But knowing about a social practice* always involves *recognizing* various distinctive ways of acting, interacting, valuing, feeling, knowing, and using various objects and technologies that constitute the *social practice.*
>
> *Take something so simple as the following sentence about basketball*: "The guard dribbled down court, held up two fingers, and passed to the open man." *You may very well know* what every word in this sentence means in terms of dictionary definitions, but you cannot read the sentence with any real worthwhile understanding unless you can *recognize*, in some sense (perhaps only in simulations in your mind), guards, dribbling, basketballs, open men, and basketball courts. *But to be able to recognize* these things is to already *know* a good deal about basketball as a game, that is, as a particular sort of *social practice. The same thing is equally* true about any sentence or text about the law, comic books, a branch of science, or anything else for that matter. (15)

If you try rewriting these paragraphs so that all the italicized terms come at the ends of sentences, you will eliminate the coherence Gee built into the published version.

SETTING PRIORITIES FOR EDITING

In all disciplines, editing your work is crucial. On the most basic level, editing includes reviewing and correcting the paper for standard English usage, clear sentence structure and style, and using an appropriate voice for your audience—but these language issues come to seem much less basic when you consider your writing from the reader's point of view. Editing is very important to readers, because those language features are the first features they see. Attempts to use a professional voice will not succeed if a paper seems poorly edited and proofread. In business and professional communication, a report that is not clear and correct will seldom be accepted as valid in content. It is particularly important that the sentences that begin and end paragraphs are correct and clear, because—as you have already seen—these will be read with particular attention by most readers. They are the sentences readers seek when skimming, and the revision process, as described above, involves using these sentences to make connections clear and convincing.

Editing sentences is easier if you distinguish between correcting errors and increasing clarity. Managers tend to think that mistakes in writing may indicate mistakes in measurement, pricing, and other more countable features of a project, whether or not that idea is true. Because few readers in professional situations are willing to read beyond surface errors, learning to edit your work is a crucial skill in any field, both in the university and in the workplace. If you think (or are told) that you make a lot of mistakes when writing, it might be useful to start by editing for correctness. But many writers start by editing for clarity because the process of comparing what you mean to say with what your sentences actually do say can help you correct some of the mistakes that tend to creep into writing.

Editing for Clarity

Sentences with clarity problems often follow the rules for correct language, but are nonetheless difficult to follow. Even though unclear sentences may distract readers or make them find a piece difficult to read, if they need the information, most readers will probably plod their way through. If you've ever had the feeling, "He knows his stuff but just can't communicate," you were probably responding to some kind of problem with clarity. However, although an unclear piece of writing may be reasonably argued and well supported, it will seldom have the impact the writer hopes for. If readers can find the information they need elsewhere, they may abandon the piece before finishing it.

FOCUS POINTS: EDITING FOR WORDINESS AND CHOPPINESS

Two major obstacles to clarity are wordiness and choppiness; the revisions below offer one possible solution—but other solutions are possible. Any handbook will offer detailed explanations and examples of how to edit for clearer style. Stylistic problems, unlike usage mistakes, are a matter of constructing better or worse sentences, not necessarily of correcting grammatical errors.

- *Wordy sentences:* Minimize nominalizations, repetition, unnecessary words, and use of the passive voice.

  Example

  The fact that the discovery of plagiarism can result in the student's failing a paper or even an entire class doesn't seem to hinder students from trying to find methods or ways to avoid writing their own papers. This persistence in the appropriation of other peoples' writing is a major frustration for teachers and instructors in all fields.

One Revision

Even though students can fail a paper or an entire course if they are discovered plagiarizing, they still seek ways to avoid writing their own papers. Instructors in all fields are highly frustrated by students' persistence in appropriating other peoples' writing.

Example

Notification of the termination of the experiment was given only at the point at which it was too late for the participants to undertake the rescheduling of their activities.

One Revision

The participants were notified that the experiment was over too late for them to reschedule their activities.

■ *Choppy sentences or "lack of flow":* Combine short sentences and rearrange the word order to put repeated or key words and concepts at the beginnings of sentences.

Example

Public education has been severely criticized. Democracy depends on informed citizens. Many teachers work hard. Students learn to think problems through when they have effective teachers.

One Revision

Public education had been severely criticized because well-educated citizens are necessary in a democracy. However, students do learn to participate in a democracy and to think problems through when they have hardworking and effective teachers.

Example

Watson and Crick discovered the shape of DNA. It took many years of research. Scientists do not always achieve such notable results. Sometimes only small discoveries are the result of a long research career.

One Revision

Watson and Crick discovered the shape of DNA after many years of research. However, scientists do not always achieve such notable results, and a long research career may result in only small discoveries.

Editing for Correctness

Most readers immediately recognize grammatical errors, even if they cannot name them. While one or two may be disregarded as due to hasty proofreading, these errors can quickly and seriously undermine your credibility, and you should work to eliminate them, even though this may take some work on your part. You probably already know that while it is always necessary to check spelling, it is not sufficient to rely solely on the spelling and grammar checking functions of a word-processing program.

An effective way to edit for correctness is to keep a personal list of grammatical errors you often make. If you find yourself making sentence errors often, ask your instructor or a tutor at your campus writing center to help you identify your patterns of error and learn what they are called, so that you can learn to recognize them yourself and look them up by name in a handbook. You can also consult an online writing lab (OWL), either at your own writing center's Web site, or elsewhere. Some widely used sites (available free for everyone to use) are

Purdue University Online Writing Lab (OWL) (owl.english.purdue.edu/owl/)

Writing at the University of Toronto (www.utoronto.ca/writing/)

Carnegie Mellon's writing resources (www-2.cs.cmu.edu/afs/cs.cmu.edu/project/fox/mosaic/people/mleone/how-to.html)

The Massachusetts Institute of Technology's Writing and Communication Center (web.mit.edu/writing/)

The University of Wisconsin Writing Center (www.wisc.edu/writing/Handbook/index.html)

Keeping a personal list of errors is not easy, but it can be effective. The suggestions below can give you a start by identifying some of the most common grammatical errors college students make, errors that can undermine the credibility of your argument. If you recognize them in your own writing, they can offer a place to start working on correcting them. This is by no means a complete list, nor does it offer grammatical explanations, but it offers a starting place for your personal list and gives you some of the language you need to look for explanations.

FOCUS POINTS: FIVE COMMON SENTENCE ERRORS

■ *Failure of agreement of subject and verb*

Incorrect

Most of the people who care about this controversy, with the exception of the occasional crackpot, has a financial stake in its outcome.

Correct

Most of the people who care about this controversy, with the exception of the occasional crackpot, have a financial stake in its outcome.

Incorrect

Coming up in the fall, there are a series of debates about cost-cutting measures in particular academic departments.

Correct

Coming up in the fall, there is a series of debates about cost-cutting measures in particular academic departments.

Incorrect

Every last one of us need to know not only how to use the technology at our disposal, but also how to anticipate our future needs.

Correct

Every last one of us needs to know not only how to use the technology at our disposal, but also how to anticipate our future needs.

■ *Disagreement of a pronoun with the noun it stands for or unclear reference of pronouns*

Incorrect

People who make up data are considered serious violators of the ethical codes not only of journalism, but also of most other professional fields, and he or she should expect to be caught and sanctioned if they try it.

Correct

People who make up data are considered serious violators of the ethical codes not only of journalism, but also of most other professional fields, and they should expect to be caught and sanctioned if they try it.

Incorrect

A writer who needs information cannot simply invent it, and the cases in which they are caught doing that should be instructive.

Correct

Writers who need information cannot simply invent it, and the cases in which they are caught inventing data should be instructive.

■ *Using object pronouns in subject positions*

Incorrect

Us women need to be careful about language issues, particularly when considering inclusive language.

Correct

We women need to be careful about language issues, particularly when considering inclusive language. *Or:* Women like us need to be careful about language issues, particularly when considering inclusive language.

Incorrect

Me and my friends prefer watching movies to reading novels.

Correct

My friends and I prefer watching movies to reading novels.

Incorrect

When various members of my department and me discuss issues of intellectual property, we do not always agree.

Correct

When various members of my department and I consider issues of intellectual property, we do not always agree. *Or:* When I discuss issues of intellectual property with members of my department, we do not always agree.

■ *Sentence fragments*

Incorrect

We worked particularly hard to reach a consensus. Because the possibilities for disagreement were so great and the consequences so serious if we could not finally hammer out an agreement.

Correct

We worked particularly hard to reach a consensus because the possibilities for disagreement were so great and the consequences so serious if we could not finally hammer out an agreement.

Incorrect

Searching for a job took a lot more time and work than I expected. Writing a résumé, meeting with recruiters, and going to onsite interviews.

Correct

Searching for a job took a lot more time and work than I expected, including writing a résumé, meeting with recruiters, and going to onsite interviews.

■ *Comma splices*

Incorrect

A professional voice takes years to develop, years of education and experience in a field, no one expects it to come quickly or naturally to even the best of students.

Correct

> A professional voice takes years to develop, years of education and experience in a field. No one expects it to come quickly or naturally to even the best of students. *Or:* A professional voice takes years to develop, years of education and experience in a field, and therefore no one expects it to come quickly or naturally to even the best of students.

Incorrect

> Because the data[2] were hard to interpret, the research group reached a stalemate at the first session, the discussion was resumed the following week with even less success at resolving the problem.

Correct

> Because the data were hard to interpret, the research group reached a stalemate at the first session; the discussion was resumed the following week with even less success at resolving the problem.

FINAL EDITING: SENTENCES, SOURCES, AND PROOFREADING

Final editing involves getting the paper ready to face its readers. Start by skimming the paper yet again, reading the introduction, first sentences of paragraphs, and the conclusion. Can you grasp the progression of the argument from this skimming? Rewrite the first sentences of the paragraphs in which the progression is not clear.

FOCUS POINTS: FINAL EDITING STRATEGIES

- When you finish revising and editing, skim the paper to check the *clarity* of those important first and last sentences of paragraphs. Revise if needed.
- Think about the sentences flagged by the grammar check in your word-processing program. You cannot rely on the grammar check very much, since it will flag many stylistic features (like the passive voice) that are actually correct, and it will misread some sentences, but it *can* alert you to errors that you have overlooked. If it flags errors on your personal list (like sentence fragments or comma splices, for example), double-check those sentences carefully.
- With a partner, read your papers aloud to each other. Mark the places where something sounds wrong, awkward, or out of place to one of you, so that the writer can return to work on it later. Listen to the tone of the paper. Does it seem appropriate for its audience?

Proofreading

Proofread when you are almost finished with the paper. Proofreading is different than editing or revision because it involves looking for small mistakes that you may have overlooked before and for errors introduced in the process of revising and editing. You may see bigger problems (which you may or may not have time to change), but while proofreading, you should particularly look for small but distracting mistakes in typing and wording that you may have missed earlier.

FOCUS POINTS: EFFECTIVE PROOFREADING

- Read the paper aloud to yourself, straight through, correcting errors as you proceed. When returning to proofreading after making a correction, backtrack a few sentences to regain your focus.

- If you can exchange papers with a friend, proofread each other's papers.
- If your instructor requires certain stylistic features (for example, not using contractions or words like *I* or *we* or *you*), run a "find" check for these words. You can also run a "find" check for apostrophes to check for errors in their use.
- Read the paper to yourself backwards, one sentence at a time. This can be a particularly effective way of catching and eliminating sentence-level mistakes.

DISCIPLINARY CONVENTIONS AND DOCUMENT DESIGN

Finally, although it might seem like a minor point, document design can be much more important than it seems at first. Effective document design, like other aspects of writing, depends on your audience and purpose and on the kind of material you are presenting. Most professions have definite expectations about how documents should look and how information should be displayed, but these expectations differ from field to field. It is worthwhile to find out the standard style manual for the field for which you are writing and to adapt your papers and presentations to that style. It is also useful to examine typical pieces of academic and workplace writing in the field you hope to enter in order to consider how these conventions look in practice.

FOCUS POINTS: DETERMINING DISCIPLINE-SPECIFIC CONVENTIONS

Ask these questions about documents in a field to help identify conventions of specific disciplines.

- See the Quick Guide to Documentation for short guides to MLA, APA, and Chicago style conventions. What features demonstrate the professionalism of a writer in the field you are working in? Will readers expect a title page, a table of contents, and a list of references or works cited? If so, where should they be placed in the document, what information should be included in them, and how should they be arranged? How should the document look on the page to create a polished, professional impression? Because computer technology has made it possible to make home-produced documents look much more polished than was possible with earlier technologies, the expectations for how even informal documents should look have escalated over the past two decades.
- Should the paper be double-spaced or single-spaced? Divided into sections or not? What information should section subtitles carry?
- How much quotation, paraphrase, or summary does the document contain? How are references managed?
- When and how are visuals used; that is, do writers in the field normally include visuals such as charts, graphs, tables, or pictures in their paper or presentation? Are they essential elements, or occasional extra features? Where are they in a typical document, and how do they look? See Appendix B for more information on designing and using visuals.
- Is the content accurate? Does the writer accurately gauge the level of understanding of the field that the audience may have?
- Is it easy to follow the paper from part to part?
- Is the significance of the inquiry or argument clear?

EXAMPLE 7.2 *Making Professional Decisions about Document Design*

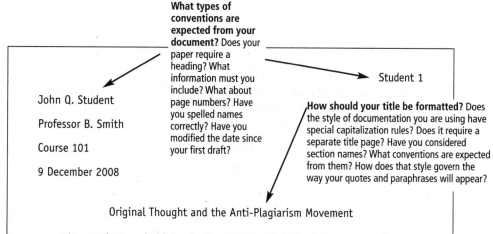

What types of conventions are expected from your document? Does your paper require a heading? What information must you include? What about page numbers? Have you spelled names correctly? Have you modified the date since your first draft?

Student 1

How should your title be formatted? Does the style of documentation you are using have special capitalization rules? Does it require a separate title page? Have you considered section names? What conventions are expected from them? How does that style govern the way your quotes and paraphrases will appear?

John Q. Student

Professor B. Smith

Course 101

9 December 2008

Original Thought and the Anti-Plagiarism Movement

As a sophomore in high school, I had the misfortune of transferring schools twice, tempting me to be initially unhappy with wherever I ended up. I ended up in a private Catholic college preparatory school in Indianapolis, Indiana. This school is well known for its scholastic fortitude as well as its athletic prominence. Because my school was so well known for its academic aptitude and integrity, its policy considering plagiarism was especially strict. Blatant plagiarism could result in expulsion.

The problem that became a major issue for me was what exactly constituted plagiarism in the first place? Unfortunately I came face to face with this issue when my sophomore English teacher approached me one day, rather upset, with the idea that I had plagiarized a paper I had written discussing the Anti-transcendentalist nature of Herman Melville. Knowing that I had not plagiarized this paper and rather shocked at the mere accusation, I started writing at a lower level than I was capable of. I eventually discovered that my teacher's accusations were based simply on the rather high level of vocabulary I had used in the Melville paper. Thinking back on this moment, I am at a loss to see how a high vocabulary is a means

Have you considered manipulating the white space of your document? Do your images, figures, and graphs blend well with your document? Does the white space give the text a fuller, richer feel, or does it appear more like space to satisfy page length requirements? Do items appear overly cramped?

What are the expectations for margins and spacing in your document? Should your margins be set at a specific width? Should you use double-spacing or single? Does your document include footnote space or have gutter requirements?

What is plagiarism?

• Using someone else's work as your own?

• Copying and pasting?

• Purchasing another's work?

What conventions govern the use of figures and images in your document? Are these additional items necessary to your text? Do you refer to them in the text? When necessary, do you label them and provide background information for them?

Exercises

7.1 REVISING

Choose the longest piece you have written about your inquiry so far, and make a revision outline from it.

1. Read it for use of key words, transitions, and connections between paragraphs.
2. Run the "find" searches for key words suggested in Focus Points: Revising for Coherence (p. 130) and Focus Points: Revising to Improve Transitions (p. 131).
3. Revise the piece using these strategies to improve its coherence.
4. Make sure you have explicitly stated the significance of the piece, and revise that statement if necessary.
5. Write a short reflection considering what you would redo or do differently if you had another week to work on the project.

7.2 EDITING

1. Reread at least four of the pieces you have written so far. Underline any sentences that seem wrong to you (either incorrect, unclear, or "unidentifiably wrong").
2. Choose one paper to reedit, and read it aloud, preferably with a partner. In each paragraph, consider where you need to work with Focus Points: Editing for Wordiness and Choppiness (p. 133), and make the necessary corrections.
3. Working with a partner or small group, or in conference with your teacher, identify the errors by name and look up solutions for the problems in any handbook.
4. Correct the errors and reread the paper.
5. Start a list with the names of at least six of your most frequent errors, so that you can edit your papers for them and look them up again when necessary.

7.3 WORKING WITH CONVENTIONS FOR DOCUMENT DESIGN

Choose one of the sources cited in your research work. Using the appropriate style manual:

1. Make a list of what seem to be the most apparent conventions in the field and a list of questions that you still have about how those conventions work.
2. Share lists with classmates working in the same general area, and compile them into a single list of observations and questions.
3. Interview a faculty member in the field about how accurate your list is, what he or she thinks makes for effective writing in the field, and what the expectations are for how a document should look (based on your list of questions).
4. Write a short account of what seem to be the most discipline-specific aspects of how documents are expected to look in this particular field.

CHAPTER 8

Adapting Writing for Professional Audiences

Even though many instructions about writing may seem to have the authority of general rules that operate everywhere, it is more useful to think about academic writing as a body of discipline-specific "conventions," or agreed-upon practices that change over time, that vary from field to field, and that need to be applied with a healthy dose of common sense. Although effective writing in all fields depends on using strategies for accurate research, clear and professional language, and a coherent presentation of evidence, these qualities vary from field to field. Effective writing depends on thoughtfully adapting to the audience, purpose, and situation for which a document is produced. Because they are shared by researchers in the field, they can not only help to develop your sense of audience, but also to establish your ethos by demonstrating your awareness of the professional expectations of a particular field. While conventions are rarely absolute, they are useful guides to normal, everyday behavior and practice in a field, and using them successfully shows that a person has enough expertise in a field to participate in its conversations. You might think about the conventions of a field as guides to thinking, rather than replacements for it.

Many conventions are so deeply engrained in a field that they are passed along but seldom discussed. They come to seem like natural and normal aspects of good writing to experienced practitioners. Becoming a member of a discipline involves learning how people in it work, and the process of learning to work within disciplinary conventions is subtler than merely learning and following rules. While there are a few written codes that embody major elements of a field's ethics (like rules against plagiarism, falsifying data, or abusing human subjects), some conventional assumptions and procedures are expected without being directly stated. For example, when people are new to a place or an institution, they often notice some conventions and miss others—sometimes in embarrassing ways. Some conventions are institution-specific. For example, whether students call faculty "Professor," "Dr.," "Mr.," and "Ms." or by their first name depends on the conventions of the particular school—and sometimes the particular department— they are in. When the expected usages are not explicitly stated, newcomers have to rely on general goodwill and good manners—and hope for the best. But they also tend to look at how other, more experienced people behave. The same is true in writing.

EXAMPLE 8.1 *Conventions Discovered*

Many conventions of speaking and writing vary from discipline to discipline in ways that are taken for granted. In the e-mail that follows, an engineering professor describes his embarrassment when asked to speak at a national conference of English professors. His e-mail to his English Department colleagues on the panel dramatizes how he discovered the significant and potentially embarrassingly different expectations for oral presentations between the two fields—expectations that were so ingrained in each field that although they were perfectly obvious to members of one academic community, they were invisible even to good friends in the other.

> E-Mail from Professor John Way (then Professor of Mechanical Engineering at the Illinois Institute of Technology) to Professor Linda Bergmann (formerly his colleague at IIT, but at that time Associate Professor of English and Director of Writing Across the Curriculum at the University of Missouri-Rolla), Dave (an English professor at IIT), and Tony (a teaching assistant).

> From: "John L. Way"
> Date: Mon, 06 Apr 1998 17:25:02 -0500
>
> Subject: Eureka!

Linda, Dave, Tony—
  I'm submitting this little drama as a candidate for one more item in Linda's list of "cultural differences."
  First, however, I'd like to thank you all for the opportunity to participate in the panel. As you will see, it was most memorable for me, and I wouldn't have missed it for anything.
  **Palmer House, early (for me) Saturday morning:
  On the way up to the third floor, I worry about appearing unprofessional during my talk by referring to a piece of paper with some ordered key words on it. I pull the page out in a futile hope that I might be able to memorize the list.
  But too soon I locate Dining Room 8, walk in and there is Linda—it is so good to see her! I'm curious about the typed sheets that she places on the table. Dave arrives and then disappears. Here's Tony, and he also has some typed pages. Was I supposed to bring a typed version of my talk to submit for a conference proceedings or something? Dave reappears and we all sit down. I feel much better because Dave doesn't . . . Ohmygod—he pulls out HIS typed pages!
  Here I sit with a few key words scribbled on a lined pad (albeit the fourth or fifth version). Maybe they'll take my typed version on Monday. Why didn't I check this out with Dave when he asked if I had any questions? Oh well, I wouldn't have thought to ask about this. Maybe I missed some instructions in the tons of conference material that I received. Too late now.
  Dave introduces us and Linda starts—BY READING FROM HER TYPED PAGES!
  Panic time! Part way through she begins to ad lib—that's a small relief. Will everyone think that I'm not interested enough to even type up

my comments? Dave reads his talk—I'll have to remember to glance down at my key words often, as if there's lots of stuff there. Tony reads his talk—maybe I can rip off a few blank pages and shuffle through them as I talk. Naw, the rest of the panel will notice.

**Eisenhower Expressway:

After a great lunch, while driving home, the phrase "read a paper" comes to mind. I have heard this phrase several times from Linda, from Dave, from the Writing Director Search Committee members. Each time I thought the phrase somewhat stilted—why don't "they" use a more descriptive phrase (as "we" do): "present a paper," or "give a presentation," or "give a talk?"

The light bulb flashes ON somewhere around Pulaski—"they" write a PAPER and then READ it! Why didn't I catch on to this earlier? It suddenly makes a great deal of sense. "They" write for a living, and reading what "they" write is the best way to talk about it. Eureka!

I believe that I can speak for most, if not all, engineering disciplines when I state that "reading a paper" is considered very poor style in our line of work. This method is practiced only by utterly terrified students presenting work at their first conference in front of Gods they have worshiped from afar. After all, it's hard to do anything BUT read with the thought "they're going to crucify me" constantly in mind.

Even though there is some small place for opinion in engineering, one's arguments CAN be proved wrong. A typical question anticipated during the discussion period might be: "Are you aware that Zamboni's Third Theorem invalidates all your work?" (Chuckle from the audience.)

A speaker's confidence and stature is perceived to be directly related to how LITTLE he/she refers to "supporting material." Come to think of it, the Propulsion group in my capstone design class (Odysseus - Manned Mission to Mars) is re-presenting their propulsion seminar to the class tomorrow precisely because they read their first presentation from typed pages (totally unacceptable—naughty, naughty—you should have known better!).

Well, this has turned out to be more of a tome than I originally intended. However, the next time any of you mention "reading a paper" in my presence, expect a knowing smile in response instead of a questioning frown.

John

PS—Linda, I apologize for using up the entire panel's lifetime supply of exclamation marks in one email!

Notice that the different disciplinary conventions for presentations are not represented as better or worse—but simply as different and appropriate to the work of each discipline.

Questions

- What conventions in each field are described in the e-mail?
- Notice that both Professor Way and Professor Bergmann to some extent violated the conventions under which they were operating. (He has written down his key words, and she departs from her written paper to talk informally with the audience.) What might this imply about how conventions are used in practice?

- Although the writer and his readers come from very different fields, they share considerable knowledge. Identify some of that shared knowledge.

- What does this story show about how conventions affect the relation between writer (or speaker) and audience? Can you see similar misunderstanding of conventions in other experiences you have had in college? Have you experienced similar misunderstandings at school or work?

PROFESSIONAL KNOWLEDGE AND PROFESSIONAL VOICE

Professional knowledge is gained through being educated for and practicing in a profession and by learning its "common knowledge," which includes specific styles and genres of writing. Researchers and practitioners in a field

- know its conventions of thought and practice and the theories on which they are based;

- have some common grounding in the research that supports the theories;

- can recognize the names of authorities and have a working understanding of how to distinguish authoritative sources from those that are not; and

- know the conventions of behavior and communication in the profession, and usually adhere to them.

Researchers learn discipline-specific language not only from textbooks and discipline-specific reading, but also from practicing and comparing their practices with those of their peers.

Professional language and writing conventions are part of what is sometimes called "domain knowledge," since field-specific knowledge is not limited to academic fields or the professions but is also used by participants in leisure activities like video game playing or sports. For instance, as the linguist James Paul Gee argues below, it takes a considerable amount of domain knowledge to understand a sentence about basketball, at least some of which can be derived from watching and listening to the game, without necessarily playing it:

> One can know a good deal about a social practice—such as arguing before the Supreme Court, carrying out an experiment in nuclear physics, or memorializing an event in gang history through graffiti—without actually being able to participate in the social practice. But knowing about a social practice always involves recognizing various distinctive ways of acting, interacting, valuing, feeling, knowing, and using various objects and technologies that constitute the social practice.
>
> Take something so simple as the following sentence about basketball: "The guard dribbled down court, held up two fingers, and passed to the open man." You may very well know what every word in this sentence means in terms of dictionary definitions, but you cannot read the sentence with any real worthwhile understanding unless you can recognize, in some sense (perhaps only in simulations in your mind), guards, dribbling, basketballs, open men, and basketball courts. But to be able to recognize

these things is already to know a good deal about basketball as a game, that is, as a particular sort of social practice. The same thing is equally true about any sentence or text about the law, comic books, a branch of science, or anything else for that matter.

We can go further. One's understanding of the sentence "The guard dribbled down court, held up two fingers, and passed to the open man" is different—in some sense, deeper and better—the more one knows and can recognize about the social practice (game) of basketball. For example, if you know a good bit about basketball, you may see that one possible meaning of this sentence is that the guard signaled a particular play by holding up two fingers and then passed to the player the play left momentarily unguarded.

But then this brings us to another important point. While you don't need to be able to enact a particular social practice (e.g., play basketball or argue before a court) to be able to understand texts from or about that social practice, you can potentially give deeper meanings to those texts if you can. This claim amounts to arguing that producers (people who can actually engage in a social practice) potentially make better consumers (people who can read or understand texts from or about the social practice). (15)

Most people with even a casual contact with basketball or American culture have enough common knowledge about basketball to keep from reading "dribble" as "drool" and "court" as "courtroom," but have less understanding (except in a very general way) of "open man" or "guard" than a fan who watches basketball games, listens to the commentary, and reads the sports pages. A person who actually plays will find even more meaning in the sentence.

ADAPTING LANGUAGE TO THE AUDIENCE AND OCCASION

Looking at a piece of writing as rhetorical work means considering how the writer (you or someone else) shaped the piece to its purpose, audience, and occasion. Writers who understand the purpose of and audience for a piece of writing can build their ethos—their voice of authority and reliability—by fitting their language to the expectations and professional expertise of a particular audience. When writing for an audience that doesn't know much about the field, they make connections between the common knowledge of the audience and key concepts in their field, and so they define and discuss those concepts in common language and popular culture. For example, James Paul Gee, in the previous excerpt from *What Video Games Can Teach Us about Learning and Literacy*, uses examples from sports and video games to introduce and explain important concepts in linguistics like "domain knowledge" and to introduce a linguist's definition of literacy, which includes social understanding as well as understanding individual words. On the other hand, an audience of professional peers would expect a researcher to draw from ongoing conversations in the field, use the field's more specialized terminology, and support claims with evidence generally accepted by other practitioners. Compare the excerpt from James Paul Gee's *Video Games*, addressed to an educated general public, with the following excerpt from his earlier book, *An Introduction to Discourse Analysis: Theory and Method*. This book, Gee explains in the introduction, is aimed at "students and researchers in other areas" (8) (probably other areas of linguistics), for people (probably scholars) who may be new to discourse analysis, and for "my colleagues in discourse studies" (8), who use discourse analysis as one of several methodologies for analyzing language:

> It is crucial to realize that to "know" a situated meaning is not merely to be able to "say certain words," e.g., "a cup of coffee," but to be able to recognize a pattern (e.g., a cup of coffee) in a variety of settings and variations. This is what makes situated meanings both contextualized and somewhat general.
>
> To see this point in another domain, one more important for education, consider again the notion of "light" in physics. First of all, our everyday cultural model for "light" is not, as we have seen, the same as the model (theory) of "light" in physics. That model is the specialized theory of electromagnetic radiation. It is more overt and articulated than most cultural models.
>
> In physics, "light" is associated with a variety of situated meanings— e.g., as a bundle of waves of different wave lengths; as particles (photons) with various special (quantum-like) properties; as a beam that can be directed in various ways and for various purposes (e.g., lasers); as colors that can mix in various fashions, and more. If one wants to start "practicing" with light, so as to learn physics, then one has to get eyes that lead to the acquisition of a few situated meanings (mid-level, contextualized patterns in one's pattern recognizer that can guide action). Otherwise, one really cannot understand what the theory of light has to explain, at least not in any way that could efficaciously guide pattern recognition and action and reflection.
>
> But I must admit now that I myself do not understand (in any embodied way) these various physically-situated meanings well enough to really have a deep understanding, despite the fact that I have read and can recite lots of the scientific theory behind light in physics. To really teach me, you would have to insure that I got experiences that allowed my mind/brain to really recognize patterns at the level of situated meanings.
>
> And what does it mean to "recognize" these? Situated meanings are correlations of various features, they are patterns that associate various features with each other, e.g., light-as-a-particle-that-behaves-in-terms-of-various-sorts-of-contrived-(experimental)-observations-in-certain-characteristic-quantum-like-ways. To recognize such things is to be able to recognize (reconstruct in terms of one's pattern-recognizing capabilities) and to be able to act-on-and-with these various features and their associations in a range of contexts. One's body and mind have to be able to be situated with (coordinated by and with) these correlated features in the world. Otherwise you have my sort of understanding. (50–51)

Because this book was written for a more specialized audience, Gee describes his research with more complexity than he anticipates would be acceptable to the more general audience. Thus, he uses the example of understanding physics, another academic domain, rather than the popular domain of basketball. In the *Video Games* book, he builds his ethos for a general audience by tempering his professional expertise with his ability to convey his ideas relatively simply, through the popular language of sports. He takes on the voice of a professor who knows how to speak to the public. In the

Introduction to Discourse Analysis, on the other hand, he builds his ethos by comparing his professional knowledge as an expert in discourse analysis with his position as a "spectator" of physics, able to comprehend and repeat some important concepts in that academic field (and even "pass a test"), but not really understanding it with the "embodied knowledge" he attributes to a physicist. In the *Video Games* book, where he is trying to introduce some of the more important conclusions of discourse analysis to the public discussion of learning and literacy, he minimizes technical jargon. In the *Introduction to Discourse Analysis,* on the other hand, Gee freely uses the technical terms of discourse analysis, like "situated meanings," "embodied recognition," and "pattern recognition," since his purpose here is to introduce students and other potential practitioners to the language and methodologies of his discipline.

AUDIENCE, PERFORMANCE, AND WRITING

Sometimes students find the concept of audience hard to apply to college writing assignments. Thinking about the following questions may help you see some specific experiences you have already had with audiences and their expectations.

1. Describe an occasion when you felt a strong sense of having an audience for something you have written or perhaps for some other thing you have done, such as participating in a musical performance, an athletic event, a presentation, a prom, or wedding. Was that audience a single person or a group of people? What did you know about their expectations, and how did that knowledge make you feel? How can an awareness of audience enhance performance? On the other hand, how does a sense of audience limit how and what you perform? How might you apply this awareness of performance to your writing?

2. How do you think the writing for the following audiences could affect the way you write?
   • an audience that needs information in order to make a crucial decision
   • an audience that is hostile to the point you are making
   • an audience that will probably agree with your point
   • an audience that has more specialized knowledge in the field than you have

3. Most students find it difficult to imagine writing for an audience with specific expectations and needs, and instead imagine a "general audience," which often boils down to no audience at all. How can you more clearly define the actual audience for which you are researching your inquiry?

VIOLATING CONVENTIONS

As noted earlier, professional conventions are often so deeply embedded in the writing process that researchers communicating to their peers do not even think about them; this was the point of Professor Way's account of his discovery of what his colleagues in English meant by "reading a paper." His concern that the audience might think he had not prepared for his presentation is a concern about the ethos he will project: will that particular audience take his conclusions seriously when he seems to be, in their terms, unprofessional? Sometimes it is easier to see disciplinary conventions when there are lapses from them, whether intended or not. When a professional researcher like Professor Way found himself fumbling through an encounter with unfamiliar conventions, he used the experience as an opportunity not only to laugh at himself and to share his discomfort with old friends and collaborators, but also to reflect on how disciplinary differences can take even experienced scholars by surprise. The key phrase in the anecdote concerns the "transparency" of disciplinary conventions, which we can see when Professor Way asks himself, "Why didn't I check this out with Dave when he asked if I had any questions? Oh well, I wouldn't have thought to ask about this." Moreover, he uses the informal language of friend to friends, a different language than he would use in a publication about mechanical engineering, and a different language than his colleagues would use in a rhetorical analysis.

Practiced writers in a field sometimes break some of the conventions and get away with it, particularly if their readers are apt to be familiar with their work already. For example, some academic writers use personal pronouns like "I" or "we" in professional publications in certain situations, even though most style guides say to avoid them. Likewise, sometimes writers tell personal stories and create a personal context for an academic argument, in order to expose and admit their own possible biases. However, few writers ignore *all* the conventions of their field when writing professional research, because this could call into question their expertise.

EXAMPLE 8.2 *Conventions at Work in "'Indians': Textualism, Morality, and the Problem of History"*

In the essay "'Indians': Textualism, Morality, and the Problem of History," Jane Tompkins uses personal pronouns and anecdotes, and tells the story of her research rather than directly arguing for its results—even though she is writing to a professional audience whom she wants to accept her conclusions.

> When I was growing up in New York City, my parents used to take me to an event in Inwood Park at which Indians—real American Indians dressed in feathers and blankets—could be seen and touched by children like me. This event was always a disappointment. It was more fun to imagine that you *were* an Indian in one of the caves in Inwood Park than to shake the hand of an old man in a headdress who was not overwhelmed at the opportunity of meeting you. After staring at the Indians for a while, we would take a walk in the woods where the caves were, and once I asked my mother if the remains of a fire I had seen in one of them might have been left by the original inhabitants. (101)

But in other matters, she follows the conventions expected of literary historians listed below.

1. Tompkins' review of previous historians' interpretations of the relations between Native Americans and colonists is organized chronologically, as most readers in English studies or history would expect it to be organized. Moreover, she clearly compares the ideas of the 30-year-old text to current thinking in the field:

   > My research began with Perry Miller. Early in the preface to *Errand into the Wilderness,* while explaining how he came to write his history of the New England mind, Miller writes a sentence that stopped me dead. He says

that what fascinated him as a young man about his country's history was "the massive narrative of the movement of European culture into the vacant wilderness of America." "Vacant"? Miller, writing in 1956, doesn't pause over the word "vacant," but to people who read his preface thirty years later, the word is shocking. In what circumstances could someone proposing to write a history of colonial New England *not* take account of the Indian presence there? (103)

She continues the chronology, pointing out that the next book starts from Miller's important (if flawed) work:

A book entitled *New England Frontier: Puritans and Indians, 1620–1675,* written by Alden Vaughan and published in 1965, promised to rectify Miller's omission.

Again, she returns to a chronological account of how historians have changed their thinking about relationships between colonists and natives:

Francis Jennings's *The Invasion of America* (1975) rips wide open the idea that the Puritans were humane and considerate in their dealings with the Indians. (106)

2. She uses a conventional citation system, *The Chicago Manual of Style* system using endnotes for citations, which was current when this article was first published in 1986. Since the article was published in an academic journal published by the University of Chicago Press, use of this style was probably mandated by the journal editors.

3. Like most literary critics and historians, she analyzes the images and points of view in the histories and personal accounts she examines.

4. She uses the kind of evidence—lots of well-chosen quotations from her sources— that is expected in her field. For example:

The fuel drums stand, in Miller's mind, for the popular misconception of what this country is about. They are "tangible symbols of [America's] appalling power," a power that everyone but Miller takes for the ulti- mate reality (p. ix). To Miller, "the mind of man is the basic factor in human history," and he will plead, all unaccommodated as he is among the fuel drums, for the intellect—the intellect for which his fellow histo- rians, with their chapters on "stoves or bathtubs, or tax laws," "the Wilmot Proviso" and "the chain store," "have so little respect" (pp. viii, ix). His preface seethes with a hatred of the merely physical and mechanical, and this hatred, which is really a form of moral outrage, explains not only the contempt with which he mentions the stoves and bathtubs but also the nature of his experience in Africa and its relation- ship to the "massive narrative" he will write. (187)

5. She also assumes—and rightly so—that her academic audience will recognize the following allusion:

Knowledge of what really happened when the Europeans and the Indians first met seemed particularly important, since the result of that encounter was virtual genocide. This was the kind of past "mistake" which, presumably, we studied history in order to avoid repeating. If studying history couldn't put us in touch with actual events and their causes, then what was to prevent such atrocities from happening again? (186)

This is a variation of the concept first articulated in the early twentieth century by the philosopher George Santayana in *The Life of Reason:* "Those who cannot remember the past are condemned to repeat it." By following most of the common practices of her professional peers and alluding to knowledge that she can reasonably assume they have in common with her, she assures her readers (the piece was first published in a prestigious professional journal, *Critical Inquiry*) that she is an experienced practitioner in the field and leads them to understand that she is violating some conventions for rhetorical impact—to emphasize her point, not because she does not know them.

DEVELOPING YOUR PROFESSIONAL VOICE

The concept of professional voice differs from field to field. A **professional voice** is developed not only through study, but also through work experience and communication within a profession. As you move into your field of study, try to identify its specific language, practices, and conventions and try to adapt them to your own writing as a student in the field.

FOCUS POINTS: FINDING CUES TO PROFESSIONAL VOICE IN VARIOUS FIELDS

■ *Look for personal/impersonal pronouns:* Writers in the sciences seldom use personal pronouns ("I") or discuss personal experiences and observations in their professional publications. They may or may not use them when making recommendations for applying results or when evaluating other researchers' work. Writers in some but not all of the humanities are more likely to use personal words and a personal tone, usually to emphasize a point or to extend an idea beyond the direct evidence.

■ *Look for professional vocabulary:* Every profession has a vocabulary that may not be common outside its field. For example, newcomers to neurology must learn what terms like "neurotransmitter" or "circadian rhythm" mean, and newcomers to rhetoric must learn the meaning of terms like "ethos" and "pathos." Even more important is discovering the words that have one meaning in everyday use and a very different meaning in a specific field. For example, most scientists avoid terms like *fact* and *prove*, when writing for each other, even though most nonscientists think that facts and proof are what science is about. Similarly, "theory" has a very different meaning for scientists than it does for those outside the field, and while many nonscientists tend to consider "theory," "hypothesis," and "opinion" to be almost synonyms, scientists distinguish clearly among them. "Modern," "criticism," and "culture" have different meanings in the humanities than they do in general conversation, and using them loosely when writing for these fields suggests a lack of expertise. In the same way, everyday words have different, specific meanings in computer science, the social sciences, and many other fields. Sometimes instructors point out the special meanings of common words in their disciplines, but like other professional conventions, sometimes professional language seems transparent to its users, and students have to pick up the meaning of words and expressions as they gain expertise in a field.

■ *Jargon* is a negative term for professional vocabulary and is sometimes used to identify the inappropriate use of professional vocabulary. Writers and speakers are apt to be accused of jargon when they use a lot of undefined professional vocabulary in a piece aimed at a general audience. Jargon can leave a nonprofessional audience confused or intimidated, rather than informed. Newcomers to a field often think it to be full of jargon until they become accustomed to hearing, reading, and using its professional vocabulary, which then comes to seem a natural feature of the field. The key for the student writer is to recognize words that have definitions particular to a field, and to use them appropriately for that particular audience.

■ *Professional arguments:* Notice what counts as evidence and how it is arranged in peer-reviewed articles you use in your research. The examples from James Paul Gee and Jane Tompkins above give some guidance in seeing this arrangement, as do the examples from the sciences and social sciences below.

■ *Professional conventions:* Getting acquainted with a professional style (like APA or MLA) is a means of developing a professional voice. It takes considerable practice to master these styles, but knowing that they exist and where to look them up is a crucial first step.

EXAMPLE 8.3 *Conventions and Argument in Science and Social Science Writing*

The following examples demonstrate variations across the curriculum as researchers adopt discipline-specific conventions to their arguments.

Similar conventions. The following passage from Francine Patterson and Wendy Gordon's "The Case for the Personhood of Gorillas" demonstrates how many argumentative documents include claims that support a thesis, reasons that support those claims, and evidence from research that sustains those reasons.

Does this individual have a claim to basic moral rights? It is hard to imagine any reasonable argument that would deny her these rights based on the description above. She is self-aware, intelligent, emotional, communicative, has memories and purposes of her own, and is certainly able to suffer deeply. There is no reason to change our assessment of her moral status if I add one more piece of information, namely that she is not a member of the human species. The person I have described—and she is nothing less than a person to those who are acquainted with her—is Koko, a 26-year-old lowland gorilla.

Patterson and Gordon's principle **claim** is that gorillas should have the same "basic moral rights" as human beings, though at this point they do not yet identify the individual they describe as a gorilla.

The authors cite self-awareness, intelligence, emotions, and other abilities as **reasons** that support the claim for moral rights.

For over 25 years, Koko has been living and learning in a language environment that includes American Sign Language (ASL) and spoken English. Koko combines her working vocabulary of over 500 signs into statements averaging three to six signs in length. Her emitted vocabulary—those signs she has used correctly on one or more occasions—is about 1000. Her receptive vocabulary in English is several times that number of words.

> The authors provide **evidence** that Koko, a gorilla, has learned to communicate—one of their reasons for asserting that gorillas have claim to moral rights.

Koko is not alone in her linguistic accomplishments. Her multi-species "family" includes Michael, an 18-year-old male gorilla. Although he was not introduced to sign language until the age of three and a half, he has used over 400 different signs. Both gorillas initiate the majority of their conversations with humans and combine their vocabularies in creative and original sign utterances to describe their environment, feelings, desires, and even what may be their past histories. They also sign to themselves and to each other, using human language to supplement their own natural communicative gestures and vocalizations.

> Further **evidence** demonstrates that the ability is not confined to one unique animal.

Discipline-specific practices (Sciences). Academic fields have their own conventions for presenting research and supporting claims. While Patterson and Gordon provide evidence that the gorillas they research demonstrate an ability to use sign language, science research also demands experimental data.

Tests have shown that the gorillas understand spoken English as well as they understand sign. In one standardized test called the Assessment of Children's Language Comprehension, novel phrases corresponding to sets of pictures were given to the gorillas under conditions in which the tester did not know the correct answers. Koko's performance (see Table 1) was twice as good as might have been expected by chance, and there was no significant difference in her performance whether the instructions were given in sign only or English only.

> By demonstrating that gorillas can understand spoken English and signs, the authors provide **empirical evidence** for their reasons.

> In the sciences, standardized tests and experiments provide **data** that are testable and repeatable.

Table 1

Koko's Performance on the Assessment of Children's
    Language Comprehension Test

Percent Correct

Number of Critical Elements	Chance	Sign + Voice	Sign Only	Voice Only	Overall Percent
1 (vocabulary)	20	72	–	–	–
2	20	70	50	50	56.7
3	20	50	30	50	43.3
4	20	50	50	30	43.3

Data are typically presented in the form of tables, graphs, and charts, which make the information easier to read and study. Data and experimentation are also critical to research in the sciences and an anticipated part of research documentation.

The results of chi-squared tests (1 degreee of freedom) indicate that Koko's performance on the ACLC in all modes and at all levels of difficulty was significantly better than chance, and that there was no significant difference in her comprehension whether the instructions were given in sign, English, or sign plus English.

The science writer must then not only explain the implications of data but must also account for the reliability of both the data and experimental methods and explain their implications by providing **discussion** and **results.** These explanations build the writer's credibility and finally link the data and evidence back to the reasons and initial claim.

Because the gorillas understand linguistic instructions and questions, we have been able to use standardized intelligence tests to further assess their abilities. Koko's scores on different [. . .]

Discipline-specific practices (Economics). Like the sciences, the social sciences require arguments that include specific claims, reason, and evidence. However, the need for data and experimentation varies depending upon the subject matter. Documents in economics also make use of figures, graphs, and charts, when necessary, but often quotes and citations dominate the visual landscape of these documents as in the example below from Davide Gualerzi's "Globalization Reconsidered," where Gualerzi argues that current competitive international economic policy favors developed countries over developing ones.

The structural adjustment and stabilization policies of the IMF [International Monetary Fund] have not been able to promote rapid growth and poverty reduction at least in a

The **claim** that adjustment and stabilization policies have been ineffective in developing countries heads this section on the Poverty Reduction Strategy Papers (PRSP).

large part of the developing world, most notably Africa but also Latin America (Argentina) and many of the transition economies (Milanovic 2002).

> The author qualifies the claim with specific **evidence** and builds the document's ethos by including a reference to other similar research (Milanovic 2002).

Faced with the seriousness of the problem, the IMF and the World Bank have devised a set of policies under the heading of the Heavily Indebted Poor Country Initiatives. More specifically, the PRSP [Poverty Reduction Strategy Papers] was introduced to give operational content to the CDF [Comprehensive Development Framework].[19] Accordingly, countries should submit poverty reduction strategy papers in order to qualify for debt relief. Cammack observes that PRSP used the language and the ideas of some NGOs [nongovernmental organizations] to support policies and priorities set in advance by the IMF and the World Bank, "a classic case of the manipulation of 'participation' as part of a strategy of securing hegemony" (Wilkinson and Hughes 2002: 47).

> Expository notes may point to additional **evidence** that point readers to information that may not need to be included in the text but that other researchers may find useful.

> Here the author provides **reasons** as to why adjustment and stabilization policies fail in developing countries and builds his credibility by appealing to an authority (Cammack).

The macroeconomic and financial framework is now supplemented by targeted poverty-relief programs and small-scale public sector expenditures, directed to the provision of public goods. It seems questionable that these changes can significantly affect poverty and social welfare (Pasha 2002). So, although the pro-poor rhetoric is now in fashion, there seems to be a fundamental continuity with the previous policy framework.

> The author offers further expert documentation and **evidence** for the claim's reasons.

> The author begins to conclude the point by explaining the **results** and implications of the failed policies he cites in his reasons and evidence.

The problem is a reorientation of macro policy, which seems [. . .]

DIRECTLY STATING THE SIGNIFICANCE OF AN INQUIRY

An important expectation that can be hard to recognize in your own work is connecting the significance of a particular inquiry to an ongoing conversation in the field or profession to whom you are writing or its larger significance in public life. Discussing the significance of a particular research project seems so commonplace to researchers that it seems natural and transparent—so conventional that it may not be mentioned. In the excerpt below, researchers Gerald Graff and Andrew Hoberek reflect on what is missing in papers that do not address the crucial questions of "So what?" or "Who cares?" Students who do not apply what they discover in their own inquiries to the larger controversies being discussed in their field of study can miss the chance to join the "conversation":

> Granted, most undergraduates won't know enough about academic conversations to initiate groundbreaking new paradigm shifts. . . . Still, in our experience, undergraduates are often more than capable of producing the kind of meta-commentary we urge, which really involves not much more than the basic rhetorical principle that what you say should have something to do with what people around you are saying. The cocktail party provides an analogy: people who walk up to a conversation, listen to what's going on to find out what the interlocutors are already talking about, and then make a contribution to this preexisting conversation generally have much more success than those who walk up, interrupt whoever is currently speaking, and launch into an unrelated discourse about whatever happens to be on their minds. (252)
>
> [Endnote: We echo here a comment by Kenneth Burke that has been widely quoted and endorsed by compositionists in which Burke compares intellectual history to a neverending parlor conversation that as individuals we enter and exit. See Burke, *The Philosophy of Literary Form: Studies in Symbolic Action*, rev. ed. (New York: Vintage, 1957), pp. 95–96.]

Readers in all fields expect writers to connect their work to ongoing work in the field, to specify what it adds to the conversations or arguments that matter in the discipline.

Exercises

8.1 WRITING FOR DIFFERENT AUDIENCES

1. Consider the kinds of "domain knowledge" you already have: a sport, an organization, an academic area, a kind of music, and so forth. Make a list of some of the jargon, practices, and assumptions that are part of that domain knowledge.
2. Write instructions about how to carry out a process or procedure in that domain to a specific person who has about the same level of "domain knowledge" as you have. This should be a real person. If you are working on a course project with another person or a group—such as creating a Web site to display the results of your inquiry—that would be the best choice for an audience. Otherwise, write to someone who shares some other domain knowledge with you.
3. Write a paragraph on the same topic to a person who knows little or nothing about the content knowledge that needs to go onto the Web site—again, write to a real person, not to people in general.
4. Compare the two versions: how are they different?
5. If they are not substantially different, rewrite them to take into account the different extent of knowledge possessed by the two audiences. Think carefully about what needs to be explained or defined for the "outsider," and what can be assumed to be common knowledge for the "insider."

6. What if your collaborator had a lot of domain or disciplinary knowledge about your topic, but knew much less than you about how to design and manage a Web site? How would this change your instructions? What might be your purpose for such a piece of writing?

8.2 READING FOR AUDIENCE

Reread Jane Tompkins' essay, "'Indians': Textualism, Morality, and the Problem of History," in the Readings; or use an academic source connected with your project. Reread either text even if you already have read it, but this time continue the analysis of adapting to a professional audience begun on pages 151–154 in this chapter by looking for the assumptions and conventions the writer is adapting to or resisting and for the ways she takes the audience into account.

1. Identify acknowledgements of audience and the writer's relation to it.
2. Mark those points where you think the writer is addressing or violating shared conventions and common knowledge.
3. Highlight cues to the author's relationship with that audience. List as many of the shared assumptions, conventions, and practices the writer uses as you can find.
4. Discuss with your group which of these assumptions and expectations you share, and which you do not. Consider how your responses have developed and changed since first encountering this piece in Chapter 1.
5. Write a response to conclude your list that reflects on the author's sense of her audience and how she shapes her work to address it.

8.3 WORKING WITH DISCIPLINARY EXPECTATIONS ABOUT ARGUMENTS

1. Take another look at one of the documents you wrote in Chapter 6. What field or discipline does it draw on most? How does the way you address your audience compare to the relation of author to audience in one of the peer-reviewed *academic* sources you cite? How does the way you address your audience compare to the relation of the author to the audience in one of the *popular* sources (i.e., magazines, newspapers) that you cite?
2. How would you describe the audience to which your document is addressed? Point out specific features in the document in which you acknowledge your relationship to your audience.
3. In what other ways could you adapt the document to the audience you are addressing? Or, is there another audience at whom it could or should be aimed? If so, describe how you would have to revise the paper to make it appropriate for that audience.

CHAPTER 9

Writing a Personal Research Narrative

As you have seen, research can be communicated in a variety of ways, depending on the nature of the audience and the purpose of the communication. Communicating in a longer paper may seem less difficult if you think of drafting as *revision* rather than starting from scratch: revising notes, responses, and ideas into a form that will communicate how you see the results of your inquiry to the specific audience you are addressing. The genres described in this chapter and the next invite you to rework your notes and previous assignments into a larger document. Writers in many fields work in this way, so that they do not have to start from a blank screen and so that they can review what they already know about a topic. This recursive approach to writing, like the recursive approach to choosing a topic and conducting research, demands that you read your own work critically and adapt your writing not only to a specific audience, but also to how your thinking has changed over the course of a research project.

As you research a question, your thinking about the topic may change substantially from the initial questions or preliminary thesis. Instead of trying to fit the results of an inquiry into a preexisting thesis, it can be more productive to adapt the thesis to the results of the inquiry. As Richard Feynman affirmed in Chapter 1, a researcher cannot know the answer to a question before conducting the research. The summaries, syntheses, and responses of your earlier research should deepen your understanding of the topic, and this work may change your ideas about it altogether.

Genres like the proposal, annotated bibliography, or literature review provide opportunities to revise earlier notes and preliminary responses to fit your increased knowledge of a field and to take into account the particular expectations of a specific audience. Longer researched papers like the I-Search paper or the argumentative research paper provoke even more rethinking and reframing of the information you have gathered, literally "re-seeing" your work, rethinking your sense of its purpose and significance, reviewing your understanding of earlier sources in light of later readings, and deciding on the most appropriate way to communicate to your audience. Sometimes experienced researchers need to produce several versions of a project before they can state with confidence and clarity what they have to say about an issue and what they have finally concluded. The practice of self- and peer-evaluation can be a help in this revising, not only from draft to draft, but also from genre to genre.

PLANNING A LONGER PAPER

While planning and preliminary writing are useful in drafting shorter papers, they are even more important to writing longer and more complex personal narratives and arguments. Few researchers ever feel ready to start writing, but if your inquiry has progressed reasonably well and your preliminary thesis statement has developed into an arguable claim or a clear perspective, you are ready to start planning a paper. If writing a longer and more formal paper seems daunting, consider how much you have to start with:

- a good sense of what has been written about your topic and who has taken what approaches to the issues it raises;
- a series of responses to some of the sources, and a point of view that may have changed over the process of the inquiry;
- some understanding of how your inquiry might fit into a conversation in the field you have researched;
- a collection of notes, summaries, syntheses, and responses to draw upon;
- a well-formatted list of references;
- knowledge of what sources you still need and when you expect to have access to them; and
- experience using the claims, reasons, and evidence that will go into the longer paper.

The process by which different researchers most effectively arrive at and organize an argument is largely a matter of personal style. Some writers think or talk through their ideas until they know exactly what they are going to say, while other writers discover their point only through the process of writing things down, seeing what they have written, and revising. Writers who prefer to think through what they are going to say before they start writing often write detailed and highly structured outlines; they make significant discoveries during this process of outlining, and may spend more time outlining than actually drafting the paper. On the other hand, writers who do most of their thinking as they write need a looser planning strategy. They might never get to writing a first draft if they had to start from a detailed outline—because they would never finish the outline.

Although there are many possibilities for variation and adaptation between tight and loose planning styles, most writers benefit from some kind of written, retrievable plan for writing a longer piece because when a writer is deeply engaged in drafting, it is very easy to forget earlier ideas. Moreover, even claims that seem final at the planning stage can become clearer through modifications that become apparent only as the narrative or argument takes a more finished shape. You will know what planning strategy works for you when you find the strategy that most efficiently (i.e., most quickly and painlessly) produces successful papers. The strategies in Chapters 9 and 10 are meant to help you identify an organizational style for handling your own work—the "best" organizational style being that with which you are most comfortable and which helps you produce the most satisfying results.

Initial Planning

You may be lucky enough to see immediately a clear pattern or organization to shape the paper from beginning to end, but more often writers have to try more than one organizational strategy. It might help to know that few writers outline papers from beginning to end. Many writers sort out main claims and reasons and then shift and arrange evidence and sources to where they seem to fit best. Like other genres of writing, both personal and argumentative research papers depend heavily on judgments by the writer.

A useful way to start planning is to quickly skim everything you have written on the topic: notes, summaries, responses, shorter papers, and self- and peer-responses. Copying pieces of work you have already done into the same file can be an effective way to help fill in a blank page, but be sure to carry references along with the pieces and to maintain clear distinctions between summaries of and responses to the sources. Also, consider how your thinking has changed in the course of the research project, and be sure that your paper reflects your final sense of the issue.

FOCUS POINTS: REVIEWING AND ORGANIZING INFORMATION

- While reviewing your previous writing and notes, *list the ideas that seem to be most important to understanding the issue*. What claims can you see yourself making? Why do you believe them? That is, what are the *reasons* for your thinking this way?

- If you have trouble identifying your reasons, try to *find them by rereading your previous work carefully*. Consider how your thinking developed—where your inquiry began and ended, and what claims marked its progress. Your short responses and syntheses can also help you see or devise convincing reasons.

- *Review the thesis statement* you have already formulated and revised in Chapter 4. Try finishing sentences like "I have reached this conclusion because. . . ." or "I am making this claim because. . . ." Make sure that "because" is followed by a reason, not a warrant or underlying assumption.

- *Use the reasons as the main divisions of the plan or outline*. Consider what seems to be the most reasonable order in which to present them. It may take several tries to identify the best shape for a narrative or argument. A few possibilities:
  - chronologically?
  - from most to least, or least to most important?
  - from local impact to wider, or vice versa?

- You might *skim your sources again*, but don't let reading distract you from writing at this point.

- It may help to *work from your list of important ideas*, cutting and pasting if you are planning on the computer, or using circles and arrows on hard copy. As you consider the order of reasons, look for major evidence to support them, and start fitting it into the list.

- *Write down the major objections* to your claims and reasons. Where and how are you going to address those objections? After the introduction and major claim? Reason by reason? Some other way? Write it down.

■ *If you have written a synthesis of sources or a history of the issue* for an earlier assignment, consider how to adapt it for the introduction.

■ *Rethink the significance of your main claim,* whether it is stated in the introduction or the conclusion—or both. Does it work for the paper as it is now taking shape? How should the significance be changed or adapted to work in the conclusion?

■ *Rearrange the parts and look for points where transitions may be needed* to show where the argument is going.

THE PERSONAL RESEARCH ("I-SEARCH") PAPER

In 1980, Ken Macrorie, a professor at Western Michigan University, published a research writing textbook called *The I-Search Paper,* which spoke of and responded to the dissatisfaction many college students and faculty felt toward traditional term paper assignments. Macrorie designed a research writing course that encouraged students to pursue their genuine interests in a heartfelt way, to extend their research from the library into the community, and to write a narrative—a story—of their research, rather than writing the typical, more formal argumentative research paper. He wanted students to experience the pleasure and pride that academic researchers experience, and he encouraged students to integrate their growing professional or domain knowledge with their personal knowledge and life experiences. Macrorie believed that the I-Search paper could—and should—replace the argumentative research paper in much undergraduate writing because it encourages students to speak with their own voice and from their own perspective.

Making this connection and experiencing this pleasure are some of the purposes for today's versions of personal research writing, which are derived from Macrorie's earlier work. Faculty have applied Macrorie's ideas in various ways: replacing the argumentative paper with an I-Search paper, assigning reflective writing at various stages of the research process, and making the I-Search paper a preliminary means for thinking through research that is then revised for an argumentative essay or formal oral presentation. However it is used, an I-Search (or personal research) paper can be a very powerful means of helping students develop and reflect upon their individual research process. Moreover, filtering research through your own experience can reveal a more personal significance for your research and its claims—an insight that can help you both to make a more meaningful and powerful argument in an assignment and to find means to use that research in other areas of your life.

Although an I-Search assignment calls for a personal narrative, like most academic writing it is written to communicate to a particular audience, not for the writer alone. Its purpose is to help you discover *and* communicate the personal and professional significance of your research to a particular audience. Although self-discovery is part of this kind of writing, the writer generally addresses an audience that cares more about what the writer has discovered and concluded than about the life story of the researcher. Therefore, instead of writing a memoir, use your personal experiences and responses to illuminate and illustrate the issue you are researching and the pattern that research has taken—much as James Paul Gee or Jane Tompkins do in their writing.

Although the personal research narrative does not take the *form* of an argument, often an argument underlies it or emerges from it. When reading a personal narrative closely, you can see the writer's ideas develop, the warrants they rely on, the reasoning that supports them, and often the development from a question or potential argument to a thesis. As in most other genres of academic writing, the conclusion of a research narrative should reflect on the significance of the inquiry and answer the "So what?" question.

Writing an Effective I-Search Paper

Look through your earlier work—notes, summaries, syntheses, and papers—reflecting on how you have modified your thinking about the issue. Think about how you moved through this process from topic to problem, argument, reasons, and evidence. This usually is a recursive process that seldom moves in a straight line, and your narrative should reflect the real process of the inquiry, not an idealized process.

Your paper should convey not only the problems you faced in understanding the topic and presenting it to an audience (false turns and all, if they demonstrate significant mistakes), but also your sense of the larger significance of what you have done. Consider how this paper might serve as groundwork for any future work. An I-Search paper can be more exploratory than argumentative, and so finding an argument may be the ending point rather than the beginning—at least of the first draft. Consider also how the professional knowledge you have gained through the inquiry impacts the common knowledge you brought to it.

Because this paper is exploratory, transitions and cues to your purpose and to your response to sources are particularly important for your readers, who need to be able to follow easily the progress of your thinking. You may need to add more cues after you have read and reviewed the first draft of the paper, as you turn your attention from reflecting on your thinking about the topic to communicating your ideas clearly to the audience.

FOCUS POINTS: KEEPING SOURCES UNDER CONTROL

Accurate and appropriate use of citations and an accurate reference list are as important in a personal research paper as in most other forms of academic writing: they show that your opinions are grounded in researched knowledge of the field.

- When starting the paper, create a separate document, entitled "Works Cited" or "References," depending on the style you are using. Each time you quote, paraphrase, summarize from, or refer to a source, immediately copy the full, formatted documentation for the source from the working bibliography into this reference file. Rather than creating a list from scratch after finishing the draft, it is much easier and more reliable to have a complete list of formatted sources ready to select into a reference list, which then merely needs to be alphabetized and proofread.

- Write your parenthetical citations (in general, authors' last names and page numbers for MLA or dates for APA) as you draft new material, as a safeguard against forgetting to reference the source later. See the Quick Guide to Documentation for more detailed instructions for in-text citations.

- Distinguish clearly between quoted text and paraphrased text as you write, and *never move a quotation into your text without quotation marks*. Then decide whether the length of the quotation requires quotation marks (three lines) or set-off formatting (more than four lines).

■ Be very careful to carry parenthetical citations with you when you cut and paste from earlier writing, to maintain the distinction between your voice and the voices of your sources, and to keep your point of view clear. Cutting and pasting from document to document can put these distinctions at risk, so stay sharply attuned to who is saying what.

EXAMPLE 9.1 *The I-Search Paper (Plagiarism Inquiry)*

This I-Search paper is the second of the series of projects proposed by one student in the sample proposal in Chapter 4. Notice in particular the progression of her thinking from the early rough notes (p. 69), to the proposal (p. 78), to the annotated bibliography (p. 113), and finally to the following personal research narrative.

Original Thought and the Antiplagiarism Movement

As a sophomore in high school, I had the misfortune of transferring schools twice, tempting me to be initially unhappy with wherever I ended up. I ended up in a private Catholic college preparatory school in Indianapolis, Indiana. This school is known for its scholastic fortitude as well as its athletic prominence. Because my school was so well known for its academic aptitude and integrity, its policy concerning plagiarism was especially strict. Blatant plagiarism could result in immediate expulsion. The problem that became a major issue for me was what exactly constituted plagiarism in the first place? Unfortunately I came face to face with this issue when my sophomore English teacher approached me one day, rather upset, with the idea that I had plagiarized a paper I had written discussing the antitranscendentalist nature of Herman Melville. Knowing that I had not plagiarized this paper and rather shocked at the mere accusation, I started writing at a lower level than I was capable of. I eventually discovered that my teacher's accusations were based simply on the rather high level of vocabulary I had used in the Melville paper. Thinking back on this moment, I am at a loss to see how a high vocabulary is a means of catching a plagiarist, so I decided to research the other methods used to deter plagiarism. But first, I thought it would be more appropriate if I were to do a little background research on the current plagiarism problems that exist in colleges and universities.

I began my research by searching scholarly journals and newspaper articles for current reports on plagiarism around the nation. Apparently plagiarism has become an important issue facing the academic world due to a recent significant hike in incidents on college campuses around the country. John Crace, in a report in *The Guardian*, a London paper, said that "cheating and plagiarism are endemic within the US academic system, with an estimated 30–35% of students engaged in some form of copying or collusion" (10). I was astounded by the possibility that so many students could be plagiarizing and wondered whether American students were being taught the importance of thinking for themselves.

The idea bothered me so much that I continued to look for a reason why plagiarism had become so prevalent in today's educational world. An article by Lauren Iacocca, in *The Daily Bruin,* focuses on how the ease of finding a surplus of information on the Internet has encouraged student plagiarism (1). This idea seemed like a valid one, but I wasn't through searching so easily.

While scouring through a few scholarly journals I ran into an article written by Mary Ellen Scribner, in the *Library Media Connection,* that addresses a few more surprising questions concerning the plagiarism problem. According to Scribner, "plagiarism is not just an American problem but is both a cultural and a global issue" (32). Scribner continues to consider other possibilities that could be causing or at least contributing to the current problem. She blames bad teaching practices, such as relying on vague, outdated, and recycled assignments; accepting incorrectly structured papers; not checking sources; and a few other possibilities as reasons for the current increase in plagiarism. Scribner also discusses a study done by Professor McCabe in 2001 at Rutgers University that reported that as many as ninety percent of students who had plagiarized off of the Web had also plagiarized from print sources (Scribner 32). According to Scribner's arguments, the Internet has been a contributing factor affecting the increase in plagiarism, but not the only factor.

This widespread perception that the Internet has made the problem of plagiarism worse led me to wonder just how many Web sites offering their services and promoting plagiarism were available to students. In my search I decided to check out a few of the Web sites that are commonly used for plagiarism and found plenty of places from which a student could plagiarize a paper by buying it from an online paper mill. A few of the sites I found are *essayfinder.com, hotessays.com, and directessays.com.* A few even claim that if they don't have an essay on a topic in their database, they will write one, for a fee of course. At this point in my exploration I have come up with a slight dilemma.

There is a surplus of Web sites that encourage students to plagiarize, yet statistics show that a majority of students who use the Internet to plagiarize also use print sources.

The question that I ponder is whether the Internet is really intensifying the growing problem of plagiarism, or just offering an alternative medium. Charles McGrath of the *New York Times* asserts, "No wonder young people are confused, and no wonder they continue to plagiarize in record numbers, with more than 40 percent of college students admitting to copying from the Internet in 2001" (33). Whether students are confused or the Internet makes it easier, plagiarism seems to be cheapening the value of personal thought.

At this point, I started investigating antiplagiarism programs and Web sites to see what they are doing to promote personal thought. I concluded that antiplagiarism programs like *turnitin.com* can scare students into doing the work rather than plagiarizing, but they leave little room for developing a positive sense of integrity in students, and they do little to develop independent thinking. For example, these programs can create an ethics of innocent until proven guilty, which students may translate into "I'm only guilty if I'm caught." Also, these programs can cost universities thousands of dollars to access. According to *Community College Week,* over 200,000 high schools, universities, and colleges spend around twelve thousand dollars per year to join plagiarism busters like *turnitin.com* ("Online Tool" 18). I think that the antiplagiarism programs that are available are too expensive, and although they do respond to the current alarm about plagiarism, they don't seem to be making any major dents in the rising plagiarism statistics.

I decided to research other antiplagiarism teaching techniques before drawing conclusions. According to Deborah Straw, teachers should make their assignments more clear and not assume that students are equipped well enough for test taking and writing more focused papers than in high school. She says that it is also imperative that teachers discuss the university's dishonesty policy with their students as well as the definition of plagiarism itself (5). Straw makes some very important observations. If a student isn't taught to recognize and avoid plagiarism, then how can he or she understand its significance? Looking back at the feedback regarding my proposal for this very paper, several students in my research group asked me what the actual definition of plagiarism is. One student even said that he believes it isn't plagiarism if he copies only a few lines from a source. Under what circumstances, and at what point in his education, should the student be blamed for this ignorance? I don't ever remember anyone explaining to me what is and is not plagiarism in my previous years of schooling, and so I could have easily made a similar mistake.

Then I turned to Rebecca Moore Howard, who seems to pick up on the responsibilities of teachers to teach students to understand plagiarism, and who seems to trust that in a good learning situation, students will do their best, original work in good faith. At this point, I am returning to my original thinking about plagiarism, that the issue is how to best develop personal responsibility and individual thinking in students. It is problematical to me that most of the pieces I've read in the popular press are devoid of pictures of decent students and teachers; they focus on combating cheating rather than building originality and integrity.

I am beginning to think that teachers have to take responsibility for teaching students about plagiarism in enough detail so that they understand clearly what it means and how to avoid it. But teachers have a difficult role in this process, too. According to Amy E. Robillard, a university composition instructor, teachers "might even find themselves defending conflicting values," wanting to support the institution on the one hand by thwarting plagiarists and students on the other by giving them a second chance, even when the university says that they should not be given one (20). Still, students need to develop a pride and confidence in their own thinking, so that to steal someone else's ideas would seem not just irresponsible, but a violation of their own minds. Students who do not or cannot take pride in their own thinking probably will not care to make clear distinctions between their own work and that of someone else.

The problem that is still bothering me is how to think about social pressures that cause plagiarism. As a society, I think we are neglecting the larger moral issues that allow plagiarism to flourish. I tend to believe that this neglect comes from problems deep within the educational system, a system in which students learn to worry more about maintaining high grade point averages than about actually learning the material. If our society taught students to think for themselves rather than chasing after higher grade point averages, plagiarism might not be so much of a problem. Could we rethink writing instruction right from the start to promote independent thinking and moral integrity—qualities that I do believe go hand in hand? On the other hand, I do not want to end up blaming all our problems on "society in general." I want to argue that teachers and students can and should start thinking differently about our responsibilities, to shift our focus from detecting and policing to develop a positive atmosphere for genuine learning.

Works Cited

Crace, John. "Higher Education: Cut and Paste Job: As Plagiarism Engulfs the US and
   Threatens the UK, a New Advisory Service Has Been Launched to Track Down Our Own
   Academic Cheats." *Guardian* [London] 15 Oct. 2002: 10. Print.

Directessays.com. Direct Essays, 2003. Web. 27 May 2007.

Essayfinder.com. The Paper Stores Enterprises, 2000. Web. 1 Sept. 2008.

Hotessays.com. Hot Essays, 2003. Web. 2 Sept. 2008.

Howard, Rebecca Moore. "Forget about Policing Plagiarism. Just Teach." *Chronicle.com*.
   Chronicle of Higher Education, 16 Nov. 2001. Web. 17 Jan. 2008.

---. "Plagiarisms, Authorships, and the Academic Death Penalty." *College English* 57.7
   (1995): 788–806. Print.

Iacocca, Lee. "Internet Encourages Student Plagiarism." *Daily Bruin* [Los Angeles] 5 Nov.
   2002: 1. Print.

McGrath, Charles. "Plagiarism: Everybody into the Pool." *New York Times* 7
   Jan. 2007: 33. Print.

"Online Tool Helps Universities, Colleges Fight Plagiarism." *Community College Week* 15.12
   (2003): 18. Print.

Robillard, Amy E. "We Won't Get Fooled Again: On the Absence of Angry Responses to
   Plagiarism in Composition Studies." *College English* 70.1 (2007): 10–31. Print.

Scribner, Mary Ellen. "An Ounce of Prevention: Defeating Plagiarism in the Information
   Age." *Library Media Connection* 21.5 (2003): 32–35. Print.

Straw, Deborah. "The Plagiarism of Generation 'Why Not?'" *Community College Week* 14.24
   (2002): 4–6. Print.

Turnitin.com. iParadigms, 2003. Web. 31 Aug. 2008.

FOCUS POINTS: RETHINKING AND REVISING THE PERSONAL RESEARCH PAPER

As with other kinds of writing for an audience, revising the personal research paper involves further adapting it to its specific audience and purpose. When revising the personal research paper, consider how potential revisions can help you adapt the results of your inquiry to other projects. If you will be writing an additional paper or using another medium for representing your research, such as an oral presentation, a PowerPoint presentation, or a Web site, consider how you might adapt the personal narrative for those genres and audiences.

To make sure your paper is as effective as it can be, read it over from start to finish. Highlight the issue you are investigating, your approach to that problem, the reasons for your conclusions, and the larger significance you find in them. If any of these aspects is missing from your paper or is not very clear, make a note in the margin or at the end of the paper. Then, read your paper again, looking for the answers to the rest of these questions.

- Is there an argument within your personal research story? Is there an argument that becomes apparent at the end of it? Should it be clearer?

- If there is an argument, either on or beneath the surface of the narrative, consider how well it is made. What are the warrants for your claims? Are they stated, and do they need to be? Is your argument grounded in warrants a group of researchers in the field would share? Are these warrants your specific audience would share? Have they changed in the process of your inquiry?

- Do common knowledge and disciplinary knowledge conflict at any point in the narrative? How is that conflict resolved?

- What is the most serious potential objection to the conclusion you arrive at or to the reasons that support it? This could be an objection that one or more of your sources has made, or it could be an objection that you now see for yourself.

- What is your response to that objection? You do not need to abandon your approach, claims, or genuine responses to the issue, but you do need to consider how you might shape your narrative to respond to potential objections and to engage people who might see it differently than you do.

- Do you use sources that rely primarily on personal knowledge or common knowledge to make important professional points? How do you defend their credibility or overcome their limitations? Do you need to do so to be convincing?

- How clearly do you indicate your position in controversies when sources disagree? Do you use sufficient cues to show how the sources support and contradict each other and your own thinking on the topic?

- Does the narrative seem sufficiently focused on your inquiry and its results, or does the inquiry seem dominated by references to yourself? Use the "find" function of your word-processing program to search for your use of the words "I" and "me." Highlight and count them. Can any of the references to yourself be eliminated without substantially changing the meaning or violating the purpose of the paper?

- What kinds of transitions do you make? How much does the narrative depend on weak transitions that show only the passage of time rather than engaging the relationships among ideas? Can you find a better way to show the progression from idea to idea?

- Are the voices in this paper clearly recognizable? Refresh your memory about intellectual property issues by reviewing Chapter 3, and then, with a small group, repeat Exercise 6.6 in Chapter 6: Listening for Voice in a Synthesis (p. 127).

FOCUS POINTS: PEER EVALUATION OF THE PERSONAL RESEARCH PAPER

For an even more effective revision strategy, exchange drafts, accompanied by your self-evaluation, with another student, and answer in writing the questions below.

■ Is the research process clear? Do you see the issue in the same way as the writer of the paper does? Do you see a coherent development to the story of the writer's thinking? Can you see a potential argument in the writer's research story?

■ Can you raise any important objections to sources or reasoning that the writer has not already raised, in either the paper or the self-evaluation? Can you suggest an alternative response to the response the writer gave?

■ Do the writer's claims seem warranted? What specific similarities or differences in assumptions (or warrants) do you see between yourself and the writer? Are they personal or professional differences? How do they affect your reading of the paper? Can you suggest changes the writer might make to address or overcome those differences?

■ Can you think of a different or larger significance to the writer's work than the writer has stated in this draft? What is it?

■ Does each use of "I" or "me" in the paper contribute to the story the writer is telling? Does the writer use the personal narrative to show what he or she has learned and how that knowledge matters? Make suggestions about where that knowledge or significance could be emphasized more, and, if relevant, how they might be adapted to a different kind of project.

FOCUS POINTS: EDITING CITATIONS AND REFERENCES

To make sure you are citing sources correctly, follow these steps.

1. Alphabetize and proofread the list of sources actually used in this paper. Give this page the appropriate title: "References" (APA) or "Works Cited" (MLA).

2. Reread the paper, checking your citations against the reference list, making sure that you have used every source that is on the list, and that a reference for each source used in the paper is on the list. Check to see that you have made clear how and why each source fits into your narrative.

3. Check your quotations against the original texts for accuracy, and check summaries and paraphrases against the original texts for possible distortions of their intended meaning. Make sure that your voice is distinct from those in your sources. If you have copied phrases of more than two words from the original, put them in quotation marks or change them into your own words. See Chapter 6 for a review of quoting, paraphrasing, and summarizing.

4. Do a "find" search for the opening parenthesis "(", and make sure that the information and punctuation in parenthetical citations are appropriate for the professional style you are using. Paste your "References" or "Works Cited" list to the end of the emerging draft of the paper.

Exercises

9.1 ANALYZING A SAMPLE PAPER

1. Read the Example 9.1 I-Search Paper (Plagiarism Inquiry), and list its use of assumptions and conventions, the kinds of knowledge it draws on, and examples of the writer's awareness of the audience and its expectations.

2. Write a paragraph of response to these issues, giving examples of where they need to be clarified or justified.

3. Evaluate this piece of student writing using the following criteria:
   - How—and how well—does the writer use key words in transition sentences?
   - Does she provide sufficient cues to her responses to maintain a consistent point of view?
   - Does she make the significance of her research project clear?
   - How clearly does her introduction provide a context for the inquiry?
   - Has she moved you to agree with her conclusions?

9.2 REVIEWING AND REVISING RESEARCH TO START A RESEARCH NARRATIVE

1. Following the suggestions about reviewing and organizing in the Focus Points: Reviewing and Organizing Information on page 159, review your materials and experiment with different organizational strategies. Assemble a list of the materials you feel must be included in the narrative.

2. Choose an organizational structure for the narrative that takes into serious consideration your progression of understanding the material of your inquiry.

3. Write a set of questions that your paper should answer about the topic.

4. Write a short reflection about how you intend to interpret your learning experience for an audience that may not know the material. This may take the form of a paragraph or a bulleted list, depending on which format seems most appropriate to your thinking at this point.

5. Write a list of reminders of ideas and sources you do not want to forget; add a note about sources that you still hope to look at, or of sources that you would add to the project if they were more easily available to you.

9.3 WRITING A PERSONAL ACCOUNT OF YOUR RESEARCH (THE I-SEARCH PAPER)

1. Write an I-Search Paper, a personal research narrative that describes the process of your research with a focus on the way your understanding of the problem and your project developed as your research progressed. Use the Writing an Effective I-Search Paper section found on page 161 to help you tell the story of your research—what you did, and more particularly what you learned about the issue from doing it. If you are going to write an argumentative paper later, your narrative should move toward the major claims of that argument and the major reasons for supporting them. If you will be working on other kinds of projects, think about how this research narrative can help you shape them.

2. Be sure to compile from your working bibliography the list of references for sources used in this narrative.

3. Revise the narrative, using the suggestions and Focus Points in this chapter as a guide.

9.4 REVISING YOUR NARRATIVE INTO ANOTHER GENRE

1. Revise your narrative to share your research with your class as an oral presentation with visuals. Consider carefully the information about oral presentations in Appendix A and the use of visuals in Appendix B. As you adapt your written work to a speaking performance, consider how this kind of presentation changes the arrangement of your research. Consider how the personal element of this project can translate into an oral performance.

2. Create a Web site that records your research and offers links to appropriate sources and visuals.

9.5 REFLECTING ON YOUR WRITING

1. Write a short reflection on what more you would like to learn from the inquiry, considering in particular what other sorts of documents it could lead to.
2. If you are assigned an argumentative research paper, consider how your approach may change with the different genre, and what materials and ideas you expect to keep.
3. If you think this inquiry is over, explain, in as much detail as possible, why it seems finished. Consider whether your response to this inquiry is evidence of its success or its failure.

CHAPTER **10**

Writing an Argumentative Research Paper

Writing a substantial argumentative research paper can be a valuable learning process, particularly if you research a topic with which you become genuinely engaged. Instead of describing your own research process, a successful argumentative paper directly joins an ongoing conversation regarding a problem about which reasonable and informed people disagree.

Writing an argumentative research paper lets you:

- use the rhetorical understanding you have developed,
- frame the research gathered in your inquiry for a particular audience,
- produce an argument that will help you experience entering the conversation of a discourse community and writing for an academic audience, and
- use conventions of a particular domain of academic research and writing.

Although each such assignment has its own requirements, the general features of this kind of paper may already be familiar to you:

- It is long enough to require a substantial inquiry.
- It makes a well-reasoned argument based on evidence from reliable sources.
- It contains an assigned number of cited sources, that is, references that are actually used in the paper, for summaries, paraphrases, or quotations. There may also be a required balance of print and online sources.
- The sources demonstrate your mastery of the research process and your growing expertise in a field; that is, they must be relevant to the argument and clearly used in relationship to it (as support for it, as alternatives to be refuted, as sources of evidence, etc.).
- The sources are cited and documented according to a specified set of scholarly conventions (normally MLA or APA).

As with other kinds of writing, the specific requirements vary from field to field and assignment to assignment, but argumentative research papers are commonly assigned in upper-level college courses, particularly in the humanities and social sciences. Because this is a student version of a kind of paper researchers in many fields write, it can help to develop understanding of the ways specific fields approach issues and use evidence, and it can offer practice in how to use, respond to, and make an argument about sources in ways appropriate for a field. This is the kind of disciplinary knowledge described in Chapter 8. Moreover, through the processes of reading, writing, and revising, researchers often discover new questions about or approaches to their topics, and working on an extended research project can introduce you to the excitement of the kinds of discovery possible in different academic fields.

REASSESSING THE THESIS

When starting an argumentative research paper, reviewing notes and responses from earlier work can help you clarify your thinking about your inquiry and decide specifically how it can be framed in this genre. By this point in your inquiry, you may have reformulated several times the thesis that you first constructed in Chapter 4, and your argument may have taken its final form. However, many writers discover their final claims only through the process of writing and rewriting a paper or series of papers, and thus they revise the emerging thesis many times. Often writers who need to start writing in order to meet a deadline use a "working or exploratory thesis" when they start writing, rather than a conclusive thesis statement that includes topic, question, and impact or significance. A working thesis tells readers what you are going to investigate, rather than what you have concluded about your research. By the time you rewrite the first draft of the argumentative paper, you should turn this exploratory statement into a definitive statement, as part of an introduction that explains how and why you pursued the inquiry.

EXAMPLE 10.1 *From Working Thesis to Final Thesis*

The proposal in Chapter 4 has a working thesis (p. 80):

> In my research project, I intend to investigate the use of international teaching assistants,
>
> in order to see whether they actually hurt the education of American undergraduates.

A thesis like this is weak because it states the question the writer intends to explore rather than the results of the inquiry, but it can be used to start an early draft if necessary. The thesis in the final draft of the argumentative paper in this chapter (p. 195), however, makes a much stronger claim and anticipates the significance of the argument:

> Obviously, many students are resistant to the idea of having TAs who are other than
>
> American-born, even students who haven't had any personal experience with international
>
> TAs. However, this resistance may stem from problems much deeper than just speaking
>
> English, and it definitely obscures the fact that international TAs are very valuable to
>
> diversity on campus.

PLANNING THE PAPER

Start with the basic organizational planning described on page 159 in Chapter 9. Then consider whether you are the kind of writer who works best from a polished outline that organizes most of your thinking, or from a more informal organizational plan that allows more room for thinking as you write.

Constructing an Outline

A planning outline is similar to the reading and revision outlines you have already worked with. An outline is a formal, hierarchical plan for organizing writing. It can be a useful way to organize material and plan an argument because it clearly shows the relationships among evidence, reasons, and claims. There are two basic writing styles for outlines: topic outlines (which are written in grammatically parallel phrases) and sentence outlines. Each has its advantages and disadvantages. It can be a bit easier to arrange and visualize the hierarchy of ideas in a topical outline because its clearly hierarchical format can help you to visualize parts of the argument and to arrange claims, reasons, and evidence at the appropriate levels. On the other hand, in a sentence outline, some of the sentences can become topic sentences of paragraphs in the paper, as they are in a revision outline. This preliminary work can put some key words and transitions in place before you start drafting the whole paper. Whatever format suits you best, start with the preliminary planning suggested in Focus Points: Reviewing and Organizing Information (Chapter 9, p. 159).

Because you are the primary audience for a planning outline, and its sole purpose is to help you organize your thinking, it may not matter very much whether you get the format exactly right. More informal outlining may also be sufficient for understanding difficult readings and for checking the coherence of your own written work. However, having some knowledge about how to construct a formal outline is useful because in many professions outlines are an important part of project proposals, making the case for the usefulness or profitability of the final work. Outlines for these public purposes need to be very well organized and clearly formulated.

Formatting Outlines

In the humanities and social sciences, researchers who use outlines usually use a number and letter format, with roman numerals indicating divisions of the largest magnitude, capital letters at the next level down, and so on—as in the example that follows.

Title

Thesis Statement: (optional)

    I. XXXXXX

        A. YYYYYYY

            1. ZZZZZZZ

            2. ZZZZZZZ

            3. ZZZZZZZ

      B. YYYYYYY

      C. YYYYYYY

          1. ZZZZZZZ

          2. ZZZZZZZ

II. XXXXX

      A. YYYYYYY

      B. YYYYYYY

          1. ZZZZZZZ

          2. ZZZZZZZ

          3. ZZZZZZZ

      C. YYYYYYY

          1. ZZZZZZZ

          2. ZZZZZZZ

          3. ZZZZZZZ

III. XXXXX

      A. YYYYYYY

          1. ZZZZZZZ

          2. ZZZZZZZ

      B. YYYYYYY

      C. YYYYYYY

In the sciences, technology, and business, the decimal outline is common.

    1. XXXXXXX

      1.1 YYYYYY

          1.1.1 ZZZZZZ

          1.1.2 ZZZZZZ

          1.1.3 ZZZZZZ

          1.1.4 ZZZZZZ

      1.2 YYYYYY

          1.2.1 ZZZZZZ

          1.2.2 ZZZZZZ

      1.3 YYYYYY

2. XXXXXXX

    2.1 YYYYYY

        2.1.1 *ZZZZZZ*

        2.1.2 *ZZZZZZ*

    2.2 YYYYYY

    2.3 YYYYYY

        2.3.1 *ZZZZZZ*

        2.3.2 *ZZZZZZ*

        2.3.3 *ZZZZZZ*

3. XXXXXXXX

    3.1 YYYYYY

        3.1.1 XXXXX

        3.1.2 XXXXX

    3.2 YYYYYY

Word-processing programs provide several other formats. The format you use might be designated by the assignment you are working on or the field you are working in. These preset formats give you the highest (main claims) level of numbering first. To get to levels for reasons and evidence, use the tab key. These formats can help you think about the different levels of magnitude of your argument and can help you manage the difference between main claims, reasons, and supporting evidence. They also take care of spacing and capitalization, leaving you to focus on the content of the argument rather than the mechanics of outlining.

However, many writers find these programmed formats unwieldy to use, particularly when the writer's ideas do not fit a strictly parallel design or when they want to cut and paste into the outline. As when using any writing technology or strategy, if you find that the preset format causes more problems than it solves, there is nothing wrong with doing the formatting yourself.

In the following outline, notice that short references to sources are incorporated into the outline, as prompts to help the writer remember where to locate appropriate information in the working bibliography and in project notes. Although formal outlining formats may not provide a place for the thesis statement, many writers find it useful to begin the outline with it. Notice that the thesis for this preliminary draft has not yet been revised to what will be its final form.

EXAMPLE 10.2 *Topic Outline*

The Problem of Negative Views of ITAs

Thesis: Even though many American undergraduates resent being taught by international

graduate students, we should look at the positive aspects of this situation.

I. Why graduate teaching assistants are used as instructors for undergraduates

    A. Classes needing instructors

        1. Started in 1940s (Ouzts)

        2. Graduate education and research valued more than undergraduate (Fox)

    B. International students needing jobs

        1. Started in 1980s (Fox, Plakans, Ouzts)

        2. Numbers large (Iowa State and Purdue Examples)

II. Complaints by American undergraduates

    A. Different customs (Sarkodie-Mensah)

        1. Large lectures rather than small classes

        2. American students' expectations

        3. Other cultural factors (Ouzts)

    B. Who complains (Plakans and Smith)

    C. Language skills

    D. Pronunciation

    E. The real problem

        1. Frustrated undergraduates

        2. Underclassmen vs. seniors (Plakans)

        3. Majors vs. nonmajors

III. Intervention strategies

    A. Programs for undergraduates

        1. Learning techniques for good communication (Oppenheim)

        2. Univ. of Missouri at Columbia (Plakans)

    B. Undergraduates participating in screening (Fox)

    C. Opportunities to interact (Plakans)

    D. Video at Texas Tech

    E. Training programs

IV. Positive aspects of international teaching assistants

    A. Diversity: Adjusting to new cultures

    B. Substitute for travel abroad

    C. Preparation for global workforce

EXAMPLE 10.3 *Sentence Outline*

The Problem of Negative Views of ITAs

Thesis: Even though many American undergraduates resent being taught by international graduate students, we should look at the positive aspects of this situation.

I. Graduate teaching assistants have been used as instructors for undergraduates since the 1940s (Ouzts 21).

   A. The foreign TA problem started in the 1980s (Fox, Plakans, Ouzts).

   B. Iowa State (Plakans) and Purdue (Fox) illustrate large numbers.

   C. ITA training programs started in the 1980s (Smith et al.).

II. The problem is that ITAs have little experience with teaching in an interactive manner (Plakans 3).

   A. American students are used to interaction.

   B. International students may be used to large lecture halls and formal manners (Sarkodie-Mensah).

   C. International students may not know that American students pay for college, and so have higher expectations for how they are treated.

   D. Even when the ITA has clear speaking patterns and pronunciation, he may have a hard time relating to students (Fox 203).

III. One problem may be that many undergraduates get disillusioned and frustrated.

   A. Failing students blame ITAs (Fox 207).

   B. Seniors accept the system (Plakans 137–39).

   C. Undergrads who learn techniques for good communication with an international teaching assistant rate the ITAs higher (Oppenheim 9).

   D. Some studies show that undergraduates are less critical of ITAs in courses in their majors.

IV. There are several possible intervention strategies to help undergraduates deal with ITAs.

   A. Michigan State uses a program in residence halls (Plakans).

   B. The University of Missouri-Columbia and Iowa State use brochures (Plakans).

   C. Fox recommends making students part of the screening and training process (217–18).

      D. Undergraduates benefit from this participation.

      E. Texas Tech has a video that stresses the positive aspects of having an international teaching assistant.

      F. Some of these interventions may not work very well (Plakans 16).

  V. There are advantages to having international teaching assistants.

      A. They are often the "cream of the crop" in their own countries.

      B. We need to learn to interact with people from other countries, but not everyone can travel to another country.

      C. We would all be better off with a more positive perspective.

Informal Paper Planning

Writers who find it difficult to use a formal outline nonetheless need to plan and organize, even though they know their plan may change significantly as they write. Informal paper plans look less orderly than outlines, because they seldom clearly show the relationship among claims, reasons, and supporting evidence—a relationship that may become clear to the writer only in the process of drafting. However, any kind of written planning can help keep the writer on track and make the process of drafting a paper easier. There are other ways in which writers document their planning, and if you have discovered one that works well for you, you may want to share it with your class.

FOCUS POINTS: CREATING AN INFORMAL PAPER PLAN

The following informal plan shows how a writer can organize ideas and evidence for an argument without arranging the ideas into a fixed hierarchy:

1. Use the preplanning strategies in the Focus Points in Chapter 9, Reviewing and Organizing Information (p. 159), to pull your information and ideas together.
2. Paste your revised thesis into a new file.
3. If you have written a synthesis or history of the issue that can be modified for an introduction, paste it in before the thesis. Be sure to clearly state the issue or controversy you are addressing: the gap that you intend to fill or the question you intend to answer. Also make sure that the introductory synthesis provides sufficient context for that issue and prepares for the thesis.
4. Write down your major claims and the main reasons to support it. Paste in pieces you have already written where you think they might fit under those claims and reasons. Think about the order in which to arrange them, and rearrange them until you see a clear progression.
5. Identify sources for reasons and evidence as you go along. Add reminders of your own thinking (short identifiers to take you to sections of your notes and parts of other papers) at places where you agree with, disagree with, or otherwise respond to the sources.

6. Make a list of things that you do not want to forget, tasks that still need to be done, and ideas about which you still feel uncertain.

7. Reread your plan, rethinking the order and arrangement of the assembled material.

8. Quickly review your notes and responses. Can you see a place for anything you have left out of this early plan? If so, paste it in at the likely place, with a note to yourself if necessary.

9. Write some final thoughts about what you foresee as strong points and problems in the paper you are planning.

EXAMPLE 10.4 *Informal Paper Plan*

The Problem of Negative Views of ITAs

Context: Undergraduates at nearly any major university will tell you they have had a teaching assistant, or TA, for a teacher. Many of those students probably had an international student as a TA, especially if they were in a math class or chemistry/biology class with labs. And many students will probably tell you they would rather have a TA who can "speak English," if they have to have a TA at all. Obviously, many students are resistant to the idea of having TAs who are other than American-born, even those who haven't had any personal experience with them.

Controversy: Why do American undergraduates resent having international students as instructors? (Chang, Fox, Plakans) How realistic are their objections? What are the advantages of having international students as teachers?

Thesis: Even though many American undergraduates resent being taught by international graduate students, we should look at the positive aspects of this situation.

Main Claims

    1. There really are two problems (which sometimes get confused):

        • Some ITAs are not prepared to teach American students (Plakans, Sarkodie-Mensah).

        • Some American students are prejudiced against international students and perceive them through their preconceptions (Fox, Smith, Ouzts, Rao, Oppenheim).

2. Both American students (Plakans, Rao, Fox, Texas Tech) and international students (Smith, Davis, Oppenheim) need training to be able to work most effectively with each other.

   • Reason: cultural misunderstandings can be overcome, but it takes effort.

3. It is valuable for American students to experience the cultural diversity that ITAs can offer (Johnson & Lollar, Goodin, Plakans).

   • Increasingly, global business expectations require cooperation among people from difficult cultures.

   • Relatively few American students get to study abroad.

Reminders

   • Find some quotes that don't make American students look really awful; I want to illustrate their misunderstanding or not appreciating international teaching assistants—but I don't want to make us look like ignorant bigots!

   • I'm not sure how to refer to the Texas Tech videotape in this paper.

Things to Do

   • I may need to find some more general articles on graduate students teaching undergraduates, so that I can put international graduate students into the context of all graduate students, American and foreign.

   • Is there anyone I can interview locally about this? Or can I just rely on general observations about how my friends (undergraduates) feel?

   • Find a background book on different kinds of American colleges and universities.

Final thoughts: I have learned a lot from having international graduate students as my teachers. They have made me think about wanting to study abroad, either during my junior year or after I finish my undergraduate work. I really want to get across the idea that while there may be problems with communication, international graduate students give us something of extra value in our education, a cross-cultural experience that we would not get otherwise. They should not have to become pseudo-Americans, although most of the ITAs I've met do want to understand and participate in American life, particularly the life at the university. We American students can learn a lot from helping the ITAs help us learn.

Reviewing the Outline or Plan

You will see how well the planning worked only when actually drafting the paper. However, it may be useful to review and revise it before you start the work of drafting. These questions can direct that revision:

- What are the strongest parts of the outline or plan? Are these the same as the parts of the proposal or other work on the issue that you really believed in? How has your thinking developed since the proposal?

- Where do your claims seem weak? Can you support them with the sources you have? Where do you need to do more research or consult your sources again?

- How clearly can you see important connections between the ideas in the paper? Add some markers to describe transitions that you should make (for example, relational terms like *addition, contrast,* or *part/whole;* or actual transition words, like *moreover, however,* and so on). These reminders can help you make clear connections when drafting.

FOCUS POINTS: PEER EVALUATION OF THE PLAN

If you share the outline or plan and self-evaluation with a partner, use these questions to guide your thinking:

- What do you think the most exciting part of the paper will be? How does that part relate to the overall organizational structure of the argument? What suggestions can you make to increase its effectiveness or impact?

- Can you see any gaps in the reasoning? Do you see any logical fallacies? What warrants does the argument rest upon? Do any of them need to be more explicitly stated or defended?

- Can you see a clear progression from reason to reason?

- Can you point out places where particularly clear transitions will be needed to move the reader from part to part?

- Does any important aspect of the argument seem to be missing? Is there any irrelevant evidence?

MOVING FROM PLANNING TO DRAFTING

Although you may have already had considerable practice writing short papers, drafting a longer paper can seem intimidating. One reason for starting to draft from an outline or plan is that it cuts the project into shorter, more manageable parts. Also, the more time and thought you spend on planning, the less time you will need to spend on the actual drafting process.

You may have heard this many times, but it bears repeating: start drafting early enough to avoid being overly rushed in meeting deadlines. Take your personal writing style and needs into account when deciding when and where to work on the paper: how much time you need, what kind of writing environment, and so on. However you draft, the first thing to decide is with what part of the paper to start. This will depend both on your own personal style of writing and also on which pieces of writing you have already done.

FOCUS POINTS: STRATEGIES FOR DRAFTING

If you already have an approach that works well for you, you should use it, but if you find that you have trouble starting or if you get stuck, one of the approaches below might help you restart the drafting process.

- Some writers *use the outline or plan to clarify their reasoning*, and then draft the paper separately, paragraph by paragraph, glancing at the outline from time to time, and adapting the outline to draft and the draft to outline as necessary. This approach often appeals to writers who like to think through their argument in detail before starting to write it.

- Some writers start by *writing a condensed version of their draft*, with only their major claims and reasons, and then revise it to fill in evidence and specific sources after they have worked their way through their ideas.

- Some writers *first draft a fairly complete and polished introduction*, in order to rethink carefully the thesis statement and assess their claims. Revising a proposal or synthesis written earlier can help move drafting this introduction along.

- Some writers start drafting by *inserting text from their own earlier writing directly into a copy of the outline or plan*. This method uses parts of the research that are already written, which can make the task of drafting seem easier. These writers start filling sentences directly into a copy of the outline, eliminating the formatting as paragraphs emerge. They may insert sections of their notes, summaries, and responses, as well as excerpts from proposals and other preliminary writing, including quotations copied from sources. This process allows a writer to see the parts of the paper that are already written and to rethink the relationship of the parts to the whole. A writer might even discover a new line of reasoning around what he or she has extracted from earlier work, and then reposition the supporting information to fit the purpose of this particular project. Researchers who write this way must be particularly careful to integrate the imported pieces into their argument smoothly and without distortion, and, as always, to keep track of references for sources. They usually need to spend more time on revision.

EXAMPLE 10.5 *Drafting into an Outline*

Here is the example sentence outline from pages 177–178 in this chapter, with the automatic formatting removed and some of the already-written parts extracted from the writer's notes and added to the outline in the early phases of drafting:

The Problem of Negative Views of ITAs

Talk to undergraduates at nearly any major university and they will tell you they have

had a teaching assistant, or TA, for a teacher. Many of those students probably had an international student as a TA, especially if they were in a math class or chemistry or biology class with labs. And many students will probably tell you they would rather have a TA who can "speak English," if they have to have a TA at all. Obviously, many students are resistant to the idea of having TAs who are other than American-born, even those who haven't had any personal experience with them. International students, who are sometimes still called foreign students, are increasing on campuses nationwide, and graduate international teaching assistants, or ITAs, are increasing as well. I am looking at research done mainly at universities in order to find out why American students have such a hard time with international teaching assistants because it helps us address how to see the situation as a positive one.

Thesis: Even though many American undergraduates resent being taught by international graduate students, we should look at the positive aspects of this situation.

   I. Graduate teaching assistants have been used as instructors for undergraduates since the 1940s (Ouzts 21).
      A. The foreign TA problem started in the 1980s (Fox, Plakans, Ouzts).
      B. Iowa State (Plakans) and Purdue (Fox) illustrate large numbers.
         In a study done by Barbara Sweeney Plakans at Iowa State University, over 72% of the undergraduates she studied had been in a course taught by an ITA. ITAs at Iowa State comprised nearly a third of all the TAs and were found mainly in math, engineering, and the physical sciences. In a study by Wanda Fox at Purdue University, about 30% of the TAs were international and found mainly in the Engineering and Science schools (190–91).
      C. ITA training programs started in the 1980s (Smith et al.).
  II. The problem is that ITAs have little experience with teaching in an interactive manner (Plakans 3).
      A. American Students are used to interaction.
      B. International students may not know that American students pay for college and have higher expectations for how they are treated.
      C. Even when the ITA has clear speech, he may have a hard time relating to students (Fox 203).
 III. One problem may be that many undergraduates get disillusioned and frustrated.

    A. Failing students blame ITAs (Fox 207).

    B. Seniors accept the system (Plakans 137–39).

    C. Undergrads who learn techniques for good communication with an international teaching assistant rate the ITAs higher (Oppenheim 9).

    D. Some studies show that undergraduates are less critical of ITAs in courses in their majors.

IV. There are several possible intervention strategies to help undergraduates deal with ITAs.

    A. Michigan State uses a program in residence halls (Plakans).

    B. The University of Missouri-Columbia and Iowa State use brochures (Plakans).

    C. Fox recommends making students part of the screening and training process (217–18).

    D. Undergraduates benefit from this participation.
    Sarkodie-Mensah states:

    "Encouraging interaction of college-bound students and TAs from other countries also will foster understanding between the two groups and will prepare the new students for some of the culture shock they will experience in the hands of the foreign TAs" (116).

    E. Texas Tech has a video that stresses the positive aspects of having an international teaching assistant. Texas Tech University put out a video in 1988 called *You and the International TA: Paths to Better Understanding*—why international teaching assistants are beneficial.

        1. statistics on the increase of international students and TAs (here to stay).

        2. interviews with TAs from Sri Lanka, Taiwan, and Peru on how American students are different.

        3. positive aspects too: friendly and more independent.

        4. Professors explain why ITAs are used, but Americans tend to be wary of people who are different or students are coming from a conservative part of the country, such as the south. (Is this a fair reason?)

F. Some of these interventions may not work very well (Plakans 16): one of the studies Plakans referred to in her study showed that undergraduates were "neutral about whether the experience of having an ITA increased cultural understanding" (16). Another showed that mentoring did not affect undergraduate acceptance and what was needed was "more informal, interpersonal contact to change attitudes and more overseas travel by undergrads" (16).

V. There are advantages to having international teaching assistants.

  A. They are often the "cream of the crop" in their own countries.

  B. We need to learn to interact with people from other countries, but not everyone can travel to another country.

  One comment by Plakans claims that the students need to give more than the ITAs regarding cultural difference:

  "I think we are placing too much of an emphasis on making these TAs conform to American ways. I'm not expecting an ITA to give up their culture just because they're here. I think we have a lot to learn just having an ITA as an instructor. There isn't much chance that you are going to go out into the business world and everyone you run into is an American. I think in a lot of cases we are being too inflexible and that bothers me. . . . Americans are just so egocentric we don't want to allow other people to be what they are." (112)

  C. We would all be better off with a more positive perspective. Most of the ITAs I've met do want to understand and participate in American life, particularly the life at the university. We American students can learn a lot from helping the ITAs help us learn.

Keep your thesis and your main reasons clearly in mind as you draft. Having a printout of your outline or plan with these elements highlighted can help you move particular parts around without losing track of the overall claim you are supporting. If you get stuck, move to an easier part to write, and come back to the problematic part later. Longer writing projects need not be written in the order in which they are read, and sometimes you will find solutions to problems when you "write around" them.

Your outline, your thesis, and your main claims may very well change in the course of your writing. As you assemble evidence for your reasons, you may find new objections to be overcome, and you may discover new reasons to support your claims. There is usually considerable discovery involved in the process of drafting. You might want to construct a revision outline (see Focus Points: Revising for Coherence in Chapter 7, p. 130) as you move from drafting to revision. Review page 161 in Chapter 9, Focus Points: Keeping Sources under Control, to make managing sources easier.

EXAMPLE 10.6 *Early Draft of an Argumentative Research Paper (with Instructor's Comments)*

Here is the first draft of a student paper on the topic of international teaching assistants and what they can offer to American students, based on the outline and paper plan above. The comments point out where the student is achieving what she seems to be aiming for, and where she needs to make her case more clearly.

The Problem of Negative Views of ITAs

Can you revise the title to give a clearer sense of how the paper will address this topic? Will the abbreviation *ITAs* come up in a key word search in a database? If not, use the full term in the title.

Talk to undergraduates at nearly any major university and they will tell you they have had a teaching assistant, or TA, for a teacher. Many of those students probably had an international student as a TA, especially if they were in a math class or chemistry/biology class with labs. And many students will probably tell you they would rather have a TA who can "speak English," if they have to have a TA at all. Obviously, many students are resistant to the idea of having TAs who are other than American-born, even those who haven't had any personal experience with them. International students, who are sometimes still called foreign students, are increasing on campuses nationwide. According to the Institute of International Education, there are nearly 600,000 international students at US campuses. Moreover, graduate international teaching assistants, or ITAs, are increasing as well. I am looking at research done mainly at universities in order to find out why American students have such a hard time with international teaching assistants because it helps us address how to see the situation as a positive one.

The thesis still states your question; try reading through your draft again to find your answer to that question, and then reformulate your thesis as the argument for your conclusion.

Graduate students started to be used as teaching assistants in the 1940s and 1950s (Ouzts 21). Possibly a quarter of all undergraduate courses at big research institutions are taught by teaching assistants (Ouzts 3), whose use has always been controversial (Fox 2), and where too much value is being placed on graduate education and research (Smith et al.). "The Foreign TA Problem," as it has been called (Plakans 4, Smith et al.), has been around since the mid-1980s.

How does the use of graduate students as teaching assistants place too much value on graduate education?

It was then that larger numbers of undergraduate courses began being taught by TAs who did not speak English as a first language. Those students came to the United States to study but couldn't get visas to work off-campus. While many would work in cafeterias and libraries, some were eligible to teach low-level introductory courses that professors wanted to be freed from anyway. So being a TA is a way satisfying the need to finance an education for the ITA and staff low-level, often required courses for the college (Fox, Plakans, Ouzts).

> It would help to give more context here—from the undergraduate's point of view as well as from the graduate students'.

In a study done by Barbara Sweeney Plakans at Iowa State University, over 72% of the undergraduates she studied had been in a course taught by an ITA. ITAs at Iowa State comprised nearly a third of all the TAs and were found mainly in math, engineering, and the physical sciences. In a study by Wanda Fox at Purdue University, about 30% of the TAs were international and found mainly in the Engineering and Science schools (190–91). A study conducted by Florence Louise Ouzts added business to the list (1) and reported that most of the ITAs getting complaints were from Taiwan, China, and India (6) and most of the complaints were in math, physics, and chemistry (30).

> Think about how topic sentences of paragraphs can contribute to your argument. Try making a revision outline of this draft, and see how well you can follow the argument.

ITA training programs have been going on since the 1980s. Smith states that since 1982, laws have been passed or state mandates required for assessing language abilities of ITAs in 18 states. Some of these assessments also include training programs. Orientation programs are short, one- to five-day training sessions, concurrent programs go along with the teaching in the first semester, pre-term and concurrent combine both (Smith et al.) She states that we need more assessment instruments to address both language and teaching skills of ITAs including student evaluations, surveys of ITAs and supervisors, and student improvement evaluation.

> I'm confused here.

> What kinds of things do ITAs report about these training programs?

In *The Professional Development of Graduate Teaching Assistants*, several authors discuss training of ITAs (Marincovich, Prostko, and Stout). They state part of the problem as being that ITAs have little experience with teaching in an interactive manner such as is common in the US. Using TAs are unique to the US (Plakans 3). In their own countries, they were probably in a very large lecture hall that was very formal. Kwasi Sarkodie-Mensah states in some countries, it is considered rude to walk in late into the classroom or raise the

> How does this information fit into the point of the paragraph? Is this related to class size and conduct?

left hand to ask a question. He says that many ITAs also don't know that
American students have to pay for their tuition instead of the government
funding them as in other countries which leads to lack of understanding about
the special circumstances of the American classroom (115–16). Fox talks about
the importance of "cultural factors" in the classroom, stating that even when
the ITA has clear speech he may have a hard time relating to the students but
students should also adapt. Fox seems to see a particular responsibility on the
undergraduate's part to overcome bias and prejudice (206).

> You have lots of good research, and you show some of your sources in conversation with each other's ideas; but where does your own thinking fit into the picture?

Plakans compared her study at Iowa State University with one
conducted by Wanda Fox at Purdue. Plakans's study and Fox's study both
researched attitudes of undergraduates who had had experiences with an
ITA. For her study, Fox developed the Questionnaire of Undergraduates about
International Teaching Assistants (QUITA) as well as interviews (190–91).
Fox's study surveyed 540 undergraduates, but only 18 of these were
freshmen (192).

One interesting finding in Plakans's study and confirmed by Smith et al. is
that when students complained about ITAs, they usually blamed the problem on
pronunciation, but her study showed that many other kinds of communication
problems were actually behind that complaint (131). Ouzts's study confirms that
cultural problems add to the problem most often cited as language-based (5).
One of the problems could be a general disillusionment and frustration with
college that many undergraduates experience in the first two years, which could
find a scapegoat in the ITA. Fox also reports that some students blamed the ITA
for their poor academic performance (207). According to Plakans, seniors will be
more lenient on ITA evaluations because they've mellowed and accepted the
system (Plakans 137–39).

A study by Nancy Ann Oppenheim suggested that students in upper levels
have more "domain knowledge" to be able to "negotiate meaning" and figure
out what the ITA is saying (vii, 212). The hypothesis of her study was that the
real problem isn't the ITAs ability to speak clearly or teach well but that
undergraduate negative and resistant attitudes were based on their perceptual
bias (7). Negative stereotyping, prejudice, and overgeneralizations learned

early, situational factors of seeing the foreign students as competition, and high emotions and insecurity are four causes she finds (22–27). She states that undergrads who learn techniques for good communication with an international teaching assistant rate the ITAs higher (9).

Plakans' study showed that undergraduates that weren't as critical had positive attitudes, believing the ITA was a good teacher, were open to cultural differences, and took some of the responsibility for good communication (132). Some other studies she refers to show that undergraduates were less critical if the ITA was teaching in a course they were majoring in (also in Oppenheim 212), that personality made a big difference in acceptance, and that the lecture topic affected comprehension more than how the ITA talked. Fox's study showed that one student could understand an ITA when the topic was discussed in casual conversation but not when the ITA talked about math (203). Ouzts states that more critical ratings came from males, from nonmajors, which contradicts some other studies, from students who hadn't studied a foreign language, and from students who expected a low grade (142).

> It's hard to see what Plakans is saying about undergrads and what she's saying about ITAs.

> What is the focus of this paragraph? How does listing results of these studies contribute to your argument?

Based on the results of her study, Plakans suggested "intervention strategies" (vii) for undergraduate students to deal with ITAs. She discusses one Michigan State approach that uses programs in residence halls conducted by an ITA and an undergraduate that talks about stereotyping, shows a video, and gets the students talking about the subject. Using this kind of program in freshmen orientation might also work. The University of Missouri-Columbia uses a brochure called "TAs at Mizzou" that gives tips on better communication. However, Plakans says that a brochure used at Iowa State was criticized by a foreign student for being discriminating, and the video used at the parents' orientation created more anxieties and questions than answering them (147–48).

> This is interesting. Could you give more details?

> Do you think the critics of these strategies are correct, given the research you have done?

Fox's study recommends making undergraduates part of a screening process for new ITAs and having them participate in the ITA training course, which would help the undergraduates feel more confident about the TA program (217–18). Plakans says that trying to get undergraduates more involved in the ITA program as well as making it clear how much the ITAs are qualified would be good but hasn't been studied. The authors in *The Professional Development of*

Graduate Teaching Assistants also state that many colleges have established conversation groups, informal lunches, and focused meetings involving role-playing (171). These opportunities make the undergraduates more comfortable with ITAs and the ITAs more confident and comfortable as teachers. Having undergraduates in a training program, according to the authors, "has the added benefit of preparing undergraduates for cultural diversity. Many undergraduates who participate view ITAs with new respect and understanding, an attitude that they may pass on to their peers" (172). They also suggest more opportunities for feedback and evaluation before the end of the semester (177), a suggestion that Fox seconds (220). For example, Sarkodie-Mensah states:

> "Encouraging interaction of college-bound students and TAs from other countries also will foster understanding between the two groups and will prepare the new students for some of the culture shock they will experience in the hands of the foreign TAs." (116)

Good introduction to quote, but do not use quotation marks when quotes are set off.

Texas Tech University put out a video in 1988 called *You and the International TA: Paths to Better Understanding*. The 30-minute video explains why international teaching assistants are beneficial. It gives statistics on the increase of international students and TAs, showing that they are something that is here to stay. Three international TAs are interviewed from Sri Lanka, Taiwan, and Peru, and each explains how different American students are, but stressing the positive aspects such as their being friendly and more independent. Professors explain why American students are resistant as being wary of people who are different or coming from a conservative part of the country, such as the south.

Could this be seen as a faulty generalization by the professors?

Joe Goodin, Dean of the College of Arts and Sciences at Texas Tech, explains how students become "sensitized to international education, international problems" in a class taught by an ITA, which is important in a globalized world becoming more interdependent. Goodin states it is important that American students go into a class taught by an ITA with the attitude that "the cultural experience" will be positive, that with "receptivity" they will end up "on the learning end" and be better off than if all TAs were American.

Let's see your point come through more clearly in this transition. Also, does this paragraph continue to describe the video, or does it go back to a more general discussion of various means of promoting cultural awareness and diversity?

The international TAs help American students understand cultural diversity.

However, one of the studies Plakans referred to in her study showed that undergraduates were "neutral about whether the experience of having an ITA increased cultural understanding" (16). Another showed that mentoring did not affect undergraduate acceptance and what was needed was "more informal, interpersonal contact to change attitudes and more overseas travel by undergrads" (Plakans 16).

Professors in the video list benefits, including being exposed to different cultures, and getting a better understanding of the world we live in. They also stress that many ITAs are the "cream of the crop" among students in their countries and earn awards here in the US. The video ends with six steps for the American student to handle difficulty understanding an ITA and four suggestions for how to speak better to the ITA, which Oppenheim stresses as the key to better relations (213). The video stresses being fair and patient and ends with the message that the international TAs are needed. The video would have been even better with student comments supporting using ITAs. One comment from Plakans's study even shows how the students need to give more than the ITAs regarding cultural difference:

> I think we are placing too much of an emphasis on making these TAs conform to American ways. I'm not expecting an ITA to give up their culture just because they're here. I think we have a lot to learn just having an ITA as an instructor. There isn't much chance that you are going to go out into the business world and everyone you run into is an American. I think in a lot of cases we are being too inflexible and that bothers me. . . . Americans are just so egocentric we don't want to allow other people to be what they are. (112)

Citing another study, Ouzts refers to the ITA having to take on a "culturally alien persona" in order to try to fit in, and Smith refers to the "Americanization" of ITAs, which shows how difficult and maybe wrong it is for the ITA to do all the accomodating.

ITAs in most colleges and universities go through training programs for GTAs, and many are specific for the international graduate student. Stephen Davis and Jason Kring describe the GTA training at their institution as a model

Is this your own critique or does it come from one of your sources? You might speculate a bit about why students were not included.

When you say "refers to," what position does that source take in regards to the enforced Americanization of ITAs?

Be sure to proofread your final draft very thoroughly. For example, since your spell-check will pick up many authors' names, make sure that they are spelled as they should be.

for GTA training. It uses GPA, background courses, a personal statement and philosophy of teaching as selection criteria, and supervisor reviews and visits to the classroom as well as other detailed curriculum materials that go into a portfolio evaluation (Davis and Kring). All of these would be good if geared specifically to ITAs.

Whether students see the ITA as a necessary evil or a benefit, it is clear that they are part of our education process. So we would all be better off with a more positive perspective, such as that of the Texas Tech video. This should start in high school, but some of the suggestions made by the researchers covered in this paper are also good. It would be best if every student had the chance to spend time in another country by themselves. But since that isn't possible, we need to find ways to show students how important it is to accept people who are different first of all, then try to understand them. Then we can help the ITA help us learn.

The conclusion might have a clearer sense of ending if it included more key terms. For instance, "some of the suggestions made by the researchers covered in this paper are also good" could be strengthened by terms like "undergraduates," "international teaching assistants," "cultural differences," "understanding," and "contact." You might consider using an evaluative term like "improving relations." Or, instead of a general term like "positive perspective," how about something more specific like "appreciation of cultural differences"?

Your appreciation of the significance of this issue is a strong point of the paper.

Works Cited

Chang, Mei-Hsia. *Native-speaking Undergraduates' Perceived and Actual Comprehension of Foreign Teaching Assistants' Spoken Language on the Spoken Proficiency English Assessment Kit (SPEAK test)*. Diss. State U of New York at Buffalo, 1993. Ann Arbor: UMI, 1993. Print.

Davis, Stephen F. and Jason P. Kring. "A Model for Training and Evaluating Graduate Teaching Assistants." *College Student Journal* 35.1 (2001): n. pag. *EBSCO*. Web. 8 August 2008.

Fox, Wanda S. "Functions and Effects of International Teaching Assistants at a Major Research Institution." Diss. Purdue U, 1991. Print.

Institute of International Education. "Open Doors 2007: International Students in the United States." *Open Doors Online*. IIE Network, 12 Nov. 2007. Web. 3 September 2008.

Johnson, Susan M., and Xia Li Lollar. "Diversity Policy in Higher Education: The Impact of College Students' Exposure to Diversity on Cultural Awareness and Political Participation." *Journal of Education Policy* 17.3 (2002): 305–20. Print.

Marincovich, Michele, Jack Prostko, and Frederic Stout, eds. *The Professional Development of Graduate Teaching Assistants*. Bolton, MA: Anker, 1998. Print.

Oppenheim, Nancy Ann. *"Living Through" an Intercultural Experience: Undergraduates Learning from Nonnative English-Speaking Teaching Assistants*. Diss. U of Texas at Austin, 1996. Ann Arbor: UMI, 1997. Print.

Ouzts, Florence Louise. *Students' Perceptions of Native and Non-native English-Speaking Graduate Teaching Assistants (GTAs)*. Diss. U of Mississippi, 1991. Ann Arbor: UMI, 1991. Print.

Peterson, Dennis M., Peter Briggs, Luiza Dreasher, David D. Horner, and Trevor Nelson. "Contributions of International Students and Programs to Campus Diversity." *New Directions for Student Services* 86 (1999): 67–77. Print.

Plakans, Barbara Sweeney. *Undergraduate Experiences with and Attitudes toward International Teaching Assistants*. Diss. Iowa State U, 1994. Ann Arbor: UMI, 1994. Print.

Sarkodie-Mensah, Kwasi. "The International Student as TA." *College Teaching* 39.3 (1991): 115–16. Print.

Smith, Rosslyn, et al. "Crossing Pedagogical Oceans: International Teaching Assistants in U.S. Undergraduate Education." *ASHE-ERIC Higher Education Report* 8 (1992): n. pag. Web. 6 Nov. 2008.

You and the International TA: Paths to Better Understanding. Writ./Prod. Rosslyn Smith. Texas Tech U, 1988. Videocassette.

This sample paper is a good first draft, with strong sources and an important point. But all first drafts need revision. To revise it, the writer needs to build in key terms, work on transitions, and build a stronger recognition of the overall argument.

FOCUS POINTS: STRATEGIES FOR REVIEWING THE ARGUMENT

1. Before reviewing the paper, put the draft aside for awhile—really.

2. Quickly read the draft through to get an overall view of what it says. Edit only when you can't stand not to. Your goal in this reading is to get the big picture, and you may lose it if you spend too long working on any one part. You may discover through this quick reading that a different organization would be more reasonable for your argument, or that you need additional reasons or evidence to support your claims. Make notes to yourself or jot down suggestions for changes on the page when you're afraid you'll forget an idea or insight. Reading out loud is a useful approach to this task, especially if you can find someone who will listen and take notes but refrain from commenting until you are finished.

3. Underline your major claim. Is it located in the statement you identified as your thesis? Do you need to revise your thesis?

4. Reread the introduction closely. You may see the context of your thesis differently after finishing the draft, since many writers find that writing is a process of discovery. If so, you may need to revise the introduction.

5. Check the support for claims against the list of logical fallacies in Chapter 1. Is the argument reasonable? Are the reasons and conclusions based on warrants your readers will accept? Do any of these assumptions need explanation or justification?

6. Think about the argument you have made. What is the most serious objection to your argument? Where and how well do you address it?

7. Identify and adjust the transitions that clarify your organization for your readers and that increase the coherence of your paper (see Focus Points: Revising to Improve Transitions Chapter 7, p. 131).

8. Run a "find" search for key words, and make sure their repetition is consistent and their placement reasonable. Do you need to add transition words to make the relationships among your ideas clearer?

9. Skim the paper, reading the introduction, first sentences, and conclusion. Can you grasp the progression of the argument from this skimming? Rewrite the first sentences of the paragraphs in which the progression is not clear. If you are not sure, make a revision outline (Chapter 7, p. 130).

10. What difference does your argument make? Do you address that further significance in your paper? Does your conclusion emphasize that significance and transmit a sense of ending?

FOCUS POINTS: QUESTIONS FOR PEER REVIEW

■ Identify the part of the paper that you find most convincing.

■ Identify points in the paper where you have trouble following the writer's argument.

■ Write a short evaluation of the introduction and conclusion. If you think they still need work, give the writer some suggestions about what seems lacking or out of place in these crucial parts of the paper.

■ Write a paragraph of response to the writer's argument, in which you state the grounds on which you agree with it and address your own sense of the significance of the point the writer has made or, if you disagree, the significance of the writer's failure to convince you in the argument.

■ Make a list of sentence-level errors you recognize—but do not correct them in the paper.

EXAMPLE 10.7 *Final Draft of the Argumentative Research Paper*

Negative Views of International Teaching Assistants: Causes and Solutions

Talk to undergraduates at nearly any major university and they will tell you they

have had a teaching assistant, or TA, for a teacher. Many of those students probably had

an international student as a TA, especially if they were in a math class or

chemistry/biology class with labs. And many students will probably tell you they would

rather have a TA who can "speak English," if they have to have a TA at all. According to

the Institute of International Education, there are nearly 600,000 international students on US campuses. Moreover, graduate international teaching assistants, or ITAs, are increasing as well. In response, many American students have gone public with their views, getting their complaints published in campus newspapers (Chang 6). Obviously, many students are resistant to the idea of having TAs who are other than American-born, even students who haven't had any personal experience with international TAs. However, this resistance may stem from problems much deeper than just speaking English, and it definitely obscures the fact that international TAs are very valuable to diversity on campus.

International students, who are sometimes still called foreign students, are increasing on campuses nationwide, and graduate international teaching assistants, or ITAs, are increasing as well. With this increase comes the opportunity for more diversity on American campuses. Our world is quickly becoming more and more connected globally thanks to technology and strong economies. We as students now have the opportunity to learn about other cultures and appreciate them, to live in a world community instead of just a local one. As graduates we will probably find jobs working side by side with people from different countries, so being exposed to diverse cultures early in college has a great benefit for adjustment later. As Susan Johnson and Xia Li Lollar state, "Universities and colleges are a place where students from homogenous backgrounds can be introduced to the diverse environment in which they will live their adult lives" (306). Not only is the benefit of learning to live with and respect others who are different ignored by many complaints against ITAs, many of those complaints may be unjustified. I am looking at research done mainly by graduate students at universities in order to find out why American students really have such a hard time with international teaching assistants, to address some of the misconceptions, and offer suggestions in order to argue that we should appreciate the diversity value of study with international TAs.

Graduate students started to be used as teaching assistants in the 1940s and 1950s (Ouzts 21). According to one author, possibly a quarter of all undergraduate courses at big research institutions are taught by teaching assistants (Ouzts 3), but another states that the figure could be as high as half (Chang 1). The use of teaching assistants has always been controversial (Fox 2), because using graduate students to teach undergraduates can be seen as placing too much value on graduate education and research (Smith et al.) at the expense of good undergraduate education. The controversy has grown with the use of international TAs. "The Foreign TA Problem," as it has been called (Chang, Plakans, Smith et al.), has been around since the mid-1980s. It was then that larger numbers of undergraduate courses began being taught by TAs who did not speak English as a first language. Those students came to the United States to study but couldn't get visas to work off-campus. While many would work in cafeterias and libraries, some were eligible to teach low-level introductory courses that professors did not have time to teach, or to serve as lab instructors, graders, and recitation section leaders. Thus, working as a teaching assistant is a way of satisfying the graduate students' need to finance their education as well as the university's need to staff low-level, often required courses for relatively low cost (Fox, Plakans, Ouzts).

In a study done by Barbara Sweeney Plakans at Iowa State University, over 72 percent of the undergraduates she studied had been in a course taught by an ITA. ITAs at Iowa State comprised nearly a third of all the TAs and were found mainly in math, engineering, and the physical sciences. In a study by Wanda Fox at Purdue University, about 30 percent of the TAs were international and found mainly in the Engineering and Science schools (190–91). A study conducted by Florence Louise Ouzts added business to the list (1) and reported that most of the ITAs getting complaints were from Taiwan, China, and India (6), and that most of the complaints were from students in sections of in math, physics, and chemistry (30).

While most ITAs are chosen because they excel in their fields, they aren't all prepared to be good teachers, let alone teachers of American students. In order to improve teaching performance, many universities have instituted ITA training programs, which orient international students to American universities and work to assess and improve their English language skills. These programs began in the 1980s. Smith et al. state that since 1982, laws have been passed or state mandates required for assessing language abilities of ITAs in 18 states. Some of these assessments also include training programs. The training includes orientation programs, which are short, one- to five-day training sessions that students take before they start teaching. Concurrent programs are given while the teaching assistants are in their first semester of teaching, and may involve some mentoring. Some training programs combine pre-term and concurrent work with teaching assistants (Smith et al.). Smith et al. observe that we need more assessment instruments to address both the language and teaching abilities of ITAs and suggest the use of student evaluations, surveys of ITAs and supervisors, and student improvement evaluation.

ITAs in most colleges and universities go through training programs initially designed for American graduate teaching assistants, although some programs are specifically designed for international graduate students. Stephen Davis and Jason Kring describe the GTA training at their institution as a model for GTA training. It uses GPA, background courses, a personal statement and philosophy of teaching as selection criteria, and supervisor reviews and visits to the classroom as well as other detailed curriculum materials that go into a portfolio evaluation. All of these would be good for international TAs if geared specifically to their needs as instructors of American undergraduates. Cai Lun Jia and Amy Aldous Bergerson report that ITAs that attending these sorts of training seminars not only value the pedagogical advice but are then able "to develop networks both among international students and across campus," which contribute greatly to their cultural experience and the way they relate to American students (92).

Using TAs is unique to the United States (Plakans 3). In their own countries, the international graduate students probably took their classes in a very large lecture hall that was very formal. Kwasi Sarkodie-Mensah states that in some countries, it is considered rude to walk in late into the classroom or raise the left hand to ask a question. He says that many ITAs also don't know that American students have to pay for their tuition instead of the government funding them as in other countries, which leads to lack of understanding about the special circumstances of the American classroom and about the expectations of American students (115–16). Wanda Fox talks about the importance of "cultural factors" in the classroom, stating that even when the ITA has clear speech, he or she may have a hard time relating to the students (203). In a similar way, Kwasi Sarkodie-Mensah states that ITAs should not "become dictators in the classroom"(116), but that American students also need to adapt their expectations to some extent. Fox seems to see a particular responsibility on the undergraduate's part to overcome bias and prejudice (206).

So, while part of the problem may rest with ITA preparation to teach American students, much of it seems to rest with American students' perceptions. Barbara Plakans compared her study at Iowa State University with one conducted by Wanda Fox at Purdue. Plakans and Fox both researched attitudes of undergraduates who had had experiences with an ITA. For her study, Fox developed the Questionnaire of Undergraduates about International Teaching Assistants (QUITA) as well as interviews (190–91). Fox surveyed 540 undergraduates, but only 18 of these were freshmen (192). Nagesh Rao also conducted a dissertation study on negative views on ITAs held by undergraduates, finding that American undergraduates are at least equally responsible for the negative views (6). And Mei-Hsia Chang studied real versus perceived comprehension of ITAs, finding that undergraduates understand what their ITAs say more than they report they do (6).

Students often use criticism of international students' language skills as a mask for other issues. One interesting finding in Plakans's study and confirmed by Smith is that when students complained about ITAs, they usually claimed that the problem was pronunciation, but her study showed that many other kinds of communication problems were actually behind undergraduates' complaints about the speaking abilities of international teaching assistants (Plakans 131). Florence Ouzts's study confirms that cultural problems add to the problem of understanding most often identified as language-based (5). Chang discusses a study that suggests that an increased attitude of consumerism and getting one's money's worth, more ITA visibility, and ethnocentrism may be at the base of many complaints (6). Rao studied the importance of undergraduate expectations when encountering an ITA. In addition, one of the problems could be a general disillusionment and frustration with college that many undergraduates experience in the first two years, which could find a scapegoat in the ITA. Fox also reports that some students blamed the ITA for their poor academic performance (207). According to Plakans, seniors tend to be more lenient on ITA evaluations because they've mellowed and accepted the system (137–39).

A study by Nancy Ann Oppenheim suggested that students in upper-level courses have more "domain knowledge" to be able to "negotiate meaning" and figure out what the ITA is saying (vii, 212). The hypothesis of her study was that the real problem isn't the ITAs' ability to speak clearly or teach well, but that undergraduate negative and resistant attitudes were based on their perceptual bias (7). She identifies four causes of this bias: (1) negative stereotyping, (2) prejudice and overgeneralizations learned early, (3) situational factors, especially seeing the foreign students as competition, and (4) high emotions and insecurity (22–27). She states that undergraduates who learn techniques for good communication with an international teaching assistant give the ITAs higher ratings (9).

Plakans' study showed that the undergraduates who were not as critical of their instructors had positive attitudes, believing the ITA was a good teacher, was open to cultural differences, and took some of the responsibility for maintaining good communication (132). Some other studies she refers to show that undergraduates were less critical if the ITA was teaching in a course they were majoring in (also in Oppenheim 212), that personality made a big difference in acceptance, and that the lecture topic affected comprehension more than how the ITA talked. Fox's study showed that one student could understand an ITA when discussing a topic in casual conversation, but not when the ITA talked about math (203). Ouzts states that more critical ratings came from males, from nonmajors (which contradicts some other studies), from students who hadn't studied a foreign language, and from students who expected a low grade (142).

Schools have devised a number of programs to help American students adjust to instructors with foreign backgrounds. Based on the results of her study, Plakans suggested "intervention strategies" (vii) to help American undergraduate students deal with ITAs. She discusses one Michigan State approach that uses programs in residence halls conducted jointly by an ITA and an undergraduate. They talk about stereotyping, show a video, and get the students talking about the subject. Using this kind of program in freshmen orientation might also work, an idea strongly suggested by Chang along with more regular intercultural activities (149). Rao suggests sending a letter informing new undergraduates that they will have international instructors (100–03). The University of Missouri-Columbia uses a brochure called "TAs at Mizzou" that gives tips on better communication. However, Plakans says that a similar brochure used at Iowa State was criticized by a foreign student for being discriminating, and the video used at the parents' orientation created more anxieties and questions than answering them (147–48).

Fox's study recommends making undergraduates part of a screening process for new ITAs and having them participate in the ITA training course, which would help the undergraduates feel more confident about the TA program (217–18). Plakans says that trying to get undergraduates more involved in the ITA program as well as making it clear how much the ITAs are qualified might be good strategies, but they have not yet been carefully studied. Rao discusses "buddy programs" that pair an ITA with an undergraduate (104). These opportunities make the undergraduates more comfortable with ITAs and the ITAs more confident and comfortable as teachers. Sarkodie-Mensah states:

> Encouraging interaction of college-bound students and TAs from
> other countries also will foster understanding between the two

groups and will prepare the new students for some of the culture shock they will experience in the hands of the foreign TAs. (116)

Texas Tech University produced a video in 1988 called *You and the International TA: Paths to Better Understanding*. The 30-minute video explains why international teaching assistants are beneficial. It gives statistics on the increase of international students and TAs, showing that they are something that is here to stay. Three international TAs—from Sri Lanka, Taiwan, and Peru—are interviewed, and each explains how different American students are from students in their home countries. However, they all stress the positive aspects of teaching in America such as American students' being friendly and more independent. Professors explain that some American students are resistant to classes with international instructors because they are wary of people who are different or because they come from conservative parts of the country, where people with different cultures or beliefs can be seen as threatening or dangerous.

Joe Goodin, Dean of the College of Arts and Sciences at Texas Tech, describes some of the positive benefits to American undergraduates from studying with international teaching assistants. He explains how students become "sensitized to international education, international problems" in a class taught by an ITA, which is important in a globalized world becoming more interdependent. Goodin states it is important that American students go into a class taught by an ITA with the attitude that "the cultural experience" will be positive, that with "receptivity" they will end up "on the learning end" and be better off than if all their TAs were American. The international TAs help American students experience and understand cultural diversity. However, one of the studies Plakans referred to in her study showed that undergraduates were "neutral about whether the experience of having an ITA increased cultural understanding" (16). Another study showed that mentoring did not affect undergraduate acceptance and suggested that what is needed is "more informal, interpersonal contact to change attitudes and more overseas travel by undergrads" (Plakans 16).

Professors in the video list benefits, including being exposed to different cultures, and getting a better understanding of the world we live in. They also stress that many ITAs are the "cream of the crop" among students in their countries and earn awards here in the United States. The video ends with six steps for the American student to handle difficulty understanding an ITA and four suggestions for how to speak more effectively to the ITA, which Oppenheim stresses as the key to better relations (213). The video stresses being fair and patient and ends with the message that that the international TAs are needed. The video would have been even better with student comments supporting using ITAs. One comment from Plakans's study even shows how the students need to learn to adapt to people from different cultures rather than expecting their teaching assistants to do all the accommodating:

> I think we are placing too much of an emphasis on making these TAs
> conform to American ways. I'm not expecting an ITA to give up their
> culture just because they're here. I think we have a lot to learn just
> having an ITA as an instructor. There isn't much chance that you are
> going to go out into the business world and everyone you run into is
> an American. I think in a lot of cases we are being too inflexible and
> that bothers me. . . . Americans are just so egocentric we don't want
> to allow other people to be what they are. (112)

Citing another study, Ouzts refers to the ITA having to take on a "culturally alien persona" in order to try to fit in, and Smith et al. refer to the "Americanization" of ITAs, which shows how difficult and maybe wrong it is for the ITA to do all the accommodating.

International students, and ITAs in particular as very visible and authoritative international students, contribute to and support American society and education. Dennis Peterson et al. discuss their "vast and various contributions," including the fact that it is because of ITAs that many required courses can be offered regularly (68). They also state that international students contribute through their spending to a strong U.S. economy, and that their home countries show their appreciation by supporting U.S. goods and services (68). Johnson and Lollar discuss their study's findings on the important influence cultural diversity exposure in education has on American students' functioning as citizens, providing better, more democratic political participation as well as the ability to handle different perspectives and disputes better (306).

But the greatest contribution international teaching assistants make to American education is the learning opportunities they provide for undergraduates. Through working with international students and teaching assistants, American students can learn about other cultures and countries, learn about the issues we face that are unique as well as common. This learning can help us in fighting stereotyping (Peterson et al. 71) and "promoting racial understanding" (Johnson and Lollar 313). This kind of learning "could be a beacon, illuminating a world of cultural differences and a common global humanity, building blocks for a just and peaceful world" (76). The key, according to Johnson and Lollar, is exposure: "the greater the exposure to diversity the more culturally aware the students" (315).

Whether students see the ITA as a necessary evil or as the benefit they are, it is clear that they are part of our education process. So we would all be better off with a more positive perspective, like that promoted by the Texas Tech video. This positive appreciation of cultural differences should start in high school, but the suggestions made by the researchers for improving relations between undergraduates and international teaching assistants are also important. It would be best if every American student had the chance to spend time in another country. But since that isn't possible, international teaching assistants can help expand the diversity of American students' experience and teach them how important it is to first accept people who are different from themselves, and then try to understand them. Then we can help the ITAs help us learn.

Works Cited

Chang, Mei-Hsia. *Native-speaking Undergraduates' Perceived and Actual Comprehension of Foreign Teaching Assistants' Spoken Language on the Spoken Proficiency English Assessment Kit (SPEAK test)*. Diss. State U of New York at Buffalo, 1993. Ann Arbor: UMI, 1993. Print.

Davis, Stephen F., and Jason P. Kring. "A Model for Training and Evaluating Graduate Teaching Assistants." *College Student Journal* 35.1 (2001): n. pag. *EBSCO*. Web. 8 August 2008.

Fox, Wanda S. "Functions and Effects of International Teaching Assistants at a Major Research Institution." Diss. Purdue U, 1991. Print.

Institute of International Education. "Open Doors 2007: International Students in the United States." *Open Doors Online*. IIE Network, 12 Nov. 2007. Web. 3 September 2008.

Jia, Cai Lun and Amy Aldous Bergerson. "Understanding the International Teaching Program: A Case Study at a Northwestern Research University." *International Education* 37.2 (2008): 77–98. Print.

Johnson, Susan M., and Xia Li Lollar. "Diversity Policy in Higher Education: The Impact

of College Students' Exposure to Diversity on Cultural Awareness and

Political Participation." *Journal of Education Policy* 17.3 (2002):

305–20. Print.

Oppenheim, Nancy Ann. *"Living Through" an Intercultural Experience: Undergraduates*

Learning from Nonnative English-Speaking Teaching Assistants. Diss. U of Texas at

Austin, 1996. Ann Arbor: UMI, 1997. Print.

Ouzts, Florence Louise. *Students' Perceptions of Native and Non-native English-Speaking*

Graduate Teaching Assistants (GTAs). Diss. U of Mississippi, 1991. Ann Arbor: UMI,

1991. Print.

Peterson, Dennis M., Peter Briggs, Luiza Dreasher, David D. Horner, and Trevor Nelson.

"Contributions of International Students and Programs to Campus Diversity." *New*

Directions for Student Services 86 (1999): 67–77. Print.

Plakans, Barbara Sweeney. *Undergraduate Experiences With and Attitudes Toward International*

Teaching Assistants. Diss. Iowa State U, 1994. Ann Arbor: UMI, 1994. Print.

Rao, Nagesh. *The Oh No! Syndrome: A Language Expectation Model of Undergraduates'*

Negative Reactions toward Foreign Teaching Assistants. Michigan State U, 1994. Ann

Arbor: UMI, 1994. Print.

Sarkodie-Mensah, Kwasi. "The International Student as TA." *College Teaching* 39.3 (1991):

115–16. Print.

Smith, Rosslyn, et al. "Crossing Pedagogical Oceans: International Teaching Assistants in

U.S. Undergraduate Education." *ASHE-ERIC Higher Education Report* 8 (1992): n. pag.

Web. 6 Nov. 2008.

You and the International TA: Paths to Better Understanding. Writ./Prod. Rosslyn Smith.

Texas Tech U, 1988. Videocassette.

Exercises

Since this chapter is devoted to writing, revising, and editing an argumentative research paper, these exercises point to various phases of that process and offer practice using the strategies for revision and editing suggested in the chapter and elsewhere in the book. Your campus writing center can offer help with the planning, drafting and editing stages of this process. Writing centers do not proofread, although they can help you learn how to do it. However, writing centers do usually provide a concerned and impartial reader, and this can help build your confidence in the knowledge you have gained from the inquiry.

10.1 PLANNING THE RESEARCH PAPER

1. Use Focus Points: Reviewing and Organizing Information (Chapter 9, p. 159) to review your inquiry and revise your thesis.
2. Use one of the planning strategies described in this chapter—either the outline or informal paper plan—to organize your argument.
3. Exchange plans with a classmate or a group, and revise your plan, anticipating how well your plan addresses the issues raised in Focus Points: Questions for Peer Review (Chapter 10, p. 194).
4. If neither of these planning strategies seems to work for you, write a paragraph explaining why, using specific examples.

10.2 DRAFTING THE RESEARCH PAPER

Working from your outline or plan as much as you can, and using whatever drafting methods (see Focus Points: Strategies for Drafting, p. 182) you find most productive, write a first draft of the paper. If you rethink issues during the process of drafting, use the comment feature to note changes and ask questions. This draft should be sufficiently focused to be ready for serious revision.

10.3 REVIEWING AND REVISING THE DRAFT

1. Reread the draft, using the questions and strategies in the Focus Points: Strategies for Reviewing the Argument (p. 193) in this chapter as a guide. Take notes or mark on the paper where changes seem necessary.
2. Reread the draft, using Focus Points: Revising for Coherence (Chapter 7, p. 130). Revising for coherence often helps you see other problems with argumentation, evidence, and language.
3. Working with another student or a group, review your argument, first using Exercise 6.6: Listening for Voice in a Synthesis (Chapter 6, p. 127) and then using Focus Points: Questions for Peer Review in this chapter (p. 194).
4. Write a short but specific description of how you plan to revise the paper, drawing from your notes on your readings of the draft, your answers to the self-review questions, and responses from your reviewers. This description need not be more than a paragraph or a bulleted list, but it should address the major changes you expect to make, any recurring problems you have found, any additional sources you need to consult, and any questions you have yet to resolve about your argument.
5. Produce a second draft of the paper, incorporating the revisions you have decided on.

10.4 EDITING THE DRAFT

1. Start editing this draft using strategies described in Focus Points: Revising to Improve Transitions (Chapter 7, p. 131) and Focus Points: Editing for Wordiness and Choppiness (Chapter 7, p. 133).
2. Check your use of sources, using Focus Points: Editing Citations and References (Chapter 9, p. 168).
3. Produce the other apparatus (title pages, acknowledgements, table of contents, etc.) that are assigned. See the Quick Guide to Documentation in this book for differences among these conventions in different professional styles. Produce a clean, revised draft that incorporates your changes.
4. Proofread your paper, following the strategies in Focus Points: Final Editing Strategies (Chapter 7, p. 137) and Focus Points: Effective Proofreading (Chapter 7, p. 137) before you submit your final draft.

10.5 PRESENTING RESEARCH BY OTHER MEANS

1. Present your research to your class as an oral presentation with visuals. Consider carefully the information about oral presentations in Appendix A and the use of visuals in Appendix B. As you adapt your written work to a speaking performance, consider how this kind of presentation changes the arrangement of your research. If you are asked to present your research orally before or while you are producing the written report, this presentation can be a useful way to clarify your ideas and give them a hearing before working them into a written form. It is very common for researchers to present a project orally before producing a written version.

2. Create a Web site that records your research and offers links to appropriate sources and visuals.

10.6 REFLECTING ON YOUR INQUIRY

1. This paper and the other projects you have carried out required a considerable amount of work from you. Think about this work in terms of the intellectual property issues raised in Chapter 3 and elsewhere in the book. How would you feel if someone submitted the paper as their own without your permission? Would you be willing to give it to someone else? To sell it? To make it available for other students to consult? Why or why not?

2. Reflect on how well the various collaborations involved in this extended inquiry worked. What could be done to make them more useful?

3. Reflect on how recursive your writing process was as you worked on this paper, that is, how often you seemed to move to an earlier part of the process as you neared your finished product.

4. What more would you like to do to pursue this inquiry, perhaps in another class? Or, if you think it is finished, why do you think so?

A Quick Guide to Documentation

MODERN LANGUAGE ASSOCIATION (MLA) STYLE

Modern Language Association (MLA) style is typically used for work done in the humanities disciplines. For more detailed information, see *The MLA Handbook for Writers of Research Papers*, 7th edition (2009).

Formatting

Spacing and Margins

1. Double-space the paper, using 1-inch margins on all sides. Use the best printer you can get access to if you are submitting a printed copy.

2. Use a plain and easily readable font (such as Times New Roman).

3. While MLA previously preferred <u>underlining</u> to *italics* to signal titles of major works, the *MLA Handbook* now recommends using only *italics*.

Titles and Title Page

1. When writing a title for a paper, think about what you have learned from searching for sources. Because databases sort by key words and by titles, you should try to get as many key words into your title as you can without making it too long and unwieldy. Putting key words in your title makes your work more easily retrievable by other researchers.

2. Although the *MLA Handbook for Writers of Research Papers* says that title pages are not required for research papers, many professors in the humanities expect them. In English classes in particular, innovative titles involving literary allusions, puns, or other sorts of word play are often invited. Very often in the humanities titles come in two parts, for example: "Funny Papers: Humor in the Writing of College Students" or "Making Fun: Comic Form and the Student Writer."

3. Make a title page only when requested; otherwise, make a double-spaced heading at the top left of the first page with your name, the instructor's name, the course, and the date. Center the title, and do not leave extra spaces before beginning the paper.

4. On the title page, if you use one, capitalize the first letter of the first and last word and of all nouns, verbs, adjectives, and adverbs in the title. Repeat the title, centered at the top of the page, on the first page of the paper.

5. Generally, teachers expect the title page to show the paper's title, the student's name, the course for which the paper is submitted, and the date due or submitted, in a form that is pleasing and clear. Some teachers encourage students to add pictures or graphics to the title page.

Pagination

1. Place page numbers on the top right of each page. Page numbering is absolutely essential. A running header with your last name preceding the page number is also required.

2. In MLA style, the title page (if there is one) is not numbered. Numbering starts on the first page of the text. Some instructors follow an older version of MLA style, which demands that no number appear on the first page. Therefore, the first visible page number is 2 on the second page.

Works Cited Page

1. Begin the works cited page on a separate page immediately following the paper. Use Works Cited, centered but not bolded, as the title. Continue the page numbering in sequence. (In shorter, informal papers with only a few sources, your teacher may suggest that you leave several spaces after the text ends and add your works cited list to the last page.)

2. Use hanging indentation, and double-space the entries without leaving extra spaces between them.

Sample MLA Title Page

Funny Papers:

Humor in the Writing of Engineering Undergraduates

John L. Shorten

English 102–03

Professor Lionel E. Jones

March 21, 2008

Acknowledgements

1. Many books have a paragraph or more of acknowledgements in their opening material, in which the author names and thanks people who have contributed to the project. These acknowledgements always include sources of funding and mention friends and colleagues who have reviewed the manuscript and aided the process of inquiry. They might also include editors, people who have helped the writer find resources, reading or writing groups that have helped the writer generate ideas, and other similar sources of assistance in the writing process.

2. Although an acknowledgements page is not required by the MLA style guide for student papers, many professors encourage or require students to write them, in order to become accustomed to recognizing publicly the collaborations that go into producing most academic writing.

3. In MLA style, the acknowledgements page should follow the title page of the report, with the title, "Acknowledgements," centered (no bold or italics).

Sample MLA Acknowledgements

Acknowledgements

I would like to acknowledge the help of my colleague John Yu for his review of an early draft of this manuscript, of Professor Janis Erikson of the history department for her help with locating sources, and of my colleagues Jennifer Smith and Yolanda Jones for their careful reading of and thoughtful responses to my final draft.

Parenthetical Citations

1. Any information, figures, ideas, arguments, theories, or other material derived from sources must be attributed to that source, whether it is used in the form of direct quotation, paraphrase, or summary (see Chapter 3). The purpose of parenthetical citation is to allow the reader to find the complete reference for the source in the list of works cited.

2. MLA requires that following the quotation or summary you provide the author's last name and the page number in parentheses, unless that information is given in the text. If you name the author before the quotation, paraphrase, or summary, you should put only the page number in parentheses afterward. The idea is to give the necessary information only once, in order to interrupt the reading as little as possible.

3. In general, avoid putting the same information both in your text and in the parenthetical citation, and remember that the less information put in parentheses the better, except for the page number.

Examples

"There is no single profile of the Good Teacher" (Rose 9).

Mike Rose does not outline one and only one set of attributes of the good teacher (9).

4. If there is no page number (as is true with some material on the Web), you cannot use one.

Examples

Alfie Kohn observes that "the long history of indignation" over grade inflation is

usually ignored.

Although there is a "long history of grade inflation," it is usually ignored (Kohn).

5. If there is more than one author with the same last name in the citations list, identify the author of the text cited by using both names in your text or by putting the first initial before the last name in parentheses.

6. If there is more than one work by the same author in the list of works cited, use a short title to refer to the work cited in your text.

Examples

Rebecca Moore Howard argues that teachers should worry more about teaching good

citation skills than tracking down plagiarists ("Forget" 24).

It has been argued that faulty citation practices can and should be distinguished from such

fraudulent activities as downloading or purchasing term papers (Howard, "Plagiarisms" 788–89).

7. Check the *MLA Handbook* when citing sources like the Bible or other religious scriptures, major public documents like the U.S. Constitution or UN Charter, or widely reprinted works like the plays of William Shakespeare. Usually these texts are cited by part and line number rather than by page number.

Creating the Works Cited List

As noted in Chapter 4, you need to collect the following information from all the sources you use; not all sources have all these features, but use common sense to collect the information available when first consulting each source:

- For all sources, record the author, title, page number(s) for the material you are using, and the year of publication; also record the editor or translator, if there is one.
- For books, record the place of publication, publisher, and edition number if you are not using the first.
- For articles in journals, record the journal name, volume and issue numbers, and page numbers for the entire article as well as for the specific page of the citation.

- For articles in magazines and newspapers, record the publication name, full date, and section number or letter for newspapers divided into sections.
- For online sources, record the required publication information for all sources that originally appeared in print, the date you accessed the site, the Web site title, the publisher, and the URL. MLA does not require the use of URLs for sites that can be easily found by through a search engine or that have part of the URL in their Web site name (e.g., *Popular Science, CIA Fact Book, CNN.com*). However, check with your instructor, as many instructors still require the URL at the end of the citation in angle brackets.
- Include a medium of publication for every entry. Although you will use *Print* and *Web* most often, you might also use other descriptors such as *DVD, Performance,* or *CD.*

General Formatting

The following guidelines and examples offer a short overview of MLA style for references. Consult the *MLA Handbook for Writers of Research Papers* for the finer points:

1. Entries should follow alphabetical order by the first word, which will usually be the last name of the author, if it is available.
2. If there is more than one source by a single author, alphabetize by the first word in the title (other than *a, an,* or *the*), and after the first entry replace the author's name with three hyphens.
3. Use hanging indentation.
4. Use double-spacing throughout, with no extra spaces between entries.
5. Continue page numbering (with the header, if you are using one) from the text of your paper, but start the Works Cited list on a new page.

Citations for Books

Standard Citations

1. Book citations look like this:

    Author's last name, first name. *Title: Subtitle if There Is One.* City of Publication:

    Publishing Company Short Name, date. Print.

2. Add a state or country if there is a possibility of ambiguity, such as with Cambridge (MA or UK?) and Springfield (Massachusetts, Illinois, Missouri, etc.?) or if the location does not seem like common knowledge, such as Cresskill, NH.

Example

Blum, Susan D. *My Word!: Plagiarism and College Culture.* Ithaca, NY: Cornell UP, 2009. Print.

3. If there are two or more authors, list them in the order they appear on the title page. Subsequent authors' names follow the standard first then last name order, which is reversed only for the first author, to make alphabetization easier. Notice the comma after both of the first author's names (whether or not "and" is used) and the period at the end of the sequence.
4. If there are more than three authors, either name the first and add *et al.* or list all the authors.

Examples

Baym, Nina, et al.

Graff, Gerald, Sally Smith, James McEwan, and Andrew Hoberek.

5. **A book with no author.** Start with the title, and alphabetize the source by the first word that is not an article.

6. **A work in an anthology (collection of essays or literary pieces) or a part of a book (such as an introduction, foreword, or afterword).** The entry begins with the author of the piece, not the editor of the collection, and the page numbers for the entire piece follow the date. In the Examples, *The Autobiography* is italicized, since it is a book-length work in its own right, whereas the title of Kleinman's article is in quotation marks.

Examples

Franklin, Benjamin. *The Autobiography. The Norton Anthology of American Literature.*

    Ed. Nina Baym et al. 5th ed. Vol. 1. New York: Norton, 1998. 523–96. Print.

Kleinman, Neil. "Don't Fence Me In: Copyright, Property, and Technology." *Communication*

    and Cyberspace: Social Interaction in an Electronic Environment. Ed. Lance Strate,

    Ronald Jacobson, and Stephanie P. Gibson. Cresskill, NH: Hampton, 1996.

    59–82. Print.

Lunsford, Andrea. Foreword. *Perspectives on Plagiarism and Intellectual Property in a Postmodern*

    World. Ed. Lise Buranen and Alice M. Roy. Albany, NY: SUNY, 1999. ix–xi. Print.

7. **Cross-references.** When you use two or more articles published in a collection or anthology, create an entry for the anthology and then reference the articles to it.

Examples

Buranen, Lise, and Alice M. Roy, eds. *Perspectives on Plagiarism and Intellectual Property*

    in a Postmodern World. Albany, NY: SUNY, 1999. Print.

Lunsford, Andrea. Foreword. Buranen and Roy ix–xii.

Spigelman, Candace. "The Ethics of Appropriation in Peer Writing Groups." Buranen and Roy

    231–40.

8. **A work with editions and volumes.**
   - Since pagination changes from edition to edition of a work, it is important to identify the edition from which you are citing, and since some works come in volumes, such as the two-volume *Norton Anthology of American Literature*, identify which volume is being used.
   - When an older work is published in a modern edition, like *Leviathan* (1651) in the Examples, the editor's name is usually given. Notice that in most cases, the entry is listed under the original author. The original date of publication is optional.

- When a book is translated, the name of the translator is added, either in place of or in addition to the editor's name.

Examples

Franklin, Benjamin. *The Autobiography. The Norton Anthology of American Literature.* Ed.

Nina Baym et al. 5th ed. Vol. 1. New York: Norton, 1998. 523–96. Print.

Freud, Sigmund. *Jokes and Their Relation to the Unconscious.* Trans. James Strachey. New

York: Norton, 1963. Print.

Modern Language Association. *MLA Style Manual and Guide to Scholarly Publishing.* 3rd ed.

New York: MLA, 2008. Print.

Hobbes, Thomas. *Leviathan.* 1651. Ed. Crawford Brough Macpherson. New York: Penguin,

1981. Print.

9. **Dissertations.** A dissertation is a sizable work written as a requirement for the Ph.D. degree. Dissertations are stored in the libraries of the universities for which they were written and are often published in paper versions or on microfilm. Usually, a young researcher rewrites the dissertation into a book or a series of articles as his or her career progresses. The first dissertation below has been published (by University Microfilms International), and the number that follows is its order number (which is optional). The second dissertation is unpublished.

Examples

Chang, Mei-Hsia. *Native-speaking Undergraduates' Perceived and Actual Comprehension of*

Foreign Teaching Assistants' Spoken Language on the Spoken Proficiency English

Assessment Kit (SPEAK test). Diss. State U of New York at Buffalo, 1993. Ann Arbor:

UMI, 1993. 9330043. Microfilm.

Fox, Wanda S. "Functions and Effects of International Teaching Assistants at a Major

Research Institution." Diss. Purdue U, 1991. Print.

Citations for Periodicals

1. **Articles in magazines and newspapers.**
   - Standard citation format is Author's last name, first name. "Title of Article." *Title of Magazine* date: pages. Print.
   - Use the full date as given on the newspaper or magazine. If the newspaper has sections (as in the Howard example below), add the section number or letter before the page number.

Examples

Boyle, James. "Who Stole the Goose?" *Syllabus* Nov. 2003: 22–24. Print.

Crace, John. "Higher Education: Cut and Paste Job: As Plagiarism Engulfs the US and

Threatens the UK, a New Advisory Service Has Been Launched to Track Down Our Own

Academic Cheats." *Guardian* [London] 15 Oct. 2002: 10. Print.

Howard, Rebecca Moore. "Forget about Plagiarism. Just Teach." *Chronicle of Higher*

Education 16 Nov. 2001: B24. Print.

2. **Scholarly journals.** Most scholarly journals are published with continuous pagination throughout a calendar or publication year. Some, however, begin pagination with each issue. Previously the *MLA Handbook* required citations that distinguished between the two, but that is not longer the case. For all scholarly
journals, include both the volume and issue numbers.

> Author's last name, first name. "Title of Article." *Title of Journal* Volume. Issue (year):
>
> pages. Print.

Examples

Schultz, Karen. "Dreams Deferred: The Personal Narratives of Four Black Kansans." *American*

Studies 4.3 (1993): 22–51. Print

Citations for Other Kinds of Sources

1. **Reference books.** Include what is available of the following information: Author
and title of the article or entry, title of the reference work, edition, date, and medium
of publication. The page and volume numbers are not necessary if the articles are
alphabetized.
   - Very familiar reference works (e.g., the *Oxford English Dictionary*) do not need
   publication information other than the edition and date.
   - If you are using a specialized disciplinary encyclopedia (e.g., the *Encyclopedia of
   Literature and Science*), the place of publication and name of the publisher can
   help your reader find the source.

Examples

Lee, Judith Yaross. "Popularization." *Encyclopedia of Literature and Science*. Ed. Pamela

Gossin. Westport, CT: Greenwood, 2002. Print.

"Popular." *The Oxford English Dictionary*. 2nd ed. 1989. Print.

2. **Personal interviews.** Include the interviewee's name, the designation *personal
interview*, and date.

Example

Howard, Rebecca Moore. Personal interview. 3 June 2003.

3. **Lectures or similar performances.** Include what is available of the following information: speaker's name; the title of the talk or a descriptive term for it; the conference, meeting, or organization sponsoring the talk; the location (place and city); the full date; and the medium.

Example

Yancey, Kathleen Blake. "Made Not Only in Words: Composition in a New Key." Conference on

College Composition and Communication, San Antonio, TX. 25 March 2004. Lecture.

4. **Film or video.**
   - Include the title, director or other identified creator (preceded by function), medium, production company, and date.
   - If you have a good reason for including the names of certain actors or participants (such as discussing them in the paper), put them after the director's name.

Example

You and the International TA: Paths to Better Understanding. Writer/Prod. Rosslyn Smith.

Narr. Joe Goodin. Texas Tech U, 1988. Videocassette.

5. **Television or radio broadcasts.**
   - Include whatever is available of the following information: title of episode in quotation marks, title of program italicized, title of series with no special punctuation, network, call letters, city of local station, and date.
   - If you have a good reason to include names of participants or performers, put them after the first title, identified by function.
   - If your reference is primarily to the work of the director, performer, or newscaster, that name can precede the title.
   - Be sure to include the publication medium (e.g., Radio, Television).

Example

The Prairie Home Companion. Host Garrison Keillor. Natl. Public Radio. WBAA, West

Lafayette, IN, 13 Dec. 2003. Radio.

Citations for Electronic Sources

Methods for citing electronic sources are still evolving as new sources are developed, as print documents are archived online, as the Web changes, and as libraries and scholars adapt to these changes. Although *The MLA Handbook* does not require the use of URLs for Web entries, unless the reference is obscure and difficult to find, some instructors may still require the use of URLs in student papers. Keep in mind that the purpose of a list of works cited is to let another researcher find your sources, so use that purpose as a guide when problems arise with citing electronic sources. In many cases, for example, no author is named for Web sites; in these cases, start with the Web page title, as you would for a print source with no identified author.

The sources you find on the Web may be archived print documents or material produced explicitly for online publication. *The MLA Handbook* recommends that you order the information in the following way:

Author's last name, first name. "Title of the Document." *Name of Larger Work or Web Site.*

Information about print publication. Information about electronic publication.

Medium (e.g., Web). Access information.

- The information about print publication follows the conventional pattern described above.
- The information about electronic publication may vary in availability. At best, include the site title italicized, the site editor, the most recent date of electronic publication, and the name of the organization that runs the site.
- If the site does not include sponsor or publisher information, use *n.p.* for *no publisher.*
- If no date of publication is given, use *n.d.* for *no date.*
- For articles that are only published online and do not provide a page number, use *n. pag.* for *no pagination.*
- Access information includes the date of access, which is very important, because sites can change considerably in even a short time.
- If your Web citation is difficult to locate or if the URL is required by your instructor, add it to the end of your citation in angle brackets followed by a period. Break URLs after the slash in order to fill entry lines. Do not allow your word processor to reformat the entry after you have typed it in.

Citations for Online Sources

1. **Web sites.** Include whatever is available of the following information: the editor or author, the title of the site, electronic publication information (version number, most recent date, publisher or sponsoring organization [*n. p.* if not known]), and access date.

Examples

Essayfinder.com. Paper Stores, 2000. Web. 1 Sept. 2008.

The Victorian Women Writers Project. Indiana U, 1995–2003. Web. 1 Aug. 2008.

2. **Article in an independent Web site (not from a database).** Include whatever is available of the following information: author; title in quotation marks; online periodical italicized or Web site title; volume number; issue number; date of publication; pages, if numbered, or *n. pag.*, if not; *Web* as medium; and date of access.

Example

Haberling, Michael. "Maintaining Academic Integrity in Online Education." *Journal of*

Distance Learning 5.1 (2002): n. pag. Web. 20 Aug. 2008.

3. **Print journal article archived on a Web site.** Include whatever is available of the following information: author, title in quotation marks, name of periodical italicized, archive sponsor, date added to archive, *Web* as medium, and date of access.

Example

Hunt, Russell. "Four Reasons to be Happy about Internet Plagiarism." *Teaching Perspectives.*

St. Thomas U, 5 Dec. 2002. Web. 19 June 2008.

4. **Print magazine or newspaper article published or archived on a Web site.** Include whatever is available of the following information: author, title in quotation marks, name of the online periodical italicized, publisher, full date of publication, *Web* as medium, and date of access. Note that sometimes the names of periodicals and online periodicals may slightly differ. Provide the online periodical name (e.g. *The Atlantic* is the name of the print periodical publication, while its online version is *TheAtlantic.com*).

Examples

Howard, Rebecca Moore. "Forget about Policing Plagiarism. Just Teach."

Chronicle.com. Chronicle of Higher Education, 16 Nov. 2001. Web.

17 Jan. 2008.

Plotz, David. "The Plagiarist: Why Stephen Ambrose Is a Vampire." *Slate.com.* Washington

Post, 11 Jan. 2002. Web. 25 Feb. 2008.

5. **E-mail messages.**
   - It is an important professional courtesy to get permission from the writer of the message or of a post to a discussion list before quoting or excerpting from it, and it is crucial if you want to use a message not addressed personally to you. For example, the e-mail from Professor Way was reproduced in Chapter 5 with his written permission.
   - Include in the citation whatever is available of the following information: writer, subject line heading in quotation marks, *Message* as descriptor, the recipient name, date of message, and *E-mail* as medium.
   - If it is an e-mail to a discussion list (listserv), cite as you would for a Web site: include subject heading, listserv name, publisher, date posted, *Web* as medium, and date of access.

Examples

Bergmann, Linda. "Re: Plagiarism and Post 9/11 Purge." *Writing Program Administration*

(WPA-L). Arizona State U, 11 Dec. 2003. Web. 15 May 2008.

Way, John. "Re: Eureka!" Message to the author. 6 Apr. 1998. E-mail.

For More Information

The best source for more information is the *MLA Handbook for Writers of Research Papers*, now in its seventh edition. It is explicitly designed for college students learning to write research papers. Most of the information in this appendix is derived from this source. The writing center in your college will have one or more copies of this handbook, and so will the library.

In addition, the online writing centers listed in Chapter 6 have information about using MLA format on their Web sites and links to other, related guides to using this style. The only way to learn to use it, though, is to work through the problems, citation by citation, always remembering your readers' needs.

AMERICAN PSYCHOLOGICAL ASSOCIATION (APA) STYLE

American Psychological Association (APA) style is typically used for work done in the social sciences and is substantially different from Modern Language Association (MLA) style, involving not only a different format for citations, but also a different approach to formatting the entire paper, and at heart a different approach to transmitting knowledge. If you are familiar with MLA style, be careful not to let the similarities make you overlook the differences.

Formatting

Spacing and Margins

1. Double-space the paper, using 1-inch margins on all sides. Use the best printer you can get access to if you are submitting a printed copy.
2. Use a plain and easily readable font (such as Times New Roman).
3. *Note:* Underlining is a mark used in typed manuscripts to indicate that type should be set in *italics*; the *APA Publication Manual* recommends using italic font unless working with a typewriter (which would be highly unusual).

Titles and Title Page

1. When writing a title for an academic research paper, think about what you have learned from searching for sources. Because databases sort by key words and by titles, try to get as many key words into your title as you can without making it too long and unwieldy. Putting key words in your title makes your work more easily retrievable by other researchers.
2. The APA manual advises that the title state the main topic, the significant variable or theoretical position, and the relation between them. For example, a good title in APA style might be "The Effects of Humor on Writing Proficiency of Undergraduate Engineering Majors," with "Effects of Humor" as the shortened title. Use the shortened title to create the running head, which is placed in the header preceding the page number. "Humor" and "writing proficiency" would be identified as key words, along with "engineering education" and other terms pointing to the paper's content.

3. In the header of the title page and on all subsequent pages, flush-left, insert a running head. Provide the shortened title, which may be 50 characters or less and must appear in all caps.

4. Be sure to include the following on the title page:
   - the author's name and institutional affiliation;
   - identification of the running head; and
   - page number preceded by running head.

Some instructors may ask for additional information on the title page, such as the name and section number of the course and the date of submission.

Pagination

1. Place page numbers in the document header on the top right of each page flush-right and following the page header. Page numbering is absolutely essential.

2. In APA style, the title page is page 1. On subsequent pages, the running head appears alongside the page number.

Sample APA Title Page

Running Head: EFFECTS OF HUMOR   1

The Effects of Humor on the Writing Proficiency of

Undergraduate Engineering Majors

Melinda W. Jones

Mindful College

Acknowledgements

1. Many publications have a paragraph or even a page of acknowledgements, in which the author names and thanks people who have contributed to the project. Although not required for student papers, many professors encourage or require

students to write acknowledgements, in order to become accustomed to recognizing publicly the collaborations that go into producing most academic writing.

2. While APA style designates a particular format for acknowledgements in professional publications, for student work, it is sufficient merely to mention those who have helped with the process of researching, writing, and revising the paper. Some instructors, however, may ask for a wider range of acknowledgements or a more formal construction of them.

3. Acknowledgements always include sources of funding and mention colleagues who have reviewed the manuscript and aided the research project. They might also include editors, people who have helped the writer find resources, reading or writing groups that have helped the writer generate ideas, and other similar sources of assistance in the writing process.

4. In APA style, place the acknowledgements in an "Author Note" on the title page.

Abstracts

1. APA style requires an Abstract. Place it after the title page. Keep your abstract short, no more than one paragraph and under 120 words as recommended by the *APA Publication Manual*, which stipulates that an abstract should be accurate, self-contained, concise and specific, nonevaluative, coherent, and readable (25–27).

2. Summarize the whole paper in the abstract: the problem, your major claim(s), the basic lines of your argument, and your conclusion.

3. Use key terms in the abstract: in professional research, abstracts are often stored in databases used by other researchers use to find sources.

Example: Abstract for the Argumentative Research Paper in Chapter 8

NEGATIVE VIEWS   2

Abstract

This paper looks at the resistance of American undergraduates to taking classes with international teaching assistants. This resistance often results from misconceptions, communication problems, and poor academic performance, as well as from prejudice against people from different cultures. Effective training of international teaching assistants can help them function more effectively in American classrooms, and programs for undergraduates can help them adjust to the cultural differences they may find when studying with instructors from other countries. International teaching assistants make an important contribution to undergraduate learning, giving American students direct experience with people from other cultures and teaching them to accept and understand people who are different from them.

Headings

APA uses a unique formatting system for section headings and subheadings. While most student papers will only require one level of headings (i.e., Abstract, Methods, Results), more advanced papers may require subheadings the document's main headings. These additional subheadings are like the subsections of an outline that go beyond the initial roman numerals (e.g., I. . . ., A. . . ., B. . . ., 1. . . ., 2. . . ., etc.).

Count how many levels you will need for your document. Then, use the guide below to determine how to format each heading level. For example, if your paper will use three levels of headings, format the first level as in line 1, those that appear in the second sublevel as in line 2, and so forth.

Level 1 Headings are Centered, Require Standard Heading Capitalization, and Appear in Bold

Level 2 Headings Appear Flush-Left, in Bold, and in Standard Heading Capitalization

Level 3 headings are indented, use paragraph capitalization (only capitalize proper nouns), appear in bold, and end with a period.

Level 4 headings are indented, placed in both boldface and italics, use paragraph capitalization (only capitalize proper nouns), and end with a period.

Level 5 headings are indented, appear in italics, use paragraph capitalization (only capitalize proper nouns), and end with a period.

Assembling Information

Collect the following information from all the sources you use; not all sources offer all of this information, but use your common sense to collect the information available when first consulting the source.

1. For all sources, record the author, title, page number(s) of the material used and the year of publication; also record the name of the editor or translator, if there is one.
2. For books, record the place of publication, publisher, and edition if it is not the first.
3. For articles in journals, record the journal name, volume and issue numbers, and page numbers.
4. For articles in magazines and newspapers, record the publication name, volume number, full date, and section number for newspapers divided into sections.
5. For online sources, record the information from the medium of initial publication, and, in most cases, add the URL and the date you accessed the site.

Parenthetical Citations

1. Attribute any information, data, figures, ideas, arguments, theories, and so on derived from sources, whether used as a direct quotation, paraphrase, or summary. Review Chapter 4 for examples of these different ways of using sources. The purpose of parenthetical citations is to allow the reader to find the complete reference for the source in the reference list.

2. Provide the author's last name and the year of publication in parentheses when introducing a summary or paraphrase, unless you have identified the author in your text, in which case you should put only the year of publication in parentheses. In general, avoid putting the same information both in your text and in the parenthetical citation, and remember that the less information you put in parentheses the better.

3. Texts by multiple authors are much more common in disciplines that use APA style than those that use MLA.
   - If a work has two authors, give both names every time you cite the source.
   - If a work has 3–5 authors, name all the authors in the first citation, and in later citations name only the first author and let "et al." represent the remaining authors.
   - If a work has six or more authors, cite only the last name of the first author, followed by "et al" and a period. (APA no longer recommends italics for "et al" but still requires that a period follow it.)

4. Quotations are less commonly used in APA style than in MLA, although practices vary from discipline to discipline. For example, researchers in education who use APA style are more apt to use direct quotations more than researchers in physiological psychology. For quotations, give page numbers in parentheses as well.

Examples

"There is no single profile of the Good Teacher" (Rose, 1995, p. 9).

Rose (1995) asserts, "There is no single profile of the Good Teacher" (p. 9).

However, a paraphrase would look like this:

Rose (1995) does not outline one and only one set of attributes of the good teacher.

5. For quotations over 40 words, end your signal phrase with a colon, then, on a separate line, type the quote without quotation marks. Indent the left margin of the quote 5 spaces or one-half inch. If multiple paragraphs appear in the quote, indent five spaces where the new paragraph begins. The parenthetical citation follows the punctuation of the quote. Normal formatting resumes after the quotation.

6. If there is no page number or author named (as is true with much material on the Web), use what information you have.

Example

Turnitin.com claims a high success rate in detecting plagiarism.

7. If there is more than one author with the same last name in your references list, be sure to identify the author of the text cited by using both first and last names in your text or by putting the first initial before the last name in the parenthetical citation.

8. Using multiple sources in one set of parentheses is a common practice in APA style, which relies more heavily on summary than quotations. Arrange these multisource citations alphabetically by the authors' last name.

Examples

Past research into plagiarism (Howard, 1995, 2001; Spigelman, 1999) indicates that . . .

Past research into plagiarism (Howard, 1995, 2001; see also Spigelman, 1999)

indicates that . . .

9. Cite personal communications that are not publicly available, such as conversations, e-mails, and personal interviews, in parentheses in the text, but do not include them in the reference list.

Examples

J. Y. Lee (personal communication, September 16, 2002) identified the business memo as a

particularly malleable form of communication.

The business memo can actually be a seen as a particularly malleable form of

communication (J. Y. Lee, personal communication, September 16, 2002).

10. Do not make an entry in the reference list for the Bible or major classical works; in-text parenthetical citations are located by parts (books, chapters, lines, acts, etc.) rather than by page numbers. Check the *Publication Manual of the American Psychological Association* if you feel uncertain when citing sources like the Bible, other scriptures, or classical texts.

Creating the References Page

General Formatting

You may need to consult the *Publication Manual of the American Psychological Association* for the finer points. These basic rules offer a start.

1. Entries should follow alphabetical order, by the first word, which will be the last name of the author if there is one.
2. If there is more than one piece by a single author, repeat the name for each reference, and order the entries by date from earliest to most recent; if an author has more than one publication in a single year, order the entries by the title (excluding *a, an,* and *the*), and put a lowercase letter after each in the parenthetical citation (e.g., 1999a and 1999b).
3. An author's single-authored publications precede publications of which he or she is first in a series of co-authors.
4. If one name appears as the first author for multiple sources with different co-authors, alphabetize by the subsequent author's last name.
5. Format the reference list with hanging indentation.
6. Use double-spacing throughout, with no extra spaces between entries.
7. Continue page numbering with the header from the text of your paper, but start the list on a new page, directly after the last page of the body of the paper.

The *APA Publication Manual* gives the following general formats for references:

1. Periodicals. Periodicals include items published on a regular basis: journals, magazines, scholarly newsletters, and so on.

> Author, A. A., Author, B. B. & Author C. C. (1994). Title of article. *Title of Periodical,*
>
> *xx,* xxx–xxx.

2. Nonperiodical publications. Nonperiodicals include items published separately: books, reports, brochures, certain monographs, manuals, and audiovisual media.

> Author, A. A. (1994). *Title of Work.* Location: Publisher.

3. Part of a nonperiodical (e.g., book chapter).

> Author, A. A., & Author, B. B. (1994). Title of chapter. In A. Editor, B. Editor, & C.
>
> Editor (Eds.), *Title of book* (pp. xxx–xxx). Location: Publisher.

4. Online Periodicals.

> Author, A. A., Author, B. B., & Author, C. C. (2000). Title of article. *Title of Periodical,*
>
> *xx,* xxx–xxx. Retrieved from URL.

Note: You do not need to provide a retrieval date unless the URL for your source is likely to change. Most URLs for scholarly journals and other periodicals are not likely to change.

5. Online document.

> Author, A. A. (2000). *Title of Work.* Retrieved month day, year, from URL.

Note: if the URL for the online document is likely to move or change, as in the case of personal Web sites, for example, provide a retrieval date (e.g., Retrieved month day, year, from URL).

6. Electronic sources include aggregated databases, online journals, Web sites or Web pages, Web- or e-mail based discussion groups, and Web- or e-mail based newsletters. (*Publication Manual of the American Psychological Association,* 2009, pp. 187–192.)

References for Books

1. General example.

> Peloso, J. (2003). *Intellectual Property.* New York: H. W. Wilson.

2. Books with multiple authors or editors. If there are two or more authors, as there very often are in fields that use APA style, list them in the order they appear on the title page. All authors' names follow the same order: last name before first and middle initials. Notice the comma after each author's name, the use of the ampersand ("&") rather than the word *and,* and the period at the end of the authorial sequence. Provide the last names and initials for the first six authors, referring to any additional authors with "et al." (Notice the period in *et al.*)

Example

McLeod, S. H., Miraglia, E., Soven, M., & Thaiss, C. (Eds.). (2001). *WAC for the new*

   millennium: Strategies for continuing writing-across-the-curriculum programs. Urbana,

   IL: NCTE Press.

3. **A book with no author.** Start with the title, and follow the general order above; only if it is designated "anonymous," should you put "Anonymous" in the author position.

4. **A piece in an anthology (collection of chapters or studies written by different authors), or a part of a book (such as an introduction, foreword, or afterword).** The entry begins with the author of the piece, not the editor of the collection. Page numbers for the entire article are used.

Examples

Franklin, B. (1998). The autobiography. In N. Baym (Ed.), *The Norton anthology of American*

   literature (5th ed., Vol. 1, pp. 523–596). New York: Norton.

Kleinman, N. (1996). Don't fence me in: Copyright, property, and technology. In L. Strate,

   R. Jacobson, & S. P. Gibson (Eds.), *Communication and cyberspace: Social interaction*

   in an electronic environment (pp. 59–82). Cresskill, NH: Hampton Press.

Lunsford, A. (1999). Foreword. In L. Buranen, & A. M. Roy (Eds.), *Perspectives on plagiarism*

   and intellectual property in a postmodern world (pp. ix–xii). Albany, NY: SUNY Press.

5. **Edition and volume.** Since pagination changes from edition to edition, it is important to identify the edition from which you are citing, and since works such as the *Norton Anthology* come in two or more volumes, you need to identify which you are citing. Edition and volume numbers are put in parentheses, immediately after the title.

6. **Editors and translators.** When a book is translated (*Jokes*) or a new edition of an older work is reedited (*Leviathan*), the date of the new edition goes in the date position, the name of the translator and/or editor is added, and a parenthetical explanation may be given to supply the original date.

Examples

Franklin, B. (1998). The autobiography. In N. Baym (Ed.), *The Norton anthology of American*

   literature (5th ed., Vol. 1, pp. 523–596). New York: Norton. (Original full edition

   published 1868)

Freud, S. (1963). *Jokes and their relation to the unconscious* (J. Strachey, Trans.). New York:

Norton. (Original work published 1905)

Hobbes, T. (1981). *Leviathan* (C. B. Macpherson, Ed.). New York: Penguin. (Original work

published 1651)

7. **Dissertations.** A dissertation is a sizable work written as a requirement for the Ph.D. degree. Dissertations are stored in the libraries of the universities for which they were written, and sometimes published in paper versions or on microfilm. Usually, a young researcher will rewrite the dissertation into a book or a series of articles as his or her career progresses, and these are considered better sources, since they are more recent and more polished. The first dissertation below has been published (by University Microfilms International) and the number that follows is its order number (which is optional). The second dissertation is unpublished, but has been abstracted in *Dissertation Abstracts International,* a collection of dissertation abstracts available in most reference collections and online.

Examples

Chang, M. (1993). Native-speaking undergraduates' perceived and actual comprehension of

foreign teaching assistants' spoken language on the Spoken Proficiency English

Assessment Kit (SPEAK test). *Dissertation Abstracts International, 54*(01), 2074A.

(UMI No. 9330043)

Fox, W. S. (1991). Functions and effects of international teaching assistants at a major

research institution (Doctoral Dissertation, Purdue University 1991). *Dissertation

Abstracts International, 52*(09), 3193A.

References for Periodicals

1. **References for articles in magazines and newspapers.** The volume numbers of magazines are noted, and months are not abbreviated. Only in newspapers do the abbreviations *p.* or *pp.* appear before the page numbers.

Examples

Boyle, J. (2003, November) Who stole the goose? *Syllabus, 7,* 22–24.

Crace, J. (2002, October 15). Higher education: Cut and paste job: As plagiarism engulfs

the US and threatens the UK, a new advisory service has been launched to track down

our own academic cheats. *The Guardian* [London], p. 10.

Howard, R. M. (2001, November 16). Forget about plagiarism: Just teach. *The Chronicle of

Higher Education,* p. B24.

2. References for scholarly journals. Most scholarly journals are published with continuous pagination throughout a calendar or publication year. Page numbers are not preceded by *p.* or *pp.*

Examples

Howard, R. M. (1995). Plagiarisms, authorships, and the academic death penalty. *College*

   English, 57, 788–806.

Johnson, S. M., & Xia, L. L. (2002). Diversity policy in higher education: The impact of

   college students' exposure to diversity on cultural awareness and political

   participation. *Journal of Education Policy, 17,* 305–320.

3. If the pagination starts again for each issue, the issue number is added after the volume number.

Example

Schultz, K. (1993). Dreams deferred: The personal narratives of four black Kansans.

   American Studies 4(3), 25–51.

References for Other Kinds of Sources

1. Reference books. Include what is available of the following information: editor of reference work, date, title of reference work, edition, volumes, place of publication and publisher.

Example

Lee, J. Y. (2002). Popularization. In P. Gossin (Ed.), *Encyclopedia of literature and science*

   (351–355). Westport, CT: Greenwood Press.

2. Lectures or other performances. Only published speeches go into a reference list; if you have used material you hear at a speech or talk, use a parenthetical citation of the kind used for personal correspondence or conversation.

3. Films or video recordings. Include the producer, director, followed by their function in parentheses, date in parentheses, title in italics, medium in brackets, production company. If you have information about how to order a recording cited, put that at the end of the citation.

Example

Smith, R. (Writer/Producer). (1988). *You and the international TA: Paths*

   to better understanding [Videocassette]. Lubbock, TX: Texas

   Tech University.

4. **Television or radio broadcasts.** Name the producer or director, date, title, medium (in brackets), and place and station of origin.

Example

Keillor, G. (Director). (2003). *The prairie home companion* [Radio series]. Minneapolis:

    Minnesota Public Radio.

Citing Electronic Sources

Methods for citing electronic sources are still evolving, as new sources are developed, as print documents are archived online, and as the Web changes and libraries and scholars adapt to those changes. Keep in mind that the purpose of lists of references is to let another researcher find your sources, and use that purpose as a guide when problems arise with citing electronic sources. When a piece of information is not available, simply record what is available, keeping the importance of easy access in mind. For example, often no author is named for Web sites; in these cases, start with the title, as you would for a print source with no identified author.

The sources you find on the Web may be archived print documents or material produced explicitly for online publication. The *Publication Manual of the American Psychological Association* (2009) recommends that you follow these two guidelines when trying to decide how to create references for online resources:

- Direct readers as closely as possible to the information being cited—whenever possible, reference specific documents rather than home or menu pages.
- Provide addresses that work (pp. 187–188).

The *APA Style Guide to Electronic References* (2007) supplements the *APA Publication Manual* and provides standards for citations that were not previously covered in previous manuals. It also includes some important changes:

- APA no longer requires a retrieval date for all online sources. If URLs are likely to remain stable, as in the case of publishers' Web sites or online scholarly journals, a retrieval date is not necessary, whereas sites that may potentially change domains or actively move content require a retrieval date.
- Many publishers now provide a **Digital Object Identifier (DOI)** for print documents that also appear online. The DOI is a unique alphanumeric code that functions as a more stable identifier than traditional URLs. APA recommends DOIs as opposed to URLs, when available.
- Formerly, APA suggested placing line breaks after slashes and other punctuation. It now recommends that line breaks occur before the punctuation and also warns writers not to place hyphens that do not already occur in the URL in order to continue one line to the next.

APA References for Online Sources

1. **An article from an online periodical with a DOI assigned.** Always include an issue number and page range (if available).

Example

Author, A. A., & Author, B. B. (Date of publication). Title of article. *Title of Journal, volume number*(issue number), page range. doi:0000000/000000000000

Note: Many—but not all—publishers will provide an article DOI, usually on the first page of the document. Some online bibliographies may provide an article's DOI, but it may be hidden "behind" a button, which may read "Article," "CrossRef," or "PubMed." This button will usually lead you to the article and the correct DOI. If you are verifying a DOI or come across a dead link but have a DOI, you can use CrossRef.org's "DOI Resolver" to find the information you are looking for.

2. **An online periodical with no DOI assigned.** Online scholarly journal articles without a DOI require a URL but do not normally require a retrieval date. Provide a retrieval date only if the information is likely to be updated or changed. Always include an issue number and page range (if available).

Example

Author, A. A., & Author, B. B. (Date of publication). Title of article. *Title of Journal, volume number*(issue number), page range. Retrieved month day, year (only necessary if the URL is likely to change), from http://www. someaddress.com/full/url/

3. **An article from an online database.** Cite database articles as you would print versions. If the database from which you retrieved your article is well-known (e.g., *PsycARTICLES*) you need not provide the database name. Give only the URL. If you do provide the database name, do not provide the URL.

Examples

Author, A. A. (date). Title of article. *Title of journal, 1*(1), page range. Retrieved from Less Well-Known Database.

Fortier, C. B. et al. (2008). Delay discrimination and reversal eyeblink classical conditioning in abstinent chronic alcoholics. *Neuropsychology, 22*(2), 196–208. Retrieved from http://www.ovid.com

4. **Online encyclopedias and dictionaries.** Encyclopedias and dictionaries usually do not provide authors' names. When no name is present, place the entry name at the beginning of the citation. Provide publication dates, if present, or specify (n.d.)—no date—if no date is present in the entry. Provide only the root URL for the site. Since these sites do not normally provide editing dates, include a retrieval date in the citation.

Example

Feminism. (n.d.). In *Encyclopaedia Britannica* online. Retrieved March 16, 2008, from http://www.britannica.com

5. **An entire Web site.** It is not necessary to provide a citation on the References page for an entire Web site. Instead, APA recommends that you include the Web site's principal URL in the text.

Example

You can find other helpful articles on this topic on the *Scientific American Mind* magazine

Web site (http://www. sciam.com/sciammind/).

6. **E-mail messages.** These are considered personal communications, which should be identified in the text but not listed as a reference.

7. **A listserv, blog, or discussion board posting.** Only posts to sites that maintain an archive should be listed as a reference. If you do not know the author's name, provide the screen name. Include identifiers like post or message numbers in brackets.

Example

Bergmann, L. S. (2003, December 11). Plagiarism and post 9/11 purge. Message posted

to Writing Program Administration (WPA-L) electronic mailing list, archived at

http://lists.asu.edu/archives/wpa-l.html

8. **Wikis.** Please note that the *APA Style Guide to Electronic References* warns writers that wikis (like Wikipedia, for example) cannot guarantee the verifiability or expertise of their entries. Cite wikis at your own risk.

Example

OLPC Peru/Arahuay. (n.d.). Retrieved May 1, 2008, from the OLPC Wiki:

http://wiki.laptop.org/go/OLPC_Peru/Arahuay

For More Information

The best source for more information is the *Publication Manual of the American Psychological Association,* which anticipates most of the questions users have about working in this style. This manual is the source of most of the information in this appendix. For electronic sources, consult the *APA Style Guide to Electronic References.* The writing center in your college will likely have copies of both, as will the college library:

Publication manual of the American Psychological Association (6th ed.). (2009). Washington, DC: American Psychological Association.

In addition, some of the online writing centers listed in Chapter 7 have information about using APA style on their Web sites and links to other, related guides to using this style. The best way to learn to use the style is to work through the problems, citation by citation, always remembering your readers' needs to use the reference list to find sources, as you have used the lists of others.

CHICAGO MANUAL OF STYLE (CMS)
NOTES AND BIBLIOGRAPHY MANUSCRIPT STYLE

Chicago Style documentation employs two basic formats: (1) a notes and bibliography system, and (2) a name-date system. Writers in the arts, history, and literature who use Chicago Style typically prefer the notes and bibliography system, while writers in the sciences favor the author-date system. Since writers in the sciences use a wide variety of documentation formats, often specific to their field or to a particular journal, this summary covers the notes and bibliography system only. For information on the author-date system, consult the *Chicago Manual of Style*, 15th edition (Chicago: University of Chicago Press), 2003, chapters 16–17.

Formatting

Spacing and Margins

1. Double-space the document vertically throughout.

2. Follow both colons and periods with a single character space.

3. Set the margins for at least 1-inch on all four sides of the document.

4. Justify only the left margin. Maintain an unjustified (sometimes referred to as "jagged" or "ragged") right margin to preserve proper word spacing.

Titles (Your Own) and Title Pages

1. When writing a title for an academic research paper, think about what you have learned from searching for sources. Because data bases sort by key words and by titles, try to get as many key words into your title as you can without making it too long and unwieldy. Putting key words in your title makes your work more easily retrievable by other researchers.

2. The notes and bibliography system employs headline-style capitalization. This means that you capitalize the first letters of the first and last words of a title, and the first letters of nouns, adverbs, and adjectives. Begin articles (*a, an, the*), prepositions (for example, *on, like, through, to*), and conjunctions (for example, *and, but, or*) with a lowercase letter.

3. If your instructor requires a title page, do not number it. Center all items on the title page. Include only the following items (when applicable) in the order listed. Each entry gets its own line.
   a. The title (followed by a colon if there is a subtitle)
   b. The subtitle (if applicable)
   c. Your full name
   d. The full names of other contributors, if any (each name gets its own line)
   e. The course name
   f. The instructor's name
   g. The date

Pagination

1. Chicago Style allows page numbers to be placed wherever the writer or publisher thinks appropriate, and many writers place them in the top right-hand corner of

the page. Your instructor may require that you also include your last name or an abbreviated title before the page number.

2. Start numbering pages on the first page of your text. Do not number the title page, if you included one.

Footnotes and Endnotes

The Chicago Style notes and bibliography system allows for two note options: footnotes and endnotes. The "Reference" function of word processing programs usually offers the choice of footnotes or endnotes and inserts them appropriately. Both footnotes and end-notes are signaled in the text by a superscripted Arabic numeral.

When given a choice, weigh the pros and cons of each option before deciding which one to use:

- Footnotes are placed on the bottom of the page on which they are referenced. Footnotes allow readers to easily find explanatory and bibliographic notes because they appear on the same page as the text. However, a large number of footnotes, particularly if they are long, can seem to crowd and dominate the page.

- Endnotes appear at the end of the document (before the Works Cited page, if there is one) on a separate page entitled "Notes" (centered, standard font). Endnotes require readers to turn to the end of the document to access them, but they conveniently gather information in one list and do not get in the way of the text.

Chicago Style uses footnotes and endnotes to provide bibliographic information for quotations, paraphrases, and works consulted. Some writers also use content notes, which are explanatory notes that provide supplemental information that may seem like digressions from the main argument.

Examples

Bibliographic Note

2. Tania Ralli, "Software Strives to Spot Plagiarism before Publication," *New York Times*, 5 September 2005, http://www.nytimes.com.

Content Note

3. Wasley specifically mentions the University of Michigan at Ann Arbor, Davidson College, Lee University, and the University of Colorado as schools that have considered whether faculty use of anti-plagiarism software is compatible with an honor code system. See Paula Wasley, "Antiplagiarism Software Takes on the Honor Code," *Chronicle of Higher Education*, 29 February 2008, A12.

Footnotes and Endnotes Use Similar Formats:

1. Indent the first line of the note five spaces or one-half inch. Use single spacing within notes, but double space between notes.

2. Number notes consecutively, using full-size, standard Arabic numbers that correspond to the superscripted numbers in the text. Follow each number with a period and one space.

3. **Exception:** Footnotes should appear in a smaller type than the rest of the text, usually 9-or 10-pt. font. Endnotes should appear in a smaller type than the rest of the text but larger than the size of a footnote, usually 10- or 11-pt. font. However, some instructors tell students to maintain a 12-pt. font throughout a document, including footnotes, endnotes, and bibliography, in which case you should adapt your practices to follow your instructor's preference.

4. For authors' names, the first name comes before the last.

5. For the first reference to a source, write a full bibliographic note, and then abbreviate later notes for that source. If you are citing a particular page or pages of the source, include page numbers.

6. When you write subsequent notes for the same source, if the note is for the *same source as the note that immediately precedes it*, use the abbreviation "*Ibid.*" (Latin for "in the same place"), followed by a comma and the page number.

Example

1. Ellen Sarkisian, *Teaching American Students: A Guide for International Faculty and Teaching Assistants in Colleges and Universities* (Cambridge, MA: Derek Bok Center for Teaching and Learning, 2006), 25.

2. Ibid., 30.

3. Ibid., 38.

7. However, when you refer to a source after the first time in a note *and it is a different source from the one in the note that directly precedes it*, use a shortened entry that includes only the author's last name, the title of the work, and the page number.

Example

1. Ellen Sarkisian, *Teaching American Students: A Guide for International Faculty and Teaching Assistants in Colleges and Universities* (Cambridge, MA: Derek Bok Center for Teaching and Learning, 2006), 25.

2. Loreto R. Prieto and Steven A. Meyers, *The Teaching Assistant Training Handbook: How to Prepare TAs for Their Responsibilities*, 3rd ed. (Stillwater, OK: New Forums Press, 2001), 15.

3. Sarkisian, *Teaching American Students: A Guide for International Faculty and Teaching Assistants in Colleges and Universities*, 25.

Constructing a Bibliography

Since in Chicago Style, full reference information is given in either footnotes or endnotes, a separate bibliography may not be necessary. However, some instructors and publishers require one.

1. Place the bibliography at the end of the document after the text or the endnotes page, if you have one. Entitle the page "Works Cited" or "Bibliography" (centered, standard font) and double space before the first entry. If using endnotes, you will have to make the bibliography a separate document, since most word processing programs automatically put endnotes at the end of the entire document, which places the bibliography *before* the endnotes.

2. Use hanging indentation, in which the first line of all entries is flush with the left margin, and subsequent lines are indented five spaces or one-half inch from the margin. You can select hanging indentation as a paragraph format option in your word processing program. Single space within entries, and double space between entries.

3. List entries in alphabetical order, by the last name of the first author. If there are several authors, follow the order used by the source. When no author or editor is identified for the source, alphabetize by the first word of the title that is not an article (*a, an, the*).

4. Put the first or only author's last name before the first name, so that you can easily alphabetize the entries by last names, and so that your readers can easily locate them. However, if a source has more than one author or editor, the names of all authors after the first should follow the regular order of first name before last name (because inversion is necessary for alphabetizing only the first author's name).

5. When including two or more works by the same author in a bibliography, use a 3-em dash ("———" or six unspaced hyphens) followed by a period and a space, instead of repeating the author's name.

Capitalization and Formatting Titles of Works in the Bibliography

1. As with your own titles, capitalize the first letters of the first and last words. Also capitalize nouns, adverbs, and adjectives. Begin articles (*a, an, the*), prepositions (for example, *on, like, through*), and conjunctions (for example, *and, but, or, to*) with lowercase letters.

2. Italicize titles of books, scholarly journals, newspapers, magazines, artwork, plays, films, conference proceedings, and musical compositions.

3. Place quotation marks around the titles of articles in periodicals, short stories, television and radio programs, essays, songs, and unpublished works.

Examples

The format of notes—both footnotes and endnotes–differs from the format of entries in the bibliography; the following examples illustrate the differences between note entries and bibliography entries.

1. Citing a book by a single author.

Notes

1. Wendy Sutherland-Smith, *Plagiarism, the Internet, and Student Learning: Improving Academic Integrity* (New York: Routledge, 2008), 15.

Bibliography

Sutherland-Smith, Wendy. *Plagiarism, the Internet, and Student Learning: Improving Academic Integrity.* New York: Routledge, 2008.

2. Citing an edited work.

Notes

2. Catherine Ross and Jane Dunphy, eds., *Strategies for Teaching Assistant and International Teaching Assistant Development: Beyond Micro Teaching* (San Francisco, CA: Jossey-Bass, 2007), 15–16.

Bibliography

Ross, Catherine, and Jane Dunphy, eds. *Strategies for Teaching Assistant and International Teaching Assistant Development: Beyond Micro Teaching.* San Francisco, CA: Jossey-Bass, 2007.

3. Citing a translated work.

Notes

3. Michel Foucault, *The Archaeology of Knowledge and the Discourse on Language,* trans. Rupert Swyer (New York: Tavistock Publications, 1972), 31.

Bibliography

Foucault, Michel. *The Archaeology of Knowledge and the Discourse on Language.* Translated by Rupert Swyer. New York: Tavistock Publications, 1972.

4. Citing a piece from an anthology.

Notes

4. Amit Ray and Erhardt Graeff, "Reviewing the Author-Function in the Age of Wikipedia," in *Originality, Imitation, and Plagiarism: Teaching Writing in the Digital Age,* ed. Martha Vicinus and Caroline Eisner (Ann Arbor, MI: University of Michigan Press, 2008), 39–47.

Bibliography

> Ray, Amit, and Erhardt Graeff. "Reviewing the Author-Function in the Age of Wikipedia."
> In *Originality, Imitation, and Plagiarism: Teaching Writing in the Digital Age,*
> edited by Martha Vicinus and Caroline Eisner. Ann Arbor, MI: University of
> Michigan Press, 2008.

5. Citing an article from a journal.

Notes

6. Rebecca Volpe, Laura Davidson, and Matthew C. Bell, "Faculty Attitudes and
Behaviors Concerning Student Cheating," *College Student Journal* 42, no. 1 (2008):
164–175.

Bibliography

> Volpe, Rebecca, Laura Davidson, and Matthew C. Bell. "Faculty Attitudes and Behaviors
> Concerning Student Cheating." *College Student Journal* 42, no. 1 (2008):
> 164–175.

When working with online versions (including databases), include the URL at the
end of the entry and end with a period.

Notes

7. Ron Scollon, "Plagiarism and Ideology: Identity in Intercultural Discourse
Plagiarism and Ideology," *Language in Society* 24, no. 1 (1995): 1–28,
http://www.jstor.org/.

Bibliography

> Scollon, Ron. "Plagiarism and Ideology: Identity in Intercultural Discourse Plagiarism
> and Ideology." *Language in Society* 24, no. 1 (1995): 1–28.
> http://www.jstor.org/.

6. Citing a Web site.

When citing a Web site, include (when the information is available) the author(s)'
name, the article's title (or title of Web page), the name of the Web site, the publication date, and the URL. If it is likely that the URL for your source will change or
become a dead link at in the near future (like for a site that updates its content
often and does not archive older items), include the date of access in the note in
parentheses after the URL.

Notes

8. Jane Sharka, "Plagiarism Stoppers: A Teacher's Guide," *Naperville Community Unit School District 203,* 7 June 2007, http://www.ncusd203.org/central/html/where/ plagiarism_stoppers.html (accessed 10 April 2009).

Bibliography

Sharka, Jane. "Plagiarism Stoppers: A Teacher's Guide." *Naperville Community Unit School District 203,* 7 June 2007. http://www.ncusd203.org/central/html/ where/plagiarism_stoppers.html.

7. Citing a sacred text.

Notes

5. John 3.5–6 (Revised Standard Version).

Bibliography

Sacred texts are usually omitted from the bibliography.

8. Citing an encyclopedia or dictionary.

List the name of the reference work first, followed by the edition number (sometimes listed by year). For works that list entries alphabetically, use the abbreviation *s.v.* (Latin abbreviation for *sub verbo,* meaning "under the word") and list the entry in quotation marks.

Notes

9. *Merriam-Webster's Collegiate Dictionary,* 11th ed., s.v. "Plagiarism."

Bibliography

Reference works are usually omitted from the bibliography.

Readings

DIGITAL PUBLISHING IS SCRAMBLING THE INDUSTRY'S RULES

Motoko Rich

When Mark Z. Danielewski's second novel, *Only Revolutions*, is published in September, it will include hundreds of margin notes listing moments in history suggested online by fans of his work. Nearly 60 of his contributors have already received galleys of the experimental book, which they're commenting about in a private forum at Mr. Danielewski's Web site, www.onlyrevolutions.com.

Yochai Benkler, a Yale University law professor and author of the new book *The Wealth of Networks: How Social Production Transforms Markets and Freedom* (Yale University Press), has gone even farther: his entire book is available—free—as a download from his Web site. Between 15,000 and 20,000 people have accessed the book electronically, with some of them adding comments and links to the online version.

Mr. Benkler said he saw the project as "simply an experiment of how books might be in the future." That is one of the hottest debates in the book world right now, as publishers, editors and writers grapple with the Web's ability to connect readers and writers more quickly and intimately, new technologies that make it easier to search books electronically and the advent of digital devices that promise to do for books what the iPod has done for music: making them easily downloadable and completely portable.

Not surprisingly, writers have greeted these measures with a mixture of enthusiasm and dread. The dread was perhaps most eloquently crystallized last month in Washington at BookExpo, the publishing industry's annual convention, when the novelist John Updike forcefully decried a digital future composed of free downloads of books and the mixing and matching of "snippets" of text, calling it a "grisly scenario."

Hovering above the discussion of all these technologies is the fear that the publishing industry could be subject to the same upheaval that has plagued the music industry, where digitalization has started to displace the traditional artistic and economic model of the record album with 99-cent song downloads and personalized playlists. Total album sales are down 19 percent since 2001, while CD sales have dropped 16 percent during the same period, according to Nielsen BookScan. Sales of single digital music tracks have jumped more than 1,700 percent in just two years. What writers think about technological developments in the literary world has a lot to do with where they are re sitting at the moment. As a researcher and scholar, Anne Fadiman, author of *The Spirit Catches You and You Fall Down* and *Ex Libris: Confessions of a Common Reader,* thinks a digital library of all books would be a "godsend" during research, allowing her to "sniff out all the paragraphs" on a given topic. But, she said: "That's not reading. For reading, you have to read a book in its entirety and I think there's no substitute for the look and feel and smell of a real book—the magic of the paper and thread and glue."

Others have a much less fixed notion of books. Lisa Scottoline, the author of 13 thrillers, the most recent of which, *Dirty Blonde,* spent four weeks on the *New York Times* hardcover fiction best-seller list earlier this spring, offers the first chapter or two of each book on her Web site; and her publisher, HarperCollins, hands out "samplers" of a few chapters of her titles in bookstores. Any of these formats are fine with her, she says. Whether its "paper, pulp, gold rimmed or digitized, I don't think you can take away from the best stories," she said.

Liberating books from their physical contexts could make it easier for them to blend into one another, a concept heralded by Kevin Kelly in an article in the *New York Times Magazine* last month. "Once text is digital, books seep out of their bindings and weave themselves together," wrote Mr. Kelly in an article that was derided by Mr. Updike in his BookExpo polemic. "The collective intelligence of a library allows us to see things we can't see in a single, isolated book."

"Does that mean *Anna Karenina* goes hand in hand with my niece's blog of her trip to Las Vegas?" asked Jane Hamilton, author of *The Book of Ruth* and a forthcoming novel, *When Madeline Was Young.* "It sounds absolutely deadly." Reading books as isolated works is precisely what she wants to do, she said. "When I read someone like Willa Cather, I feel like I'm in the presence of the divine," Ms. Hamilton said. "I don't want her mixed up with anybody else. And I certainly don't want to go to her Web site."

For unknown authors struggling to capture the attention of busy readers, however, the Web offers an unprecedented way to catapult out of obscurity. Glenn Greenwald, a lawyer who started a political blog, "Unclaimed Territory," just eight months ago, was recruited by a foundation financed by Working Assets, a credit card issuer and telecommunications company, to write a book this spring. Mr. Greenwald promoted the result, called *How Would a Patriot Act? Defending American Values From a President Run Amok,* on his own blog and his publisher e-mailed digital galleys to seven other influential bloggers, who helped to send it to the No. 1 spot on Amazon.com before it was even published. This Sunday it will hit No. 11 on the *New York Times* nonfiction paperback best-seller list. "I think people who are sort of on the outside of the institutions and new voices entering will be a lot more excited about this technology," Mr. Greenwald said. "That's one of the effects that technology always has. It democratizes things and brings in new readers and new authors."

For many authors, the question of how technology will shape book publishing inevitably leads to the question of how writers will be paid. Currently, publishers pay authors an advance against royalties, which are conventionally earned at the rate of 15 percent of the cover price of each copy sold.

But the Internet makes it a lot easier to spread work free. "I've had pieces put up on Web sites legally and otherwise that get hundreds of thousands of hits, and believe me I sit around thinking 'Boy, if I got a dollar every time that somebody posted an op-ed that

I wrote, I'd be a very happy writer,'" said Daniel Mendelsohn, author of the forthcoming book *The Lost: A Search for Six of Six Million*, a memoir about his hunt to discover what happened to relatives who were killed in the Holocaust.

Mr. Mendelsohn said he understood that technological shakeups take time to play out, and that he can't bemoan every lost penny. "But as an author who creates texts that people consume, I want my authorship to be recognized and I want to get compensated," he said.

Mr. Benkler, the Yale professor and author, argues that people will continue to pay for books if the price is low enough. "Even in music, price can compete with free," Mr. Benkler said. "The service has to be sufficiently better and the moral culture needs to be one where, as an act of respect, when the price is reasonable, you pay. Its not clear to me why, if people are willing to pay 99 cents for a song they won't be willing to pay $3 for a book."

He argues that without the costs of paper and physical book production, publishers could afford to give authors a higher cut of the sale price as royalties.

In the context of history, the changes that today's technology will impose on literary society may not be as earth-shattering as some may think. In fact, books themselves are a relatively new construct, inheritors of a longstanding oral storytelling culture. Mass-produced books are an even newer phenomenon, enabled by the invention of the printing press that likely put legions of calligraphers and bookbinders out of business.

That history gives great comfort to writers like Vikram Chandra, whose 1,000-page novel, *Sacred Games,* will be published in January. Mr. Chandra, a former computer programmer who already reads e-books downloaded to his pocket personal computer, said he saw no point in resisting technology. "I think circling the wagons and defending the fortress metaphors are a little misplaced," he said. "The barbarians at the gate are usually willing to negotiate a little, and the guys in the fort usually end up yelling that 'we are the only good things in the world and you guys don't understand it,' at which point the barbarians shrug, knock down your walls with their amazingly powerful weapons, and put a parking lot over your sacred grounds.

"If they are in a really good mood," he added, "they put up a pyramid of skulls."

Mr. Danielewski said that the physical book would persist as long as authors figure out ways to stretch the format in new ways. *Only Revolutions,* he pointed out, tracks the experiences of two intersecting characters, whose narratives begin at different ends of the book, requiring readers to turn it upside down every eight pages to get both of their stories. "As excited as I am by technology, I'm ultimately creating a book that can't exist online," he said. "The experience of starting at either end of the book and feeling the space close between the characters until you're exactly at the halfway point is not something you could experience online. I think that's the bar that the Internet is driving towards: how to further emphasize what is different and exceptional about books."

REWRITING HISTORY: SNARED IN THE WEB OF A WIKIPEDIA LIAR

Katharine Q. Seelye

According to Wikipedia, the online encyclopedia, John Seigenthaler Sr. is 78 years old and the former editor of the *Tennessean* in Nashville. But is that information, or anything else in Mr. Seigenthaler's biography, true?

The question arises because Mr. Seigenthaler recently read about himself on Wikipedia and was shocked to learn that he "was thought to have been directly involved in the Kennedy assassinations of both John and his brother Bobby."

"Nothing was ever proven," the biography added.

Mr. Seigenthaler discovered that the false information had been on the site for several months and that an unknown number of people had read it, and possibly posted it on or linked it to other sites.

If any assassination was going on, Mr. Seigenthaler (who is 78 and did edit the *Tennessean*) wrote last week in an op-ed article in *USA Today*, it was of his character.

The case triggered extensive debate on the Internet over the value and reliability of Wikipedia, and more broadly, over the nature of online information.

Wikipedia is a kind of collective brain, a repository of knowledge, maintained on servers in various countries and built by anyone in the world with a computer and an Internet connection who wants to share knowledge about a subject. Literally hundreds of thousands of people have written Wikipedia entries.

Mistakes are expected to be caught and corrected by later contributors and users.

The whole nonprofit enterprise began in January 2001, the brainchild of Jimmy Wales, 39, a former futures and options trader who lives in St. Petersburg, Fla. He said he had hoped to advance the promise of the Internet as a place for sharing information.

It has, by most measures, been a spectacular success. Wikipedia is now the biggest encyclopedia in the history of the world. As of Friday, it was receiving 2.5 billion page views a month, and offering at least 1,000 articles in 82 languages. The number of articles, already close to two million, is growing by 7 percent a month. And Mr. Wales said that traffic doubles every four months.

Still, the question of Wikipedia, as of so much of what you find online, is: can you trust it?

And beyond reliability, there is the question of accountability. Mr. Seigenthaler, after discovering that he had been defamed, found that his "biographer" was anonymous. He learned that the writer was a customer of BellSouth Internet, but that federal privacy laws shield the identity of Internet customers, even if they disseminate defamatory material. And the laws protect online corporations from libel suits.

He could have filed a lawsuit against BellSouth, he wrote, but only a subpoena would compel BellSouth to reveal the name.

In the end, Mr. Seigenthaler decided against going to court, instead alerting the public, through his article, "that Wikipedia is a flawed and irresponsible research tool."

Mr. Wales said in an interview that he was troubled by the Seigenthaler episode, and noted that Wikipedia was essentially in the same boat. "We have constant problems where we have people who are trying to repeatedly abuse our sites," he said.

Still, he said, he was trying to make Wikipedia less vulnerable to tampering. He said he was starting a review mechanism by which readers and experts could rate the value of various articles. The reviews, which he said he expected to start in January, would show the site's strengths and weaknesses and perhaps reveal patterns to help them address the problems.

In addition, he said, Wikipedia may start blocking unregistered users from creating new pages, though they would still be able to edit them.

The real problem, he said, was the volume of new material coming in; it is so overwhelming that screeners cannot keep up with it.

All of this struck close to home for librarians and researchers. On an electronic mailing list for them, J. Stephen Bolhafner, a news researcher at the *St. Louis Post-Dispatch*, wrote, "The best defense of the Wikipedia, frankly, is to point out how much bad information is available from supposedly reliable sources."

Jessica Baumgart, a news researcher at Harvard University, wrote that there were librarians voluntarily working behind the scenes to check information on Wikipedia. "But, honestly," she added, "in some ways, we're just as fallible as everyone else in some areas because our own knowledge is limited and we can't possibly fact-check everything."

In an interview, she said that her rule of thumb was to double-check everything and to consider Wikipedia as only one source.

"Instead of figuring out how to 'fix' Wikipedia—something that cannot be done to our satisfaction," wrote Derek Willis, a research database manager at the *Washington Post*, who was speaking for himself and not the *Post*, "we should focus our energies on educating the Wikipedia users among our colleagues."

Some cyberexperts said Wikipedia already had a good system of checks and balances. Lawrence Lessig, a law professor at Stanford and an expert in the laws of cyberspace, said that contrary to popular belief, true defamation was easily pursued through the courts because almost everything on the Internet was traceable and subpoenas were not that hard to obtain. (For real anonymity, he advised, use a pay phone.)

"People will be defamed," he said. "But that's the way free speech is. Think about the gossip world. It spreads. There's no way to correct it, period. Wikipedia is not immune from that kind of maliciousness, but it is, relative to other features of life, more easily corrected."

Indeed, Esther Dyson, editor of *Release 1.0* and a longtime Internet analyst, said Wikipedia may, in that sense, be better than real life.

"The Internet has done a lot more for truth by making things easier to discuss," she said. "Transparency and sunlight are better than a single point of view that can't be questioned."

For Mr. Seigenthaler, whose biography on Wikipedia has since been corrected, the lesson is simple: "We live in a universe of new media with phenomenal opportunities for worldwide communications and research, but populated by volunteer vandals with poison-pen intellects."

VIRTUES AND VICTIMS

David Brooks

All great scandals occur twice, first as Tom Wolfe novels, then as real-life events that nightmarishly mimic them. And so after *I Am Charlotte Simmons*, it was perhaps inevitable that Duke University would have to endure a mini-social explosion involving athletic thugs, resentful townies, nervous administrators, male predators, aggrieved professors, binge drinking and lust gone wild.

If you wander through the thicket of commentary that already surrounds the Duke lacrosse scandal, the first thing you notice is how sociological it is. In almost every article and piece of commentary, the event is portrayed not as a crime between individuals but as a clash between classes, races, and sexes.

"This whole sordid party scene played out at the prestigious university is deeply disturbing on a number of levels, including those involving gender, race, and the notion of athletic entitlement and privilege," a *USA Today* columnist wrote.

"The collisions are epic: black and white, town and gown, rich and poor, privilege and plain, jocks and scholars," a CBS analyst observed.

The key word in the coverage has been "entitlement." In a thousand different ways commentators have asserted (based on no knowledge of the people involved) that the lacrosse players behaved rancidly because they felt privileged and entitled to act as they pleased.

The main theme shaping the coverage is that inequality leads to exploitation. The whites felt free to exploit the blacks. The men felt free to exploit women. The jocks felt free to exploit everybody else. As a Duke professor, Houston Baker, wrote, their environment gave the lacrosse players "license to rape, maraud, deploy hate speech and feel proud of themselves in the bargain."

It could be that this environmental, sociological explanation of events is entirely accurate. But it says something about our current intellectual climate that almost every reporter and commentator used these mental categories so unconsciously and automatically.

Several decades ago, American commentators would have used an entirely different vocabulary to grapple with what happened at Duke. Instead of the vocabulary of sociology, they would have used the language of morality and character.

If you were looking at this scandal through that language, you would look at the e-mail message one of the players sent on the night in question. This is the one in which a young man joked about killing strippers and cutting off their skin.

You would say that the person who felt free to send this message to his buddies had crashed through several moral guardrails. You would surmise that his character had been corroded by shock jocks and raunch culture and that he'd entered a nihilistic moral universe where young men entertain each other with bravura displays of immoralism. A community so degraded, you might surmise, is not a long way from actual sexual assault.

You would then ask questions very different from the sociological ones: How have these young men slipped into depravity? Why have they not developed sufficient character to restrain their baser impulses?

The educators who used this vocabulary several decades ago understood that when you concentrate young men, they have a tropism toward barbarism. That's why these educators cared less about academics than about instilling a formula for character building. The formula, then called chivalry, consisted first of manners, habits and self-imposed restraints to prevent the downward slide.

Furthermore, it was believed that each of us had a godlike and a demonic side, and that decent people perpetually strengthened the muscles of their virtuous side in order to restrain the deathless sinner within. If you read commencement addresses from, say, the 1920s, you can actually see college presidents exhorting their students to battle the beast within—a sentiment that if uttered by a contemporary administrator would cause the audience to gape and the earth to fall off its axis.

Today that old code of obsolete chivalry is gone, as is a whole vocabulary on how young people should think about character.

But in *I Am Charlotte Simmons*, Wolfe tried to steer readers back past the identity groups to the ghost in the machine, the individual soul. Wolfe's heroine is a modern girl searching for honor in a world where the social rules have dissolved, and who commits "moral suicide" because she is unprepared for what she faces.

Many critics reacted furiously to these parts of Wolfe's book. And we are where we are.

SHOW ME THE SCIENCE

Daniel C. Dennett

President Bush, announcing this month [August 2005] that he was in favor of teaching about "intelligent design" in the schools, said, "I think that part of education is to expose people to different schools of thought." A couple of weeks later, Senator Bill Frist of Tennessee, the Republican leader, made the same point. Teaching both intelligent design and evolution "doesn't force any particular theory on anyone," Mr. Frist said. "I think in a pluralistic society that is the fairest way to go about education and training people for the future."

Is "intelligent design" a legitimate school of scientific thought? Is there something to it, or have these people been taken in by one of the most ingenious hoaxes in the history of science? Wouldn't such a hoax be impossible? No. Here's how it has been done.

First, imagine how easy it would be for a determined band of naysayers to shake the world's confidence in quantum physics—how weird it is!—or Einsteinian relativity. In spite of a century of instruction and popularization by physicists, few people ever really get their heads around the concepts involved. Most people eventually cobble together a justification for accepting the assurances of the experts: "Well, they pretty much agree with one another, and they claim that it is their understanding of these strange topics that allows them to harness atomic energy, and to make transistors and lasers, which certainly do work. . . ."

Fortunately for physicists, there is no powerful motivation for such a band of mischief-makers to form. They don't have to spend much time persuading people that quantum physics and Einsteinian relativity really have been established beyond all reasonable doubt.

With evolution, however, it is different. The fundamental scientific idea of evolution by natural selection is not just mind-boggling; natural selection, by executing God's traditional task of designing and creating all creatures great and small, also seems to deny one of the best reasons we have for believing in God. So there is plenty of motivation for resisting the assurances of the biologists. Nobody is immune to wishful thinking. It takes scientific discipline to protect ourselves from our own credulity, but we've also found ingenious ways to fool ourselves and others. Some of the methods used to exploit these urges are easy to analyze; others take a little more unpacking.

A creationist pamphlet sent to me some years ago had an amusing page in it, purporting to be part of a simple questionnaire:

Test Two

Do you know of any building that didn't have a builder? [YES] [NO]

Do you know of any painting that didn't have a painter? [YES] [NO]

Do you know of any car that didn't have a maker? [YES] [NO]

If you answered YES for any of the above, give details:

Take that, you Darwinians! The presumed embarrassment of the test-taker when faced with this task perfectly expresses the incredulity many people feel when they confront Darwin's great idea. It seems obvious, doesn't it, that there couldn't be any designs without designers, any such creations without a creator.

Well, yes—until you look at what contemporary biology has demonstrated beyond all reasonable doubt: that natural selection—the process in which reproducing entities must compete for finite resources and thereby engage in a tournament of blind trial and error from which improvements automatically emerge—has the power to generate breathtakingly ingenious designs.

Take the development of the eye, which has been one of the favorite challenges of creationists. How on earth, they ask, could that engineering marvel be produced by a series of small, unplanned steps? Only an intelligent designer could have created such a brilliant arrangement of a shape-shifting lens, an aperture-adjusting iris, a light-sensitive image surface of exquisite sensitivity, all housed in a sphere that can shift its aim in a hundredth of a second and send megabytes of information to the visual cortex every second for years on end.

But as we learn more and more about the history of the genes involved, and how they work—all the way back to their predecessor genes in the sightless bacteria from which multicelled animals evolved more than a half-billion years ago—we can begin to tell the story of how photosensitive spots gradually turned into light-sensitive craters that could detect the rough direction from which light came, and then gradually acquired their lenses, improving their information-gathering capacities all the while.

We can't yet say what all the details of this process were, but real eyes representative of all the intermediate stages can be found, dotted around the animal kingdom, and we have detailed computer models to demonstrate that the creative process works just as the theory says.

All it takes is a rare accident that gives one lucky animal a mutation that improves its vision over that of its siblings; if this helps it have more offspring than its rivals, this gives evolution an opportunity to raise the bar and ratchet up the design of the eye by one mindless step. And since these lucky improvements accumulate—this was Darwin's insight—eyes can automatically get better and better and better, without any intelligent designer.

Brilliant as the design of the eye is, it betrays its origin with a tell-tale flaw: the retina is inside out. The nerve fibers that carry the signals from the eye's rods and cones (which sense light and color) lie on top of them, and have to plunge through a large hole in the retina to get to the brain, creating the blind spot. No intelligent designer would put such a clumsy arrangement in a camcorder, and this is just one of hundreds of accidents frozen in evolutionary history that confirm the mindlessness of the historical process.

If you still find Test Two compelling, a sort of cognitive illusion that you can feel even as you discount it, you are like just about everybody else in the world; the idea that natural selection has the power to generate such sophisticated designs is deeply counterintuitive. Francis Crick, one of the discoverers of DNA, once jokingly credited his colleague Leslie Orgel with "Orgel's Second Rule": Evolution is cleverer than you are. Evolutionary biologists are often startled by the power of natural selection to "discover" an "ingenious" solution to a design problem posed in the lab.

This observation lets us address a slightly more sophisticated version of the cognitive illusion presented by Test Two. When evolutionists like Crick marvel at the cleverness of the process of natural selection they are not acknowledging intelligent design. The designs found in nature are nothing short of brilliant, but the process of design that generates them is utterly lacking in intelligence of its own.

Intelligent design advocates, however, exploit the ambiguity between process and product that is built into the word "design." For them, the presence of a finished product (a fully evolved eye, for instance) is evidence of an intelligent design process. But this tempting conclusion is just what evolutionary biology has shown to be mistaken.

Yes, eyes are for seeing, but these and all the other purposes in the natural world can be generated by processes that are themselves without purposes and without intelligence. This is hard to understand, but so is the idea that colored objects in the world are composed of atoms that are not themselves colored, and that heat is not made of tiny hot things.

The focus on intelligent design has, paradoxically, obscured something else: genuine scientific controversies about evolution that abound. In just about every field there are challenges to one established theory or another. The legitimate way to stir up such a storm is to come up with an alternative theory that makes a prediction that is crisply denied by the reigning theory—but that turns out to be true, or that explains something that has been baffling defenders of the status quo, or that unifies two distant theories at the cost of some element of the currently accepted view.

To date, the proponents of intelligent design have not produced anything like that. No experiments with results that challenge any mainstream biological understanding. No observations from the fossil record or genomics or biogeography or comparative anatomy that undermine standard evolutionary thinking.

Instead, the proponents of intelligent design use a ploy that works something like this. First you misuse or misdescribe some scientist's work. Then you get an angry rebuttal. Then, instead of dealing forthrightly with the charges leveled, you cite the rebuttal as evidence that there is a "controversy" to teach.

Note that the trick is content-free. You can use it on any topic. "Smith's work in geology supports my argument that the earth is flat," you say, misrepresenting Smith's work. When Smith responds with a denunciation of your misuse of her work, you respond, saying something like: "See what a controversy we have here? Professor Smith and I are locked in a titanic scientific debate. We should teach the controversy in the classrooms." And here is the delicious part: you can often exploit the very technicality of the issues to your own advantage, counting on most of us to miss the point in all the difficult details.

William Dembski, one of the most vocal supporters of intelligent design, notes that he provoked Thomas Schneider, a biologist, into a response that Dr. Dembski characterizes as "some hair-splitting that could only look ridiculous to outsider observers."

What looks to scientists—and is—a knockout objection by Dr. Schneider is portrayed to most everyone else as ridiculous hair-splitting.

In short, no science. Indeed, no intelligent design hypothesis has even been ventured as a rival explanation of any biological phenomenon. This might seem surprising to people who think that intelligent design competes directly with the hypothesis of non-intelligent design by natural selection. But saying, as intelligent design proponents do, "You haven't explained everything yet," is not a competing hypothesis. Evolutionary biology certainly hasn't explained everything that perplexes biologists. But intelligent design hasn't yet tried to explain anything.

To formulate a competing hypothesis, you have to get down in the trenches and offer details that have testable implications. So far, intelligent design proponents have conveniently sidestepped that requirement, claiming that they have no specifics in mind about who or what the intelligent designer might be.

To see this shortcoming in relief, consider an imaginary hypothesis of intelligent design that could explain the emergence of human beings on this planet:

> About six million years ago, intelligent genetic engineers from another galaxy visited Earth and decided that it would be a more interesting planet if there was a language-using, religion-forming species on it, so they sequestered some primates and genetically re-engineered them to give them the language instinct, and enlarged frontal lobes for planning and reflection. It worked.

If some version of this hypothesis were true, it could explain how and why human beings differ from their nearest relatives, and it would disconfirm the competing evolutionary hypotheses that are being pursued.

We'd still have the problem of how these intelligent genetic engineers came to exist on their home planet, but we can safely ignore that complication for the time being, since there is not the slightest shred of evidence in favor of this hypothesis.

But here is something the intelligent design community is reluctant to discuss: no other intelligent-design hypothesis has anything more going for it. In fact, my far-fetched hypothesis has the advantage of being testable in principle: we could compare the human and chimpanzee genomes, looking for unmistakable signs of tampering by these genetic engineers from another galaxy. Finding some sort of user's manual neatly embedded in the apparently functionless "junk DNA" that makes up most of the human genome would be a Nobel Prize–winning coup for the intelligent design gang, but if they are looking at all, they haven't come up with anything to report.

It's worth pointing out that there are plenty of substantive scientific controversies in biology that are not yet in the textbooks or the classrooms. The scientific participants in these arguments vie for acceptance among the relevant expert communities in peer-reviewed journals, and the writers and editors of textbooks grapple with judgments about which findings have risen to the level of acceptance—not yet truth—to make them worth serious consideration by undergraduates and high school students.

So get in line, intelligent designers. Get in line behind the hypothesis that life started on Mars and was blown here by a cosmic impact. Get in line behind the aquatic ape hypothesis, the gestural origin of language hypothesis and the theory that singing came before language, to mention just a few of the enticing hypotheses that are actively defended but still insufficiently supported by hard facts.

The Discovery Institute, the conservative organization that has helped to put intelligent design on the map, complains that its members face hostility from the established scientific journals. But establishment hostility is not the real hurdle to intelligent design. If intelligent design were a scientific idea whose time had come, young scientists would be dashing around their labs, vying to win the Nobel Prizes that surely are in store for anybody who can overturn any significant proposition of contemporary evolutionary biology.

Remember cold fusion? The establishment was incredibly hostile to that hypothesis, but scientists around the world rushed to their labs in the effort to explore the idea, in hopes of sharing in the glory if it turned out to be true.

Instead of spending more than $1 million a year on publishing books and articles for non-scientists and on other public relations efforts, the Discovery Institute should finance its own peer-reviewed electronic journal. This way, the organization could live up to its self-professed image: the doughty defenders of brave iconoclasts bucking the establishment.

For now, though, the theory they are promoting is exactly what George Gilder, a long-time affiliate of the Discovery Institute, has said it is: "Intelligent design itself does not have any content."

Since there is no content, there is no "controversy" to teach about in biology class. But here is a good topic for a high school course on current events and politics: Is intelligent design a hoax? And if so, how was it perpetrated?

OUTSOURCING HOMEWORK

At $9.95 a Page, You Expected Poetry?

Charles McGrath

"Damn!" a little comic-strip balloon says. "I'll have to cancel my Saturday night date to finish my term paper before the Monday deadline."

Well, no, she won't—not if she's enterprising enough to enlist Term Paper Relief to write it for her. For $9.95 a page she can obtain an "A-grade" paper that is fashioned to order and "completely non-plagiarized." This last detail is important. Thanks to search engines like Google, college instructors have become adept at spotting those shopworn, downloadable papers that circulate freely on the Web, and can even finger passages that have been ripped off from standard texts and reference works.

A grade-conscious student these days seems to need a custom job, and to judge from the number of services on the Internet, there must be virtual mills somewhere employing armies of diligent scholars who grind away so that credit-card-equipped undergrads can enjoy more carefree time together.

How good are the results? With first semester just getting under way at most colleges, bringing with it the certain prospect of both academic and social pressure, the *Times* decided to undertake an experiment in quality control of the current offerings. Using her own name and her personal e-mail address, an editor ordered three English literature papers from three different sites on standard, often-assigned topics: one comparing and contrasting Huxley's *Brave New World* and Orwell's *1984*; one discussing the nature of Ophelia's madness in *Hamlet*; and one exploring the theme of colonialism in Conrad's *Lord Jim*.

A small sample, perhaps, but one sufficient, upon perusal, to suggest that papers written to order are just like the ones students write for themselves, only more so— they're poorly organized, awkwardly phrased, thin on substance, but masterly in the ancient arts of padding and stating and restating the obvious.

If they're delivered, that is. The *Lord Jim* essay, ordered from SuperiorPapers.com, never arrived, despite repeated entreaties, and the excuse finally offered was a high-tech variant of "The dog ate my homework." The writer assigned to the task, No. 3323, was "obviously facing some technical difficulties," an e-mail message explained, "and cannot upload your paper." The message went on to ask for a 24-hour extension, the wheeziest stratagem in the procrastinator's arsenal, invented long before the electronic age.

The two other papers came in on time, and each grappled, more or less, with the assigned topic. The Orwell/Huxley essay, prepared by Term Paper Relief and a relative bargain at $49.75 for five pages, begins: "Although many similarities exist between Aldous Huxley's *A Brave New World* and George Orwell's *1984*, the works books [sic] though they deal with similar topics, are more dissimilar than alike." That's certainly a relief, because we couldn't have an essay if they weren't.

Elsewhere the author proves highly adept with the "on the one hand/on the other" formula, one of the most valuable tools for a writer concerned with attaining his assigned word count, and says, for example, of *Brave New World*: "Many people consider this Huxley's most important work: many others think it is his only work. This novel has been praised and condemned, vilified and glorified, a source of controversy, a subject for sermons, and required reading for many high school students and college undergraduates. This novel has had twenty-seven printings in the United States alone and will probably have twenty-seven more."

The obvious point of comparison between the two novels is that where Orwell's world is an authoritarian, police-state nightmare, Huxley's dystopia is ostensibly a paradise, with drugs and sex available on demand. A clever student might even pick up some extra credit by pointing out that while Orwell meant his book as a kind of predictive warning, it is Huxley's world, much more far-fetched at the time of writing, that now more nearly resembles our own.

The essay never exactly makes these points, though it gets close a couple of times, declaring at one point that "the two works vary greatly." It also manages to remind us that Orwell's real name was Eric Blair and that both he and his book "are misunderstood to this day."

The paper does make a number of embarrassing spelling errors ("dissention," "anti-semetic") but William H. Pritchard, an English professor at Amherst, who read the paper at the *Times*'s request, shrewdly suggested that, in this day of spell check, they may have been included deliberately, to throw suspicious teachers off the track. If confronted with such a paper from one of his own students, he wrote in an e-mail message, he probably wouldn't grade it at all but would instead say "come see me" (shuddering at the prospect).

The Hamlet essay was a trick assignment, or perhaps a poorly worded one. Ophelia's genuine madness, as opposed to Hamlet's feigned craziness, has become a touchstone in Shakespeare studies, especially among feminist and gender studies scholars who read in Ophelia's songs and fragmentary utterances a coded response to the irrationality and sexual repression of the Elizabethan patriarchy.

The author of the four-page paper, supplied by Go-Essays for $127.96, approaches the question more literally and concludes, not incorrectly, that Ophelia is literally driven crazy by her father, brother and lover—or as the essay puts it: "Thus, in critical review of the play, Ophelia mentally suffers from the scars of unwanted love and exploitation rather than any singular or isolated cause."

The paper goes on to repeat this point with so much plot summary and quotation from the text that it soars right to the assigned length. It's also written in language so stilted and often ungrammatical ("Hamlet is obviously hurt by Ophelia's lack of affection to his vows of love") that it suggests the author may not be a native speaker of English, and even makes you suspect that some of these made-to-order term papers are written by the very same people who pick up the phone when you call to complain about your credit card bill.

Stephen Greenblatt, a Shakespeare scholar at Harvard and a confessed "soft touch," said the grade he would give this paper "would depend, at least to some extent, on whether I thought I was reading the work of a green freshman—in which case I would probably give it a D+ and refer the student to the writing lab for counseling—or an English major, in which case I would simply fail it."

He added: "If I had paid for this, I would demand my money back."

As it happens, a refund is just what Superior Papers offered, along with a 10 percent discount on a new paper. Term paper writing is an arduous business, we need to remember, and we shouldn't expect too much. As the author of the Orwell/Huxley essay says: "It is so often that one wants something and in wanting romanticizes it, thus bringing disappointment when the end is finally obtained. They serve as a reminder that it is necessary to have pain to compare with joy, defeat to compare with victory, and problems in order to have solutions."

CLASSROOM DISTINCTIONS

Tom Moore

In the past year or so I have seen Matthew Perry drink 30 cartons of milk, Ted Danson explain the difference between a rook and a pawn, Hilary Swank remind us that white teachers still can't dance or jive talk. In other words, I have been confronted by distorted images of my own profession—teaching. Teaching the post-desegregation urban poor, to be precise.

Although my friends and family (who should all know better) continue to ask me whether my job is similar to these movies, I find it hard to recognize myself or my students in them.

So what are these films really about? And what do they teach us about teachers? Are we heroes, villains, bullies, fools? The time has come to set the class record straight.

At the beginning of Ms. Swank's new movie, *Freedom Writers,* her character, a teacher named Erin Gruwell, walks into her Long Beach, Calif., classroom, and the camera pans across the room to show us what we are supposed to believe is a terribly shabby learning environment. Any experienced educator will have already noted that not only does she have the right key to get into the room but, unlike the seventh-grade science teacher in my current school, she has a door to put the key into. The worst thing about Ms. Gruwell's classroom seems to be graffiti on the desks, and crooked blinds.

I felt like shouting, *Hey, at least you have blinds!* My first classroom didn't, but it did have a family of pigeons living next to the window, whose pane was a cracked piece of plastic. During the winter, snowflakes blew in. The pigeons competed with the mice and cockroaches for the students' attention.

This is not to say that all schools in poor neighborhoods are a shambles, or that teaching in a real school is impossible. In fact, thousands of teachers in New York City somehow manage to teach every day, many of them in schools more underfinanced and chaotic than anything you've seen in movies or on television (except perhaps the most recent season of *The Wire*).

Ms. Gruwell's students might backtalk, but first they listen to what she says. And when she raises her inflection just slightly, the class falls silent. Many of the students I've known won't sit down unless they're repeatedly asked to (maybe not even then), and they don't listen just because the teacher is speaking; even "good teachers" are occasionally drowned out by the din of 30 students simultaneously using language that would easily earn a movie an NC-17 rating.

When a fight breaks out during an English lesson, Ms. Gruwell steps into the hallway and a security guard immediately materializes to break it up. Forget the teacher—this guy was the hero of the movie for me.

If I were to step out into the hallway during a fight, the only people I'd see would be some students who'd heard there was a fight in my room. I'd be wasting my time waiting for a security guard. The handful of guards where I work are responsible for the safety of five floors, six exits, two yards and four schools jammed into my building.

Although personal safety is at the top of both teachers' and students' lists of grievances, the people in charge of real schools don't take it as seriously as the people in charge of movie schools seem to.

The great misconception of these films is not that actual schools are more chaotic and decrepit—many schools in poor neighborhoods are clean and orderly yet still don't have enough teachers or money for supplies. No, the most dangerous message such films promote is that what schools really need are *heroes.* This is the Myth of the Great Teacher.

Films like *Freedom Writers* portray teachers more as missionaries than professionals, eager to give up their lives and comfort for the benefit of others, without need of compensation. Ms. Gruwell sacrifices money, time, and even her marriage for her job.

Her behavior is not represented as obsessive or self-destructive, but driven—necessary, even. She is forced into making these sacrifices by the aggressive neglect of the school's administrators, who won't even let her take books from the bookroom. The film applauds Ms. Gruwell's dedication, but also implies that she has no other choice. In order to be a good teacher, she has to be a hero.

Freedom Writers, like all teacher movies this side of *The Prime of Miss Jean Brodie,* is presented as a celebration of teaching, but its message is that poor students need only love, idealism, and martyrdom.

I won't argue the need for more of the first two, but I'm always surprised at how, once a Ms. Gruwell wins over a class with clowning, tears, rewards, and motivational speeches, there is nothing those kids can't do. It is as if all the previously insurmountable obstacles students face could be erased by a 10-minute pep talk or a fancy dinner. This trivializes not only the difficulties many real students must overcome, but also the hard-earned skill and tireless effort real teachers must use to help those students succeed.

Every year young people enter the teaching profession hoping to emulate the teachers they've seen in films. (Maybe in the back of my mind I felt that I could be an inspiring teacher like Howard Hesseman or Gabe Kaplan.) But when you're confronted with the reality of teaching not just one class of misunderstood teenagers (the common television and movie conceit) but four or five every day, and dealing with parents, administrators, mentors, grades, attendance records, standardized tests, and individual education plans for children with learning disabilities, not to mention multiple daily lesson plans—all without being able to count on the support of your superiors—it becomes harder to measure up to the heroic movie teachers you thought you might be.

It's no surprise that half the teachers in poor urban schools, like Erin Gruwell herself, quit within five years. (Ms. Gruwell now heads a foundation.)

I don't expect to be thought of as a hero for doing my job. I do expect to be respected, supported, trusted, and paid. And while I don't anticipate that Hollywood will stop producing movies about gold-hearted mavericks who play by their own rules and show the suits how to get the job done, I do hope that these movies will be kept in perspective.

While no one believes that hospitals are really like *ER* or that doctors are anything like *House,* no one blames doctors for the failure of the health care system. From No Child Left Behind to City Hall, teachers are accused of being incompetent and underqualified, while their appeals for better and safer workplaces are systematically ignored.

Every day teachers are blamed for what the system they're just a part of doesn't provide: safe, adequately staffed schools with the highest expectations for all students. But that's not something one maverick teacher, no matter how idealistic, perky, or self-sacrificing, can accomplish.

DANGLING PARTICLES

Lisa Randall

Science plays an increasingly significant role in people's lives, making the faithful communication of scientific developments more important than ever. Yet such communication is fraught with challenges that can easily distort discussions, leading to unnecessary confusion and misunderstandings.

Some problems stem from the esoteric nature of current research and the associated difficulty of finding sufficiently faithful terminology. Abstraction and complexity are not signs that a given scientific direction is wrong, as some commentators have suggested, but are instead a tribute to the success of human ingenuity in meeting the increasingly complex challenges that nature presents. They can, however, make communication more difficult. But many of the biggest challenges for science reporting arise because in areas of evolving research, scientists themselves often only partly understand the full implications of any particular advance or development. Since that dynamic applies to most of the scientific developments that directly affect people's lives—global warming, cancer research, diet studies—learning how to overcome it is critical to spurring a more informed scientific debate among the broader public.

Ambiguous word choices are the source of some misunderstandings. Scientists often employ colloquial terminology, which they then assign a specific meaning that is impossible to fathom without proper training. The term "relativity," for example, is intrinsically misleading. Many interpret the theory to mean that everything is relative and there are no absolutes. Yet although the measurements any observer makes depend on his coordinates and reference frame, the physical phenomena he measures have an invariant description that transcends that observer's particular coordinates. Einstein's theory of relativity is really about finding an invariant description of physical phenomena. Indeed, Einstein agreed with the suggestion that his theory would have been better named "Invariantentheorie." But the term "relativity" was already too entrenched at the time for him to change.

"The uncertainty principle" is another frequently abused term. It is sometimes interpreted as a limitation on observers and their ability to make measurements. But it is not about intrinsic limitations on any one particular measurement; it is about the inability to precisely measure particular pairs of quantities simultaneously. The first interpretation is perhaps more engaging from a philosophical or political perspective. It's just not what the science is about.

Scientists' different use of language becomes especially obvious (and amusing) to me when I hear scientific terms translated into another language. "La théorie des champs" and "la théorie des cordes" are the French versions of "field theory" and "string theory." When I think of "un champs," I think of cows grazing in a pasture, but when I think of "field theory" I have no such association. It is the theory I use that combines quantum mechanics and special relativity and describes objects existing throughout space that create and destroy particles. And string theory is not about strings that you tie around your finger that are made up of atoms; strings are the basic fundamental objects out of which everything is made. The words "string theory" give you a picture, but that picture can sometimes lead to misconceptions about the science.

Most people think of "seeing" and "observing" directly with their senses. But for physicists, these words refer to much more indirect measurements involving a train of theoretical logic by which we can interpret what is "seen." I do theoretical research on string theory and particle physics and try to focus on aspects of those theories we might experimentally test. My most recent research is about extra dimensions of space. Remarkably, we can potentially "see" or "observe" evidence of extra dimensions. But we won't reach out and touch those dimensions with our fingertips or see them with our eyes. The evidence will consist of heavy particles known as Kaluza-Klein modes that travel in extra-dimensional space. If our theories correctly describe the world, there will be a precise enough link between such particles (which will be experimentally observed) and extra dimensions to establish the existence of extra dimensions.

Even the word "theory" can be a problem. Unlike most people, who use the word to describe a passing conjecture that they often regard as suspect, physicists have very specific ideas in mind when they talk about theories. For physicists, theories entail a definite physical framework embodied in a set of fundamental assumptions about the world that lead to a specific set of equations and predictions—ones that are borne out by successful predictions. Theories aren't necessarily shown to be correct or complete immediately. Even Einstein took the better part of a decade to develop the correct version of his theory of general relativity. But eventually both the ideas and the measurements settle down and theories are either proven correct, abandoned or absorbed into other, more encompassing theories.

The very different uses of the word "theory" provide a field day for advocates of "intelligent design." By conflating a scientific theory with the colloquial use of the word, creationists instantly diminish the significance of science in general and evolution's supporting scientific evidence in particular. Admittedly, the debate is complicated by the less precise nature of evolutionary theory and our inability to perform experiments to test the progression of a particular species. Moreover, evolution is by no means a complete theory. We have yet to learn how the initial conditions for evolution came about—why we have 23 pairs of chromosomes and at which level evolution operates are only two of the things we don't understand. But such gaps should serve as incentives for questions and further scientific advances, not for abandoning the scientific enterprise.

This debate might be tamed if scientists clearly acknowledged both the successes and limitations of the current theory, so that the indisputable elements are clearly isolated. But skeptics have to acknowledge that the way to progress is by scientifically addressing the missing elements, not by ignoring evidence. The current controversy over what to teach is just embarrassing.

"Global warming" is another example of problematic terminology. Climatologists predict more drastic fluctuations in temperature and rainfall—not necessarily that every place will be warmer. The name sometimes subverts the debate, since it lets people argue that their winter was worse, so how could there be global warming? Clearly "global climate change" would have been a better name.

But not all problems stem solely from poor word choices. Some stem from the intrinsically complex nature of much of modern science. Science sometimes transcends this limitation: remarkably, chemists were able to detail the precise chemical processes involved in the destruction of the ozone layer, making the evidence that chlorofluorocarbon gases (Freon, for example) were destroying the ozone layer indisputable.

How to report scientific developments on vital issues of the day that are less well understood or in which the connection is less direct is a more complicated question. Global weather patterns are a case in point. Even if we understand some effects of carbon dioxide in the atmosphere, it is difficult to predict the precise chain of events that a marked increase in carbon dioxide will cause.

The distillation of results presented to the public in such cases should reflect at least some of the subtleties of the most current developments. More balanced reporting would of course help. Journalists will seek to offer balance by providing an opposing or competing perspective from another scientist on a given development. But almost all newly discovered results will have some supporters and some naysayers, and only time and more evidence will sort out the true story. This was a real problem in the global warming debate for a while: the story was reported in a way that suggested some scientists believed it was an issue and some didn't, even long after the bulk of the scientific community had recognized the seriousness of the problem.

Sometimes, as with global warming, the claims have been underplayed. But often it's the opposite: a cancer development presented as a definite advance can seem far more exciting and might raise the status of the researcher far more than a result presented solely as a partial understanding of a microscopic mechanism whose connection to the disease is uncertain. Scientists and the public are both at fault. No matter how many times these "breakthroughs" prove misleading, they will be reported this way as long as that's what people want to hear.

A better understanding of the mathematical significance of results and less insistence on a simple story would help to clarify many scientific discussions. For several months, Harvard was tortured by empty debates over the relative intrinsic scientific abilities of men and women. One of the more amusing aspects of the discussion was that those who believed in the differences and those who didn't used the same evidence about gender-specific special ability. How could that be? The answer is that the data shows no substantial effects. Social factors might account for these tiny differences, which in any case have an unclear connection to scientific ability. Not much of a headline when phrased that way, is it?

Each type of science has its own source of complexity and potential for miscommunication. Yet there are steps we can take to improve public understanding in all cases. The first would be to inculcate greater understanding and acceptance of indirect scientific evidence. The information from an unmanned space mission is no less legitimate than the information from one in which people are on board.

This doesn't mean never questioning an interpretation, but it also doesn't mean equating indirect evidence with blind belief, as people sometimes suggest. Second, we might need different standards for evaluating science with urgent policy implications than research with purely theoretical value. When scientists say they are not certain about their predictions, it doesn't necessarily mean they've found nothing substantial. It would be better if scientists were more open about the mathematical significance of their results and if the public didn't treat math as quite so scary; statistics and errors, which tell us the uncertainty in a measurement, give us the tools to evaluate new developments fairly.

But most important, people have to recognize that science can be complex. If we accept only simple stories, the description will necessarily be distorted. When advances are subtle or complicated, scientists should be willing to go the extra distance to give proper explanations and the public should be more patient about the truth. Even so, some difficulties are unavoidable. Most developments reflect work in progress, so the story is complex because no one yet knows the big picture.

But speculation and the exploration of ideas beyond what we know with certainty are what lead to progress. They are what makes science exciting. Although the more involved story might not have the same immediate appeal, the truth in the end will always be far more interesting.

WHAT EVERY STUDENT KNOWS: THOU SHALL NOT COPY
Robert Rivard

I don't envy the job of my colleagues at KENS-TV. Parting ways with Albert Flores, the station's popular, longtime chief meteorologist, had to hurt—both inside the culture and with viewers.

Network affiliates live and die by the ratings book, and serious money is at stake with small shifts in viewership among the leading stations.

Give station management credit for making a principled and costly decision they could have justifiably sidestepped.

Editors at the *Express-News* faced no such dilemma when we decided to stop publishing Flores' weather column after an alert copy editor discovered he was putting his name on the work of others. No readers canceled their subscriptions, although a few did threaten. Even if there had been cancellations, I know editors would have been free to act.

Yes, the *Express-News* would fire anyone—myself, a columnist, a reporter—caught purloining the work of others and passing it off as our own.

I don't know the details of Flores' departure from KENS, but clearly it occurred in the aftermath of events here. The newspaper did not employ Flores. We did not compensate him for his column. We do not employ or compensate KENS meteorologist Bill Taylor, whose weather column appears twice a week in the *Express-News*.

KENS management, in turn, does not employ or compensate *Express-News* writers, such as columnist Edmund Tijerina, who appear on their news programs. Both companies are equal partners in MySanAntonio.com, our shared news and information Web site, but the talent exchange is just that, a collaboration.

We share something else in common. Both the *Express-News* and KENS are feeling the heat from unhappy viewers and readers.

I've personally read more than 125 e-mails and letters now, the majority of them critical of editors and KENS management. To sum up our critics: We like Albert and do not think he deserved to lose his column or his job.

Many of those protesting our decision scare me.

What's wrong with what he did, anyway, they demand? Doesn't everyone do it, both at the *Express-News* and throughout society? Who do we think we are, acting against such a popular television personality? Isn't plagiarism something only journalists think is wrong?

Thank God for the teachers who have written in our defense.

They know better than others how hard it is to teach children today that it is both wrong and nearsighted to go to the Internet and steal information rather than do original work. If parents stop caring about such ethical trespasses, what can we expect when our children become adults?

We learn early in life, as schoolchildren, the difference between inappropriate copying, on the one hand, and legitimate background research and original work on the other hand.

All writers, from sixth-graders to Pulitzer Prize winners, rely in some part on the work of other published sources. We also learn at an early age how to give credit, how to attribute, and how to take an idea and build on it in our words, based on our own original thinking.

We learn not to copy Samuel Clemens when writing a book report about Tom Sawyer and Huck Finn. Later, as high school and college students, we are reminded of the consequences of filching material to fake a term paper.

Albert Flores surely learned the same lessons early in life. He may have been part entertainer, but he also was part journalist, someone we relied on during times of severe weather, someone we trusted.

What was he thinking when he visited Internet sites and cut and pasted entire passages by other meteorologists and writers, then placed his own name over the work and told his editor at the *Express-News* his column was ready?

He didn't lift a few phrases. He didn't borrow a few ideas. He didn't forget marginal attribution. He systematically lifted his writing from other sources and passed it off as his own.

He told me and he told a reporter that he was sorry, but he also claimed not to understand why he was in such trouble. He never publicly acknowledged that he is a plagiarist. He lost our trust.

The newspaper's credibility is, perhaps, its single most valuable asset. No individual, no matter how high his ratings or readership, is bigger than that. Editors are caretakers of that credibility.

We understand that many "fans" of Albert Flores want to see us give him a second chance. We took no joy in our action, and the fact our newspaper published plagiarized material is painful to all of us here.

Albert Flores and his column are not coming back. He will have to find his second chance elsewhere. To find it, he first will have to admit what he did.

RISE OF THE PLAGIOSPHERE

Ed Tenner

The 1960s gave us, among other mind-altering ideas, a revolutionary new metaphor for our physical and chemical surroundings: the biosphere. But an even more momentous change is coming. Emerging technologies are causing a shift in our mental ecology, one that will turn our culture into the plagiosphere, a closing frontier of ideas.

The Apollo missions' photographs of Earth as a blue sphere helped win millions of people to the environmentalist view of the planet as a fragile and interdependent whole. The Russian geoscientist Vladimir Vernadsky had coined the word "biosphere" as early as 1926, and the Yale University biologist G. Evelyn Hutchinson had expanded on the theme of Earth as a system maintaining its own equilibrium. But as the German environmental scholar Wolfgang Sachs observed, our imaging systems also helped create a vision of the planet's surface as an object of rationalized control and management—a corporate and unromantic conclusion to humanity's voyages of discovery.

What NASA did to our conception of the planet, Web-based technologies are beginning to do to our understanding of our written thoughts. We look at our ideas with less wonder, and with a greater sense that others have already noted what we're seeing for the first time. The plagiosphere is arising from three movements: Web indexing, text matching, and paraphrase detection.

The first of these movements began with the invention of programs called Web crawlers, or spiders. Since the mid-1990s, they have been perusing the now billions of pages of Web content, indexing every significant word found, and making it possible for Web users to retrieve, free and in fractions of a second, pages with desired words and phrases.

The spiders' reach makes searching more efficient than most of technology's wildest prophets imagined, but it can yield unwanted knowledge. The clever phrase a writer coins usually turns out to have been used for years, worldwide—used in good faith, because until recently the only way to investigate priority was in a few books of quotations. And in our accelerated age, even true uniqueness has been limited to 15 minutes. Bons mots that once could have enjoyed a half-life of a season can decay overnight into clichés.

Still, the major search engines have their limits. Alone, they can check a phrase, perhaps a sentence, but not an extended document. And at least in their free versions, they generally do not produce results from proprietary databases like LexisNexis, Factiva, ProQuest, and other paid-subscription sites, or from free databases that dynamically generate pages only when a user submits a query. They also don't include most documents circulating as electronic manuscripts with no permanent Web address.

Enter text-comparison software. A small handful of entrepreneurs have developed programs that search the open Web and proprietary databases, as well as e-books, for suspicious matches. One of the most popular of these is Turnitin; inspired by journalism scandals such as the *New York Times'* Jayson Blair case, its creators offer a version aimed at newspaper editors. Teachers can submit student papers electronically for comparison with these databases, including the retained texts of previously submitted papers. Those passages that bear resemblance to each other are noted with color highlighting in a double-pane view.

Two years ago I heard a speech by a New Jersey electronic librarian who had become an antiplagiarism specialist and consultant. He observed that comparison programs were so thorough that they often flagged chance similarities between student papers and other documents. Consider, then, that Turnitin's spiders are adding 40 million pages from the public Web, plus 40,000 student papers, each day. Meanwhile Google plans to scan millions of library books—including many still under copyright—for its Print database. The number of coincidental parallelisms between the various things that people write is bound to rise steadily.

A third technology will add yet more capacity to find similarities in writing. Artificial-intelligence researchers at MIT and other universities are developing techniques for identifying nonverbatim similarity between documents to make possible the detection of nonverbatim plagiarism. While the investigators may have in mind only cases of brazen paraphrase, a program of this kind can multiply the number of parallel passages severalfold.

Some universities are encouraging students to precheck their papers and drafts against the emerging plagiosphere. Perhaps publications will soon routinely screen submissions. The problem here is that while such rigorous and robust policing will no doubt reduce cheating, it may also give writers a sense of futility. The concept of the biosphere exposed our environmental fragility; the emergence of the plagiosphere perhaps represents our textual impasse. Copernicus may have deprived us of our centrality in the cosmos, and Darwin of our uniqueness in the biosphere, but at least they left us the illusion of the originality of our words. Soon that, too, will be gone.

FORGET ABOUT POLICING PLAGIARISM. JUST *TEACH.*

Rebecca Moore Howard

If you are a professor in the United States and you have a pulse, you have heard about the problems of Internet plagiarism. Exactly what you have heard may vary, depending on what you have read, whom you have been listening to, and how you have been filtering the information or opinions that you have encountered. But everyone is worried about it—and for good reason.

Students can gain easy online access to an astonishing array of ready-made term papers, and for a fee, they can get custom-written papers within 48 hours from online sites. Send in the assignment and a credit-card number, download the attachment when the finished paper comes back two days later, print it out, and presto! Assignment completed. Fifteen-page paper on Plato's attitudes toward Homer? No problem.

Professors cannot always spot plagiarism, especially if a student gets a paper from a closed, subscribers-only Web site or hires an online ghostwriter. But often, they manage a digitized gotcha. No longer do they need to spend arduous days in the library, searching for the sources of a suspect paper. In faculty lounges, professors brag to each other about the speed and ease with which they located downloaded papers.

Actually, a whole gotcha industry has sprung up.

Turnitin.com. Plagiarism.org—each week brings news of another Web site that will help catch the miscreants. Never mind that some of the sites fail to distinguish between quoting and unattributed copying; never mind that they blur the distinctions between omitting quotation marks and downloading an entire paper; never mind that some require the professor to violate students' intellectual-property rights by contributing students' papers to the program's database.

What drives all the new sites and the professors' anxiety is the concern that ethics, integrity, and honesty are flying out the window on digitized wings. That is a legitimate concern to which we must collectively attend.

But professors should also be worried about even more compelling issues. In our stampede to fight what the *New York Times* calls a "plague" of plagiarism, we risk becoming the enemies rather than the mentors of our students; we are replacing the student-teacher relationship with the criminal-police relationship. Further, by thinking of plagiarism as a unitary act rather than a collection of disparate activities, we risk categorizing all of our students as criminals. Worst of all, we risk not recognizing that our own pedagogy needs reform. Big reform.

I use the word "stampede" deliberately. We are in danger of mass hysteria on the plagiarism issue, hysteria that simplifies categories and reduces multiple choices to binaries. It appears that the Internet is making cheating easier; hence, it appears that the Internet is encouraging bad morals; hence, it appears that morality is in precipitous decline. And there we are at the ramparts, trying to hold back the attack. We see ourselves in a state of siege, holding the line against the enemy.

All those who worked to get advanced academic degrees in order to police young adults, please raise your hands. No hands? Then let's calm down and get back to the business of teaching.

We like the word "plagiarism" because it seems simple and straightforward: Plagiarism is representing the words of another as one's own, our college policies say, and we tell ourselves, "There! It's clear. Students are responsible for reading those policies and observing their guidelines."

Then, when a "plague" of plagiarism comes along and we believe academic integrity itself is under attack, things get even simpler. Encouraged by digital dualisms, we forget that plagiarism means many different things: downloading a term paper, failing to give proper credit to the source of an idea, copying extensive passages without attribution, inserting someone else's phrases or sentences—perhaps with small changes—into your own prose, and forgetting to supply a set of quotation marks.

If we ignore those distinctions, we fail to see that most of us have violated the plagiarism injunctions in one way or another, large or small, intentionally or inadvertently, at one time or another. The distinctions are just not that crisp. We have to pull back from the mass hysteria and remember that the P-word covers a wide variety of behaviors, circumstances, and motivations. Accidentally omitting a set of quotation marks is not the same as submitting a downloaded paper.

Now, a downloaded paper is something that no professor should tolerate. It has to be punished. We assign papers so that our students will learn from the experience of writing them; if they do not write them, they do not learn. We have to protect education; we have to demand that our students learn. But even as we're catching and punishing plagiarists in our classes, we have to ask ourselves why they are plagiarizing. Some of the possible answers to that question are not very appealing. But just as we cannot ignore students' plagiarism, we cannot ignore these possibilities, either:

- It is possible that students are cheating because they don't value the opportunity of learning in our classes. Some of that is cultural, of course. Today's students are likely to change jobs many times before they retire, so they must earn credentials for an array of job possibilities, rather than immersing themselves in a focused, unchanging area of expertise. The fact that many of them are working long hours at outside jobs only exacerbates the problem.

- It is possible that our pedagogy has not adjusted to contemporary circumstances as readily as have our students. Rather than assigning tasks that have meaning, we may be assuming that students will find meaning in performing assigned tasks. How else can one explain giving the same paper assignment semester after semester to a lecture class of 100 students? Such assignments expect that students will gain something from the act of writing, but they do not respond to the needs and interests of the students in a particular section of the class. They are, in that sense, inauthentic assignments.

We expect authentic writing from our students, yet we do not write authentic assignments for them. We beg our students to cheat if we assign a major paper and then have no further involvement with the project until the students turn in their work. Assigning and grading a paper leaves out a crucial middle: working and talking with students while they draft those papers. You're too busy? Then what about dividing your students into small groups that you, a teaching assistant, or a tutor can meet with, or that can respond to their members' work before the papers reach you?

We deprive our students of an authentic audience if we assign papers that are due at the end of the term and that the students never see again. We deprive them of an interested audience if we scrawl a grade and "good work" on a paper—and nothing else. We deprive them of a respectful audience if we tear apart the style, grammar, and mechanics of their papers, marking every error and accusing them of illiteracy for their split infinitives, without ever talking with them about what they were trying to accomplish, how they might achieve their goals, and why all the style, grammar, and mechanics matter anyhow.

I raise those possibilities for myself as well as for my colleagues. I have not only witnessed those practices; I have engaged in them. They are, in fact, temptations to which we regularly succumb, just as our students may succumb to the temptation to plagiarize.

Do professors' shortcomings excuse students' textual transgressions? No. But they do demand that we recognize and reform pedagogy that encourages plagiarism because it discourages learning. We have to be ethical, too.

So do our institutions. If professors' working conditions are such that they cannot give, work with students on, and respond to authentic writing assignments, then the working conditions need to change—whether that means cutting class size, reducing teaching load, or placing more emphasis on teaching in decisions about hiring and promotion. Writing is an invaluable means of learning. Professors must demand that their students do the writing that they are submitting as their own; professors must assign essays that foster learning; and institutions must ensure that their professors' working conditions make good teaching possible.

THE DANGEROUS MYTH OF GRADE INFLATION
Alfie Kohn

Grade inflation got started . . . in the late '60s and early '70s . . . The grades that faculty members now give . . . deserve to be a scandal.
—*Professor Harvey Mansfield, Harvard University, 2001*

Grades A and B are sometimes given too readily—Grade A for work of no very high merit, and Grade B for work not far above mediocrity. . . . One of the chief obstacles to raising the standards of the degree is the readiness with which insincere students gain passable grades by sham work.
—*Report of the Committee on Raising the Standard, Harvard University, 1894*

Complaints about grade inflation have been around for a very long time. Every so often a fresh flurry of publicity pushes the issue to the foreground again, the latest example being a series of articles in the *Boston Globe* last year that disclosed—in a tone normally reserved for the discovery of entrenched corruption in state government—that a lot of students at Harvard were receiving A's and being graduated with honors.

The fact that people were offering the same complaints more than a century ago puts the latest bout of harrumphing in perspective, not unlike those quotations about the disgraceful values of the younger generation that turn out to be hundreds of years old. The long history of indignation also pretty well derails any attempts to place the blame for higher grades on a residue of bleeding-heart liberal professors hired in the '60s. (Unless, of course, there was a similar countercultural phenomenon in the 1860s.)

Yet on campuses across America today, academe's usual requirements for supporting data and reasoned analysis have been suspended for some reason where this issue is concerned. It is largely accepted on faith that grade inflation—an upward shift in students' grade-point averages without a similar rise in achievement—exists, and that it is a bad thing. Meanwhile, the truly substantive issues surrounding grades and motivation have been obscured or ignored.

The fact is that it is hard to substantiate even the simple claim that grades have been rising. Depending on the time period we're talking about, that claim may well be false. In their book *When Hope and Fear Collide* (Jossey-Bass, 1998), Arthur Levine and Jeanette Curteon tell us that more undergraduates in 1993 reported receiving A's (and fewer reported receiving grades of C or below) compared with their counterparts in 1969 and 1976 surveys. Unfortunately, self-reports are notoriously unreliable, and the numbers become even more dubious when only a self-selected, and possibly unrepresentative, segment bothers to return the questionnaires. (One out of three failed to do so in 1993; no information is offered about the return rates in the earlier surveys.)

To get a more accurate picture of whether grades have changed over the years, one needs to look at official student transcripts. Clifford Adelman, a senior research analyst with the U.S. Department of Education, did just that, reviewing transcripts from more than 3,000 institutions and reporting his results in 1995. His finding: "Contrary to the widespread lamentations, grades actually declined slightly in the last two decades." Moreover, a report released just this year by the National Center for Education Statistics revealed that fully 33.5 percent of American undergraduates had a grade-point average of C or below in 1999–2000, a number that ought to quiet "all the furor over grade inflation," according to a spokesperson for the Association of American Colleges and Universities. (A review of other research suggests a comparable lack of support for claims of grade inflation at the high-school level.)

However, even where grades are higher now as compared with then—which may well be true in the most selective institutions—that does not constitute proof that they are inflated. The burden rests with critics to demonstrate that those higher grades are undeserved, and one can cite any number of alternative explanations. Maybe students are turning in better assignments. Maybe instructors used to be too stingy with their marks and have become more reasonable. Maybe the concept of assessment itself has evolved, so that today it is more a means for allowing students to demonstrate what they know rather than for sorting them or "catching them out." (The real question, then, is why we spent so many years trying to make good students look bad.) Maybe students aren't forced to take as many courses outside their primary areas of interest in which they didn't fare as well. Maybe struggling students are now able to withdraw from a course before a poor grade appears on their transcripts. (Say what you will about that practice, it challenges the hypothesis that the grades students receive in the courses they complete are inflated.)

The bottom line: No one has ever demonstrated that students today get A's for the same work that used to receive B's or C's. We simply do not have the data to support such a claim.

Consider the most recent, determined effort by a serious source to prove that grades are inflated: *Evaluation and the Academy: Are We Doing the Right Thing*? a report released this year by the American Academy of Arts and Sciences. Its senior author is Henry Rosovsky, formerly Harvard's dean of the faculty. The first argument offered in support of the proposition that students couldn't possibly deserve higher grades is that SAT scores have dropped during the same period that grades are supposed to have risen. But this is a patently inapt comparison, if only because the SAT is deeply flawed. It has never been much good even at predicting grades during the freshman year in college, to say nothing of more-important academic outcomes. A four-year analysis of almost 78,000 University of California students, published last year by the UC president's office, found that the test predicted only 13.3 percent of variation in freshman grades, a figure roughly consistent with hundreds of previous studies. (I outlined numerous other problems with the test in "Two Cheers for an End to the SAT," *The Chronicle*, March 9, 2001.)

Even if one believes that the SAT is a valid and valuable exam, however, the claim that scores are dropping is a poor basis for the assertion that grades are too high. First, it is difficult to argue that a standardized test taken in high school and grades for college course work are measuring the same thing. Second, changes in aggregate SAT scores mostly reflect the proportion of the eligible population that has chosen to take the test. The American Academy's report states that average SAT scores dropped slightly from 1969 to 1993. But over that period, the pool of test takers grew from about one-third to more than two-fifths of high-school graduates—an addition of more than 200,000 students.

Third, a decline in overall SAT scores is hardly the right benchmark against which to measure the grades earned at Harvard or other elite institutions. Every bit of evidence I could find—including a review of the SAT scores of entering students at Harvard over the past two decades, at the nation's most selective colleges over three and even four decades, and at all private colleges since 1985—uniformly confirms a virtually linear rise in both verbal and math scores, even after correcting for the renorming of the test in the mid-1990s. To cite just one example, the latest edition of *Trends in College Admissions* reports that the average verbal-SAT score of students enrolled in all private colleges rose from 543 in 1985 to 558 in 1999. Thus, those who regard SAT results as a basis for comparison should expect to see higher grades now rather than assume that they are inflated.

The other two arguments made by the authors of the American Academy's report rely on a similar sleight of hand. They note that more college students are now forced to take remedial courses, but offer no reason to think that this is especially true of the relevant student population—namely, those at the most selective colleges who are now receiving A's instead of B's.

Finally, they report that more states are adding high-school graduation tests and even standardized exams for admission to public universities. Yet that trend can be explained by political factors and offers no evidence of an objective decline in students' proficiency. For instance, scores on the National Assessment of Educational Progress, known as "the nation's report card" on elementary and secondary schooling, have shown very little change over the past couple of decades, and most of the change that has occurred has been for the better. As David Berliner and Bruce Biddle put it in their tellingly titled book *The Manufactured Crisis* (Addison-Wesley, 1995), the data demonstrate that "today's students are at least as well informed as students in previous generations." The latest round of public-school bashing—and concomitant reliance on high-stakes testing—began with the Reagan administration's *Nation at Risk* report, featuring claims now widely viewed by researchers as exaggerated and misleading.

Beyond the absence of good evidence, the debate over grade inflation brings up knotty epistemological problems. To say that grades are not merely rising but inflated—and that they are consequently "less accurate" now, as the American Academy's report puts it—is to postulate the existence of an objectively correct evaluation of what a student (or an essay) deserves, the true grade that ought to be uncovered and honestly reported. It would be an understatement to say that this reflects a simplistic and outdated view of knowledge and of learning.

In fact, what is most remarkable is how rarely learning even figures into the discussion. The dominant disciplinary sensibility in commentaries on this topic is not that of education—an exploration of pedagogy or assessment—but rather of economics. That is clear from the very term "grade inflation," which is, of course, just a metaphor. Our understanding is necessarily limited if we confine ourselves to the vocabulary of inputs and outputs, incentives, resource distribution, and compensation.

Suppose, for the sake of the argument, we assumed the very worst—not only that students are getting better grades than did their counterparts of an earlier generation, but that the grades are too high. What does that mean, and why does it upset some people so?

To understand grade inflation in its proper context, we must acknowledge a truth that is rarely named: The crusade against it is led by conservative individuals and organizations who regard it as analogous—or even related—to such favorite whipping boys as multicultural education, the alleged radicalism of academe, "political correctness" (a label that permits the denigration of anything one doesn't like without having to offer a reasoned objection), and too much concern about students' self-esteem. Mainstream media outlets and college administrators have allowed themselves to be put on the defensive by accusations about grade inflation, as can be witnessed when deans at Harvard plead nolo contendere and dutifully tighten their grading policies.

What are the critics assuming about the nature of students' motivation to learn, about the purpose of evaluation and of education itself? (It is surely revealing when someone reserves time and energy to complain bitterly about how many students are getting A's—as opposed to expressing concern about, say, how many students have been trained to think that the point of going to school is to get A's.)

"In a healthy university, it would not be necessary to say what is wrong with grade inflation," Harvey Mansfield asserted in an opinion article last year (*The Chronicle*, April

6, 2001). That, to put it gently, is a novel view of health. It seems reasonable to expect those making an argument to be prepared to defend it, and also valuable to bring their hidden premises to light. Here are the assumptions that seem to underlie the grave warnings about grade inflation:

The professor's job is to sort students for employers or graduate schools. Some are disturbed by grade inflation—or, more accurately, grade compression—because it then becomes harder to spread out students on a continuum, ranking them against one another for the benefit of postcollege constituencies. One professor asks, by way of analogy, "Why would anyone subscribe to *Consumers Digest* if every blender were rated a "'best buy'"?

But how appropriate is such a marketplace analogy? Is the professor's job to rate students like blenders for the convenience of corporations, or to offer feedback that will help students learn more skillfully and enthusiastically? (Notice, moreover, that even consumer magazines don't grade on a curve. They report the happy news if it turns out that every blender meets a reasonable set of performance criteria.)

Furthermore, the student-as-appliance approach assumes that grades provide useful information to those postcollege constituencies. Yet growing evidence—most recently in the fields of medicine and law, as cited in publications like *The Journal of the American Medical Association* and the *American Educational Research Journal*—suggests that grades and test scores do not in fact predict career success, or much of anything beyond subsequent grades and test scores.

Students should be set against one another in a race for artificially scarce rewards. "The essence of grading is exclusiveness," Mansfield said in one interview. Students "should have to compete with each other," he said in another.

In other words, even when no graduate-school admissions committee pushes for students to be sorted, they ought to be sorted anyway, with grades reflecting relative standing rather than absolute accomplishment. In effect, this means that the game should be rigged so that no matter how well students do, only a few can get A's. The question guiding evaluation in such a classroom is not "How well are they learning?" but "Who's beating whom?" The ultimate purpose of good colleges, this view holds, is not to maximize success, but to ensure that there will always be losers.

A bell curve may sometimes—but only sometimes—describe the range of knowledge in a roomful of students at the beginning of a course. When it's over, though, any responsible educator hopes that the results would skew drastically to the right, meaning that most students learned what they hadn't known before. Thus, in their important study, *Making Sense of College Grades* (Jossey-Bass, 1986), Ohmer Milton, Howard Pollio, and James Eison write, "It is not a symbol of rigor to have grades fall into a 'normal' distribution; rather, it is a symbol of failure—failure to teach well, failure to test well, and failure to have any influence at all on the intellectual lives of students." Making sure that students are continually re-sorted, with excellence turned into an artificially scarce commodity, is almost perverse.

What does relative success signal about student performance in any case? The number of peers that a student has bested tells us little about how much she knows and is able to do. Moreover, such grading policies may create a competitive climate that is counterproductive for winners and losers alike, to the extent that it discourages a free exchange of ideas and a sense of community that's conducive to exploration.

Harder is better (or higher grades mean lower standards). Compounding the tendency to confuse excellence with victory is a tendency to confuse quality with difficulty—as evidenced in the accountability fad that has elementary and secondary education in its grip just now, with relentless talk of "rigor" and "raising the bar." The same confusion shows up in higher education when professors pride themselves not on the intellectual depth and value of their classes but merely on how much reading they assign, how hard their tests are, how rarely they award good grades, and so on. "You're going to have to work in here!" they announce, with more than a hint of machismo and self-congratulation.

Some people might defend that posture on the grounds that students will perform better if A's are harder to come by. In fact, the evidence on this question is decidedly mixed. Stringent grading sometimes has been shown to boost short-term retention as measured by multiple-choice exams—never to improve understanding or promote interest in learning. The most recent analysis, released in 2000 by Julian R. Betts and Jeff Grogger, professors of economics at the University of California at San Diego and at Los Angeles, respectively, found that tougher grading was initially correlated with higher test scores. But the long-term effects were negligible—with the exception of minority students, for whom the effects were negative.

It appears that something more than an empirical hypothesis is behind the "harder is better" credo, particularly when it is set up as a painfully false dichotomy: Those easy-grading professors are too lazy to care, or too worried about how students will evaluate them, or overly concerned about their students' self-esteem, whereas we are the last defenders of what used to matter in the good old days. High standards! Intellectual honesty! No free lunch!

The American Academy's report laments an absence of "candor" about this issue. Let us be candid, then. Those who grumble about undeserved grades sometimes exude a cranky impatience with—or even contempt for—the late adolescents and young adults who sit in their classrooms. Many people teaching in higher education, after all, see themselves primarily as researchers and regard teaching as an occupational hazard, something they're not very good at, were never trained for, and would rather avoid. It would be interesting to examine the correlation between one's view of teaching (or of students) and the intensity of one's feelings about grade inflation. Someone also might want to examine the personality profiles of those who become infuriated over the possibility that someone, somewhere, got an A without having earned it.

Grades motivate. With the exception of orthodox behaviorists, psychologists have come to realize that people can exhibit qualitatively different kinds of motivation: intrinsic, in which the task itself is seen as valuable, and extrinsic, in which the task is just a means to the end of gaining a reward or escaping a punishment. The two are not only distinct but often inversely related. Scores of studies have demonstrated, for example, that the more people are rewarded, the more they come to lose interest in whatever had to be done in order to get the reward. (That conclusion is essentially reaffirmed by the latest major meta-analysis on the topic: a review of 128 studies, published in 1999 by Edward L. Deci, Richard Koestner, and Richard Ryan.)

Those unfamiliar with that basic distinction, let alone the supporting research, may be forgiven for pondering how to "motivate" students, then concluding that grades are often a good way of doing so, and consequently worrying about the impact of inflated grades. But the reality is that it doesn't matter how motivated students are; what matters is how students are motivated. A focus on grades creates, or at least perpetuates, an extrinsic orientation that is likely to undermine the love of learning we are presumably seeking to promote.

Three robust findings emerge from the empirical literature on the subject: Students who are given grades, or for whom grades are made particularly salient, tend to display less interest in what they are doing, fare worse on meaningful measures of learning, and avoid more-challenging tasks when given the opportunity—as compared with those in a nongraded comparison group. College instructors cannot help noticing, and presumably being disturbed by, such consequences, but they may lapse into blaming students ("grade grubbers") rather than understanding the systemic sources of the problem. A focus on whether too many students are getting A's suggests a tacit endorsement of grades that predictably produces just such a mind-set in students.

These fundamental questions are almost completely absent from discussions of grade inflation. The American Academy's report takes exactly one sentence—with no citations—to dismiss the argument that "lowering the anxiety over grades leads to better learning," ignoring the fact that much more is involved than anxiety. It is a matter of why a student learns, not only how much stress he feels. Nor is the point just that low grades hurt some students' feelings, but that grades, per se, hurt all students' engagement with learning. The meaningful contrast is not between an A and a B or C, but between an extrinsic and an intrinsic focus.

Precisely because that is true, a reconsideration of grade inflation leads us to explore alternatives to our (often unreflective) use of grades. Narrative comments and other ways by which faculty members can communicate their evaluations can be far more informative than letter or number grades, and much less destructive. Indeed, some colleges—for example, Hampshire, Evergreen State, Alverno, and New College of Florida—have eliminated grades entirely, as a critical step toward raising intellectual standards. Even the American Academy's report acknowledges that "relatively undifferentiated course grading has been a traditional practice in many graduate schools for a very long time." Has that policy produced lower-quality teaching and learning? Quite the contrary: Many people say they didn't begin to explore ideas deeply and passionately until graduate school began and the importance of grades diminished significantly.

If the continued use of grades rests on nothing more than tradition ("We've always done it that way"), a faulty understanding of motivation, or excessive deference to graduate-school admissions committees, then it may be time to balance those factors against the demonstrated harms of getting students to chase A's. Ohmer Milton and his colleagues discovered—and others have confirmed—that a "grade orientation" and a "learning orientation" on the part of students tend to be inversely related. That raises the disturbing possibility that some colleges are institutions of higher learning in name only, because the paramount question for students is not "What does this mean?" but "Do we have to know this?"

A grade-oriented student body is an invitation for the administration and faculty to ask hard questions: What unexamined assumptions keep traditional grading in place? What forms of assessment might be less destructive? How can professors minimize the salience of grades in their classrooms, so long as grades must still be given? And: If the artificial inducement of grades disappeared, what sort of teaching strategies might elicit authentic interest in a course?

To engage in this sort of inquiry, to observe real classrooms, and to review the relevant research is to arrive at one overriding conclusion: The real threat to excellence isn't grade inflation at all; it's grades.

THE BURNING QUESTION

Robert Macfarlane

The effects of climate change are now perceptible in language as well as in degrees Celsius. On Banks Island, in the Canadian High Arctic, environmental shifts are happening so fast that the Inuvialuit inhabitants do not have the words to describe what they now see around them. New species of fish, bird, and insect have migrated north to the island, following the isobars. Autumn thunder and lightning have been witnessed from Banks for the first time. "Permafrost" is no longer tolerable as a term, for the ground-ice is melting: in Sachs Harbour, the main settlement on Banks, buildings are subsiding and road surfaces are slushing up.

There have been disappearances as well as arrivals on Banks. The permafrost melt has caused an inland lake to drain into the sea. The intricate stages of hardening through which the sea-ice around Banks cycles—frazil, grease, nilas, gray—are no longer being fulfilled in many places during summer, for the temperature of the sea water is spiking above the key freeze-point of 28.6°F.

The Inuvialuit culture is unprepared for these rapid fluxes. Old words (the name of an inland lake) are now unaccompanied by their phenomena; new phenomena (a fork of flame in a previously lightningless sky) are unaccompanied by words.

Contemplation of the situation on Banks Island prompts a broader question about the relationship of climate change and language. Where is the literature of climate change? Where is the creative response to what Sir David King, the government's chief scientific adviser, has famously described as "the most severe problem faced by the world"?

Cultural absences are always more difficult to document than cultural outpourings. But the deficiency of a creative response to climate change is increasingly visible. It becomes unignorable if we contrast it with the abundance of literature produced in response to the other great eschatological crisis of the past half-century—the nuclear threat.

The authoritative bibliography of American and British nuclear literature runs to over 3,000 items: it includes Ian McEwan's oratorio "Or Shall We Die", JG Ballard's *The Terminal Beach*, Martin Amis's *Einstein's Monsters,* Raymond Briggs's *When The Wind Blows,* as well as work by Edward Abbey, Ray Bradbury, Upton Sinclair, Neville Shute. This literature did not only annotate the politics of the nuclear debate, it helped to shape it. As well as feeding off that epoch of history, it fed into it.

There is nothing like this intensity of literary engagement with climate change. Climate change still exists principally as what Ballard has called "invisible literature": that is, the data buried in "company reports, specialist journals, technical manuals, newsletters, market research reports, internal memoranda." It exists as paper trail, as data stream. It also exists, of course, as journalism, as conversation, and as behaviour. But it does not yet, with a few exceptions, exist as art. Where are the novels, the plays, the poems, the songs, the libretti, of this massive contemporary anxiety?

The question is pressing. For an imaginative repertoire is urgently needed by which the causes and consequences of climate change can be debated, sensed, and communicated. Bill McKibben, author of the premonitory classic *The End of Nature* (1989), has written of how individuals would not act against climate change—altering their habits of consumption, lobbying policy-makers—until they felt "fear in their guts." Literature has a role to play in inducing this gut feeling, for one of its special abilities is that of allowing us to entertain hypothetical situations—alternative lives, or futures, or landscapes—as though they were real. It has a unique capacity to help us connect present action with future consequence.

The problem is that climate change is not—not yet—apocalyptic in its consequences. Apocalypse comes swiftly and charismatically, and as such offers great opportunities for the literary imagination. This is attested to by the extent and age of the literature of apocalypse, beginning with Revelation, with its war-chant rhythms, its grim mandala-like structure, its incantation of massive death foretold.

By contrast, climate change occurs discreetly and incrementally, and as such, it presents the literary imagination with a series of difficulties: how to dramatise aggregating detail, how to plot slow change. Though the cumulative impact of climate change may be catastrophic, and may push us into a post-natural world, this is not yet scientifically certain. And so climate change does not yet have its millenarian icons: the grim brilliance of the nuclear flash point (a sudden sunrise which is really the last dusk), or the plump red button beneath its clear plastic flip-case, or the kitchen-table fallout shelter.

Indeed, any literature of climate change would, for the time being, have to steer determinedly away from apocalyptic scenarios. For the modern environmental movement has, in the past, tried to bring about social change by harnessing the power of nightmares. In the 1970s and early 1980s in particular, dire dystopian predictions were made about over-population, imminent Gulf Stream shut-off, and sudden sea-level rises. All were proved wrong, and the damage to the credibility of environmentalism is unrepaired. Climate-change sceptics gladly trip off a list of these zealously envisaged catastrophes: lurid acts of fairground clairvoyance which have never come true.

So any literary response to the present situation would need to be measured and prudent, and would need to find ways of imagining which remained honest to the scientific evidence. It might require, one would think, forms which are chronic—which unfold within time—and are therefore capable of registering change, and weighing its consequences. And it might require literary languages which are attentive to the creep of change; which practise a vigilance of attention and a precision of utterance (one thinks back to Thoreau, recording the day each year on which Walden Pond first froze, or of Ruskin, in his home on the shores of Coniston, making painstaking daily measurements of the blueness of the sky, to check the effects of air-pollution upon its colour, or of Gilbert White ascertaining the different keys in which owls of different woods hooted). But presumably there would be room, too, for more bumptious vernaculars: for satire, say, or for polemic. Might John le Carré, who took on the global pharmaceutical industry so angrily and well in *The Constant Gardener,* do the same for the politics of climate change?

An odd parallel with our current situation can be found in the 19th century. For the Victorians of the later 1800s lived in the fear-shadow of their version of climate change: global cooling. In 1862, the physicist William Thomson—better known as Lord Kelvin—made public his belief that the sun was cooling without renewal of its energy. Owing to the irreversible seep of entropy, Thomson announced, the solar system was condemned to what was christened "Heat Death." The Earth would slowly lose the benefit of its lantern and radiator, and would gradually become encased in ice. A "universal winter," as Thomas Huxley put it, would ensue.

Solar physics immediately became a hot topic of discussion among Victorians, who were appalled at this demonstration of the universe's indifference to humanity. And the idea of global cooling precipitated quickly into the literary culture of the period. It can be found, among other places, in the work of Samuel Butler, James Thomson, Richard Jefferies, William Morris, GF Watts, Thomas Huxley, Charles Darwin (who noted in his autobiography that he found it "intolerable" that humanity should be "doomed to complete annihilation after such long-continued slow progress"), John Ruskin ("I want to believe in Apollo—but can't—the sun is said to be getting rusty (is not it?)," he wrote anxiously in a letter to a friend on 19 November 1862), Thomas Hardy, and HG Wells (in *The War of the Worlds* it is the cooling of the solar system that forces the Martians to "carry warfare sunwards"). The annual death of the sun at the solstice, and the daily death of the sun at sunset, took on new and sinister resonances within fiction and poetry of the period. Old myths—especially the Norse myths of Ragnarok and Balder, in which a young hero dies in his youthful vigour—were rehabilitated, and used to trope the sun's extermination.

There are differences between then and now, of course; not least that what frightened the Victorians was the universe's passivity to human action, whereas what frightens us is its reactiveness. But it is clear that Victorian worries at Heat Death, and the prospects for life on a cooling Earth, led to a great cultural output, which partly debated the science and partly dramatised it. "Imaginative figuration and scientific inquiry," wrote Gillian Beer, in a fine essay on the subject, "operated in inseparable co-operation with one another." It is a "co-operation" which has not happened in our period.

But signs of change exist; initiatives are afoot. David Buckland's visionary Cape Farewell project has recently sailed artists—including Antony Gormley, McEwan, and Rachel Whiteread—to the Arctic, with the aim of "illustrating the workings of this crucial part of the planet, and engaging the public and schools in the debate about climate change." The RSA has launched an excellent "Arts & Ecology" programme, with the aim of bringing together environmentalists, scientists, and writer-thinkers "to explore the roles and responsibilities of contemporary art in ecology"; among their events is a public discussion on climate change and literature. The exemplary Open Democracy Web site is hosting a climate change debate. The latest edition of *Granta* magazine this month carries a feature called "The Weather Where You Are," in which writers across the world describe the meteorological shifts they have witnessed. And a fortnight ago, I was part of an unorthodox conference, hosted by the Environmental Change Institute at Oxford University, at which 30 scientists and 30 artists—including McEwan, Philip Pullman, Caryl Churchill, and Gretel Ehrlich—were brought together to discuss how art and science might collaborate in fighting climate change.

So perhaps the cultural climate is changing. Or, perhaps, cultural change will be overtaken by the climate. For the effects of global warming may not remain discreet and incremental for long. Sudden climatic step changes may soon become evident, which radically displace precipitation patterns, changing the moisture economies of whole territories, with drastic consequences. Last month, for instance, a senior Chinese environmentalist predicted that China's "arid-north, wet-south" geographical paradigm would invert within 15 years. It has also been proposed, but not proved, that the severity of Hurricane Katrina was exacerbated by climate change. It has been shown that human influence more than doubled the risk of harm occurring during the murderous European heat-wave of 2003. In the future, indeed, it may become hard for writers not to take climate change as their subject.

SOMETIMES DESIGN MUST FAIL TO SUCCEED

Henry Petroski

Design pervades our campuses. Professors design courses, curricula, and research programs. Administrators design forms to be filled out. Development staff members design fund-raising campaigns. Students design schedules with no classes on Monday morning or all day Friday. Facilities and transportation offices design parking lots with too few spaces.

We cannot escape design—nor the reality that it is difficult to produce anything that is without fault or critics. That is nowhere so clear as in the area of campus planning and architecture. At my institution, Duke University, where historically the university chapel had been the geographical center of a campus whose Gothic stone architecture was of a whole, problems of design arose in the wake of World War II.

At that time, campus officials decided to relocate Duke's engineering school from what was then a separate women's campus to the main campus. The location chosen was down the hill from the chapel. Here, out of sight of the main quadrangle, an anomalous red-brick Georgian-style building was constructed at the intersection of what came to be known as Research and Science Drives.

Before long, other brick-faced science buildings were constructed up the street. At a time when C.P. Snow was lamenting the divide between the two cultures of the sciences and the humanities, here was a campus being physically changed to promote their separation.

The engineering school was out of sight and out of mind, hidden behind a thick stand of trees. Whether by conscious design or not, that natural buffer effectively segregated the scientists from the humanists.

Half a century later, engineering had risen to a new prominence—driven in part by its receptivity to campuswide interdisciplinary research programs—and an expansion involving a new group of buildings was proposed. Locating those buildings was part of the campus-planning challenge. The university decided to place them across the street from the original Georgian-style building that engineers had come to refer to affectionately as Old Red, and, reaching back to an idea in an earlier master plan, to close off Science Drive to make a new engineering quadrangle.

The new buildings, which would move the center of gravity of engineering closer to that of the university, were clad in darker brick and stone, symbolically bridging the gap between the two architectures. Around the same time, the library and the divinity school were also expanding, leaving fewer trees standing to hide the growing engineering school from the campus proper. In a stroke of design genius, two wings of the new engineering complex were connected by elevated walkways that together formed an archway looking out from the new quad. Beyond, another archway through the new library building provided a grand entrance to the main campus quadrangle. The two archways were connected by a long, wide set of stairs that invites communication between the formerly separated cultures.

As architecturally successful as the new design is, however, it does have its flaws—as does every design. When the wind is blowing, the archways can channel it to such ferocious velocities that walking through the archways or up or down the stairs is a struggle. The problem need not have been as great, since the development of excessively windy conditions around new buildings—especially closely spaced ones—is not unknown. But as it is, book bags catch the wind, which twists lighter ones around in the hand like clothes on a line. By the way a professor's book bag flaps, it is possible to speculate on who is carrying home a laptop or a heavy stack of papers to grade, and who an empty lunch sack.

In fact, even the best designs can be full of surprises. At Case Western Reserve University, the Weatherhead School of Management is housed in a striking building designed by Frank Gehry. The smoothly curving sides of the signature structure make it into a piece of sculpture, but one winter, shortly after the building was occupied, its stainless steel facade began to shed large chunks of snow and ice onto the sidewalk below. The potentially dangerous situation caused the sidewalk to be closed until a solution could be found. (As I understand it, that solution was to retrofit the building with devices that would melt snow before it could accumulate and prevent any ice from forming.)

The most aesthetically successful designs can turn into functionally embarrassing failures. Another Gehry building, the Walt Disney Concert Hall in Los Angeles, opened to rave reviews. But some neighbors across the street were less than enthusiastic when the summer sun reflected off the polished surface of its cladding and into their condominiums—blinding them and raising the temperature in their living rooms by 15 degrees. The offending section of the facade was covered with a nonreflecting fabric while a permanent solution—such as dulling the finish—was discussed.

The surest way to produce a successful design is to anticipate most completely how it can fail to satisfy those who will use or be affected by it. That is obviously more easily said than done, for design is a complicated matter, involving aesthetic, functional, economic, sociological, and cultural considerations. Yet designers can decrease their chances of overlooking some detail that can turn an otherwise successful design into an embarrassingly flawed one by studying failures as much as they do successes.

In the early 19th century, suspension bridges were so flexible and subject to being damaged or destroyed by the wind that British engineers did not think them suitable for carrying railroad trains, and sought to develop alternative forms. Thus, in the 1840s, Robert Stephenson designed an enormous wrought-iron tubular-girder bridge to carry train traffic across the Menai Strait in northwest Wales.

But John Roebling, the German-born engineer whose bicentennial is being celebrated this year, took failed suspension bridges as data to be analyzed and distilled into lessons for building a successful suspension bridge. Beautiful contemporary etchings clearly show how Roebling designed his Niagara Gorge suspension bridge, which was completed in the mid-1850s, with a heavy truss and stay cables to hold firm under heavy trains and steady against gusty winds. Stephenson watched Roebling's experiment with great interest and wrote him, "If your bridge succeeds, mine is a magnificent blunder," because it was so less efficient a structure. Roebling's bridge did succeed, of course, and he went on to apply similar principles to his masterpiece, the Brooklyn Bridge. Stephenson's massive tubular solution quickly became extinct.

Even exact duplication of a successful design is no guarantee that it will be successful in a new context. Imagine that Gehry's Weatherhead School had been a copy of a building constructed on a campus where it never snows and ice never forms. The problems experienced in Cleveland would never have revealed themselves in such a situation. Had the building performed perfectly in that warmer climate, there might be the expectation that it would do so also in the colder one. However, unless the problem with snow and ice had been anticipated and obviated, such as by installing heating elements to prevent any accumulation in the first place, it would eventually reveal itself.

Similarly, imagine if Gehry's Disney Hall had been constructed in a location where the sun did not strike the polished surface or where there were no condominiums across the street. The problem with the solar reflection and heating might not have revealed itself to be a flaw at all. Given the positive experience with the structure, subsequent buildings might have been designed and built, perhaps with an increasing use of polished stainless-steel cladding applied in even more complex curves. In time, one might expect that the conjunction of the sun's rays, the polished face, and nearby residences would be such that the latent flaw would be made manifest.

The presence of a latent failure mode in an elaborate engineering structure can have much more dire consequences than in a less complex architectural design. An overlooked failure mode in an airplane, space shuttle, or bridge can lead to a catastrophe that claims lives. Thus, engineering students must be taught the importance of understanding failure and anticipating it. Jack V. Matson, a professor at Pennsylvania State University, believes so strongly in conveying the role of failure in successful design that he has expected students in his course known as Failure 101 to fail in order to pass. He has wanted them to be able "to disassociate failures resulting from their attempts to succeed from being failures themselves." His approach has been to emphasize that "innovation requires that you go beyond the known into the unknown, where there might be trap doors and blind alleys. You've got to map the unknown. You map it by making mistakes."

One way engineering professors help students learn to map the unknown is by giving them examinations full of problems that test the limits of their knowledge. An exam in which even one student gets a perfect score may be considered poorly designed, for that student may not have learned anything from taking it. Indeed, students who do score perfectly may come to the false conclusion that they have been studying more than was necessary—an impression of which they are often disabused on the next exam. But students whose errors are pointed out—and emphatically so by the deduction of points—not only learn that they made those errors, which they are not likely to repeat, but also that they should study harder for the next exam.

Success and failure have a paradoxical relationship. Too close a reliance on models of success tends to lead to ultimate failure. But careful thinking about failures, both past examples and future possibilities, is the surest way to produce a successful design. That is especially the case when engineers and others are engaged in the design of truly innovative structures and systems. Clearly, when something is being tried for the first time, there is by definition no successful example on which to model it. However, there is always the valuable legacy of flawed designs and outright failures of analogous designs upon which the conscientious designer should be willing and able to draw.

A HISTORIAN EXPLAINS WHY SOMEONE ELSE'S WRITING WOUND UP IN HER BOOK

Doris Kearns Goodwin

I am a historian, with the exception of being a wife and mother, it is who I am. And there is nothing I take more seriously.

In recent days, questions have been raised about how historians go about crediting their sources, and I have been caught up in the swirl. Ironically, the more intensive and far-reaching a historian's research, the greater the difficulty of citation. As the mountain of material grows, so does the possibility of error.

Fourteen years ago, not long after the publication of my book *The Fitzgeralds and the Kennedys*, I received a communication from author Lynne McTaggart pointing out that material from her book on Kathleen Kennedy had not been properly attributed. I realized that she was right. Though my footnotes repeatedly cited Ms. McTaggart's work, I failed to provide quotation marks for phrases that I had taken verbatim, having assumed that these phrases, drawn from my notes, were my words, not hers. I made the corrections she requested, and the matter was completely laid to rest—until last week, when the *Weekly Standard* published an article reviving the issue. The larger question for those of us who write history is to understand how citation mistakes can happen.

The research and writing for this 900-page book, with its 3,500 footnotes, took place over 10 years. At that time, I wrote my books and took my notes in longhand, believing I could not think well on a keyboard. Most of my sources were drawn from a multitude of primary materials: manuscript collections, private letters, diaries, oral histories, newspapers, periodicals, personal interviews. After three years of research, I discovered more than 150 cartons of materials that had been previously stored in the attic of Joe Kennedy's Hyannis Port house. These materials were a treasure trove for a historian— old report cards, thousands of family letters, movie stubs and diaries, which allowed me to cross the boundaries of time and space. It took me two additional years to read, categorize, and take notes on these documents.

During this same period, I took handwritten notes on perhaps 300 books. Passages I wanted to quote directly were noted along with general notes on the ideas and story lines of each book. Notes on all these sources were then arranged chronologically and kept in dozens of folders in 25 banker's boxes. Immersed in a flood of papers, I began to write the book. After each section and each chapter was completed, I returned the notes to the boxes along with notations for future footnoting. When the manuscript was finished, I went back to all these sources to check the accuracy of attributions. As a final protection, I revisited the 300 books themselves. Somehow in this process, a few of the books were not fully rechecked. I relied instead on my notes, which combined direct quotes and paraphrased sentences. If I had had the books in front of me, rather than my notes, I would have caught mistakes in the first place and placed any borrowed phrases in direct quotes.

What made this incident particularly hard for me was the fact that I take great pride in the depth of my research and the extensiveness of my citations. The writing of history is a rich process of building on the work of the past with the hope that others will build on what you have done. Through footnotes you point the way to future historians.

The only protection as a historian is to institute a process of research and writing that minimizes the possibility of error. And that I have tried to do, aided by modern technology, which enables me, having long since moved beyond longhand, to use a computer for both organizing and taking notes. I now rely on a scanner, which reproduces the passages I want to cite, and then I keep my own comments on those books in a separate file so that I will never confuse the two again. But the real miracle occurred when my college-age son taught me how to use the mysterious footnote key on the computer, which makes it possible to insert the citations directly into the text while the sources are still in front of me, instead of shuffling through hundreds of folders four or five years down the line, trying desperately to remember from where I derived a particular statistic or quote. Still, there is no guarantee against error. Should one occur, all I can do, as I did 14 years ago, is to correct it as soon as I possibly can, for my own sake and the sake of history. In the end, I am still the same fallible person I was before I made the transition to the computer, and the process of building a lengthy work of history remains a complicated but honorable task.

Source: Doris Kearns Goodwin, "How I Caused That Story," *Time*, February 4, 2002. Copyright TIME Inc. Reprinted by permission. TIME is a registered trademark of Time Inc. All rights reserved.

THE 600 FACES OF EVE

Patricia J. Williams

How I became a 100-year-old, motorcycle riding, white evangelical hip-hop member of a steel drum band begins with my consideration of why today's generation of young people are not a visible political presence when the entire civil rights movement is going quietly to its grave.

I have spent a lot of time hoping, waiting for a new wave of the civil rights movement to take hold, a movement embodying the civic energy of the 1960s as reinvigorated by the youth of today. I wonder why there is such apathy.

My students are, on the whole, less anxious about this than I am. They tell me that activism hasn't disappeared—it's just all happening in cyberspace. The Internet is their commons. I am glad to hear it, and when I think about MoveOn.org, it seems reasonable that there might be real movement by real bodies. At the same time, as anyone in academia knows, those of college age and below are online all the time. Even in class, the laptops are burning up—they're taking notes ostensibly, checking cites and sources not sites and solitaire, the busy little bees. Yet however genuinely engaged in their classes they may be, it is also true that often we teachers can't see their lips moving anymore, just the tips of their noses over the raised tops of their laptop screens. They speak, they interact, but always a part of their heads, a slab of their faces, an ear or an eye, is sucked into those powerful machines. You can see them receding—heads, necks, arms, torsos disappearing into the fog. Sometimes I just want to pull them out by their feet and manacle them to their chairs.

Recently, I joined Facebook and MySpace, two of the more popular networking sites, to see if I could incorporate some of it into a lecture, nudge them back to what I think of as the real world, from the inside out. For all the much-discussed—and valid—questions of sexual predation, what was most striking to me about the social climate of these sites are the invisible hands that seem to be guiding what goes on. It's often said of MySpace, for example, that the participants "choose" to foreground their interests so as to be connected to other like-minded souls. But you don't just choose by wandering and grazing—you proceed by filling out themed questionnaires and following links and pursuing guided suggestions. If you choose a Paris Hilton–themed path, you might be asked how often you go shopping. If you choose hip-hop, you're asked to "fess up to the acts of a true thug." The jokey, formulaic questions demand to know if you've ever smoked or used drugs or committed a crime, or what, by the way, your sexual orientation is. They ask how you see yourself dying and on what date, how many guns you own, how many orgasms you have in a day and how much money you make. Who would you be if you were a famous dictator? Do you like Hello Kitty? What would you name your own personal police force? The sites analyze and organize your personality as though rendering a horoscope, based not on the stars but on what your dream car would be.

It doesn't seem unreasonable to question Rupert Murdoch's ownership of MySpace more closely, given its structured invitations for people to sort themselves into cascading ranks of adolescent sexism and sexiness, foul gangsta language and multiple temptations to transgression. If I were a data miner, I'd be in there every day, grazing and hunting and gathering, sorting and profiling and pre-empting for a rainy day.

To say that these sites are not private understates the problem. "Going public" implies a group so massive that some anonymity is guaranteed; you can lose yourself in a crowd in real space. But cyberspace is like entering an obsessively unforgiving world with no capacity to forget. Even if the human administrators mean you well, the machines are inherently promiscuous and literal-minded. If you are a white Episcopalian from the suburbs of Connecticut who wears polo shirts and plaid boating shorts, you may find yourself cruelly redirected along life's cyber-path if you disguise yourself as a Confederate flag-loving Wiccan headed for Chocolate City in your Escalade with the gun rack and spinning hubcaps. (Try it out! You could be both these people and more!)

This is lots of fun, assuming there are no consequences. If there are overseers with stern standards and no sense of humor—well then, that could make a difference. Small droppings of letters and slurrings of words could have life-changing consequences—my spell-checker recently changed "Jerry Falwell" to "Jerry Falafel." At present, such errors are as frequent as dust bunnies—particularly for those with common last names—yet determine whether you get to vote, whether your welfare check is cut off or your insurance processed, or whether you spend years in the stalls of Guantánamo Bay. We need some process—due process—enabling us to distinguish ourselves in this Kafkaesque landscape.

In the meantime, a generation raised on the Net is becoming adept at proliferating many different identities for one life. The medium invites all of us to generate multiple brands of ourselves. It makes me wonder, this evolution into a high-tech future: In a world given over to purchase, cover and disguise, might the pursuit of ideas not be nearly as important as a talent for manipulating appearances according to the urgencies of escape or the conveniences of entering new markets?

A friend whose grandfather fled pogroms and fascism spoke of what it took to live in those times: "They had to speak six languages," he said. My students will survive by having 600 e-identities. They will have more colors than a chameleon, changing race and gender, upgrading religion, downsizing dreams, outsourcing home as a page. They live in a land so unimaginable to me as to earn the label "foreign"—even as I tootle around it on my newly imagined motorbike. "You have 733 new friends," blinks the screen of my computer, gleefully, gaily, as though I really, really do have 733 friends. The thrumming steel drums of my newfound identity notwithstanding, I feel lonely. This is not about substantive engagement, but numbers. It's ruled by assortive principles and the misplaced faith that an actuarial table is any kind of community—beloved, political or "other" wise.

THIS PEN FOR HIRE: GRINDING OUT PAPERS FOR COLLEGE STUDENTS

Abigail Witherspoon

I am an academic call girl. I write college kids' papers for a living. Term papers, book reports, senior theses, take-home exams. My "specialties": art history and sociology, international relations and comparative literature, English, psychology, "communications," Western philosophy (ancient and contemporary), structural anthropology, film history, evolutionary biology, waste management and disposal, media studies, and pre-Confederation Canadian history. I throw around allusions to Caspar Weinberger and Alger Hiss, Sacco and Vanzetti, Haldeman and Ehrlichman, Joel Steinberg and Baby M. The teaching assistants eat it up. I can do simple English or advanced jargon. Like other types of prostitutes, I am, professionally, very accommodating.

I used to tell myself I'd do this work only for a month or two, until I found something else. But the official unemployment rate in this large Canadian city where I live is almost 10 percent, and even if it were easy to find a job, I'm American, and therefore legally prohibited from receiving a paycheck. So each day I walk up the stairs of a rotting old industrial building to an office with a sign on the window: TAILORMADE ESSAYS, WRITING AND RESEARCH. The owner, whom I'll call Matthew, claims that he started the business for ghostwriters, speech-writers, and closet biographers, and only gradually moved into academic work as a sideline. But even Grace, the oldest surviving writer on Tailormade's staff, can't remember anybody ever writing much other than homework for students at one university or another.

This is a good city for Tailormade. Next door is the city's university and its tens of thousands of students, a school that was once somewhat better when not all of its computer-registered classes numbered in the hundreds. Orders come in from Vancouver, Calgary, Winnipeg. There are plenty of essay services in the States, of course; they advertise in campus newspapers and the back pages of music magazines. Some of the big ones have toll-free phone numbers. They're sprinkled all over: California, Florida, New Jersey. But we still get American business too. Orders come in here from Michigan, Vermont, Pennsylvania; from Illinois, Wisconsin, upstate New York, sometimes California; from Harvard, Cornell, and Brown. They come in from teachers' colleges, from people calling themselves "gifted students" (usually teenagers at boarding schools), and, once in a while, from the snazzy places some of our customers apparently vacation with their divorced dads, like Paris.

Matthew runs the business with his wife, Sylvia. Or maybe she is his ex-wife, nobody's exactly sure. When you call Tailormade—it's now in the phone book—you hear Sylvia say that Tailormade is Canada's foremost essay service; that our very qualified writers handle most academic subjects; and that we are fast, efficient, and completely confidential. Sylvia speaks loudly and slowly and clearly, especially to Asian customers. She is convinced that everyone who phones the office will be Asian, just as she's convinced that all Asians drive white Mercedes or black BMWs with cellular phones in them. From my personal experience, I find the Asian customers at least more likely to have done the assigned reading.

Matthew and Sylvia are oddly complementary. Matthew, gentle and fumbly, calls out mechanically, "Thank you, sir, ma'am, come again" after each departing back slinking down the hall. Sylvia asks the Chinese customers loudly, "SIMPLE ENG-LISH?" She tells the uncertain, "Well, don't show up here till you know what you want," and demands of the dissatisfied, "Whaddya mean you didn't like it? You ordered it, din'cha?"

This afternoon, October 10, I'm here to hand in a paper and fight it out with the other writers for more assignments. Some of us are legal, some aren't. Some have mortgages and cars, some don't. All of us are hungry. The office is jammed, since it's almost time for midterms. Tailormade does a brisk business from October to May, except for January. The chairs are full of customers studiously filling out order forms. You can always tell who is a student and who is a writer. The students are dressed elegantly and with precision; the writers wear ripped concert T-shirts or stained denim jackets with white undershirts peeking out. The students wear mousse and hair gel and nail polish and Tony Lama western boots and Tourneau watches and just the right amount of makeup. They smell of Escape, Polo for men, and gum. The writers smell of sweat, house pets, and crushed cigarettes. Four of the other writers are lolling in their chairs and fidgeting; work usually isn't assigned until all the order forms have been filled out, unless somebody requests a topic difficult to fill. Then Matthew will call out like an auctioneer: "Root Causes of the Ukrainian Famine? Second year? Anyone? Grace?" or "J. S. Mill's Brand of Humane Utilitarianism? Third year? Henry, that for you?" as some customer hovers in front of the desk, eyes straight ahead. Someone else in the room might idly remark that he or she took that course back in freshman year and it was a "gut" or a "real bird."

I suspect that each of us in the Tailormade stable of hacks sorts out the customers differently: into liberal-arts students and business students; into those that at least do the reading and those that don't bother; into those that have trouble writing academic English and those that just don't care about school; into those that do their assignments in other subjects and those that farm every last one of them out to us; into the struggling and inept versus the rich, lazy, and stupid. But for Matthew and Sylvia, the clientele are divisible, even before cash versus credit card, or paid-up versus owing, into Asian customers and non-Asian ones. There's been an influx of wealthy immigrants from Hong Kong in recent years, fleeing annexation. Matthew and Sylvia seem to resent their presence and, particularly, their money. Yet they know that it's precisely this pool of customers—who have limited written English language skills but possess education, sophistication, ambition, cash, and parents leaning hard on them for good grades—that keeps the business going.

When I hand in my twelve pages on "The Role of Market Factors in the Development of the Eighteenth-Century Fur Trade," Matthew tells me, "This lady's been patiently waiting without complaining." I must be very late. Turning to the client, he picks up one of my sheets and waves it. "At least it's a nice bib," he points out to her. "Look at that." Although I wasn't provided with any books for this essay, I managed to supply an extensive bibliography. I can't remember what I put on it.

I'm still waiting for an assignment. In fact, all the writers are still waiting. We often wait at the bar around the corner; Tailormade has its own table there, permanently reserved. But we all have to get ourselves to the office eventually to pick up assignments. Grace, the oldest writer and by now, probably, the best, sits sorrowfully by the window, her long gray hair falling into her lap and her head jammed into her turtleneck, on her thin face a look of permanent tragedy. Grace gets up at three in the morning to work; she never forgets a name, a fact, or an assignment; she has a deep, strange love for Japanese history and in ten years here has probably hatched enough pages and research for several doctoral dissertations in that field. Elliott, another writer, reclines near the door, his little dog asleep under his chair. He uses the dog as an icebreaker with the clients, especially young women. He is six and a half feet tall and from somewhere far up in the lunar landscape of northern Ontario. He has a huge head of blond hair down to his eyes and pants as tight as a rock star's. Elliott is the business writer. He specializes in finance, investment, management, and economics. He lives out of a suitcase; he and the little dog, perhaps practicing fiscal restraint, seem to stay with one of a series of girlfriends. When the relationship comes to an end, Elliott and the little dog wind up back in the office, where they sleep in the fax room and Elliott cranks out essays on his laptop. Henry and Russell, two other writers, twist around, changing position, the way travelers do when they're trying to nap on airport lounge chairs. They both look a little like El Greco saints, although perhaps it just seems that way to me because lately I've been doing a lot of art history papers. They both have long skinny legs, long thin white nervous twiddling hands, long thin faces with two weeks' worth of unintentional beard. Henry points out how good Russell looks, and we all agree. Russell is forty. He has a new girlfriend half his age who has, he says, provided a spiritual reawakening. Before he met her, Russell drank so much and held it so badly that he had the distinction of being the only staff member to be banned from the bar around the corner for life. Henry, by contrast, looks terrible. He's always sick, emaciated, coughing, but he invariably manages to meet his deadlines, to make his page quotas, and to show up on time.

We used to have another writer on staff, older even than Russell or Grace, who smoked a pipe, nodded a lot, and never said anything. He was a professor who'd been fired from some school, we were never really sure where. Eventually, he went AWOL and started an essay-writing service of his own. He's now Tailormade's main competition. The only other competitors, apparently, worked out of a hot-dog stand parked next to a campus bookstore. Nobody knows whether they're open anymore.

In general, there is a furtiveness about the way we writers talk to one another, the way we socialize. In the office, we're a little like people who know each other from A.A. meetings or rough trade bars encountering each other on a Monday morning at the photocopy machine. It's not because we're competing for work. It's not even because some of us are illegal and everyone else knows it. It is, if anything, collective embarrassment. We know a lot more than Matthew and Sylvia do. They sit dumbly as we bullshit with the clients about their subjects and assignments ("Ah, introductory psychology! The evolution of psychotherapy is a fascinating topic . . . ever read a guy called Russell Jacoby?") in order to impress them and get them to ask for us. This must be the equivalent of the harlots' competitive bordello promenade. But we work for Matthew and Sylvia. They have the sense to pit us against each other, and it works. We can correct their pronunciation of "Goethe" and they don't care. They know it makes no difference. I suspect they have never been farther away than Niagara Falls; neither of them may have even finished high school. It doesn't matter. The laugh's on us, of course: they own the business.

OCTOBER 12, 1994. A tall gangly kid comes in for a twenty-page senior history essay about the ancient local jail. It involves research among primary sources in the provincial archives, and I spend a week there, going page by page through the faded brown script of the warden's prison logbooks of the 1830s. Agitators are being executed for "high treason" or "banished from the realm," which, I assume, means being deported. Once in a while there's a seductive joy to a project. You forget that you've undertaken it for money, that it isn't yours.

Most of the time, though, all I think about is the number of pages done, the number to go. Tailormade charges twenty dollars Canadian a page for first- and second-year course assignments, twenty-two a page for third- and fourth-year assignments, twenty-four for "technical, scientific, and advanced" topics. "Technical, scientific, and advanced" can mean nuclear physics, as it does in September when there is no business. Or it can mean anything Matthew and Sylvia want it to, as it does in March. Most major spring-term essays are due when final exams begin, in April, and so in March kids are practically lined up in the office taking numbers and spilling out into the hall. The writers get half, in cash: ten and eleven bucks a page; twelve for the technical, scientific, and advanced.

There's one other charge: if the client doesn't bring in her or his own books, except in September and January, she or he is "dinged," charged an extra two dollars a page for research. When the writers get an assignment, we ask if there are books. If there are, it saves us time, but we have to lug them home, and often they're the wrong books. If there are no books, we have to go to the libraries and research the paper ourselves. "Client wants twelve pages on clinical social work intervention," Matthew and Sylvia might tell us. "She has a reading list but no books. I think we can ding her." "He wants a book report on something called Gravity's Rainbow? Doesn't have the book, though. I'm gonna ding him."

OCTOBER 13. I am assigned a paper on the French philosopher Michel Foucault. The client has been dinged; I have to find some books. Foucault's *Discipline and Punish* and *Madness and Civilization* are hot properties in the pubic library system. They are not to be found anywhere. *Perhaps* is a hot property, too; he's all over everyone's syllabus.

I warn the client about this in the office. "If you don't find anything by the guy, call me," he says. He gives me his home phone number. "Only, please don't say you're from the essay service. Say you're . . . a classmate of mine." I promise to be discreet. Most of the clients get scared when you call them at home; most never give out their numbers. I don't blame them.

It was different, though, when I was a university student in the early 1980s. I wasn't aware of anyone who bought his or her homework anywhere, although it must have happened. It was about that time that Tailormade was putting up signs on the telephone poles outside the university's main classroom buildings. It advertised just outside the huge central library as well as outside the libraries of three or four smaller schools a few minutes' drive away. This burst of entrepreneurial confidence almost led to the service's undoing. In a spectacular cooperative sting operation among the security departments of the various schools, the office was raided. This event has become a sort of fearsome myth at Tailormade, discussed not unlike the way Syrians might occasionally mention the Israeli raid on Entebbe. Matthew and Sylvia were hauled off to court and a dozen or so clients were thrown out of their respective universities. Matthew and Sylvia, however, must have hired the right Lawyer: they were allowed to reopen, provided that they stayed away from campuses and that they stamped every page of every essay TAILORMADE ESSAY SERVICE: FOR RESEARCH PURPOSES ONLY. Now the clients take the stamped essays home, retype them, and print them out on high-end laser printers much better than ours. If the client is obnoxious, complains, or is considered a whiner, each typewritten page will be stamped in the middle. If the client is steady and has good credit, each page will be stamped in the margin so that the stamp can be whited out and the pages photocopied.

By the time Tailormade reopened, I had moved back to this country after some years at home in the States. I had no money and no prospects of a legal job. I came in, handed Matthew a résumé, spent a couple of weeks on probationary trial, and then began a serious career as a hack. "What are your specialties?" Matthew had asked me. I told him I'd majored in history and political science as an undergraduate. Over time, as my financial situation grew worse, my "specialties" grew to include everything except math, accounting, economics, and the hard sciences.

OCTOBER 23. Three weeks ago I was assigned an essay on the establishment and growth of political action committees among the Christian right. I am earnest about this one; I actually overprepare. I want to document, with carefully muted horror, the word of Paul Laxalt and direct mail, the arm-twisting of members of Congress on the school prayer issue. My contempt for the client was mixed with pity: he knew not how much he was missing. Only afterward do I realize that after doing an essay I take seriously, I still expect, as in college, to get something back with a mark on it, as a reward or at least as an acknowledgment. I hear nothing, of course. I feel oddly let down. I'm certain it got the client an A. Today, the same client stops in to order something else and helpfully points out what he thinks I could have done to improve the essay I'd written for him.

OCTOBER 25. This summer, a woman wanted me to write about how aboriginal peoples' systems of law and justice were better developed than those of conquering colonials. I took books with titles like *The Treaties of Canada with the Indians of Manitoba and the North-West Territories, 1880* to the beach. After finishing the client's reading material, I still had no idea what aboriginal peoples thought about law or anything else;

she had given me only books about the conquering colonials. So the paper went on, for twenty-odd pages, about the conquering colonials. Now she wants me to rewrite it. The time I will spend on this second version waters my pay down to about a dollar an hour.

NOVEMBER 8. I will not go into any of the university's libraries. I will not risk running into anyone I know, anyone who might think I'm one of those perpetual graduate students who never finished their dissertations and drift pathetically around university libraries like the undead, frightening the undergraduates. It would be as bad to be thought one of these lifelong grad students as to be suspected of being what I am. So I use the public libraries, usually the one closest to my apartment, on my street corner. It's a community library, with three wonderful librarians, three daily newspapers, and remarkably few books. If I haven't been given the books already, if the client has been dinged and I have to do research on my own, I come here. I have my favorite chair. The librarians assume I am a "mature" and "continuing" community college student, and make kind chitchat with me.

Sometimes, when I can't find any of the sources listed in the library's computer and don't have time to go to a real library, I use books barely appropriate for the essay: books for "young adults," which means twelve-year-olds, or books I have lying around my apartment—like Jane Jacobs's *The Death and Life of Great American Cities*, H. D. F. Kitto's *The Greeks*, Eduardo Galeano's *Open Veins of Latin America*, Roy Medvedev's book on Stalin or T. H. White's on John Kennedy, books by J. K. Galbraith, Lewis Mumford, Christopher Lasch, Erich Fromm. Books somewhere between the classic and the old chestnut; terrific books, yet with no relation to the topic at hand. But they're good for the odd quote and name-drop, and they can pad a bibliography. Sometimes I can't get away with this, though, and then I have no choice but to go back to an actual place of research, like the archives.

The archives are, in fact, a difficult place for me. They are full of oak tables, clicking laptops, whirring microfiche readers, and self-assured middle-aged men working with pretty young women whose hair is pinned up in nineteenth-century styles. Perhaps some of them are lovers, but certainly all of them are graduate students with their profs. I, by contrast, am a virtual student, a simulacrum.

NOVEMBER 16. I have also been pulling at least one or two all-nighters a week for three weeks now. They're very much like the all-nighters I did as an undergraduate. I eat licorice nibs for energy and drink molehill coffee for caffeine. You make molehill coffee by pouring an entire half cup of coffee grounds, the finer the better, in a number 4 paper filter, one filter per cup. At midnight the razzy voice of Tom Waits is temporarily replaced by the BBC news hour. It would be great to be able to speak just like the BBC newscaster, Somebody hyphen-Jones. If I sounded like that I'm sure I would be able to get credit, somehow, for writing about the birth of the Carolingian Renaissance, or the displacement of the samurai in Tokugawa times, or the inadequacies of the Treaty of Versailles.

I know by experience that if I start writing at midnight I can time my output: first page by the BBC's second news summary, second page by the financial news on the half hour, third page finished by the time they read the rugby scores. Except that the first page, the one with the thesis paragraph in it, is the hardest to write, and it clocks in at well over fifteen minutes.

At two-thirty I hit a wall. The molehill coffee still hasn't kicked in yet, or else it did and I didn't notice, and now it's worn off, or else I've just built up a fatal tolerance to the stuff, like a crack addict. I begin to fall asleep in my chair, even with my headphones on. I turn up the music and blast it through the headphones. This works for the time being. I plug along. I can't really remember what I said in my thesis paragraph, but I am not going to worry about it. The client wants fifteen pages, and when I find myself on the fourteenth I'll read the thing over and brace myself, if I have to, for a bow-out. Bow-outs, like legal fine print, allow you to dart gracefully out of the large ambitious thesis statement you've started the essay with: "The topic of bird evolution is an enormous one; I have been able to touch on just one or two interesting controversies within it." "Space does not permit a detailed discussion of all the internal contradictions within Sri Lanka's postcolonial history." And so on. Nine and a half pages down. Five and a half to go. I can still barely remember what I said in my thesis statement. I can barely remember what this paper is about. I want to put my head down for a minute on the keyboard, but God only knows what it would end up typing.

NOVEMBER 18. Things are picking up for Christmas vacation; everything, it seems, is due December 5 or December 15. The essay order form asks, "Subject & Level," "Topic," "No. of Pages," "Footnotes," "Bibliography," and then a couple of lines marked "Additional Information," by far the most common of which is "Simple English." As the year rolls on, we hacks will all, out of annoyance, laziness, or just boredom, start unsimplifying this simple English; by April it will approach the mega-watt vocabulary and tortured syntax of the Frankfurt School. But people hand these papers in and don't get caught, people who have difficulty speaking complete sentences in English; perhaps this is because classes and even tutorials are so big they never have to speak. But in December we're all still on pretty good behavior, simple instead of spiteful. I've just handed in an assignment in "Simple English," a paper titled "Mozart's Friendship with Joseph and Johann Michael Haydn and Its Impact on Mozart's Chamber Music." It reads, in part:

> Mozart was undeniably original. He was never derivative. That was part of his genius. So were the Haydn brothers. All of them were totally unique.

The little library on my corner didn't have much on Mozart or the Haydn brothers. As a result, one of the items in my bibliography is a child's book with a cardboard pop-up of a doughy-looking little Mozart, in a funky pigtail and knee breeches, standing proudly beside a harpsichord.

NOVEMBER 22. I'm assigned an overnight rush essay on the causes of the English Civil War. It may sound perverse, but I love rush essays. We get paid a dollar more a page (two for technical, Scientific, and advanced), and if it's lousy we can always say, "Well, you wanted it in a hurry." Although I majored in history, I never took any courses on the English Civil War; I figured, wrongly, that Shakespeare's histories would take care of that. Now I find myself reading the books I took out from the little corner library, not for quotes, or to form an opinion on the roots, germination, feeding, and watering of the war, but just to find out what the hell went on. I find out enough to write five pages. It takes me all night.

NOVEMBER 23. I am handing in something entitled "Sri Lanka: A Study in Ethnic Division and Caste Co-optation," which Sylvia assigned me, over the phone, a week ago. "The girl says to tell you that she's Sri Lankan." Last year I wrote a senior sociology thesis on "The Italian-Canadian Family: Bedrock of Tradition or Agent of Change?" With that one I heard, "The girl says to tell you that she's Italian." I wanted to ask Sylvia if the client knew I wasn't, but I was afraid she'd interpret that as meaning I didn't want the work and she'd give it to someone else.

DECEMBER 2. Occasionally there is an assignment the writers fight for. This week somebody—not me—gets to take home *Fanny Hill* and *Lady Chatterley's Lover*, and get paid for it. I guess some kids really, really hate to read.

DECEMBER 5. A bad assignment: unnecessarily obscure, pedantic, pointless. Certain courses seem to consist of teaching kids the use of jargon as though it were a substitute for writing or thinking well. Often there is an implied pressure to agree with the assigned book. And many are simply impossible to understand; I often take home a textbook or a sheaf of photocopies for an assignment and see, next to a phrase such as "responsible acceptance of the control dimension," long strings of tiny Chinese characters in ballpoint pen. No wonder the students find the assignments incomprehensible; they are incomprehensible to me.

DECEMBER 8. I hand in a paper on Machiavelli. "How'd it go?" asked the client, a boy in a leather bomber jacket reading John Grisham. I begin to go on about how great one of the books was, a revisionist biography called Machiavelli in Hell. I am hoping, with my scholarly enthusiasm, to make the client feel particularly stupid. "It's an amazing book," I tell him. "It makes a case for Machiavelli actually being kind of a liberal humanist instead of the cynical guy everybody always thinks he was—amazing." "That's good," the kid says. "I'm glad you're enjoying yourself on my tab. Did you answer the essay question the way you were supposed to?"

DECEMBER 16. Every so often clients come in with an opinion they want us to replicate. The freshman sociology and political science essays are already starting to rain in: a deluge of "Show why immigrants are a dead weight on the economy and take jobs away from us"; "Show why most social programs will become too expensive for an aging population"; "Show why gun control can be interpreted as an infringement on civil rights"; "Show the Pacific Rim's single-handed assault on North American economies," I ignore them. I write, depending on my mood, about the INS's unequal criteria for refugee status, or the movie *Roger and Me*, or the NRA's political clout. For instance, there is today's assignment: to describe Locke's influence, as an Enlightenment figure, on our own time. I think this is baloney. I talk about how the postwar military-industrial complex proves that God really did give the world, whatever Locke thought, to the covetous and contentious instead of to the industrious and the rational. No one's ever complained about finding my opinion in a paper instead of their own. Now I realize this isn't because I've persuaded anybody of anything. It's just laziness: there are some customers who actually retype their stamped essays without bothering to read them.

DECEMBER 27. During Christmas vacation, friends of mine invite me to a party. Some people will be there whom we know from college; they are in the process of becoming successful, even making it big. It will be important to project confidence, the illusion of fulfilling my abandoned early promise. "What do I say," I ask my friends, "when somebody asks me what I do for a living?"

"Tell them you're a writer."

My friend Lisa sticks by me loyally all evening. When people ask me, "What is it you do?" Lisa answers for me quickly: "She's a writer."

"Oh, what is it you write?"

"Essays," I say, spitefully, drunkenly. Lisa thinks fast.

"Articles," she says. "She writes articles, on Sri Lanka, and Machiavelli, and the English Civil War."

"Isn't that interesting," they say, leaving us for the guacamole.

JANUARY 10, 1995. School has been back in session for a week now. The only work that is in are essays from the education students. I hate these assignments. I have trouble manipulating the self-encapsulated second language in which teaching students seem compelled to write. But it's after Christmas, and I'm broke. Education assignments all involve writing up our customers' encounters in their "practicum." Teaching students work several times a week as assistant teachers in grade school classrooms; instead of getting paid for this work, they pay tuition for it. Unfortunately, these expensive practice sessions don't seem to go well. My first such assignment was to write "reflections" on a "lesson plan" for a seventh-grade English. class. The teaching student had given me some notes, and I had to translate these into the pedagogical jargon used in her textbooks. The idea seems to be that you have to say, as obscurely as possible, what you did with your seventh-grade kids and what you think about what you did:

> Preliminary Lesson Formulations: My objectives were to integrate lesson content with methodology to expand students' receptiveness and responsiveness to the material and to one another by teaching them how to disagree with one another in a constructive way. The class will draw up a T-chart covering "Disagreeing in an Agreeable Way," roughly in the manner of Bennett et al. Check for understanding. When the students discuss this, they are encouraged to listen to one another's language carefully and "correct" it if the wording is unhelpful, negative, or destructive. I shared my objectives with the class by asking them to read a fable and then divide into pairs and decide together what the moral was. Clearly, this is the "Think-Pair-Share" technique, as detailed in Bennett et al. The three strategies in use, then, are: (1) pair and sharing; (2) group discussion of the fable with mind-mapping; (3) group discussion of ways of disagreement. The teacher, modeling, divides the board in two with a line.

"Pair and share" seemed to mean "find a partner." I had no idea what "mind-mapping" or a "T-chart" was supposed to be. And come to think of it, after reading the fable, I had no idea what the moral was.

JANUARY 18. Somebody is applying to the graduate program in family therapy at some university somewhere and wants us to write the application. "She's my friend," said the young woman sitting across from Matthew at the desk. "She wants to start her own private practice as a therapist, right? So she can buy a house, right? And if you're a psychiatrist you have to go all the way through med school, right? So she's given me some notes for you about her here—she only needs one credit for her B.A. in psychology, and she volunteered at a shelter one summer. She wants you to tell them all that. Maybe make up some other things."

"See," Matthew tells me after she leaves. "If you ever go to one of those therapists, that's something you should think about."

JANUARY 20. When I first started this work, friends of mine would try to comfort me by telling me it would teach me to write better. Actually, academic prostitution, just like any other kind, seems to bring with it diseases, afflictions, vices, and bad habits. There is, for instance, the art of pretending you've read a book you haven't. It's just like every speed-reading course ever offered by the Learning Annex: read the introduction, where the writer outlines what he's going to say, and the conclusion, where he repeats what he's said.

In his book *The Technological Society,* Jacques Ellul begins by defining the technical simply as the search for efficiency. He claims, however, that technique itself is subdivided into three categories: the social, the organizational, and the economic.

This is all on the book's first four pages. Sometimes—often—I find myself eating up as much space as possible. There are several ways to do this. One is to reproduce lengthy, paragraph-long quotes in full; another is to ramble on about your own apparently passionate opinion on something. Or you start talking about the United States and what a handbasket it's going to hell in. This is equally useful, for different reasons, on either side of the border. You can ask rhetorical questions to obsessive excess. ("Can Ellul present the technical in such a reductionist way? Can he really define technique in such a way? And is it really valid to distinguish between the social and the organizational?" etc.) And there's always the art of name-dropping as a way to fill pages and convince the teaching assistant that your client has read something, even if it wasn't what was on the syllabus.

Certainly, as writers from Eduardo Galeano to Andre Gunder Frank to Noam Chomsky to Philip Agee to Allan Frankovich to Ernesto Laclau document, the CIA has long propped up the United Fruit Company.

At least you can make the client feel stupid. It's the third week of January, my apartment is cold, and I am bitter.

FEBRUARY 8. I'm learning, as the environmentalists tell us, to reuse and recycle. It's easier when I adapt a paper, with minor changes, on the same topic for different classes, or when I use the same paper for the same class again the following year. I've never worried much about a recycled essay being recognized: the pay for teaching assistants is low enough, and the burnout rate high enough, that the odds are substantially against the same person reading and grading papers for the same course two years in a row. Some topics just seem to beg for recycling: freshmen are forever being asked to mull over the roles of determinism, hubris, and moral responsibility in the Oedipus cycle; sociology and philosophy majors, the ethics of abortion. There are essays on shantytowns in developing countries, export-oriented economies in developing countries, structural adjustment in developing countries, and one only has to make the obvious case that the three are interrelated to be able to extend the possibilities for parts of essays in any of those three categories to resurface magically within another. Other essays can be recycled with just a little tinkering to surmount minor differences in topic or in emphasis: for instance, "Italian Fascists in North America," to which "The Italian-Canadian Family" lends itself nicely; "Taboo-Breaking in Racine and Ford," which re-emerges, after minor cosmetic surgery, as "Master-Slave Relationships in Ford and Racine: What They Tell Us about Lust, Fate, and Obligation." And so on.

FEBRUARY 15. I'm sitting on the floor with a pile of old magazines, cutting out pictures of Oreo cookies and Wendy's burgers. This is Andy's essay. It's not an essay, actually, it's a food bingo chart. I have to find a large sheet of cardboard, divide it into squares, and glue on pictures of what is recognizably food. Andy is another education student: he wants to teach junior kindergarten, and his assignment is, apparently, to teach the little tots where food comes from, or what it is, or that advertising is a vital component of each of the four basic food groups, or something. I come into Tailormade with food bingo under my arm. I've gotten some strange looks on the subway. It nets me twenty-five bucks.

MARCH 7. I was supposed to turn in an essay today, one I don't have. I fell asleep at the keyboard last night and accidentally slept through the whole night, headphones and all.

MARCH 16. There's a regular customer whose course load would be appropriate for the resume of a U.N. secretary general. She's taking several courses on developing economies, including one referred to by other clients in the same class as "Third World Women." And one on the history of black Americans from Reconstruction to the present. I wrote her a twenty-five-page history of the early years of the civil-rights movement. She was sitting in the office when I handed it in. "Interesting course, isn't it?" she asked. She requested me again. I wrote her a paper on Costa Rica, one on dowry murders in India, one on the black leader W. E. B. Du Bois. "It's a great course, isn't it?" she asked me when she got the paper on dowry murders. "He seems like a fascinating guy," she said the day she collected W. E. B. Du Bois. "Somebody told me he wound up in Ghana." Today I take a shortcut across the university campus on my way to the essay service and see her with a group of other students. I make a direct beeline for her and I smile. I watch her blanch, look around, try to decide whether to pretend not to know me, decide that maybe that isn't a good idea. She gives me a stricken look and a big toothy grin.

MARCH 26. One day I'm given five pages on the Treaty of Versailles. Last year at the same time, I was assigned a paper on the same topic. A memorable paper. Two days after I turned it in, there was a camera crew outside. It turned out to be the local cable station for kids, doing an "expose" on cheating. We taped it when it came on. It featured kids sitting in shadow, faces obscured, 60 Minutes style.

"There she is, the little rat," Sylvia glowered at the time. The pretty young fake client handed my paper to some professor sitting behind a desk and asked, "What do you think about this? Is it better or worse than what you would normally get? Would you assume that it was a real paper or one that had been bought?"

"Well . . . it's a credible paper," said the professor. "I mean, one wouldn't think it was . . . synthetic unless one had reason to."

"What kind of grade would you give it?"

"Oh, I'd give it . . . a B minus."

"Please." I was really offended. Elliott comforted me. "Well, he has to say that. Now that he knows it's ours, he can't admit it's an A paper even if he wants to."

We all sat tight and waited for every professor within fifty miles to call us, threatening death. But professors don't watch cable shows for teenagers; neither do ambitious young teaching assistants. Instead, the show turned out to be a free advertising bonanza. Soon the phone rang off the hook with kids calling up and asking, "You mean, like, you can write my term paper for me if I pay you?"

APRIL 16. Today, working on a paper, I was reminded that there are good professors. They're the ones who either convince the kids the course content is inherently interesting and get them to work hard on the assignments or who figure out ways to make the assignments, at least, creative events to enjoy. But students with shaky language skills falter at surprises, even good ones; lazy students farm the assignments out no matter what they are. Such assignments are oddly comforting for me: I can almost pretend the two of us are talking over the clients' heads. When I'm alone in my room, in front of the computer and between the headphones, it's hard not to want to write something good for myself and maybe even for the imaginary absentee professor or appreciative T.A., something that will last. But when I'm standing in the crowded Tailormade office, next to someone elegant and young and in eight hundred bucks' worth of calfskin leather, someone who not only has never heard of John Stuart Mill and never read *Othello* but doesn't even know he hasn't, doesn't even mind that he hasn't, and doesn't even care that he hasn't, the urge to make something that will last somehow vanishes.

APRIL 28. The semester is almost at an end. Exams have started; the essays have all been handed in. Elliott and Russell begin their summer jobs as bike couriers. Henry, like me, is illegal; but he confides to me that he's had enough. "You can only do so much of this," he says. I know, I tell him. I know.

EXCERPT FROM *POSSIBLE LIVES: THE PROMISE OF PUBLIC EDUCATION IN AMERICA*

Mike Rose

Our journey begins in Los Angeles and the surrounding LA Basin. The movement of the chapter forecasts the movement of the book, traveling through region and community, finding good work in a range of places, arising out of specific histories and cultural conditions, abundant and varied. The LA chapter presents a number of classrooms in relatively quick succession, for I want at the outset to render the complexity of public education in urban America, the overwhelming needs of these schools condemned and abandoned by so many, yet the many kinds of teaching and learning achieved within them. Subsequent chapters proceed at a different pace, but the scheme is the same: a series of portraits of classrooms, each good on its own terms, yet part of a larger social fabric.

I also want to introduce during our time in Los Angeles some of the themes that will re-emerge as we continue the journey: the relation of classroom to community and learning to identity; the nature of a teacher's knowledge and the social and moral dimensions of that knowledge; the role of the teacher as culture broker, boundary mediator; the intricate mix of courage, hope, and thoughtfulness among our nation's youth and the threats to and misrepresentations of those riches; the grounding of the public school in local economy, politics, and social structure; the joy of intellectual work and the role of public institutions in fostering it. We will encounter as well the educational issues that were much in the news as I traveled through the LA Basin and across the country—school restructuring, standards and testing, multiculturalism, and the like—for they have become part of the sociopolitical terrain of schooling. Many treatments of them, unfortunately, tend toward the polemical or the sensational. They will emerge here in the more nuanced contexts of classrooms and the teacher-student encounter.

From Los Angeles I travel south to Calexico, California, a small city on the Mexican border that reveals some of the educational possibilities of bicultural life in the United States and presents, as well, an occasion to reflect on teacher education and development.

The third stop in the journey, a long arc cross country from the base of California to the Chesapeake Bay, takes us along North Avenue in inner-city Baltimore, where science, reading, writing, and the African-American experience intersect in a first-grade classroom. Then a six-hundred-mile angle west and a little north to Chicago, the industrial Midwest. We'll make our way through a number of schools, observing, as we will throughout the journey, a range of teaching styles and classroom events, from an advanced placement class analyzing *As I Lay Dying* to a group of sixth-graders putting their day in order. All this takes place in the midst of chaotic school politics and a movement to reform the way schools are structured and governed. It is this reform impulse that takes me back across the Northeast to New York City, to interview nine first-year principals trying to create a new kind of public high school in the largest school system in the nation. There is much said about school reform these days, but we hear infrequently from the people struggling to make it work. We will get close to the day-to-day human reality of social change.

From New York, I fly south and west into one of the early frontiers of the Republic, the Commonwealth of Kentucky. We'll hear from young teachers about to begin their careers, the dreams and uncertainties that consume them, and then travel into the Eastern Coal Field to watch two veteran teachers work through their own uncertainty as they forge an American studies curriculum around independent research projects and computer technology. Farther south to Mississippi, via commuter plane and Greyhound bus to Tupelo, Hattiesburg, Jackson, and a series of small towns in the Delta, where physics, algebra, and the humanities provide the opportunity to consider race, gender, sexual orientation, and school prayer. From Mississippi in sharp angle over the Great Plains, into Western Montana, to a one-room schoolhouse near the ghost town of Polaris in Beaverhead County. The country school, the foundation of public education in rural America. From Polaris we travel to an experimental preschool in Missoula that integrates children with and without disabilities, providing them, at a young age, the opportunity to live across the boundaries of ability. Straight south, then, over the Rockies, to Tucson for a summer enrichment program at the University of Arizona, one example of the many ways colleges and universities—and other public and private institutions—can contribute to the public schools. Here students from the Navajo and Hopi reservations study Greek tragedy, Native American literature, and contemporary novels, writing, in the process, their own defining stories and poetry and plays.

Together, the chapters form an anthology of educational possibility, a series of occasions to think about the future of our public schools. So, though the chapters offer a number of portraits of good teachers, there is no single profile of the Good Teacher; though they offer a number of accounts of skilled practice, I recommend no final list of good practices, no curricular framework or set of instructional guidelines. Such profiles and lists have value: they can suggest direction and generate discussion. But they also have a tendency to be stripped of context, to become rigid prescriptions, at times reduced to slogan or commodity. As we move from classroom to classroom, along the packed hallways of the big city school, along the highway beyond the city, I hope not so much for prescription as for an opening up of the way we think and talk about public schools. What we come to know, we know by settling in, staying a while, watching and listening. There may be no uniform road signs on this journey, but there are rest stops, places to take stock, to reflect on the slowly developing landscape of decency and achievement, to try to leave behind the reductive charts and the stultifying, dismissive language, and ponder the intricate mix of mind and mayhem that defines the classroom.

"INDIANS": TEXTUALISM, MORALITY, AND THE PROBLEM OF HISTORY

Jane Tompkins

When I was growing up in New York City, my parents used to take me to an event in Inwood Park at which Indians—real American Indians dressed in feathers and blankets—could be seen and touched by children like me. This event was always a disappointment. It was more fun to imagine that you *were* an Indian in one of the caves in Inwood Park than to shake the hand of an old man in a headdress who was not overwhelmed at the opportunity of meeting you. After staring at the Indians for a while, we would take a walk in the woods where the caves were, and once I asked my mother if the remains of a fire I had seen in one of them might have been left by the original inhabitants. After that, wandering up some stone steps cut into the side of the hill, I imagined I was a princess in a rude castle. My Indians, like my princesses, were creatures totally of the imagination, and I did not care to have any real exemplars interfering with what I already knew.

I already knew about Indians from having read about them in school. Over and over we were told the story of how Peter Minuit had bought Manhattan Island from the Indians for twenty-four dollars' worth of glass beads. And it was a story we didn't mind hearing because it gave us the rare pleasure of having someone to feel superior to, since the poor Indians had not known (as we eight-year-olds did) how valuable a piece of property Manhattan Island would become. Generally, much was made of the Indian presence in Manhattan; a poem in one of our readers began: "Where we walk to school today / Indian children used to play," and we were encouraged to write poetry on this topic ourselves. So I had a fairly rich relationship with Indians before I ever met the unprepossessing people in Inwood Park. I felt that I had a lot in common with them. They, too, liked animals (they were often named after animals); they, too, made mistakes— they liked the brightly colored trinkets of little value that the white men were always offering them; they were handsome, warlike, and brave and had led an exciting, romantic life in the forest long ago, a life such as I dreamed of leading myself. I felt lucky to be living in one of the places where they had definitely been. Never mind where they were or what they were doing now.

My story stands for the relationship most non-Indians have to the people who first populated this continent, a relationship characterized by narcissistic fantasies of freedom and adventure, of a life lived closer to nature and to spirit than the life we lead now. As Vine Deloria, Jr., has pointed out, the American Indian Movement in the early seventies couldn't get people to pay attention to what was happening to Indians who were alive in the present, so powerful was this country's infatuation with people who wore loincloths, lived in tepees, and roamed the plains and forest long ago.[1] The present essay, like these fantasies, doesn't have much to do with actual Indians, though its subject matter is the histories of European-Indian relations in seventeenth-century New England. In a sense, my encounter with Indians as an adult doing "research" replicates the childhood one, for while I started out to learn more about Indians, I ended up preoccupied with a problem of my own.

This essay enacts a particular instance of the challenge poststructuralism poses to the study of history. In simpler language, it concerns the difference that point of view makes when people are giving accounts of events, whether at first- or second-hand. The problem is that if all accounts of events are determined through and through by the observer's frame of reference, then one will never know, in any given case, what really happened.

I encountered this problem in concrete terms while preparing to teach a course in colonial American literature. I'd set out to learn what I could about the Puritans' relations with American Indians. All I wanted was a general idea of what happened between the English settlers and the natives in seventeenth-century New England; poststructuralism and its dilemmas were the furthest thing from my mind. I began, more or less automatically, with Perry Miller, who hardly mentions the Indians at all, then proceeded to the work of historians who had dealt exclusively with the European-Indian encounter. At first, it was a question of deciding which of these authors to believe, for it quickly became apparent that there was no unanimity on the subject. As I read on, however, I discovered that the problem was more complicated than deciding whose version of events was correct. Some of the conflicting accounts were not simply contradictory, they were completely incommensurable, in that their assumptions about what counted as a valid approach to the subject, and what the subject itself was, diverged in fundamental ways. Faced with an array of mutually irreconcilable points of view, points of view which determined what was being discussed as well as the terms of the discussion, I decided to turn to primary sources for clarification, only to discover that the primary sources reproduced the problem all over again. I found myself, in other words, in an epistemological quandary, not only unable to decide among conflicting versions of events but also unable to believe that any such decision could, in principle, be made. It was a moral quandary as well. Knowledge of what really happened when the Europeans and the Indians first met seemed particularly important, since the result of that encounter was virtual genocide. This was the kind of past "mistake" which, presumably, we studied history in order to avoid repeating. If studying history couldn't put us in touch with actual events and their causes, then what was to prevent such atrocities from happening again?

For a while, I remained at this impasse. But through analyzing the process by which I had reached it, I eventually arrived at an understanding which seemed to offer a way out. This essay records the concrete experience of meeting and solving the difficulty I have just described (as an abstract problem, I thought I had solved it long ago). My purpose is not to throw new light on antifoundationalist epistemology—the solution I reached is not a new one—but to dramatize and expose the troubles antifoundationalism gets you into when you meet it, so to speak, in the road.

My research began with Perry Miller. Early in the preface to *Errand into the Wilderness*, while explaining how he came to write his history of the New England mind, Miller writes a sentence that stopped me dead. He says that what fascinated him as a young man about his country's history was "the massive narrative of the movement of European culture into the vacant wilderness of America."[2] "Vacant"? Miller, writing in 1956, doesn't pause over the word "vacant," but to people who read his preface thirty years later, the word is shocking. In what circumstances could someone proposing to write a history of colonial New England *not* take account of the Indian presence there?

The rest of Miller's preface supplies an answer to this question, if one takes the trouble to piece together its details. Miller explains that as a young man, jealous of older compatriots who had had the luck to fight in World War I, he had gone to Africa in search of adventure. "The adventures that Africa afforded," he writes, "were tawdry enough, but it became the setting for a sudden epiphany" (p. vii). "It was given to me," he writes, "disconsolate on the edge of a jungle of central Africa, to have thrust upon me the mission of expounding what I took to be the innermost propulsion of the United States, while supervising, in that barbaric tropic, the unloading of drums of case oil flowing out of the inexhaustible wilderness of America" (p. viii). Miller's picture of himself on the banks of the Congo furnishes a key to the kind of history he will write and to his mental image of a vacant wilderness; it explains why it was just there, under precisely these conditions, that he should have had his epiphany.

The fuel drums stand, in Miller's mind, for the popular misconception of what this country is about. They are "tangible symbols of [America's] appalling power," a power that everyone but Miller takes for the ultimate reality (p. ix). To Miller, "the mind of man is the basic factor in human history," and he will plead, all unaccommodated as he is among the fuel drums, for the intellect—the intellect for which his fellow historians, with their chapters on "stoves or bathtubs, or tax laws," "the Wilmot Proviso" and "the chain store," "have so little respect" (pp. viii, ix). His preface seethes with a hatred of the merely physical and mechanical, and this hatred, which is really a form of moral outrage, explains not only the contempt with which he mentions the stoves and bathtubs but also the nature of his experience in Africa and its relationship to the "massive narrative" he will write.

Miller's experiences in Africa are "tawdry," his tropic is barbaric because the jungle he stands on the edge of means nothing to him, no more, indeed something less, than the case oil. It is the nothingness of Africa that precipitates his vision. It is the barbarity of the "dark continent," the obvious (but superficial) parallelism between the jungle at Matadi and America's "vacant wilderness" that releases in Miller the desire to define and vindicate his country's cultural identity. To the young Miller, colonial Africa and colonial America are—but for the history he will bring to light— mirror images of one another. And what he fails to see in the one landscape is the same thing he overlooks in the other: the human beings who people it. As Miller stood with his back to the jungle, thinking about the role of mind in human history, his failure to see that the land into which European culture had moved was not vacant but already occupied by a varied and numerous population, is of a piece with his failure, in his portrait of himself at Matadi, to notice *who* was carrying the fuel drums he was supervising the unloading of.

The point is crucial because it suggests that what is invisible to the historian in his own historical moment remains invisible when he turns his gaze to the past. It isn't that Miller didn't "see" the black men, in a literal sense, any more than it's the case that when he looked back he didn't "see" the Indians, in the sense of not realizing they were there. Rather, it's that neither the Indians nor the blacks *counted* for him, in a fundamental way. The way in which Indians can be seen but not counted is illustrated by an entry in Governor John Winthrop's journal, three hundred years before, when he recorded that there had been a great storm with high winds "yet through God's great mercy it did no hurt, but only killed one Indian with the fall of a tree."[3] The juxtaposition suggests that Miller shared with Winthrop a certain colonial point of view, a point of view from which Indians, though present, do not finally matter.

A book entitled *New England Frontier: Puritans and Indians, 1620–1675*, written by Alden Vaughan and published in 1965, promised to rectify Miller's omission. In the outpouring of work on the European-Indian encounter that began in the early sixties, this book is the first major landmark, and to a neophyte it seems definitive. Vaughan acknowledges the absence of Indian sources and emphasizes his use of materials which catch the Puritans "off guard."[4] His announced conclusion that "the New England Puritans followed a remarkably humane, considerate, and just policy in their dealings with the Indians" seems supported by the scope, documentation, and methodicalness of his project (*NEF*, p. vii). The author's fair-mindedness and equanimity seem everywhere apparent, so that when he asserts "the history of interracial relations from the arrival of the Pilgrims to the outbreak of King Philip's War is a credit to the integrity of both peoples," one is positively reassured (*NEF*, p. viii).

But these impressions do not survive an admission that comes late in the book, when, in the course of explaining why works like Helen Hunt Jackson's *Century of Dishonor* had spread misconceptions about Puritan treatment of the Indians, Vaughan finally lays his own cards on the table.

> The root of the misunderstanding [about Puritans and Indians] . . . lies[s] in a failure to recognize the nature of the two societies that met in seventeenth-century New England. One was unified, visionary, disciplined, and dynamic. The other was divided, self-satisfied, undisciplined, and static. It would be unreasonable to expect that such societies could live side by side indefinitely with no penetration of the more fragmented and passive by the more consolidated and active. What resulted, then, was not—as many have held—a clash of dissimilar ways of life, but rather the expansion of one into the areas in which the other was lacking. [*NEF*, p. 323]

From our present vantage point, these remarks seem culturally biased to an incredible degree, not to mention inaccurate: Was Puritan society unified? If so, how does one account for its internal dissensions and obsessive need to cast out deviants? Is "unity" necessarily a positive culture trait? From what standpoint can one say that American Indians were neither disciplined nor visionary, when both these characteristics loom so large in the ethnographies? Is it an accident that ways of describing cultural strength and weakness coincide with gender stereotypes—active/passive, and so on? Why is one culture said to "penetrate" the other? Why is the "other" described in terms of "lack"?

Vaughan's fundamental categories of apprehension and judgment will not withstand even the most cursory inspection. For what looked like evenhandedness when he was writing *New England Frontier* does not look that way anymore. In his introduction *to New Directions* in *American Intellectual History*, John Higham writes that by the end of the sixties

> the entire conceptual foundation on which [this sort of work] rested [had] crumbled away. . . . Simultaneously, in sociology, anthropology, and history, *two* working assumptions . . . came under withering attack: first, the assumption that societies tend to be integrated, and second, that a shared

culture maintains that integration. . . . By the late 1960s all claims issued in the name of an "American mind" . . . were subject to drastic skepticism.[5]

"Clearly," Higham continues, "the sociocultural upheaval of the sixties created the occasion" for this reaction.[6] Vaughan's book, it seemed, could only have been written before the events of the sixties had sensitized scholars to questions of race and ethnicity. It came as no surprise, therefore, that ten years later there appeared a study of European-Indian relations which reflected the new awareness of social issues the sixties had engendered. And it offered an entirely different picture of the European-Indian encounter.

Francis Jennings's *The Invasion of America* (1975) rips wide open the idea that the Puritans were humane and considerate in their dealings with the Indians. In Jennings's account, even more massively documented than Vaughan's, the early settlers lied to the Indians, stole from them, murdered them, scalped them, captured them, tortured them, raped them, sold them into slavery, confiscated their land, destroyed their crops, burned their homes, scattered their possessions, gave them alcohol, undermined their systems of belief, and infected them with diseases that wiped out 90 percent of their numbers within the first hundred years after contact.[7]

Jennings mounts an all-out attack on the essential decency of the Puritan leadership and their apologists in the twentieth century. The Pequot War, which previous historians had described as an attempt on the part of Massachusetts Bay to protect itself from the fiercest of the New England tribes, becomes, in Jennings's painstakingly researched account, a deliberate war of extermination, waged by whites against Indians. It starts with trumped-up charges, is carried on through a series of increasingly bloody reprisals, and ends in the massacre of scores of Indian men, women, and children, all so that Massachusetts Bay could gain political and economic control of the southern Connecticut Valley. When one reads this and then turns over the page and sees a reproduction of the Bay Colony seal, which depicts an Indian from whose mouth issue the words "Come over and help us," the effect is shattering.[8]

But even so powerful an argument as Jennings's did not remain unshaken by subsequent work. Reading on, I discovered that if the events of the sixties had revolutionized the study of European-Indian relations, the events of the seventies produced yet another transformation. The American Indian Movement, and in particular the founding of the Native American Rights Fund in 1971 to finance Indian litigation, and a court decision in 1975 which gave the tribes the right to seek redress for past injustices in federal court, created a climate within which historians began to focus on the Indians themselves. "Almost simultaneously," writes James Axtell, "frontier and colonial historians began to discover the necessity of considering the American natives as real determinants of history and the utility of ethnohistory as a way of ensuring parity of focus and impartiality of judgment.[9] In Miller, Indians had been simply beneath notice; in Vaughan, they belonged to an inferior culture; and in Jennings, they were the more or less innocent prey of power-hungry whites. But in the most original and provocative of the ethnohistories, Calvin Martin's *Keepers of the Game*, Indians became complicated, purposeful human beings, whose lives were spiritually motivated to a high degree.[10] Their relationship to the animals they hunted, to the natural environment, and to the whites with whom they traded became intelligible within a system of beliefs that formed the basis for an entirely new perspective on the European-Indian encounter.

Within the broader question of why European contact had such a devastating effect on the Indians, Martin's specific aim is to determine why Indians participated in the fur trade which ultimately led them to the brink of annihilation. The standard answer to this question had always been that once the Indian was introduced to European guns, copper kettles, woolen blankets, and the like, he literally couldn't keep his hands off them. In order to acquire these coveted items, he decimated the animal populations on which his survival depended. In short, the Indian's motivation in participating in the fur trade was assumed to be the same as the white European's—a desire to accumulate material goods. In direct opposition to this thesis, Martin argues that the reason why Indians ruthlessly exploited their own resources had nothing to do with supply and demand, but stemmed rather from a breakdown of the cosmic world-view that tied them to the game they killed in a spiritual relationship of parity and mutual obligation.

The hunt, according to Martin, was conceived not primarily as a physical activity but as a spiritual quest, in which the spirit of the hunter must overmaster the spirit of the game animal before the kill can take place. The animal, in effect, *allows* itself to be found and killed, once the hunter has mastered its spirit. The hunter prepared himself through rituals of fasting, sweating, or dreaming which revealed the identity of his prey and where he can find it. The physical act of killing is the least important element in the process. Once the animal is killed, eaten, and its parts used for clothing or implements, its remains must be disposed of in ritually prescribed fashion, or the game boss, the "keeper" of that species, will not permit more animals to be killed. The relationship between Indians and animals, then, is contractual; each side must hold up its end of the bargain, or no further transactions can occur.

What happened, according to Martin, was that as a result of diseases introduced into the animal population by Europeans, the game suddenly disappeared, began to act in inexplicable ways, or sickened and died in plain view, and communicated their diseases to the Indians. The Indians, consequently, believed that their compact with the animals had been broken and that the keepers of the game, the tutelary spirits of each animal species whom they had been so careful to propitiate, had betrayed them. And when missionization, wars with the Europeans, and displacement from their tribal lands had further weakened Indian society and its belief structure, the Indians, no longer restrained by religious sanctions, in effect, turned on the animals in a holy war of revenge.

Whether or not Martin's specific claim about the "holy war" was correct, his analysis made it clear to me that, given the Indians' understanding of economic, religious, and physical processes, an Indian account of what transpired when the European settlers arrived here would look nothing like our own. Their (potential, unwritten) history of the conflict could bear only a marginal resemblance to Eurocentric views. I began to think that the key to understanding European-Indian relations was to see them as an encounter between wholly disparate cultures, and that therefore either defending or attacking the colonists was beside the point since, given the cultural disparity between the two groups, conflict was inevitable and in large part a product of mutual misunderstanding.

But three years after Martin's book appeared, Shepard Krech III edited a collection of seven essays called *Indians, Animals, and the Fur Trade*, attacking Martin's entire project. Here the authors argued that we don't need an ideological or religious explanation for the fur trade. As Charles Hudson writes,

The Southeastern Indians slaughtered deer (and were prompted to enslave and kill each other) because of their position on the outer fringes of an expanding modern world-system. . . . In the modern world-system there is a core region which establishes *economic* relations with its colonial periphery. . . . If the Indians could not produce commodities, they were on the road to cultural extinction. . . . To maximize his chances for survival, an eighteenth-century Southeastern Indian had to . . . live in the interior, out of range of European cattle, forestry, and agriculture. . . . He had to produce a commodity which was valuable enough to earn him some protection from English slavers.[11]

Though we are talking here about Southeastern Indians, rather than the subarctic and Northeastern tribes Martin studied, what really accounts for these divergent explanations of why Indians slaughtered the game are the assumptions that underlie them. Martin believes that the Indians acted on the basis of perceptions made available to them by their own cosmology; that is, he explains their behavior as the Indians themselves would have explained it (insofar as he can), using a logic and a set of values that are not Eurocentric but derived from within Amerindian culture. Hudson, on the other hand, insists that the Indians' own beliefs are irrelevant to an explanation of how they acted, which can only be understood, as far as he is concerned, in the terms of a Western materialist economic and political analysis. Martin and Hudson, in short, don't agree on what counts as an explanation, and this disagreement sheds light on the preceding accounts as well. From this standpoint, we can see that Vaughan, who thought that the Puritans were superior to the Indians, and Jennings, who thought the reverse, are both, like Hudson, using Eurocentric criteria of description and evaluation. While all three critics (Vaughan, Jennings, and Hudson) acknowledge that Indians and Europeans behave differently from one another, the behavior differs, as it were, within the order of the same: all three assume, though only Hudson makes the assumption explicit, that an understanding of relations between the Europeans and the Indians must be elaborated in European terms. In Martin's analysis, however, what we have are not only two different sets of behavior but two incommensurable ways of describing and assigning meaning to events. This difference at the level of explanation calls into question the possibility of obtaining any theory-independent account of interaction between Indians and Europeans.

At this point, dismayed and confused by the wildly divergent views of colonial history the twentieth-century historians had provided, I decided to look at some primary materials. I thought, perhaps, if I looked at some firsthand accounts and at some scholars looking at those accounts, it would be possible to decide which experts were right and which were wrong by comparing their views with the evidence. Captivity narratives seemed a good place to begin, since it was logical to suppose that the records left by whites who had been captured by Indians would furnish the sort of firsthand information I wanted.

I began with two fascinating essays based on these materials written by the ethno-historian James Axtell, "The White Indians of Colonial America" and "The Scholastic Philosophy of the Wilderness."[12] These essays suggest that it would have been a privilege to be captured by North American Indians and taken off to Canada to dwell in a wigwam for the rest of one's life. Axtell's reconstruction of the process by which Indians taught European captives to feel comfortable in the wilderness, first taking their shoes away and giving them moccasins, carrying the children on their backs, sharing the scanty food supply equally, ceremonially cleansing them of their old identities, giving them Indian clothes and jewelry, assiduously teaching them the Indian language, finally adopting them into their families, and even visiting them after many years if, as sometimes happened, they were restored to white society—all of this creates a compelling portrait of Indian culture and helps to explain the extraordinary attraction that Indian culture apparently exercised over Europeans.

But, as I had by now come to expect, this beguiling portrait of the Indians' superior humanity is called into question by other writings on Indian captivity—for example, Norman Heard's *White into Red*, whose summation of the comparative treatment of captive children east and west of the Mississippi seems to contradict some of Axtell's conclusions:

> The treatment of captive children seems to have been similar in initial stages. . . . Most children were treated brutally at the time of capture. Babies and toddlers usually were killed immediately and other small children would be dispatched during the rapid retreat to the Indian villages if they cried, failed to keep the pace, or otherwise indicated a lack of fortitude needed to become a worthy member of the tribe. Upon reaching the village, the child might face such ordeals as running the gauntlet or dancing in the center of a throng of threatening Indians. The prisoner might be so seriously injured at this time that he would no longer be acceptable for adoption.[13]

One account which Heard reprints is particularly arresting. A young girl captured by the Comanches who had not been adopted into the family but used as a slave had been peculiarly mistreated. When they wanted to wake her up the family she belonged to would take a burning brand from the fire and touch it to her nose. When she was returned to her parents, the flesh of her nose was completely burned away, exposing the bone.[14]

Since the pictures drawn by Heard and Axtell were in certain respects irreconcilable, it made sense to turn to a firsthand account to see how the Indians treated their captives in a particular instance. Mary Rowlandson's "The Soveraignty and Goodness of God," published in Boston around 1680, suggested itself because it was so widely read and had set the pattern for later narratives. Rowlandson interprets her captivity as God's punishment on her for failing to keep the Sabbath properly on several occasions. She sees everything that happens to her as a sign from God. When the Indians are kind to her, she attributes her good fortune to Divine Providence; when they are cruel, she blames her captors. But beyond the question of how Rowlandson interprets events is the question of what she saw in the first place and what she considered worth reporting. The following passage, with its abrupt shifts of focus and peculiar emphases, makes it hard to see her testimony as evidence of anything other than the Puritan point of view:

> Then my heart began to fail: and I fell weeping, which was the first time to my remembrance, that I wept before them. Although I had met with so much Affliction, and my heart was many times ready to break, yet could I not shed one tear in their sight: but rather had been all this while in a maze, and like one astonished: but not I may say as, Psal. 137.1. *By the Rivers of Babylon, there we sate down; yea, we wept when we remembered Zion.* There one of them asked

me, why I wept, could hardly tell what to say: yet I answered, they would kill me: No, said he, none will hurt you. Then came one of them and gave me two spoon-fulls of Meal to comfort me, and another gave me half a pint of Pease; which was more worth than many Bushels at another time. Then I went to see King Philip, he bade me come in and sit down, and asked me whether I would smoke it (a usual Complement nowadayes among Saints and Sinners) but this no way suited me. For though I had formerly used Tobacco, yet I had left it ever since I was first taken. It seems to be a Bait, the Devil layes to make men loose their precious time: I remember with shame, how formerly, when I had taken two or three pipes, I was presently ready for another, such a bewitching thing it is: But I thank God, he has now given me power over it; surely there are many who may be better imployed than to ly sucking a stinking Tobacco-pipe.[15]

Anyone who has ever tried to give up smoking has to sympathize with Rowlandson, but it is nonetheless remarkable, first, that a passage which begins with her weeping openly in front of her captors, and comparing herself to Israel in Babylon, should end with her railing against the vice of tobacco; and, second, that it has not a word to say about King Philip, the leader of the Indians who captured her and mastermind of the campaign that devastated the white population of the English colonies. The fact that Rowlandson has just been introduced to the chief of chiefs makes hardly any impression on her at all. What excites her is a moral issue which was being hotly debated in the seventeenth century: to smoke or not to smoke (Puritans frowned on it, apparently, because it wasted time and presented a fire hazard). What seem to us the peculiar emphases in Rowlandson's relation are not the result of her having *screened out* evidence she couldn't handle, but of her way of constructing the world. She saw what her seventeenth-century English Separatist background made visible. It is when one realizes that the biases of twentieth-century historians like Vaughan or Axtell cannot be corrected for simply by consulting the primary materials, since the primary materials are constructed according to *their* authors' biases, that one begins to envy Miller his vision at Matadi. Not for what he didn't see—the Indian and the black—but for his epistemological confidence.

Since captivity narratives made a poor source of evidence for the nature of European-Indian relations in early New England because they were so relentlessly pietistic, my hope was that a better source of evidence might be writings designed simply to tell Englishmen what the American natives were like. These authors could be presumed to be less severely biased, since they hadn't seen their loved ones killed by Indians or been made to endure the hardships of captivity, and because they weren't writing propaganda calculated to prove that God had delivered his chosen people from the hands of Satan's emissaries.

The problem was that these texts were written with aims no less specific than those of the captivity narrative, though the aims were of a different sort. Here is a passage from William Wood's *New England's Prospect*, published in London in 1634.

To enter into a serious discourse concerning the natural conditions of these Indians might procure admiration from the people of any civilized nations, in regard of their civility and good natures. . . . These Indians are of affable, courteous and well disposed natures, ready to communicate the best of their wealth to the mutual good of one another; . . . so . . . perspicuous is their love . . . that they are as willing to part with a mite in poverty as treasure in plenty. . . . If it were possible to recount the courtesies they have showed the English, since their first arrival in those parts, it would not only steady belief, that they are a loving people, but also win the love of those that never saw them, and wipe off that needless fear that is too deeply rooted in the conceits of many who think them envious and of such rancorous and inhumane dispositions, that they will one day make an end of their English inmates.[16]

However, in a pamphlet published twenty-one years earlier, Alexander Whitaker of Virginia has this to say of the natives:

These naked slaves . . . serve the divell for feare, after a most base manner, sacrificing sometimes (as I have heere heard) their own Children to him. . . . They live naked in bodie, as if their shame of their sinne deserved no covering: Their names are as naked as their bodie: They esteem it a virtue to lie, deceive and steale as their master the divell teacheth to them.[17]

According to Robert Berkhofer in *The White Man's Indian*, these divergent reports can be explained by looking at the authors' motives. A favorable report like Wood's, intended to encourage new emigrants to America, naturally represented Indians as loving and courteous, civilized and generous, in order to allay the fears of prospective colonists. Whitaker, on the other hand, a minister who wishes to convince his readers that the Indians are in need of conversion, paints them as benighted agents of the devil. Berkhofer's commentary constantly implies that white men were to blame for having represented the Indians in the image of their own desires and needs.[18] But the evidence supplied by Rowlandson's narrative, and by the accounts left by early reporters such as Wood and Whitaker, suggests something rather different. Though it is probably true that in certain cases Europeans did consciously tamper with the evidence, in most cases there is no reason to suppose that they did not record faithfully what they saw. And what they saw was not an illusion, was not determined by selfish motives in any narrow sense, but was there by virtue of a *way* of seeing which they could no more consciously manipulate than they could choose not to have been born. At this point, it seemed to me, the ethnocentric bias of the firsthand observers invited an investigation of the cultural situation they spoke from. Karen Kupperman's *Settling with the Indians* (1980) supplied just such an analysis.

Kupperman argues that Englishmen inevitably looked at Indians in exactly the same way that they looked at other Englishmen. For instance, if they looked down on Indians and saw them as people to be exploited, it was not because of racial prejudice or antique notions about savagery, it was because they looked down on ordinary English men and women and saw them as subjects for exploitation as well.[19] According to Kupperman, what concerned these writers most when they described the Indians were the insignia of social class, of rank, and of prestige. Indian faces are virtually never described in the earliest accounts, but clothes and hairstyles, tattoos and jewelry, posture and skin color are. "Early modern Englishmen believed that people can create their own identity, and that therefore one communicates to the world through signals such as dress and other forms of decoration who one is, what group or category one belongs to."[20]

Kupperman's book marks a watershed in writings on European-Indian relations, for it reverses the strategy employed by Martin two years before. Whereas Martin had performed an ethnographic analysis of Indian cosmology in order to explain, from within, the Indians' motives for engaging in the fur trade, Kupperman performs an ethnographic study of seventeenth-century England in order to explain, from within, what motivated Englishmen's behavior. The sympathy and understanding that Martin, Axtell, and others extend to the Indians are extended in Kupperman's work to the English themselves. Rather than giving an account of "what happened" between Indians and Europeans, like Martin, she reconstructs the worldview that gave the experience of one group its context. With her study, scholarship on European-Indian relations comes full circle.

It may well seem to you at this point that, given the tremendous variation among the historical accounts, I had no choice but to end in relativism. If the experience of encountering conflicting versions of the "same" events suggests anything certain it is that the attitude a historian takes up in relation to a given event, the way in which he or she judges and even describes "it"—and the "it" has to go in quotation marks because, depending on the perspective, that event either did or did not occur—this stance, these judgments and descriptions are a function of the historian's position in relation to the subject. Miller, standing on the banks of the Congo, couldn't see the black men he was supervising because of his background, his assumptions, values, experiences, goals. Jennings, intent on exposing the distortions introduced into the historical record by Vaughan and his predecessors stretching all the way back to Winthrop, couldn't see that Winthrop and his peers were not racists but only Englishmen who looked at other cultures in the way their own culture had taught them to see one another. The historian can never escape the limitations of his or her own position in history and so inevitably gives an account that is an extension of the circumstances from which it springs. But it seems to me that when one is confronted with this particular succession of stories, cultural and historical relativism is not a position that one can comfortably assume. The phenomena to which these histories testify—conquest, massacre, and genocide, on the one hand; torture, slavery, and murder on the other—cry out for judgment. When faced with claims and counterclaims of this magnitude one feels obligated to reach an understanding of what actually did occur. The dilemma posed by the study of European-Indian relations in early America is that the highly charged nature of the materials demands a moral decisiveness which the succession of conflicting accounts effectively precludes. That is the dilemma I found myself in at the end of this course of reading, and which I eventually came to resolve as follows.

After a while it began to seem to me that there was something wrong with the way I formulated the problem. The statement that the materials on European-Indian relations were so highly charged that they demanded moral judgment, but that the judgment couldn't be made because all possible descriptions of what happened were biased, seemed to contain an internal contradiction. The statement implied that in order to make a moral judgment about something, you have to know something else first—namely, the facts of the case you're being called upon to judge. My complaint was that their perspectival nature would disqualify any facts I might encounter and that therefore I couldn't judge. But to say as I did that the materials I had read were "highly charged" and therefore demanded judgment suggests both that I was reacting to something real—to some facts—*and* that I judged them. Perhaps I wasn't so much in the lurch morally or epistemologically as I had thought. If you—or I—react with horror to the story of the girl captured and enslaved by Comanches who touched a firebrand to her nose every time they wanted to wake her up, it's because we read this as a story about cruelty and suffering, and not as a story about the conventions of prisoner exchange or the economics of Comanche life. The *seeing* of the story as a cause for alarm rather than a droll anecdote or a piece of curious information is evidence of values we already hold, of judgments already made, of facts already perceived as facts.

My problem presupposed that I couldn't judge because I didn't know what the facts were. All I had, or could have, was a series of different perspectives, and so nothing that would count as an authoritative source on which moral judgments could be based. But, as I have just shown, I did judge, and that is because, as I now think, I did have some facts. I seemed to accept as facts that ninety percent of the native American population of New England died after the first hundred years of contact, that tribes in eastern Canada and the northeastern United States had a compact with the game they killed, that Comanches had subjected a captive girl to casual cruelty, that King Philip smoked a pipe, and so on. It was only where different versions of the same event came into conflict that I doubted the text was a record of something real. And even then, there was no question about certain major catastrophes. I believed that four hundred Pequots were killed near Saybrook, that Winthrop was the Governor of the Massachusetts Bay Colony when it happened, and so on. My sense that certain events, such as the Pequot War, did occur in no way reflected the indecisiveness that overtook me when I tried to choose among the various historical versions. In fact, the need I felt to make up my mind was impelled by the conviction that certain things *had* happened that shouldn't have happened. Hence it was never the case that "what happened" was completely unknowable or unavailable. It's rather that in the process of reading so many different approaches to the same phenomenon I became aware of the difference in the attitudes that informed these approaches. The awareness of the interests motivating each version cast suspicion over everything, in retrospect, and I ended by claiming that there was nothing I could know. This, I now see, was never really the case. But how did it happen?

Someone else, confronted with the same materials, could have decided that one of these historical accounts was correct. Still another person might have decided that more evidence was needed in order to decide among them. Why did I conclude that none of the accounts was accurate because they were all produced from some particular angle of vision? Presumably there was something in my background that enabled me to see the problem in this way. That something, very likely, was poststructuralist theory. I let my discovery that Vaughan was a product of the fifties, Jennings of the sixties, Rowlandson of a Puritan worldview, and so on lead me to the conclusion that all facts are theory dependent because that conclusion was already a thinkable one for me. My inability to come up with a true account was not the product of being situated nowhere; it was the product of certitude that existed *somewhere else*, namely, in contemporary literary theory. Hence, the level at which my indecision came into play was a function of particular beliefs I held. I was never in a position of epistemological indeterminacy, I was never *en abyme*. The idea that all accounts are perspectival seemed to me a superior standpoint from which to view all the versions of "what happened," and to regard with sympathetic condescension any person so old-fashioned and benighted as to believe that there really was some way of arriving at the truth. But this skeptical standpoint was just as firm as any other. The fact that it was also seriously disabling—it prevented me from coming to any conclusion about what I had read—did not render it any less definite.

At this point something is beginning to show itself that has up to now been hidden. The notion that all facts are only facts within a perspective has the effect of emptying statements of their content. Once I had Miller and Vaughan and Jennings, Martin and Hudson, Axtell and Heard, Rowlandson and Wood and Whitaker, and Kupperman; I had Europeans and Indians, ships and canoes, wigwams and log cabins, bows and arrows and muskets, wigs and tattoos, whiskey and corn, rivers and forts, treaties and battles, fire and blood—and then suddenly all I had was a metastatement about perspectives. The effect of bringing perspectivism to bear on history was to wipe out completely the subject matter of history. And it follows that bringing perspectivism to bear in this way on any subject matter would have a similar effect; everything is wiped out and you are left with nothing but a single idea—perspectivism itself.

But—and it is a crucial but—all this is true only if you believe that there is an alternative. As long as you think that there are or should be facts that exist outside of any perspective, then the notion that facts are perspectival will have this disappearing effect on whatever it touches. But if you are convinced that the alternative does not exist, that there really are no facts except as they are embedded in some particular way of seeing the world, then the argument that a set of facts derives from some particular worldview is no longer an argument against that set of facts. If all facts share this characteristic, to say that any one fact is perspectival doesn't change its factual nature in the slightest. It merely reiterates it.

This doesn't mean that you have to accept just anybody's facts. You can show that what someone else asserts to be a fact is false. But it does mean that you can't argue that someone else's facts are not facts *because they are only the product of a perspective*, since this will be true of the facts that you perceive as well. What this means then is that arguments about "what happened" have to proceed much as they did before poststructuralism broke in with all its talk about language-based reality and culturally produced knowledge. Reasons must be given, evidence adduced, authorities cited, analogies drawn. Being aware that all facts are motivated, believing that people are always operating inside some particular interpretive framework or other is a pertinent argument when what is under discussion is the way beliefs are grounded. But it doesn't give one any leverage on the facts of a particular case.[21]

What this means for the problem I've been addressing is that I must piece together the story of European-Indian relations as best I can, believing this version up to a point, that version not at all, another almost entirely, according to what seems reasonable and plausible, given everything else that I know. And this, as I've shown, is what I was already doing in the back of my mind without realizing it, because there was nothing else I *could* do. If the accounts don't fit together neatly, that is not a reason for rejecting them all in favor of a metadiscourse about epistemology; on the contrary, one encounters contradictory facts and divergent points of view in practically every phase of life, from deciding whom to marry to choosing the right brand of cat food, and one decides as best one can given the evidence available. It is only the nature of the academic situation which makes it appear that one can linger on the threshold of decision in the name of an epistemological principle. What has really happened in such a case is that the subject of debate has changed from the question of what happened in a particular instance to the question of how knowledge is arrived at. The absence of pressure to decide what happened creates the possibility for this change of venue.

The change of venue, however, is itself an action taken. In diverting attention from the original problem and placing it where Miller did, on "the mind of man," it once again ignores what happened and still is happening to American Indians. The moral problem that confronts me now is not that I can never have any facts to go on, but that the work I do is not directed toward solving the kinds of problems that studying the history or European-Indian relations has awakened me to.

Notes

1. See Vine Deloria, Jr., *God Is Red* (New York, 1973), pp. 39–56.
2. Perry Miller, *Errand into the Wilderness* (Cambridge, Mass., 1964), p. vii; all further references will be included in the text.
3. This passage from John Winthrop's *Journal* is excerpted by Perry Miller in his anthology *The American Puritans: Their Prose and Poetry* (Garden City, N.Y., 1956), p. 43. In his headnote to the selections from the *Journal*, Miller speaks of Winthrop's "characteristic objectivity" (p. 37).
4. Alden T. Vaughan, *New England Frontier: Puritans and Indians, 1620–1675* (Boston, 1965), pp. vi–vii; all further references to this work, abbreviated *NEF*, will be included in the text.
5. John Higham, intro. to *New Directions in American Intellectual History*, ed. Higham and Paul K. Conkin (Baltimore, 1979), p. xii.
6. Ibid.
7. See Francis Jennings, *The Invasion of America: Indians, Colonialism, and the Cant of Conquest* (New York, 1975), pp. 3–31. Jennings writes: "The so-called settlement of America was a *resettlement*, reoccupation of a land made waste by the diseases and demoralization introduced by the newcomers. Although the source data pertaining to populations have never been compiled, one careful scholar, Henry D. Dobyns, has provided a relatively conservative and meticulously reasoned estimate conforming to the known effects of conquest catastrophe. Dobyns has calculated a total aboriginal population for the western hemisphere within the range of 90 to 112 million, of which 10 to 12 million lived north of the Rio Grande" (p. 30).
8. Jennings, fig. 7, p. 229; and see pp. 186–229.
9. James Axtell, *The European and the Indian: Essays in the Ethnohistory of Colonial North America* (Oxford, 1981), p. viii.
10. See Calvin Martin, *Keepers of the Game: Indian-Animal Relationships and the Fur Trade* (Berkeley and Los Angeles, 1978).
11. See the essay by Charles Hudson in *Indians, Animals, and the Fur Trade: A Critique of "Keepers of the Game,"* ed. Shepard Krech III (Athens, Ga., 1981), pp. 167–69.
12. See Axtell, "The White Indians of Colonial America" and "The Scholastic Philosophy of the Wilderness," *The European and the Indian*, pp. 168–206 and 131–67.
13. J. Norman Heard, *White into Red: A Study of the Assimilation of White Persons Captured by Indians* (Metuchen, N.J., 1973), p. 97.
14. See ibid., p. 98.
15. Mary Rowlandson, "The Soveraignty and Goodness of God, Together with the Faithfulness of His Promises Displayed; Being a Narrative of the Captivity and Restauration of Mrs. Mary Rowlandson (1676)," in *Held Captive by Indians: Selected Narratives, 1642–1836*, ed. Richard VanDerBeets (Knoxville, Tenn., 1973), pp. 57–58.
16. William Wood, *New England's Prospect*, ed. Alden T. Vaughan (Amherst, Mass., 1977), pp. 88–89.
17. Alexander Whitaker, *Goode Newes from Virginia* (1613), quoted in Robert F. Berkhofer, Jr., *The White Man's Indian: Images of the American Indian from Columbus to the Present* (New York, 1978), p. 19.
18. See, for example, Berkhofer's discussion of the passages he quotes from Whitaker (*The White Man's Indian*, pp. 19, 20).

19. See Karen Ordahl Kupperman, *Settling with the Indians: The Meeting of English and Indian Cultures in America, 1580–1640* (Totowa, N.J., 1980), pp. 3, 4.

20. Ibid., p. 35.

21. The position I've been outlining is a version of neopragmatism. For an exposition, see *Against Theory: Literary Studies and the New Pragmatism*, ed. W.J.T. Mitchell (Chicago, 1985).

EXCERPT FROM "GRAPHICAL INTEGRITY," *THE VISUAL DISPLAY OF QUANTITATIVE INFORMATION*

Edward Tufte

WHAT IS DISTORTION IN A DATA GRAPHIC?

A graphic does not distort if the visual representation of the data is consistent with the numerical representation. What then is the "visual representation" of the data? As physically measured on the surface of the graphic? Or the *perceived* visual effect? How do we know that the visual image represents the underlying numbers?

One way to try to answer these questions is to conduct experiments on the visual perception of graphics—having people look at lines of varying length, circles of different areas, and then recording their assessments of the numerical quantities.

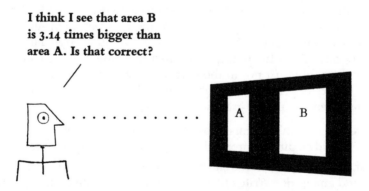

Such experiments have discovered very approximate power laws relating the numerical measure to the reported perceived measure. For example, the perceived area of a circle probably grows some what more slowly than the actual (physical, measured) area:

the reported perceived area = (actual area)^x, where x = .8 $\pm$ .3,

A discouraging result. Different people see the same areas somewhat differently; perceptions change with experience; and perceptions are context-dependent.[1] Particularly disheartening is the securely established finding that the reported perception of something as clear and simple as line length depends on the context and what other people have already said about the lines.[2]

Misperception and miscommunication are certainly not special to statistical graphics,

Source: Drawing by CEM; copyright 1961, *The New Yorker*.

but what is a poor designer to do? A different graphic for each perceiver in each context? Or designs that correct for the visual transformations of the average perceiver participating in the average psychological experiment?

One satisfactory answer to these questions is to use a table to show the numbers. Tables usually outperform graphics in reporting on small data sets of 20 numbers or less. The special power of graphics comes in the display of large data sets.

At any rate, given the perceptual difficulties, the best we can hope for is some uniformity in graphics (if not in the perceivers) and some assurance that perceivers have a fair chance of getting the numbers right. Two principles lead toward these goals and, in consequence, enhance graphical integrity:

> The representation of numbers, as physically measured on the surface of the graphic itself, should be directly proportional to the numerical quantities represented.

> Clear, detailed, and thorough labeling should be used to defeat graphical distortion and ambiguity. Write out explanations of the data on the graphic itself. Label important events in the data.

> Violations of the first principle constitute one form of graphic misrepresentation, measured by the

$$\text{Lie Factor} = \frac{\text{size of effect shown in graphic}}{\text{size of effect in data}}$$

If the Lie Factor is equal to one, then the graphic might be doing a reasonable job of accurately representing the underlying numbers. Lie Factors greater than 1.05 or less than .95 indicate substantial distortion, far beyond minor inaccuracies in plotting. The logarithm of the Lie Factor can be taken in order to compare overstating (log LF > 0) with understating (log LF < 0) errors. In practice almost all distortions involve overstating, and Lie Factors of two to five are not uncommon.

Here is an extreme example. A newspaper reported that the U.S. Congress and the Department of Transportation had set a series of fuel economy standards to be met by automobile manufacturers, beginning with 18 miles per gallon in 1978 and moving in steps up to 27.5 by 1985, an increase of 53 percent:

$$\frac{27.5 - 18.0}{18.0} \times 100 = 53\%$$

This line, representing 18 miles per gallon in 1978, is 0.6 inches long.

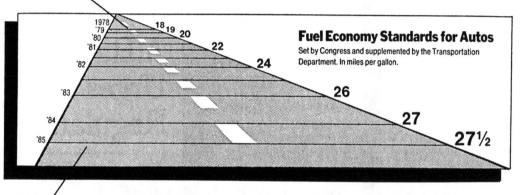

This line, representing 27.5 miles per gallon in 1985, is 5.3 inches long.

Source: © 1978 The New York Times. Reprinted by permission.

The magnitude of the change from 1978 to 1985 is shown in the graph by the relative lengths of the two lines:

$$\frac{5.3 - 0.6}{0.6} \times 100 = 783\%$$

Thus the numerical change of 53 percent is presented by some lines that changed 783 percent, yielding

$$\text{Lie Factor} = \frac{783}{53} = 14.8$$

which is too big.

The display also has several peculiarities of perspective:

- On most roads the future is in front of us, toward the horizon, and the present is at our feet. This display reverses the convention so as to exaggerate the severity of the mileage standards.

- Oddly enough, the dates on the left remain a constant size on the page even as they move along with the road toward the horizon.

- The numbers on the right, as well as the width of the road itself, are shrinking because of two simultaneous effects: the change in the values portrayed and the change due to perspective. Viewers have no chance of separating the two.

It is easy enough to decorate these data without lying:

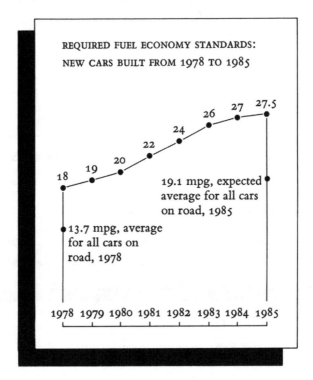

The non-lying version, in addition, puts the data in a context by comparing the new car standards with the mileage achieved by the mix of cars actually on the road. Also revealed is a side of the data disguised and mispresented in the original display: the fuel economy standards require gradual improvement at start-up, followed by a doubled rate from 1980 to 1983, and flattening out after that.

Sometimes decoration can help editorialize about the substance of the graphic. But it is wrong to distort the data measures—the ink locating values of numbers—in order to make an editorial comment or fit a decorative scheme. It is also a sure sign of the Graphical Hack at work. Here are many decorations but no lies:

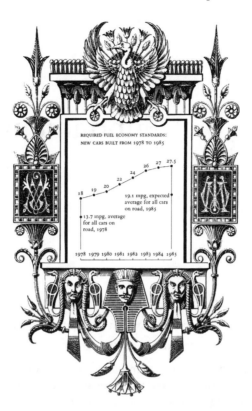

REQUIRED FUEL ECONOMY STANDARDS:
NEW CARS BUILT FROM 1978 TO 1985

27.5
27
26
24
22
20
19
18

19.1 mpg, expected
average for all cars
on road, 1985

13.7 mpg, average
for all cars on
road, 1978

1978 1979 1980 1981 1982 1983 1984 1985

---

1. The extensive literature is summarized in Michael Macdonald-Ross, "How Numbers Are Shown: A Review of Research on the Presentation of Quantitative Data in Texts," *Audio-Visual Communication Review*, 25 (1977), 359–409. In particular, H. J. Meihoefer finds great variability among perceivers; see "The Utility of the Circle as an Effective Cartographic Symbol," *Canadian Cartographer*, 6 (1969), 105–117; and "The Visual Perception of the Circle in Thematic Maps: Experimental Results," ibid., 10 (1973), 63–84.
2. S. E. Asch, "Studies of Independence and Submission to Group Pressure. A Minority of One Against a Unanimous Majority," *Psychological Monographs* (t956), 70.

Fundamentals of Oral Presentations

■ What advantages do you have when listening to a speaker who is present?

■ How is your response different when listening to a distant or recorded speaker?

■ What do these differences imply about how speaking differs from writing?

Public speaking adds the elements of memory and performance to the other aspects of written composition. If you are anxious about speaking before an audience, it may take many experiences talking in public to overcome that anxiety, and even if you feel comfortable, it takes practice to give an organized and articulate presentation. One reason to present research orally is to gain experience speaking to a group who knows and cares about what you are presenting—a sympathetic audience. One of the major differences between speaking and writing is captured in the phrase "working with an audience," because many experienced speakers use audience response to shape their talks. As a writer you may be able to *imagine* the reader's response, but when you speak before a group, you can usually *see* their actual response and adjust your presentation as your talk unfolds. This ability to respond to the audience explains why only a few professions expect you to "read a paper"; more commonly, speakers are asked to "give a talk."

You will be most able to sense the audience response and adjust your talk to it if you are well prepared, with a clear understanding of what you want to say, in what order, and why. Good speakers work from an outline, whether written on paper, or as in the case of Professor Way in Chapter 8, clearly worked out in the mind. Some speakers like to put the main points of their outline on file cards, while others print them out in large type on full-sized sheets of paper. An outline for an oral presentation of the argumentative research paper on international teaching assistants in Chapter 10 could look like the following sample.

The Problem of Negative Views of ITAs

Thesis: Even though many American undergraduates resent being taught by international graduate students, we should look at the positive aspects of this situation.

I. Complaints: English proficiency

II. Purpose and Extent of ITAs

- Iowa State: over 72% undergrads took at least one course with ITA

- Purdue: 30% TAs are ITAs—mostly in science & math

- Began in 1980s: Universities need instructors/International students
  need jobs

III. What causes complaints?

- Language

- Communication

- Failure

- Prejudice

IV. Are complaints justified?

- Language assessments mandated in 18 states since 1982: training programs

- Iowa State Questionnaire

V. Training ITAs

- Learning American customs and educational practices

- Orientation and ongoing programs

VI. Training American undergraduates

- Texas Tech Video

- Michigan State—residence halls—video and discussion

- Univ. of Missouri-Columbia—brochure

VII. Positive value of ITAs

- Diversity: Adjusting to new cultures

- Substitute for travel abroad

- Cream of crop

- Preparation for global workforce

A very experienced speaker would omit most of the bullet points except for those that record specific quantities and percentages, which are easy to forget when speaking. Compare this speaking outline to the planning outlines in Chapter 10 (pp. 175–178). An outline for an oral presentation should resemble a topic outline more than a sentence outline, although it can include facts and figures that you might forget.

It is even better to put those facts and figures into handouts or slides so that the speaker's attention can be focused more on interpreting the data than repeating it correctly. Other slides for this talk could include pictures of international teaching assistants in the classroom and charts or graphs that highlight information drawn from the sources. Your speaking notes, in short, should be as brief as possible, written to remind you of the order you are planning to follow and of a few key details you might forget. You can also add notes to yourself concerning when to change slides or distribute handouts, or how to pronounce difficult names. Using a different font or color for this kind of note lets you recognize it easily. If you use Microsoft PowerPoint to construct visuals, you can make speaker's notes as you prepare your slides. Make sure, however, that they are *notes*—not a transcript.

PURPOSE

Many of the techniques used in writing research can be adapted to oral presentations. Three elements that demand some special consideration are purpose, audience, and performance.

The topic and general purpose of the talks assigned in this book are extensions of the research and writing assignments: either to inform your audience about your research results, or, in the case of the proposal narrative assigned in Chapter 4, Exercise 4.4 (p. 82) to make a case for your project. Start by looking for a pattern in the material that suggests a reasonable order in which to present information. Define a specific purpose for the talk, tell it in your introduction, and repeat it as your talk develops. Remind yourself why you are talking and what you want your audience to do with the information you give, and let that purpose drive your talk. Deviations into side issues are particularly confusing in oral communication because the attention of the listeners typically varies as the talk progresses.

AUDIENCE

In planning your talk, it is crucial to state your topic and purpose directly at the beginning and to tell your audience how you are going to proceed. Take a look at the strategies in Focus Points: Real-Time Note-Taking (Chapter 4, p. 73). When you are the speaker, you face an audience with similar needs to understand the information and follow the organization. Your audience will want to know not only what you are going to talk about, but why, right from the start. Think of your audience as asking, "What is this good for?" and be prepared to discuss its significance at the outset. Use the introduction as a map that shows the audience how you will navigate through the talk. Then, repeat throughout the talk the key terms you developed in the introduction so that when members of your audience drift in attention they can find their way back to your point. Use transitional words and phrases liberally to remind them where you are as you move through the material. Particularly useful in oral presentations are "string phrases" like "the first reason, the second reason, the third and final reason" or "the first stage, the second stage, the last stage"—and so on. Notice that these phrases not only track the movement from part to part, but also prompt you to repeat a key term of the progression. Conclude by reviewing what you have said and repeating your point and purpose.

TRANSITIONAL CUES IN ORAL PRESENTATIONS

The same transitional cues you worked with in Chapter 7 Focus Points: Revising to Improve Transitions (p. 131) are even more important in oral presentations and need to be repeated more often.

- **Addition:** *Moreover, furthermore, in addition, also, and, not only . . . but also, first . . . second . . . third*
- **Negation or contrast:** *However, on the other hand*
- **Cause and effect:** *Thus, therefore, hence*
- **Part and whole:** *One aspect is* x, *and an equally important aspect is* y; *one explanation is* x *and another is* y.
- **Repetition:** *i.e., in other words, that is, to restate the question;* repeated key words
- **Extension:** *This implies [suggests, shows, etc.] that; we can infer [conclude, argue, etc.] that . . .*

You can ask questions more freely to make transitions in oral presentations than in written work, particularly in making transitions between major parts of a talk. For example, *"How, then, can we use this new understanding of the life cycle of the termite? One application is. . . ."*

PERFORMANCE

Oral presentations must be performed well to be effective. You may want to practice your talk with a research group or some of your friends, or at least speak it out loud to yourself. You will never give quite the same talk twice when you speak from notes, but practice gives you a sense of how your presentation sounds, and the response of a practice audience will improve your understanding about how best to shape the presentation. You might think of your practice speeches as drafts for the final talk, drafts that allow you to rework your thinking and establish clearer transitions for the actual performance. They also allow you to see what you can keep in your memory and what needs to be written down in your speaking notes or in slides or handouts. Practicing can also help you learn to keep track of time as you talk.

While memory is important in public presentation, you should not try to memorize a speech word for word for the same reason you should not read from a script. Experienced speakers watch for the reactions of the audience. Although you need a set agenda for a formal talk, and although you may be using prepared slides or handouts, you should remain flexible enough to stop, repeat yourself, give more evidence, or do more to establish your context if the audience is not following you. You can tell that your audience is not following you if they keep looking away from you or your slides, or if they seem puzzled or unresponsive. It is far better to see and respond to expressions of puzzlement, approval, and excitement than to ignore them and strictly follow a memorized outline, even though you run the risk of getting off task and not finding a way to return. If the audience seems puzzled, you can ask if they understand what you are saying, whether you should rephrase it, or if they have questions. If the audience seems bored, try to recast your material to better fit the occasion by highlighting what made *you* find the material interesting (e.g., your finding unexpected data, a paradoxical situation, a personal interest, etc.). The more oral presentations you give, the easier it becomes to adapt to your audience without losing your point.

PANEL PRESENTATIONS

A panel presentation usually consists of three or four speakers talking on similar topics or different aspects of the same topic. For example, the panel Professor Way writes about in his e-mail in Chapter 8 involved four speakers presenting different points of view about an engineering writing program his university had developed. Panels are very common means of presentations at professional meetings and some community forums because they allow for a diversity of perspectives. They almost always leave time for questions and responses from the audience.

Preparing for a panel presentation is similar to preparing for an individual talk, including writing notes and creating handouts and visuals, except that the speaker needs to keep in mind the topics other panelists will cover. Sometimes panels clearly assign specific aspects of a topic to each speaker; at other times, panels bring together separate research projects under a general topic heading. It can be useful to circulate drafts or outlines of the talks among the panelists in advance so that every member can prepare to acknowledge or respond to the other talks. When speaking on a panel, it is crucial to keep to your time limit so that there is time for each speaker to talk and time for questions and answers. Panels usually have a chair whose function is to introduce the topic and speakers, provide a rationale for the presentations, serve as timekeeper for the speakers, and lead the question and answer session at the end.

QUESTION AND ANSWER PERIODS

Most panels and many talks allow time for questions and discussion from the audience, and often this is the most interesting part of a talk for speakers and audience alike. Usually someone other than the speaker is responsible for soliciting questions and keeping track of the time: either the chair of the panel, the person who introduced the speaker, or an appointed respondent who opens the discussion with a prepared response. In panel presentations, when questions are taken depends on the field as well as on the ground rules set by the organization sponsoring the panel. In the sciences, it is usual to take questions after each talk. In the humanities, on the other hand, it is more usual to hold all questions until the end, although in some cases, a chair might allow a few specific questions about individual talks before moving on to the next speaker. Before the panel begins, the chair should announce when questions will be taken. If you are listening to a panel presentation, it can be useful to jot down questions for the earlier speakers because it is easy to forget them when listening to the subsequent talks. In most situations, asking questions is considered to be a compliment to the speaker, and experienced speakers are often disappointed if no one responds to them.

Of course, first-time speakers often worry about questions, but you can prepare to answer them by thinking about what you might ask yourself and by previewing your talk with a group of fellow students. You might even suggest questions that you would like to be asked so that if questions do not come from the audience at large one of your group members can get them started. Remember that answers to questions are not expected to be as formal as a prepared talk; it's all right to be speculative, to admit that you do not have the data to answer a question, and to defer your answer to another speaker.

USING VISUALS IN ORAL PRESENTATIONS

Oral presentations are easier to follow when they are supplemented by visuals—slides and/or handouts—to help keep the audience focused. Visuals for oral presentations should follow general principles of unity, coherence, and emphasis—and must be adapted to the conventions and expectations of the particular occasion and field. As you plan visuals for oral presentations, think about what information can be communicated more effectively visually than orally and about how to coordinate the oral and visual elements. The "appropriate visuals" depend on the format you choose, the topic you have researched, and the length of time you have to speak, as well as on the technological resources available to the speakers. The point is to keep your audience attentive, interested, and informed.

DESIGNING VISUALS FOR ORAL PRESENTATIONS

Whether to use projected visuals as part of a talk and what their content should be depend on the discipline you are working in and the purpose and location of the talk. In some fields, particularly business and engineering, projected visuals are an expected part of presentations, and speakers often make slides that show titles, subtitles, and major points as well as data. In informal discussions, participants sometimes create visuals on the spot, drawing on a white or black board or flip chart—or on a sheet of paper. In disciplines like art history, pictures are crucial adjuncts to lectures and are carefully scripted into talks; similarly, historians often rely on maps to make their points understandable. On the other hand, in English literature and similar text-centered fields, lectures with projected visuals are rarer, although sometimes pictures or quotations from texts will be projected or distributed on handouts.

Even though the visual part of an oral presentation can be an important adjunct to the presentation, it is not meant to replace explanations you give while speaking. In most cases, the audience should be focused more on the talk than on the supporting materials. Use visuals:

- when they clearly illustrate a principle better than a spoken or written explanation can, such as using a chart to illustrate trends and changes;
- when they provide a powerful impact and enhance your argument, such as using photographs or pictures to illustrate a principle or fact or to make a person, place, or problem seem real; and/or
- when they provide an essential visual framework for a complex argument, such as a topic outline.

Think about your talk as "wrapping around" the projected visuals; never read from the projections, but do refer to them. Avoid using packaged clip art or other "filler"; they distract the audience from your argument and can undermine your credibility. Also resist the temptation to bring much movement into presentations when using a program like Microsoft PowerPoint, even though it is easy to do, unless there is a meaningful purpose for that movement.

FOCUS POINTS: PLANNING VISUALS

- Remember that the visual elements of a talk should complement and reinforce the talk. They should not repeat it, and a speaker should never read from the visual presentation. However, you *can* arrange the slides to maintain the order you have established for the talk and use them as the basis for your notes.

- A presentation program like PowerPoint, with its prompts and organizing templates, can be a big help for novice speakers; more experienced speakers, however, sometimes find that it constrains their thinking too much to be useful.

- A note of warning: If a talk depends on visuals, be sure to bring a back-up. If you plan to talk from a computer projection, bring transparencies that can be used on an overhead projector or handouts of your slides, so that your audience can follow the talk if a server goes offline or if it takes too long to get a good interface between the computer and the projector.

Slides

In this context, the term *slides* is used as a generic term for each unit of a projected visual presentation. The term derives from the days when scientists and other presenters would assemble a carousel of photographic slides to accompany an oral presentation, and this is the source of the term *slideshow* in PowerPoint. Today the term *slide* is more often used for computer projections and transparencies shown by an overhead projector, rather than for literal photographic slides. Slides are effective means to present examples, quotations, charts, graphs, and pictures and to outline major sections and subsections of a talk. Slides are also particularly helpful for the speaker. The physical reality of a prepared visual presentation can help novice speakers resist the temptation to speak from copious notes or a written text. The principles for creating and using slides are the same, no matter what media are used.

FOCUS POINTS: LAYOUT OF SLIDES

- When creating visuals for oral presentations, consider how your audience will be viewing the presentation.

- If you are projecting a PowerPoint presentation or showing visuals on transparencies, your audience will not be able to perceive fine details in graphs or charts.

- While you can use pictures or patterns for backgrounds, avoid backgrounds that are irrelevant or too busy, which will make your text difficult to read and your visuals difficult to understand.

- A general rule in creating visuals for oral presentations is to use the "rule of six," which is based on research that shows that audiences have difficulty seeing and comprehending slides or transparencies that contain more than six elements. For example, slides that contain only text should not contain more than six lines of text or six bullet points.

FOCUS POINTS: FONTS AND COLOR

- Use sans serif fonts (such as Arial or Helvetica) at least 20 points or higher. Restrict yourself to at most two fonts per presentation. If you need to show contrast, use a larger or smaller font size or bold the text.

- If you know the room you will be presenting in, choose a background that matches the lighting in the room. Use darker colors for presentations to be shown in darkened rooms and lighter colors in lighted rooms.

- In general, do not count on a very dark room because in most cases listeners need light to take notes or follow your handouts.
- Maintain a consistent background color throughout the presentation, and choose fonts in a color that contrasts effectively with the background. Limit the number of colors in a presentation to three or four, and use them consistently throughout the presentation. Do not change colors unless there is a compelling reason for the change.
- Illustrations and photographs, on the other hand, may contain as many colors as the original.

FOCUS POINTS: CHARTS AND GRAPHS

- Charts, graphs, illustrations, or other pictures should consist of no more than six elements.
- In most cases, show each chart or graph on its own slide, with a descriptive title, making it as simple as possible without oversimplifying or distorting the data.
- Use as little writing as possible, keeping the audience focused as much as possible on the visual.
- Use colors the same way in charts and graphs as they are used in text slides, limiting them to three or four colors, and choose contrasting colors to emphasize the important aspects of your data.
- Make sure that charts and graphs stand out in sharp contrast from their backgrounds.
- You can see how well your visuals work if you test them beforehand under conditions as similar to the presentation site as possible. Check to see that the audience will be able to read the title and legends for charts and graphs and to understand the relationship between the data from a distance. You may have to adjust the scale for bars on a bar chart, increase the contrast of colors of the pieces of a pie chart, or enlarge the size of the lines on a graph. You might decide to enlarge or shrink an illustration or picture to better fit the slide.

Handouts

Handouts distributed to the audience can also be a very useful visual supplement to an oral presentation. Presentation programs like PowerPoint allow speakers to produce handouts of slides with from one to nine slides to the page. (Although nine slides are possible, if the slides have much detail, six per page is usually a better option; be aware that if the printing is too small, many viewers will be distracted by trying to read it.) With handouts, as with slides, keep your audience focused on you and your presentation, not on the handouts. Think carefully about when to distribute them so that they will be a complement to rather than a distraction from your talk.

FOCUS POINTS: USING HANDOUTS

- If your handouts consist of copies of the slides, it can be useful to distribute them at the beginning of the talk, since listeners appreciate being able to take notes and compose questions directly on them. Also, distribute at the beginning of a talk any handouts that contain quotations or citations for texts you discuss in depth so that your audience will not be distracted from what you are saying by wondering whether they have the correct spelling of a name or by not clearly remembering an important quotation.

■ Handouts can be used in addition to or instead of projections when you discuss detailed material like a budget, résumé, or series of quotations, that is, material that needs to be read closely and carefully. These handouts also should usually be distributed at the beginning of the talk.

■ If you have a handout that gives your audience practice with an idea or technique you are discussing, you can distribute it (or have a colleague distribute it) at the point at which it is going to be used.

■ Handouts that supplement the talk rather than contribute to it directly—like a complete bibliography, a complete text of the talk, a related publication, or a page of information for contact or follow-up—should be distributed after the talk so that the audience will not turn its attention to the new information on the pages and away from you.

■ Good handouts are often reproduced and redistributed by members of the audience to friends and co-workers who could not attend a presentation, and so a handout for general distribution at a talk should contain the name of the speaker on every page and should maintain its readability through at least two generations of photocopying.

Fundamentals of Visual Design

In this era of expanding computer use, there has been not only a profusion of new sources of information, but also the increasing expectation that professionals in all fields be able to present information and make arguments in electronic media. The concept of visual literacy has grown in importance because of the expansion of the World Wide Web to the point where most professionals need the ability to convey information on well-developed Web sites and to use presentation graphics like Microsoft PowerPoint proficiently; these are now standard skills of the professional workforce, and you should expect to use them or to supervise people who use them. The overall principles of good design presented in this Appendix are meant to apply to various media and should continue to be applicable as media change in the future.

One way to start thinking about visual design is reflecting on what you already know about it:

■ What happens when a story is moved from one medium to another, for example, when a novel is turned into a movie? What kinds of changes are involved in moving from a written text to a visually rich medium? To a medium with sound?

■ When assembling a piece of equipment or doing other work that involves following instructions, do you depend more on the written text or on pictures and diagrams? When you read a piece that includes pictures, charts, and/or graphs, do you read the text first or look at the visuals first? What does this tell you about yourself as a reader and user of information? What kinds of accommodations might be necessary to communicate effectively with people who have a different style of processing information?

■ Think about some Web sites you have used in your research in this course and in other facets of your life. What makes a site user-friendly? What makes a site exciting? Confusing? Look at some commercial Web sites and make a list of features you find useful and another list of features you find useless and (even worse) annoying or confusing.

MAKING RESEARCH VISIBLE

Visuals can be a powerful way to complement the results of research in academic writing. When used appropriately, they can make compelling arguments that support your written or oral argument. On the other hand, inappropriate visuals can detract from a compelling argument. Just as you choose words carefully when creating an argument, you also need to make deliberate and thoughtful choices when creating visuals. Effective visual design techniques can be applied to print and online documents; they increase the professionalism of your writing and your credibility as a researcher.

Visuals are especially useful in situations where an illustration can help your audience understand a complex concept, such as:

- reporting research or emphasizing concepts in oral presentations,
- reporting statistical information in print and online documents,
- illustrating processes or instructions, and/or
- documenting an unfamiliar context (e.g., maps or photographs).

Using a chart or graph to present statistics or figures can help your audience understand the information more clearly than simply reporting the information in words. A diagram can let your audience visualize a complex procedure or replicate an experiment, and a map or photograph can help them see an unfamiliar terrain. Because visuals form an important part of how individuals process information and navigate on the World Wide Web, well-designed Web sites take advantage of visual design techniques. Moreover, on the Web, visuals can be animated, allowing you to illustrate change over time, show the rotation of a three-dimensional object, integrate short video clips of a complex procedure, or play movies or music that relate to your purpose.

However, in professional situations, poorly designed or inappropriate visuals can damage your credibility. For example, simply adding packaged clip art to an existing research paper will not enhance your argument and may in fact detract from the point you are making. Your readers may suspect that you are using the clip art to fill space and avoid developing your argument. Visuals should always be in accord with the seriousness of your topic and the professional expectations of your audience. If you use cute animated graphics on your Web page, your audience may not take your argument seriously, and nonessential blinking and spinning merely distract most viewers from your point. Bad design can result in charts that are difficult to read and confusing to your audience, leaving them unable to understand your purpose, or leading to serious misinterpretation of your data.

Like other features of researched writing, appropriate use of visuals depends on the specific rhetorical context of your research, that is, your audience and purpose. Most disciplines in the sciences and social sciences rely extensively on the use of tables, figures, and other types of visuals to present information, both in written documents and oral presentations.

FOCUS POINTS: WHEN TO USE VISUALS

- Use visuals when they will enhance the presentation of your research.
- Use visuals when they form a compelling part of your argument.
- Use visuals that correspond to the general practices of your field.

■ Never use visuals just because you can.

■ When you create visuals, design them well.

Because conventions for using visuals vary from field to field, pay particular attention to how visuals are used by your sources—particularly academic sources.

To get a sense of these conventions, choose several sources you are consulting in your research and examine when and how they use visuals to present information, using the following questions to guide your examination.

■ When are visuals used?

■ When are visuals *not* used?

■ How do the visuals contribute to the overall argument of the research?

■ What kinds of data or concepts do the visuals present or illustrate? What is the pattern of their use?

■ Where are the visuals situated within specific documents? For example, are they included in the main body of a document or presentation, or on separate pages in the text or at the end?

■ How are the visuals designed? What fonts, colors, and design techniques do they use?

■ Are the visuals easy to read and understand? What about them makes them easy to understand? If not, what makes them difficult?

■ Find the guidelines for the design and placement of visuals for the style you are using (MLA or APA) in a style guide, manual, or handbook. Do the visuals in your sources conform to the recommended guidelines for good visual design? How or how not?

GRAPHS, CHARTS, AND TABLES

Graphs and charts are visual representations of numerical information, and should be designed to suit their purpose and the medium in which they will be represented. They should be designated as figures in the order in which they are referred to in the written text (i.e., Fig. 1, Fig. 2, etc.), and the figure itself should be given a title that states its purpose.

Graphs

Graphs are used to represent the changing relationships between different pieces of information, such as comparing quantities and showing changes over time, as in, for example, a graph that shows the change in student population at a university over the last five years. Scientists frequently use graphs to report the results of experiments or observations, particularly when they are showing change over time. See Figure B.1.

Charts

Charts are also visual representations of numbers or quantities, but they highlight the relationship between various parts of a whole, like a pie chart illustrating the percentages of students majoring in various subjects in a university. Charts also tend to use differing visual elements to represent numerical information, while graphs tend to use

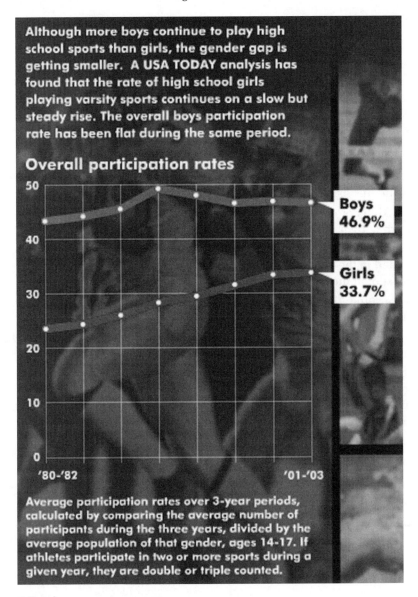

Although more boys continue to play high school sports than girls, the gender gap is getting smaller. A USA TODAY analysis has found that the rate of high school girls playing varsity sports continues on a slow but steady rise. The overall boys participation rate has been flat during the same period.

Overall participation rates

Boys 46.9%

Girls 33.7%

'80-'82   '01-'03

Average participation rates over 3-year periods, calculated by comparing the average number of participants during the three years, divided by the average population of that gender, ages 14-17. If athletes participate in two or more sports during a given year, they are double or triple counted.

FIGURE B.1 Graph
Line graph showing the change in participation in boys and girls high school sports over three-year periods.
Source: Juan Tomassie, *USA TODAY*. Reprinted with permission.

points, bars, or lines. Newspapers, magazines, and other periodicals use charts quite frequently to report on percentages and opinions. See Figures B.2 and B.3.

Tables
Tables are rows and columns of information arranged to show patterns or trends. Tables are most often used to present and compare a series of related numerical data but can also be used for comparing other quantities as well. For example, when comparing the

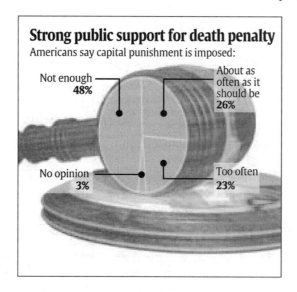

FIGURE B.2 Chart

Pie chart showing percentage breakdown of American opinions about the imposition of capital punishment.

Source: Gallup Poll; by Steven Snyder and Robert W. Ahrens, *USA TODAY*. Reprinted with permission.

FIGURE B.3 Chart

Bar graph/chart showing purchases of travel made online.

Source: Jupiter Media Metrix; by Shannon Reilly and Sam Ward, *USA TODAY*. Reprinted with permission.

TABLE B.1 Comparison of Candidate Positions

Candidate's Name	Parking	Cafeteria food
Jessica Hope Johnson	In favor of building more garages	Wants to increase variety in cafeteria options
Jeremy Franklin	Against building more garages	Thinks existing options are just fine

positions of several candidates on the same issues, you could make a table that presents each candidate and his or her position on an issue. This table would allow readers to grasp quickly how the candidates' positions compared to each other. Table B.1 shows the information described in the last two sentences.

Tables have labels that help readers understand the purpose of each column or row. In Table B.1, the labels include one explaining that the candidates' names will be down the column on the left, and two explaining which issue will be discussed. These labels prevent repeating information and help readers understand what is being compared. Make sure that you include column headings and/or row headings (when appropriate) to label the data being presented and demonstrate the relationship between the data points.

CHOOSING THE RIGHT TYPE OF VISUAL ELEMENT

It is important to choose the most appropriate type of graph or chart for displaying information, and this will depend on the data available to display, on the relationship the parts of the data have to each other, on the professional situation you are in, and on the medium you are using.

Charts, tables, and illustrations serve different purposes in a document. A table and a chart can show the same information, but a chart illustrates the overall relationship between the data in a more visually oriented way than a table. The audience gets less precise detail in a chart than in a table because they do not have easy access to the numerical amounts. For example, think about the difference between a table of sales figures for a ten-year period and a line graph for that same data. The line graph illustrates the relationship, but it's more difficult to determine the precise dollar amounts. The table shows the precise dollar amounts, but the reader has to work harder to construct an image of the relationships among the data.

Choosing a chart or a table depends on what aspect of the data is most important to the argument. If you want readers to focus primarily on the relationships among data rather than to focus on exact numerical quantities, choose a chart or graph to present your information. If being able to refer to exact quantities is important, or if you are showing the relationship between groups of ideas rather than groups of numbers, use a table. Charts and graphs are good at showing change over time and representing the parts of a whole. Tables are good at setting items of information next to each other for detailed comparisons and study. They also make good quick references for readers.

Diagrams and illustrations illustrate complex processes and can help readers visualize processes and equipment. Drawn illustrations, maps, and reproductions of photographs can bring reality to a face, a scene, or a location, giving a sense of immediacy and reality to information that might otherwise seem abstract.

The medium and context of presentation are also important factors in choosing and creating visuals. For example:

- A visual created to be projected on a screen during an oral presentation must be legible from a distance and cannot include fine gradations of detail.
- A visual that forms part of a written text will be read up close, and so can include more complex details.
- A visual created for a Web site needs to be in a form that all web browsers can read, as well as being a size that will fit comfortably into browser windows.

FOCUS POINTS: INCORPORATING VISUALS

- The visuals should be of a size that is easy to read, even if this means moving them to their own page. Visuals that take up half a page or more are best located on separate pages placed after (or facing, in a book) the page to which they are most relevant or grouped in an appendix at the end of the document. In both cases, a pointer to the visual's location should be placed in the text, such as "see Fig. 1 for more details," and the visual should be numbered and given a title.
- All visuals should be clearly numbered and titled, with a brief explanation that indicates the data they are presenting and their purpose in the document. Legends for charts and graphs should be clearly visible and easy to read.
- The sources for visuals that you did not create yourself should be clearly acknowledged when the visual is mentioned in the caption or under the title of the visual and in your reference list.
- The style of visuals should match the overall style of the print document. This means that the fonts, colors, and other elements of visuals should match those in your print document.
- Color is an important choice when integrating visuals into print documents. While color can add interest and appeal, you need to consider whether you will be able to print the document in color. If so, then you can use color in your visuals (or choose color photographs or illustrations). Always do a test printing. If you plan to print your document on a black-and-white printer, or if your printout may be photocopied, make sure that the visuals show up well in black and white. This may mean redesigning your visuals in grayscale or using colors that print acceptably in grayscale. For example, a pie chart that places a dark color like blue next to a light color like light green shows up as dark gray and light gray in grayscale, with sufficient contrast so that the reader could easily tell them apart. However, two light colored pie pieces placed next to each other, such as light yellow and light green, would both show up as light gray when printed in grayscale, making them difficult to distinguish.
- Pay special attention to how photographs or illustrations look when you print the document; like other visuals, photographs incorporated into a document should be crisp and legible. If you use color visuals on a document that is likely to be photocopied, make sure that the document remains clear when copied in black and white.

■ Be conservative in choosing fonts. In print documents, use the same fonts (at the same point size and with the same emphases) for labels in your visuals as you use in your document. Fonts in visuals and charts should be no smaller than 10-point type. If you are using color, use colors that match the colors already in use in the document; if you have not used color yet, choose colors that you think will effectively convey the document's tone. As in all visuals, if you are using color, choose contrasting colors to emphasize important information, and limit your color palette to no more than four colors.

THE ETHICS OF VISUAL DESIGN

Logical errors—both intentional and unintentional—can creep into visual representations of information as well. Although we sometimes think so, pictures are not inherently more credible than words. Good design of visual elements like charts, graphs, and tables lets writers communicate certain kinds of information clearly and efficiently. Bad design, even if deception is not intended, can lead to disastrous failure of communication. Visuals that miss or insufficiently emphasize important information can keep readers from seeing important relationships. For example, Edward Tufte, an advocate for effective and honest technical design, describes how the Space Shuttle *Challenger* disaster in 1986 can in part be attributed to a poorly designed table passed from engineers to managers (39–45). Tufte observes that all charts and graphs show relationships between numbers, and that good design makes the most important relationship clear. In the *Challenger* table, previous shuttle failures were arranged by date rather than by temperature, thus obscuring the increased vulnerability of the shuttle as temperatures decreased. Although this table was quickly assembled, the problem was *not* that the chart was not particularly polished nor attractive; engineers on tight deadlines often hand-draw visuals on the spot to clarify their ideas. Instead, the problem was that the information was not arranged to show the crucial relationship between temperatures and failures.

Visuals can also be *designed* to be deceptive, as described in Chapter 1, pages 15–16, and in the excerpt from Tufte's book, page 303.

INTELLECTUAL PROPERTY AND VISUALS FROM THE WEB

In general, treat intellectual property on the Web in the same way you would treat it in print or anywhere else: it is necessary to give credit to your sources and not to alter or distort them to suit your needs. However, just as books are not "free," even if they were borrowed from the library, material on the Web belongs to somebody. Copyright of Web resources is a hotly contested issue. You cannot scan printed text, pictures, or visuals protected by copyright onto your Web pages, and you cannot simply download materials from other sites into your own. Putting materials onto a Web site is a means of publishing them, and so uses that are considered fair use in a paper written for a class may not be fair use on a Web site open to the public at large or even to a limited network.

If you want to download pictures, images, or other Web materials, check the Web site's use policy. Many academic and organization sites allow noncommercial users to download text and images, provided they are not changed and the source information accompanies the downloaded material. Sites that want to maintain control over how their materials are used will have a use policy and expect you to follow it. For example, the Purdue University Online Writing Lab (OWL) has a detailed fair use policy reachable by a link at the bottom of every item (owl .english.purdue.edu/owl/resource/551/01), and its policy distinguishes between commercial and noncommercial users, describes who may use what material under what circumstances, and defines appropriate practices for users who want to link the OWL to their own Web sites. If you want to download materials for which you can not find an explicit use policy, you must contact the site's Webmaster to explain how you want to use it and ask permission. Commercial sites tend to guard their materials much more closely than academic or organizational sites and will probably expect you to pay for most uses of their materials.

You are ordinarily free to link to other sites (as compared to downloading their material) because that's the way the Web normally works. However, it is a good idea to check a site's use guidelines in order to follow its stated preferences for how links should be established.

RESOURCES AND LINKS

Presentation Design Resources

Rabb, Margaret Y. *The Presentation Design Book*. 2nd ed. Chapel Hill, NC: Ventana Press, 1993.
Tufte, Edward. *The Cognitive Style of PowerPoint*. Cheshire, CT: Graphics Press, 2003.

Creating Effective Slide Presentations

(See the resources for creating graphs and charts as well.)

Effective Presentations (www.kumc.edu/SAH/OTEd/jradel/effective.html)

Information Design for Presentations—Part I (masterview.ikonosnewmedia.com/ masterview6.htm)

Information Design for Presentations—Part II (masterview.ikonosnewmedia .com/masterview7.htm)

Resources and Tools for Creating PowerPoint Presentations (masterview .ikonosnewmedia.com/sitemap.htm)

Visual and Print Design Resources

Lohr, Linda. *Creating Graphics for Learning and Performance: Lessons in Visual Literacy*. Columbus, OH: Merril-Prentice Hall, 2003. Print.
Parker, Roger C. *The One-Minute Designer*. 2nd ed. New York: Hungry Minds, 1997. Print.
Tufte, Edward. *Envisioning Information*. Cheshire, CT: Graphics Press, 1990. Print.
—. *The Visual Display of Quantitative Information*. 2nd ed. Cheshire, CT: Graphics Press, 2002. Print.
—. *Visual Explanations: Images and Quantities, Evidence and Narrative*. Cheshire, CT: Graphics Press, 1997. Print.
Wilde, Richard, and Judith Wilde. *Visual Literacy: A Conceptual Approach to Graphic Problem Solving*. New York: Watson-Guptil Publications, 1991. Print.
Williams, Robin. *The Non-Designers Design Book*. Berkeley, CA: PeachPit Press, 1994. Print.

Design and Production Checklists for Print Design and Publishing
www.newentrepreneur.com/Resources/Worksheets/Print_Design_Wk_Sht/
print_design_wk_sht.html

Desktop Publishing's Twelve Most Common Mistakes
www.newentrepreneur.com/Resources/Articles/DTP_12_most_common/
dtp_12_most_common.html

Graphics Tutorials
en.wikipedia.org/wiki/Wikipedia:Graphics_tutorials
www.yourhtmlsource.com/images/

Creating Graphs and Charts—A Bibliography of Online Resources
tc.eserver.org/dir/Design/Graphic-Design/Charts-and-Graphs

Databases

Note: Academic library databases usually include full-text access to newspapers read nationally and internationally, such as the *New York Times*, the *Times* (London), the *Washington Post*, the *Wall Street Journal*, the *Economist*, and so on. Because subscriptions are often included in the library's purchase of databases, students usually have free access to both recent and archived articles provided by these sources, *but only when you reach them through the library database*. If you access these newspapers directly online, they may charge for access to the same articles.

These lists do not include the many dictionaries, encyclopedias, and other reference sources (both general and related to specific fields) to which most university libraries subscribe. To discover which particular specialized sources you can access, go to your library's Web site, click on "databases," and sort by field.

GENERAL DATABASES (INCLUDING NEWS)

Academic Search Premier: *References for sources in all fields, including sources in journals, magazines, and newspapers, 1984–present; and many full-text sources, 1990–present.*

AccuNet/AP Multimedia Archive: *News photos, continuously updated, 1840s–present.*

Archive Finder: *Guide to archives, manuscripts, and special collections.*

Black Studies Center: *References relevant to Black Studies, including the* Chicago Defender. *Some full-text articles.*

Books In Print®: *References for all in-print and forthcoming books published in the United States, 1985–present.*

Contemporary Authors: *Biographical information and references for twentieth- and twenty-first–century writers.*

Current Contents: *Tables of contents and references from important academic journals and books in the sciences, social sciences, and arts and humanities.*

Digital United States Congressional Serial Set: *Full text of U.S. Government publications, 1789–1969.*

GPO Access U.S.: *References and some full texts from U.S. Federal Register, 1993–present.*

Historical Abstracts: *References for sources in world history (1450–present, other than United States and Canada).*

Historical Statistics of the United States: *References and some full-text sources for quantitative historical information, 1500–2000.*

Index Islamicus: *References for sources on Islam, the Middle East, other Muslim countries, 1906–present.*

International Index to Black Periodicals: *References for and some full texts of sources covering cultural, economic, historical, religious, social, and political issues in the discipline of Black Studies.*

JSTOR: The Scholarly Journal Archive: *Full texts of sources in a large number of academic journals. Most college and university libraries subscribe to JSTOR, and your library's online catalog entries may contain direct links to online journal subscriptions through JSTOR—a great resource for most researchers.*

LexisNexis Academic: *References and some full-text sources for news and other publications in fields such as business, medicine, and the law.*

LexisNexis Environmental (Universe): *References, abstracts, and full texts of sources for information about the environment; full texts of news and commentary; and full texts of relevant laws and legal decisions.*

LexisNexis Statistical: *References and some full-text sources for statistical information (U.S. Government and other sources considered reliable), 1972–present.*

MasterFILE Premier: *References to general-public sources related to many fields, in magazines and other general interest periodicals, including a collection of reference books, biographies, images (flags, maps, photos), 1984–present; some full-text sources, 1990–present.*

Periodicals Index Online and Periodical Archive Online: *The* Index *provides references for academic journals in the humanities and social sciences, starting with their first volumes (including articles in many languages), 1665–present; some references have links to full-text sources in* Periodicals Archive Online *and* JSTOR.

PressDisplay: *Full texts of 450 newspapers (international), from up to the past 60 days.*

Proquest Research Library: *References and some full texts for general-public sources in fields including business, education, literature, political science, and psychology, 1986–present.*

Reader's Guide Full Text: *References and some full texts for general-public sources relevant to many fields, 1890–present; some full-text sources, 1994–present.*

Web of Science: *References and abstracts for and some full texts in the sciences, social sciences, arts and humanities, 1977–present.*

WorldCat: *Catalog of library holdings worldwide, including books and other materials, 1000–present. This can be a useful tool when trying to locate books your own library does not own.*

Women's Studies International: *References and some full-text sources in social sciences, the arts, humanities, and gender studies, 1972–present.*

ARTS AND HUMANITIES (INCLUDING HISTORY)

ACLS Humanities E-Book: *Full texts of frequently cited books in several fields of history, eighteenth through twenty-first centuries.*

Art Index/Full Index: *Full texts of sources in art, architecture, fashion design, graphic arts, landscape architecture, 1984–present.*

Arts and Humanities Citation Index: *References for arts and humanities and some related science and technology sources, 1977–present.*

BAS (Bibliography of Asian Studies): *References for humanities and social sciences concerning East, Southeast, and South Asia, 1971–present.*

Children's Literature Comprehensive Database: *Full-text reviews of children's books.*

Contemporary Authors: *Biographical information and references for twentieth- and twenty-first–century literature.*

Essay and General Literature Index: *References for essays and chapters in anthologies and multiauthor collections in the humanities and social sciences, 1985–present.*

Film and Television Literature Index: *References and some full texts from film and television periodicals (international), both academic and for the general public, 1973–present.*

Humanities Abstracts/Full Text: *References and some full-text sources for arts, communications, history, linguistics, literature, religion, 1907–present.*

MLA (Modern Language Association) International Bibliography: *References and some full sources in literature (in all modern languages) and criticism, including articles about drama, film, folklore, linguistics, and rhetoric/composition, 1926–present.*

Music Index Online: *References for international music periodicals, including most styles and genres of music and about the music industry, 1978–present.*

Project Muse: *Full texts of sources in academic journals in the arts, humanities, and social sciences, 1990–present.*

BUSINESS, MANAGEMENT, AND ECONOMICS

ABI/Inform Dateline Business: *References and full-text sources in economics and business publications, 1985–present.*

ABI/Inform Trade & Industry, Business, Economics: *References for and full-text trade and industry periodicals and newsletters, 1971–present.*

Business Source Premier: *References for and some full-text magazine and journal sources in business and management, 1965–present.*

CCH Internet Research Network: *References for and some full-text sources in securities, banking, trade, federal energy, transportation, legal information concerning product liability and safety laws.*

EconLibrary.com: *References for academic journals in accounting, economics, and finance.*

EconLit: *References for and abstracts of U.S. and international sources in economics, 1969–present.*

Factiva: *References for and some full-text sources for general business news; also commentary, pictures, stock quotes, and general information about industries.*

General BusinessFile ASAP: *References for and some full-text academic journal articles in business and management, 1980–present.*

Hospitality and Tourism Complete: *References for academic research and industry news in this field.*

IBIS World: *Full-text reports on industries in U. S. and some global industries, for past two years.*

International Abstracts of Human Resources: *References and abstracts for sources in academic journals, 1994–present.*

MarketResearch.com Academic: *References for current and historical sources on markets and industries and full-text sources over a year old.*

Mergent Web Manuals/Mergent WebReports: *References for and full texts of archived documents from corporations and industries (international), 1960–present.*

NTIS (National Technical Information Service): *References for and some full texts of research sponsored by the U.S. government, and some international information in business and in science technology developments relevant to business, 1964–present.*

ProQuest Historical Annual Reports: *Reproductions of annual reports of over 800 companies, 1844–present.*

Regional Business News: *References for and some full texts of business journals, newspapers, and newswires from all U.S. urban and rural areas, 1993–present.*

Wilson Business Abstracts: *References and abstracts for and some full texts of sources related to business, 1982–present.*

HEALTH AND MEDICINE

AIDSearch: *References for academic sources related to AIDS, 1980–present.*

BIOSIS Previews: *References for sources in life sciences and biomedical research, 1926–present.*

ComDisDome: Communication Sciences and Disorders: *References for varied useful resources and sources in fields such as language pathology, audiology, and communication, 1997–present.*

Ergonomic Abstracts: *References and abstracts for academic sources in ergonomics and human factors, including fields of health and safety, human factors engineering, human/computer interactions, industrial engineering, occupational psychology, and occupational and physical therapy, 1985–present.*

Health and Safety Science Abstracts: *References and abstracts for academic sources in public health, safety, and industrial hygiene, 1981–present.*

Health Business, FullTEXT: *Full texts of sources in health care administration, 1985–present.*

Health Source: Consumer Edition: *References for and some full texts of sources for the general public, 1985–present.*

Health Source: Nursing/Academic Edition: *References for and some full texts of academic and professional sources in fields related to nursing and allied health, 1975–present.*

ILO Encyclopaedia of Occupational Health and Safety: *Full-text entries with references; provides an important guide to the field.*

International Pharmaceutical Abstracts (IPA): *References and abstracts for sources in pharmacy and pharmaceuticals, 1970–present.*

MEDLINE: *References for academic sources in medicine, dentistry, nursing, and similar fields, 1964–present.*

Nursing Clinics of North America: *Full texts of sources giving latest diagnostic and therapeutic information, 2002–present.*

PsycINFO: *References for and some full texts of sources in psychology and such related fields as medicine, psychiatry, neuroscience, nursing, pharmacology, physiology, and so on, 1806–present.*

Sport Discuss: *References for sources in sports medicine, health, and psychology, 1975–present.*

Toxicology Abstracts: *References and abstracts for and some full texts of sources about toxic substances—industrial, agricultural, household, pharmaceutical—and substance abuse, 1981–present.*

TOXLINE *References and abstracts for and some full texts of sources about toxic substances, 1999–present.*

Virology and AIDS Abstracts: *References and abstracts and some full texts, including most international sources on virology in humans, animals, and plants, 2000–present.*

SCIENCE, TECHNOLOGY, AND ENGINEERING

ACM Online Guide to Computing Literature: *References for academic sources in computer science, 1985–present.*

Aerospace and High Technology Database: *References and abstracts for and some full-text sources in aeronautics, astronautics, and related space fields, 1962–present.*

AGRICOLA: *References for and some full-text sources in agriculture and related fields, including veterinary medicine, 1970–present.*

Animal Behavior Abstracts: *References and abstracts for and some full-text sources in animal behavior, including neurophysiology, behavioral ecology, genetics, applied ethology, and so on, 1982–present.*

Applied Science and Technology Abstracts/Full Text: *References and abstracts for and some full texts of sources in industrial and mechanical arts, 1983–present.*

Biological & Agricultural Index Plus: *References for and some full-text sources in Biology, Agriculture, and related disciplines, 1983–present.*

Biological Abstracts and Biological Abstracts/RRM: *References and abstracts for academic sources in the life sciences, 1969–present.*

Civil Engineering Abstracts: *References for and some full-text academic sources in civil engineering, 1966–present.*

Encyclopedia of Life Sciences Online (Nature): *Full-text resource aimed at undergraduate and graduate students, 2002–present.*

Engineering Research Database: *References for sources in civil, earthquake, environmental, mechanical, and transportation engineering, 1966–present.*

Food Science and Technology Abstracts (FSTA): *References for sources in food science, food technology, and human nutrition, 1969–present.*

General Science Full Text: *Full texts of sources in general science, 1994–present; some sources from 1982–1994.*

GeoRef Earth Sciences: *References for and some full-text sources in fields related to geology, 1785–present.*

High Technology Research Database with Aerospace: *References for sources in aeronautics, astronautics, space science, and related fields, 1962–present.*

IEEE Xplore: *References for sources and some full texts of IEEE (Institute of Electrical and Electronics Engineers—a large and influential professional organization) journals, conferences, and standards, 1988–present.*

INSPEC: *References for and some full texts of sources in communications, computers and computing, control engineering, electrical engineering, electronics, information technology, physics, 1898–present.*

Merck Index: *Much-consulted guide to drugs (human and veterinary) and to other biological and chemical substances, including natural, industrial, and agricultural, and environmentally significant products.*

Meteorological & Geoastrophysical Abstracts: *References and abstracts for and some full texts of academic sources in areas of geology, meteorology, oceanography, environmental science, and related areas, 1974–present.*

Science Citation Index: *References and abstracts from academic journals in science and technology, 1945–present.*

Science Online: *Full texts of sources in* Science, Science Express *(preprint version of* Science), *and other science Web sites.* Science *is a leading academic journal read by many scientists in all specializations. Preprints are articles that have been accepted for publication but not yet published in print form.*

Technology Research Database: *References and abstracts and some full texts of academic sources in all fields of technology and engineering, 1962–present.*

SOCIAL SCIENCES (INCLUDING COMMUNICATION AND EDUCATION)

ComIndex: *References for sources in communication studies.*

ERIC: *A major resource in education-related disciplines, providing references for and some full texts of sources, 1992–present; some articles dating back to 1966.*

Family & Society Studies Worldwide: *References for sources in the social sciences related to family and gender, 1970–present.*

Linguistics and Language Behavior Abstracts: *References and abstracts for and some full texts of academic sources in linguistics and language study, 1973–present.*

Social Sciences Abstracts/Full Text: *References and abstracts for and some full texts of academic sources in anthropology, area studies, family studies, law and criminology, political science, psychology, sociology, women's studies, and so on, 1907–present.*

Social Sciences Citation Index: *References for and some full texts from academic journals in the social sciences, 1977–present.*

Sociological Abstracts: *References and abstracts for academic sources in activism and action research, community organization, demographics, family studies, feminist studies, gerontology, media, political science, social security programs, sociology, 1974–present.*

Worldwide Political Science Abstracts: *References and abstracts for and some full-text sources in political science, international relations, law, sociology, economics, public administration, and public policy, 1975–present; some coverage 1960–1974 and less from earlier years.*

Notes

Chapter 1

1. The concept of warrants comes from Toulmin (95 ff.).

2. Bazerman writes of their "humble but proud authorial presence: the humble servants of nature and their discipline, filling in only a small piece of a vast puzzle and subject to the hard evidence of nature and the cold judgment of their peers—yet the proud originators of claims that have the potential ring of natural truth and nearly universal acceptance" (180).

Chapter 3

1. See also Rebecca Moore Howard's essay in the Readings.

Chapter 6

1. This formula is derived from the instructions for formulating a thesis in Booth, Colomb, and Williams, *The Craft of Research*.

Chapter 7

1. Williams calls this putting old information before new, which is a helpful way to remember it (Williams 26).

2. Sometimes students don't notice that data is plural (datum is the singular version)—but most faculty do notice.

Bibliography

Booth, Wayne C., Gregory G. Colomb, and Joseph M. Williams. *The Craft of Research*. 2nd ed. Chicago: U of Chicago P, 2003. Print. Chicago Guides to Writing, Editing, and Publishing.

Bronowski, Jacob. "Honest Jim and the Tinker Toy Model." *The Nation*. 18 March 1968: 381–82. Rpt. in *The Double Helix: A Personal Account of the Discovery of the Structure of DNA*. Ed. Gunther S. Stent. New York: Norton, 1980. 200–04. Print.

Davis, Michael. "Who Should Teach Workplace Ethics?" *Teaching Philosophy* 13.1 (1990): 21–36. Print.

Feynman, Richard P. "The Value of Science." *The Pleasure of Finding Things Out: The Best Short Works of Richard P. Feynman*. Ed. Jeffrey Robbins. Cambridge, MA: Perseus, 1999. 141–50. Print.

Franklin, Benjamin. *Autobiography of Benjamin Franklin*. 1868. New York: Dover, 1996. Print.

Gee, James Paul. *An Introduction to Discourse Analysis: Theory and Method*. New York: Routledge, 1999. Print.

—. *What Video Games Have to Teach Us about Learning and Literacy*. New York: Palgrave, 2003. Print.

Graff, Gerald, and Andrew Hoberek. "Opinion: Hiding It from the Kids (With Apologies to Simon and Garfunkel)." *College English* 62.2 (1999): 242–54. Print.

Gualerzi, Davide. "Globalization Reconsidered: Foreign Direct Investment and Global Governance." *International Journal of Political Economy* 36.1 (2007): 3–29. Print.

Howard, Rebecca Moore. "Plagiarism, Authorship, and the Academic Death Penalty." *College English* 57.7 (1995): 788–806. Print.

Kohn, Alfie. "The Dangerous Myth of Grade Inflation." *Chronicle.com*. *Chronicle of Higher Education*, 8 Nov. 2002. Web. 17 Aug. 2008.

Kuhn, Thomas. *The Structure of Scientific Revolutions*. 2nd ed. Chicago: U of Chicago P, 1970. Print. Intl. Encyc. of Unified Science 2.2.

Macrorie, Ken. *The I-Search Paper*. Portsmouth, NH: Boynton-Cook, 1980. Print.

Mallon, Thomas. *Stolen Words: Forays into the Origins and Ravages of Plagiarism*. New York: Ticknor, 1989. Print.

MLA Handbook for Writers of Research Papers. 7th ed. New York: MLA, 2009. Print.

Patterson, Francine, and Wendy Gordon. "The Case for the Personhood of Gorillas." *The Great Ape Project: Equality Beyond Humanity*. Ed. Paola Cavalieri and Peter Singer. New York: St. Martin's, 1993. 58–79. Print.

Rose, Mike. *Possible Lives: The Promise of Public Education in America*. New York: Penguin, 1996. Print.

Sperber, Murray. *Beer and Circus: How Big-Time College Sports Is Crippling Undergraduate Education*. New York: Holt, 2000. Print.

Tompkins, Jane. "'Indians': Textualism, Morality, and the Problem of History." *Critical Inquiry* 13.1 (1986): 101–19. Print.

Toulmin, Stephen E. *The Uses of Argument*. Cambridge, UK: Cambridge UP, 1958. Print.

Tufte, Edward. *The Visual Display of Quantitative Information*. 2nd ed. Cheshire, CT: Graphics, 2001. Print.

Watson, J. D., and F. H. C. Crick. "A Structure for Deoxyribose Nucleic Acid." *Nature* 171 (April 25, 1953): 337–38. Rpt. in Charles Bazerman, "What Written Knowledge Does: Three Examples of Academic Discourse." *Philosophy of the Social Sciences* 11 (1981): 361–87. Rpt. in *Landmark Essays on Writing Across the Curriculum*. Ed. Charles Bazerman and David R. Russell. Davis, CA: Hermagoras, 1994. 159–88. Print.

Williams, Joseph. *Style: Lessons in Clarity and Grace*. 9th ed. New York: Addison, 2006. Print.

Zerubavel, Eviatar. *Social Mindscapes: An Invitation to Cognitive Sociology*. Cambridge, MA: Harvard UP, 1997. Print.

Credits

Text Credits

p. 22, p. 260: Alfie Kohn, "The Dangerous Myth of Grade Inflation." Copyright 2002 by Alfie Kohn. Reprinted from *The Chronicle of Higher Education*, November 8, 2002, with the author's permission. For more information—including extended references—please see www.alfiekohn.org. **p. 241:** David Brooks, "Virtues and Victims." From *The New York Times*, Op-Ed, April 9, 2006. © 2006 The New York Times. All rights reserved. Used by permission and protected by the Copyright Laws of the United States. The printing, copying, redistribution, or retransmission of the Material without express written permission is prohibited. **p. 243:** Daniel C. Dennett, "Show Me the Science," *The New York Times*, Op-Ed, August 28, 2005. © 2005, The New York Times. Reprinted by permission. **p. 273:** Doris Kearns Goodwin, "How I Caused That Story," *Time*, February 4, 2002. Copyright TIME Inc. Reprinted by permission. TIME is a registered trademark of Time Inc. All Rights Reserved. **p. 258:** Rebecca Moore Howard, "Forget About Policing Plagiarism. Just Teach" from *The Chronicle of Higher Education*, November 16, 2001. Reprinted by permission of the author. **p. 267:** Robert Macfarlane, "The Burning Question," *The Guardian*, September 24, 2005. Reprinted by permission of the author. **p. 247:** Charles McGrath, "Outsourcing Homework: At $9.95 a Page, You Expected Poetry?" From *The New York Times*, Op-Ed, September 10, 2006. © 2006 The New York Times. All rights reserved. Used by permission and protected by the Copyright Laws of the United States. The printing, copying, redistribution, or retransmission of the Material without express written permission is prohibited. **p. 249:** Tom Moore, "Classroom Distinctions," *The New York Times*, Op-Ed, January 19, 2007. © 2007, The New York Times. Reprinted by permission. Drawing by Phil Marden, © 2007, The New York Times. Reprinted by permission. **p. 270:** Henry Petroski, "Sometimes Design Must Fail to Succeed" from *The Chronicle of Higher Education*, April 28, 2006. Reprinted by permission of the author. **p. 251:** Lisa Randall, "Dangling Particles," *The New York Times*, Op-Ed, September 18, 2005. © 2005, The New York Times.

Reprinted by permission. **p. 237:** Motoko Rich, "Digital Publishing Is Scrambling the Industry's Rules." From *The New York Times*, June 5, 2006. © 2006 The New York Times. All rights reserved. Used by permission and protected by the Copyright Laws of the United States. The printing, copying, redistribution, or retransmission of the Material without express written permission is prohibited. **p. 255:** Robert Rivard, "What Every Student Knows: Thou Shall Not Copy," *San Antonio Express-News Online*, November 10, 2002. Copyright 2002 by San Antonio Express-News. Reproduced with permission of San Antonio Express-News in the format Textbook via Copyright Clearance Center. **p. 287:** Mike Rose, excerpt from the Introduction to *Possible Lives: The Promise of Public Education in America*. Copyright © 1995 by Mike Rose. Reprinted by permission of Houghton Mifflin Harcourt Publishing Company. All rights reserved. **p. 239:** Katharine Q. Seelye, "Rewriting History: Snared in the Web of a Wikipedia Liar." From *The New York Times*, December 4, 2005. © 2005 The New York Times. All rights reserved. Used by permission and protected by the Copyright Laws of the United States. The printing, copying, redistribution, or retransmission of the Material without express written permission is prohibited. **p. 256:** Ed Tenner, "Rise of the Plagiosphere," *Technology Review*, June 2005. Reprinted by permission of Wrights Reprints. **p. 289:** Jane Tompkins, "'Indians': Textualism, Morality, and the Problem of History," *Critical Inquiry* 13.1 (1986): 101-19. Copyright © 1986, The University of Chicago Press. Reprinted by permission of the publisher, The University of Chicago Press. **p. 274:** Patricia Williams, "The 600 Faces of Eve." Reprinted with permission from the July 31, 2006, issue of *The Nation*. For subscription information, call 1-800-333-8536. Portions of each week's Nation magazine can be accessed at http://www.thenation.com. **p. 276:** Abigail Witherspoon, "This Pen for Hire: Grinding Out Papers for College Students," *Harper's Magazine*, June 1995. Copyright © 1995 by Harper's Magazine. All rights reserved. Reproduced from the June issue by special permission.

Photo Credits

p. 10 (bottom): North Wind Picture Archives. **p. 15:** Photograph courtesy of the National Archives and Records Administration. **pp. 30–31:** William Clark, from *Academic Charisma and the Origins of the Research University*. Copyright © 2006 by the University of Chicago. Reprinted by permission of the University of Chicago Press. **p. 32:** *College English*. Editorial staff page from *College English*, Volume 71, Number 4, March 2009. Reprinted by permission of National Council of Teachers of English. **p. 33:** Copyright © 2009 Condé Nast Publications. All rights reserved. Originally published in *The New Yorker*. Reprinted by permission. **p. 34:** Table of Contents from *Leviathan*, Volume 9, Number 3, October 2007. Reprinted by permission of Wiley-Blackwell. **p. 41 (top):** Screenshot, "Best French Films of the 1950s," http://www.filmsdefrance.com/Best_1950s.html. Used by permission of FilmsDeFrance.com. **p. 41 (bottom):** Screen shot, "How to get in touch" from http://filmsdefrance.com/feedback.html. Used by permission of FilmsDeFrance.com. **p. 42 (top and bottom):** Screen shot from The University of Wisconsin Press. Neupert, Richard. *A History of the New French Wave Cinema*. 2007 by the Board of Regents of the University of Wisconsin System. Reprinted courtesy of The University of Wisconsin Press. **p. 90:** Patricia L. Tenpenny et al., "In Search of Inadvertent Plagiarism, *The American Journal of Psychology* 111.4 (1998): 529–559. **p. 91:** Database search results from *Science*, www.sciencemag.org. Reprinted by permission of The American Association for the Advancement of Science (AAAS). **p. 92:** OCLC WorldCat database screenshot is used with permission of OCLC Online Computer Library Center, Inc.) WorldCat® is a registered trademark of OCLC Online Computer Library Center, Inc. **p. 303:** Edward R. Tufte, from *The Visual Display of Quantitative Information*, 2nd ed. (Cheshire, Connecticut: Graphics Press LLC, 1983, 2001). Reprinted by permission of Graphics Press LLC. **p. 304:** Drawing by CEM; copyright 1961, *The New Yorker*. **p. 305:** © 1978 The New York Times. Reprinted by permission. **p. 306:** Edward R. Tufte, from *The Visual Display of Quantitative Information*, 2nd ed. (Cheshire, Connecticut: Graphics Press LLC, 1983, 2001). Reprinted by permission of Graphics Press LLC. **p. 307:** Edward R. Tufte, from *The Visual Display of Quantitative Information*, 2nd ed. (Cheshire, Connecticut: Graphics Press LLC, 1983, 2001). Reprinted by permission of Graphics Press LLC. **p. 320:** Juan Tomassie, USA TODAY. Reprinted with permission. **p. 321 (top):** Gallup Poll; by Steven Snyder and Robert W. Ahrens, *USA TODAY*. Reprinted with permission. **p. 321 (bottom):** Jupiter Media Metrix; by Shannon Reilly and Sam Ward, *USA TODAY*. Reprinted with permission.

Index

S